OCEAN
YACHTMASTER

The essential coursebook for
the RYA Ocean Yachmaster certificate

SECOND EDITION

PAT LANGLEY-PRICE & PHILIP OUVRY

ADLARD COLES NAUTICAL
London

This edition published 2002 by Adlard Coles Nautical
an imprint of A & C Black (Publishers) Ltd
37 Soho Square, London W1D 3QZ
www.adlardcoles.co.uk

First published in Great Britain by Adlard Coles 1984
Reprinted 1988 (twice), 1989
Reprinted by Adlard Coles Nautical 1991, 1992
Revised edition 1996
Second edition 2002

ISBN 1-7136-6220-4

A CIP catalogue record for this book is available from the
British Library.

Photoset by CG Graphic Service, Tring, Herts
Printed and bound in Great Britain by
Butler & Tanner Ltd, Frome and London

CONTENTS

Note for American Readers

The books used for sight reductions are the same as the American ones shown below:

ENGLISH	AMERICAN
NP 401 *Sight Reduction Tables for Marine Navigation*	HO 229 published by US Naval Oceanographic Office
AP 3270 Vol 1 *Sight Reduction Tables for Air Navigation.*	HO 249 *Star Tables for Air Navigation*
AP 3270 Vol 3 *Sight Reduction Tables for Air Navigation.*	HO 249 *Sight Reduction Tables for Air Navigation*

Norie's Tables are international

The Nautical Almanac (NP 314) is a joint publication of Her Majesty's Stationery Office (UK) and the USA Government Printing Office. Both editions are identical.

Further details of these and other publications can be found on pages 144–46.

Foreword

As one who had to struggle in his early days with the intricacies and complexity of spherical trigonometry and astro navigation, I am well placed to appreciate the value of a comprehensive, clearly written handbook for the novice. Here is just such a book, with all the tables and examples necessary for putting theory into practice. It also includes valuable chapters on ocean passage planning and meteorology.

The study of these subjects is imperative for those who go far offshore in yachts or ships, as no electronic aids are 100% reliable. However, this knowledge must be consolidated by practical experience and one cannot be considered as qualified until one has swung a sextant and regularly obtained accurate results at sea. Good reading and Bon Voyage.

Admiral Sir John Fieldhouse, GCB GBE ADC
The First Sea Lord, Chief of Naval Staff.

Acknowledgements

The authors wish to thank the following: the Controller of Her Majesty's Stationery Office for permission to reproduce extracts from NP314–80, the Nautical Almanac, and AP3270, Sight Reduction Tables for Air Navigation, Volume 1 and Volume 3; HM Stationery Office and the Hydrographer of the Navy for permission to reproduce extracts from NP401(4), Sight Reduction Tables for Marine Navigation, and BA charts 5055 and 5333A; Imray Laurie Norie and Wilson Ltd. for permission to reproduce extracts from Norie's Nautical Tables; Telesonic Marine Ltd. and Tamaya & Co. Ltd. for photographs; George Philip & Son Ltd. for charts of the northern and southern hemispheres; and, the Royal Yachting Association for permission to reproduce part of G15.

Introduction

Nowadays all over the world more people than ever are going to sea in small boats. Many do not venture out of sight of land; but others, lured by the challenge of the oceans, think of the day that they will set out on their first ocean voyage.

To make such a trip, knowledge of celestial navigation is required. This need not be in the form of a mystical science understood only by the ancient mariner; nor a memory test involving extensive complicated mathematical formulae. It is not difficult to learn enough about celestial navigation to find your position provided you have some knowledge of coastal navigation and the ability to use tabulated information and do simple arithmetic.

The microchip age, with its computerised systems is revolutionising navigation and will continue to do so. There will always be a place for the navigator who can navigate simply with the minimum of equipment, such as a nautical almanac, a sextant and a reliable timepiece. There is also the personal satisfaction when it all works out right and the boat arrives safely at its destination.

This book attempts to explain in some detail the various methods of finding the boat's position. The publications used generally have an identical equivalent in the United States of America or are available world wide (see Chapter 15); a list of these US equivalents is given on page vi.

The explanations are set out to be understood both by a beginner, studying alone or on a celestial navigation course and by the more experienced navigator who wishes to expand his horizons.

The reader should consider each of the methods of finding the observed position and then select that which best suits his needs.

Calculations for twilight are normally worked out to the nearest minute of time and for azimuth to the nearest degree.

Ocean passages are not only navigation out of sight of land. The ideal time of the year for a passage is governed by the weather en route. Chapter 14 covers the background knowledge needed in order to decide on the optimum route and the optimum time of year for a passage.

The Royal Yachting Association/Department of Transport Ocean Yachtmaster syllabus, as shown in RYA publication G15, is fully covered together with much additional information.

Some prior knowledge in coastal navigation and coastal meteorology has been assumed. The companion volume *Yachtmaster*, covers the information necessary. *World Cruising Routes* and *World Cruising Handbook*, both by Jimmy Cornell, (both published by Adlard Coles Nautical) and *Weather Predicting Simplified* by Michael Carr are essential reading at the planning stage of an extended cruise across the world's oceans.

A series of specimen forms (Sight Reduction Forms) to assist in orderly calculation of results is included in Appendix E. Depending upon the method selected, the reader can adapt these forms for his own use.

The authors are keen that this book should be complete and unambiguous to navigators world wide and would welcome, through the publisher, any correspondence which would enable future editions to be improved.

Second edition

In this second edition various factors have been taken into account. *The Macmillan Reeds Nautical Almanac* has replaced earlier editions but no longer includes alternative methods of calculation for ocean navigation. However the alternative methods shown in earlier editions of *Reeds Nautical Almanac* are relevant and are included.

The use of the Global Positioning System (GPS) for navigation is fully operational which has resulted in increased sophisticated technical solutions both to navigation and to distress and safety operations. Moreover, the Global Maritime Distress and Safety System is fully operational commercially and should be installed on every ocean-going craft. Similar technology gives access to up-to-date weather forecasts. However, it is important that the ocean navigator understands the basic theory of astronavigation and world weather patterns, just in case there is a failure of the electronic systems.

Chapter One

No Landmarks

If you were in the Northern Hemisphere and were asked to point to the Pole Star (Polaris), at which part of the sky would you point? Certainly towards the north and up in the sky somewhere. At any time the angle between the horizon and the Pole Star (known as altitude) is nearly the same as the observer's latitude, so in fact you could estimate its height in the sky fairly accurately.

For many years seamen in the northern hemisphere have found Polaris by identifying a constellation of seven stars called the Plough (Ursa Major). The end two stars of this constellation (the pointers) point towards the north and towards the position of Polaris (see Fig. 1.1).

The earth is a free spinning gyro, the axis of which will always maintain its direction in space. Thus the axis through the north and south poles always points in the same direction. In the northern hemisphere Polaris sits conveniently near this axis and thus represents a fixed point in the night sky. The Plough, if we could observe it over a 24 hour period, would appear to move in a circular orbit around Polaris. All other stars would also appear to move in a similar orbit but, for some, because of their distance from Polaris, part of their orbit would be obscured by the earth's horizon and they would appear to rise to the east and set to the west. Of course, the stars are stationary, but because the earth is rotating in an easterly direction, they appear to move through the sky. As movement is relative, it is convenient to regard the earth as stationary with the stars (and other heavenly bodies) rotating around it. Further, we can imagine the earth being the centre of a celestial sphere of infinite radius with all other stars situated on its surface. The centre of this sphere and the centre of the earth are the same point.

Let us now look at how we define a position on the celestial sphere.

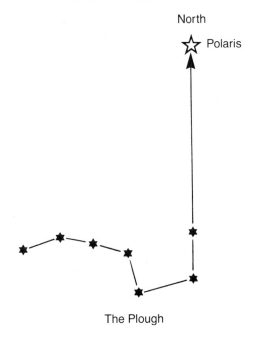

North

Polaris

The Plough

Fig 1.1 The Plough. The two stars at the end of this constellation point towards the north.

On earth, position is defined by latitude north or south of the equator and longitude east or west of the Greenwich meridian. If we projected the earth's north and south poles and its equator outwards on to the celestial sphere they would become the celestial north and south poles and the celestial equator. (The celestial equator is also known as the equinoctial.) We could then start to define the position of a star in degrees north or south of the celestial equator, though this measurement is known as declination rather than latitude, with parallels of declination instead of parallels of latitude (see Fig. 1.2).

What about celestial east and west? We need a similar datum meridian to the Greenwich meridian on earth. The meridian chosen passes through a point on the celestial sphere called the First Point of Aries or just Aries (represented by the sign ♈). Celestial meridians are annotated in degrees west of Aries.

The angle subtended at the celestial pole between the meridian which passes through the First Point of Aries and the meridian upon which the star lies is the hour angle of that star.

For a star, this hour angle is called the sidereal hour angle (SHA) (see Fig. 1.3).

The choice of the celestial datum meridian was not quite as arbitrary as the choice of the Greenwich datum meridian. Because

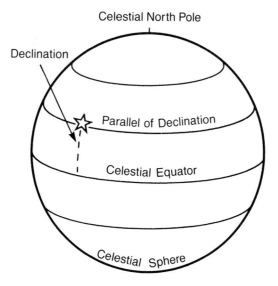

Fig 1.2 Declination. The declination of a star is measured from the celestial equator.

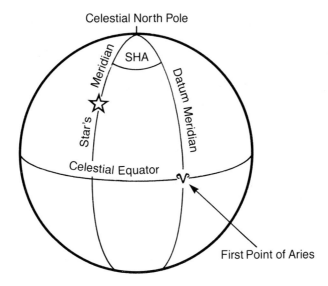

Fig 1.3 Sidereal Hour Angle. This is the angle subtended at the celestial pole between the meridian passing through the First Point of Aries and the star's meridian.

the earth's axis is tilted at an angle to the sun, as the sun moves along its annual apparent track on the celestial sphere (known as the ecliptic) its declination changes, so that it appears overhead in different latitudes at different times of the year, which is why the seasons occur. The plane of the ecliptic is inclined at an angle of 23° 27′ to the plane of the celestial equator (this angle being known as the obliquity of the ecliptic) (see Fig. 1.4). The sun's declination is 0° when it is over the equator, increasing throughout the year to 23° 27′ north and south.

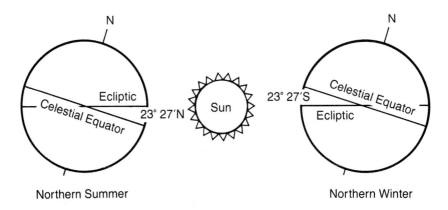

Fig 1.4 The Ecliptic. This is the sun's apparent track on the celestial sphere, and is inclined at an angle of 23° 27′ to the plane of the celestial equator.

As the sun travels along the ecliptic it passes through the constellations of Aries, Taurus, Gemini, Cancer, Leo, Virgo, Libra, Scorpio, Sagittarius, Capricorn, Aquarius and Pisces: the signs of the Zodiac. The ecliptic crosses the celestial equator at two points corresponding to the Spring (or Vernal) Equinox in March and the Autumnal Equinox in September.

When early astronomical observations were made the ecliptic intersected the celestial equator as the sun appeared to pass over the first star in the constellation of Aries. This point, called the First Point of Aries (FPA), was selected as the datum meridian (see Fig. 1.5). Due to a slight backward movement of the point of intersection of the ecliptic and the celestial equator, the sun's path no longer crosses the celestial equator in the constellation of Aries, but in the constellation of Pisces.

Although the stars are more or less fixed in space with a constant SHA and declination, the sun, moon and planets constantly move across the celestial sphere, so it is necessary that their hour angles and declinations are computed for specific times, and recorded in nautical

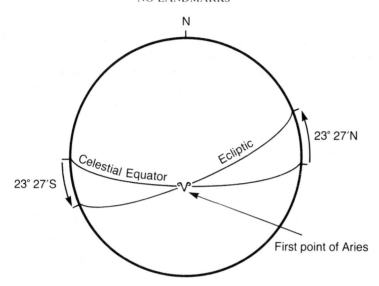

Fig 1.5 The First Point of Aries. This point was selected by early astronomers as the datum meridian on the celestial sphere, because at that time the ecliptic intersected the celestial equator as the sun appeared to pass over the first star in the constellation of Aries.

almanacs. As these times are related to Greenwich Mean Time (GMT), also known as Universal Time (UT), the recorded hour angle is measured from the Greenwich meridian and is known as the Greenwich Hour Angle (GHA). (A more detailed explanation is in Chapter Two.)

We can now define the position of a heavenly body in the celestial sphere by the co-ordinates declination and hour angle (similar to latitude and longitude on earth). How can we make use of this information? Suppose we draw a line from a star to the centre of the earth. The point where this line intersects the earth's surface is called the geographical position (GP) of the star (see Fig. 1.6). Similarly, a line projected from the earth's centre through our position on the earth's surface would reach the celestial sphere at a point (vertically above our position) called our zenith (see Fig. 1.7). The angle subtended at the earth's centre between the star and our zenith point on the celestial sphere is the same as that between the geographical position of the star and our position on the earth's surface (see Fig. 1.8). Knowing the earth's radius, the distance in miles can be determined between these corresponding points on earth. Distance in miles is, of course, meaningless on the celestial sphere. If we could determine the angular distance (in degrees and minutes) from the position of the star (which we will call X) to our zenith (which we will call Z) and we knew the position of the star, then we could fix the

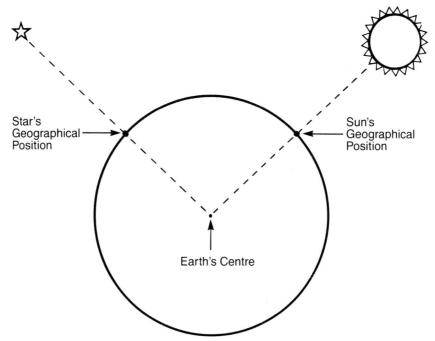

Fig 1.6 The Geographical Position of a star is the point where the line from that star to the centre of the earth meets the earth's surface.

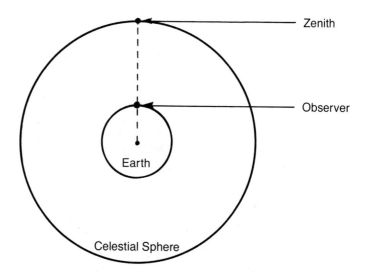

Fig 1.7 The Observer's Zenith: the point where a line projected from the earth's centre through the observer's position on the earth's surface, meets the celestial sphere.

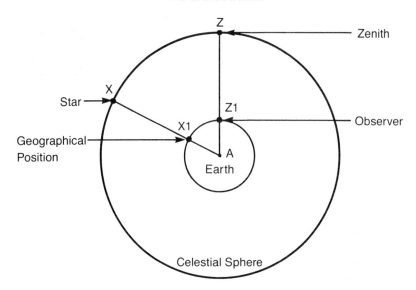

The angle subtended at A between X1 and Z1 is the same as the angle subtended at A between X and Z.

Fig 1.8 Zenith and Geographical Position.

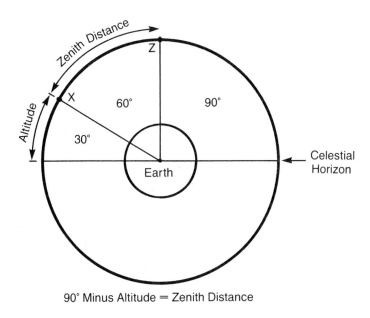

90° Minus Altitude = Zenith Distance

Fig 1.9 Zenith distance.

position of our zenith. If our position on earth is not precisely known
but we could determine (by measurement) the position of our zenith
(Z) then we could deduce our terrestrial position. We know the SHA
and declination of X. Can we determine (by measurement) the angle
between X and Z, convert it into equivalent terrestrial distance in
miles and plot this distance from the star's geographical position?
Unfortunately we cannot look vertically above our heads and find the
exact position of our zenith in the sky. However at 90° to our zenith
there is a plane through the centre of the earth which when projected
onto the celestial sphere forms a great circle called the celestial
horizon. If we could determine the angle between this horizon and
the star and subtract that angle from 90° we would then have the
angular distance between X and Z (which is called the zenith distance
[ZD]) (see Fig. 1.9). The angle between the visible horizon and the
star can be measured with a sextant. It is known as the sextant
altitude of the star. Corrections are made for the refraction of the
visible horizon, and the height of the observer's eye above sea level to
obtain the true altitude which is the altitude of the star above the
celestial horizon.

PZX triangle

Refer to Fig. 1.10. The angle subtended at P (the elevated pole)
between PZ (the observer's meridian) and PX (the star's meridian) is
the local hour angle (LHA) of the star. At any specific time we can
determine the LHA for any heavenly body.

The angular distance PX (called the polar distance) is 90° minus
(or plus) declination (dependent upon whether the star is on the same
or opposite side of the celestial equator as the observer's zenith). The
angular distance PZ (called co-latitude) is 90° minus the latitude of
the observer's position on the earth's surface. (Although the PZX
triangle is part of the celestial sphere, terrestrial polar distance can be
used to find angular distance PZ because, as shown in Fig. 1.8, the
angular distance is measured from the earth's centre and is the same
whether it is on the earth's surface or on the celestial sphere.)

Using the appropriate formula or a set of tables we can calculate
the length of the remaining side (ZX), of the triangle PZX. Side ZX
is the zenith distance (ZD).

We know already that we can measure a true altitude and thus find
a true zenith distance so why do we need to calculate one? Although
we know the geographical position of the star and the angular
distance we are from it, this distance when converted into miles may
be as much as 7000. It would clearly be impossible to measure such a

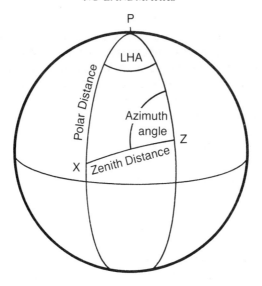

Fig 1.10 The PZX triangle.

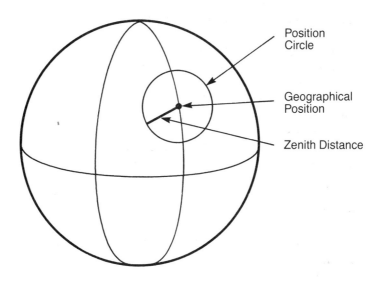

Fig 1.11 The Position Circle.

distance on our chart. The geographical position may not even be on the chart we are using. Also, unless we could determine the direction of the star's geographical position very accurately, we would know only that we were on a position circle the centre of which was the star's geographical position (see Fig. 1.11).

However, by comparing the calculated and true zenith distances we can determine the distance between the true position circle and the calculated one.

Example 1.

True zenith distance (TZD)	50° 18'·1
Calculated zenith distance, (CZD)	50° 24'·7
Angular difference	6'·6

In this case, the angular difference is 6'·6, which is equivalent to a distance of 6·6 nautical miles on the earth's surface.

This distance (known as the intercept) is named 'towards' or 'away' dependent upon whether the true position circle lies nearer to, or further away from, the geographical position than the calculated position circle. In the example, the intercept is 'towards', so we are 6·6 nautical miles nearer to the geographical position than the DR or chosen position indicated.

In practice, altitude (90° minus zenith distance) can be used to determine the intercept (see Fig. 1.12).

On a chart of the earth's surface the calculated position circle passes through our dead reckoning position, or a specially chosen position near our dead reckoning position, and so we can plot the intercept from that position, provided we can determine the direction of the star's geographical position.

Azimuth

Refer to Fig. 1.10. The angle subtended at Z between the meridian through Z and the great circle passing through the star (X) and the zenith (Z) indicates the direction the star is bearing from Z.

This angle, called the azimuth angle, is measured eastward or westward through 180° and from north or south according to the elevated pole.

For plotting purposes a bearing (called an azimuth), measured eastward from north through 360° is required. A comparison between azimuth angle and azimuth is shown in Fig. 1.13.

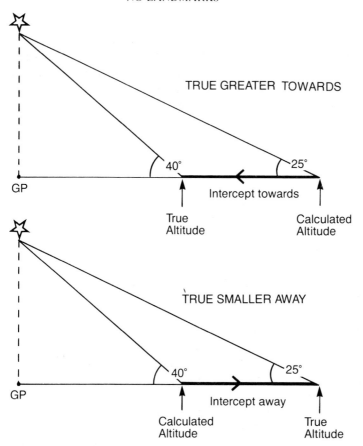

TRUE GREATER TOWARDS

40°   25°

Intercept towards

True   Calculated
Altitude   Altitude

TRUE SMALLER AWAY

40°   25°

Intercept away

Calculated   True
Altitude   Altitude

The rule True Greater Towards and True Smaller Away applies to angular differences of altitudes. For zenith distances (90°–altitude) the rule is reversed.

Fig 1.12 Intercept.

The intercept is plotted along the line of azimuth. As only an infinitely small part of the position circle is required, it can be plotted as a straight position line at 90° to the azimuth (see Fig. 1.14).

Although the azimuth calculated from the tables is accurate, a small error extended over the distance from the star's geographical position can produce a large position error, hence we cannot use the azimuth to pinpoint our position on the position line. Therefore to find the observed position, it is necessary to take at least two sights and plot at least two position lines.

A compass bearing of the star could be taken, but this would not be accurate enough for plotting purposes.

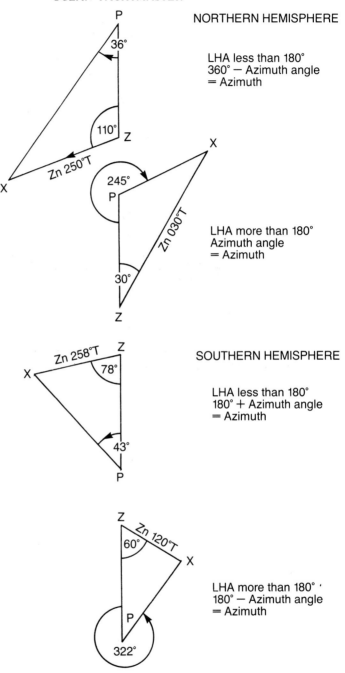

NORTHERN HEMISPHERE

LHA less than 180°
360° − Azimuth angle
= Azimuth

LHA more than 180°
Azimuth angle
= Azimuth

SOUTHERN HEMISPHERE

LHA less than 180°
180° + Azimuth angle
= Azimuth

LHA more than 180° ˙
180° − Azimuth angle
= Azimuth

X = Heavenly Body   Z = Azimuth Angle   Zn = Azimuth

Fig 1.13 Azimuth.

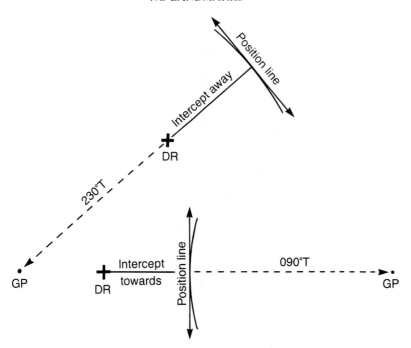

Because only a small portion of the position circle's circumference is used, this can be represented as a straight line.

Fig 1.14 Position Line.

QUESTION PAPER 1

1.1 What is the Ecliptic?

1.2 What is the First Point of Aries?

1.3 Define:
   a. Declination.
   b. Sidereal Hour Angle.

1.4 Compare the true and calculated altitudes to find the intercept, and determine whether it is away or towards the geographical position:

True Altitude	Calculated Altitude
50° 06'·7	50° 17'·4
36° 08'·1	36° 20'·3
71° 01'·0	70° 54'·5
15° 26'·7	15° 10'·6
28° 51'·2	29° 00'·3
51° 20'·4	51° 10'·1

Answers on page 154.

Chapter Two

Hour Angles

Look again at the PZX triangle in Fig. 1.10. The angle subtended at P (the elevated pole) between the meridians through Z (the observer's zenith) and X (the heavenly body) is the local hour angle (LHA) of X (the heavenly body). When a heavenly body, for instance the sun, is on the observer's meridian its LHA is 0° (Fig. 2.1a) but as the sun's position changes due to the apparent westerly rotation of the celestial sphere, its LHA increases steadily through 360° during 24 hours until it is again on the observer's meridian (Fig. 2.1b).

Local hour angle is needed to find calculated altitude and azimuth from the tables.

It is not feasible to tabulate in an almanac the LHA of all heavenly bodies, but it is possible to tabulate the hour angles with reference to the Greenwich meridian of the main heavenly bodies used for navigation. The angle subtended at the elevated pole between the Greenwich meridian and the heavenly body's geographical position is known as the Greenwich Hour Angle (GHA) and it is measured westwards through 360° (see Fig. 2.2).

The *Nautical Almanac (NP 314)* tabulates the GHA of Aries, the four navigational planets (Venus, Mars, Jupiter and Saturn), the sun and the moon, daily for each hour, with an 'Increments and Corrections' table at the back of the almanac for minutes and seconds.

The LHA is found by applying the observer's longitude to the GHA found in the almanac. If an observer is west of Greenwich a heavenly body will cross the Greenwich meridian before it reaches the observer's meridian, so the GHA will be greater than the LHA. If an observer is east of Greenwich, a heavenly body will cross the observer's meridian before it crosses the Greenwich meridian, so

a)

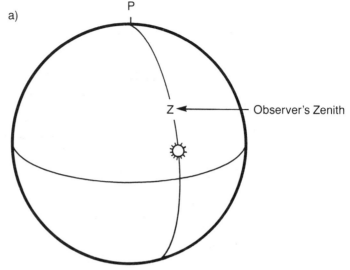

The sun is on the observer's meridian

LHA 0°

b)

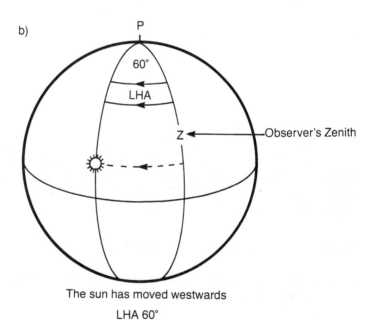

The sun has moved westwards

LHA 60°

Fig 2.1 Local Hour Angle.

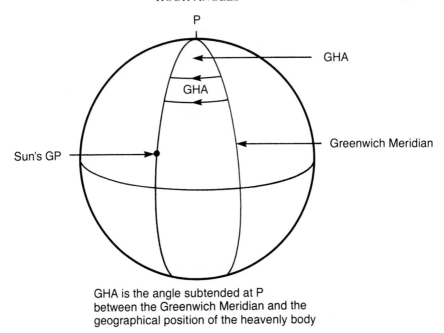

GHA is the angle subtended at P
between the Greenwich Meridian and the
geographical position of the heavenly body

Fig 2.2 Greenwich Hour Angle.

the GHA will be less than the LHA. The difference between GHA
and LHA is equivalent to the observer's longitude which is
measured from the Greenwich meridian. In longitude west, GHA
minus longitude will equal LHA, but in longitude east, GHA plus
longitude will equal LHA (see Fig. 2.3).

Example 2 (Use Extract Nos. 1 and 2)

What is the LHA of the sun on March 7th at 08h 46m 03s GMT in
the following longitudes?

(a) 85° 24'·7W
(b) 15° 07'·4E

The GHA for 08 hours is found on the daily page in the *Nautical
Almanac* for March 7th, 8th and 9th. The column headed 'Sun' is
used.

a)

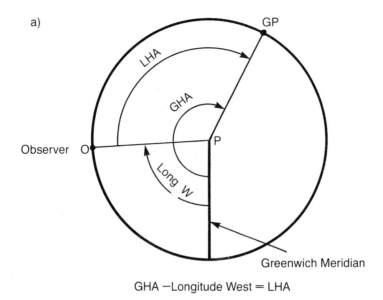

GHA −Longitude West = LHA

b)

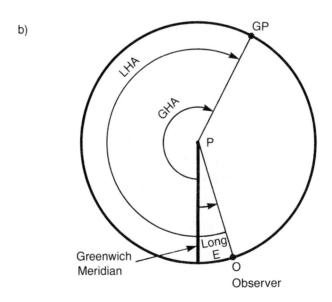

GHA + Longitude East = LHA

Fig 2.3 Deriving LHA from GHA and Longitude.

1980 MARCH 7, 8, 9 (FRI., SAT., SUN.)

G.M.T.	SUN	
	G.H.A.	Dec.
d h	° ′	° ′
7 00	177 13.2	S 5 18.0
01	192 13.4	17.0
02	207 13.5	16.0
03	222 13.7 ··	15.1
04	237 13.8	14.1
05	252 14.0	13.1
06	267 14.1	S 5 12.1
07	282 14.3	11.2
08	297 14.4	10.2
F 09	312 14.6 ··	09.2
R 10	327 14.7	08.2
I 11	342 14.9	07.3
D 12	357 15.0	S 5 06.3
A 13	12 15.2	05.3
Y 14	27 15.3	04.4
15	42 15.5 ··	03.4
16	57 15.6	02.4
17	72 15.8	01.4
18	87 15.9	S 5 00.5
19	102 16.1	4 59.5
20	117 16.2	58.5
21	132 16.4 ··	57.5
22	147 16.6	56.6
23	162 16.7	55.6
8 00	177 16.9	S 4 54.6
01	192 17.0	53.6
02	207 17.2	52.7
03	222 17.3 ··	51.7
04	237 17.5	50.7
05	252 17.6	49.7
06	267 17.8	S 4 48.8
07	282 17.9	47.8
S 08	297 18.1	46.8
A 09	312 18.2 ··	45.8
T 10	327 18.4	44.9
U 11	342 18.6	43.9
R 12	357 18.7	S 4 42.9
D 13	12 18.9	41.9
A 14	27 19.0	41.0
Y 15	42 19.2 ··	40.0
16	57 19.3	39.0
17	72 19.5	38.0

Extract Number 1

The day in large type and the hours (00h to 23h) in smaller type are shown down the left hand side of the page for each day. The increment for 46m 03s is found from the 'Increments and Corrections' table at the back of the almanac under the heading 'Sun and Planets'.

46^m INCREMENTS AND CORRECTIONS

46^m	SUN PLANETS	ARIES	MOON	v or Corrⁿ d		v or Corrⁿ d		v or Corrⁿ d	
s	° ′	° ′	° ′	′	′	′	′	′	′
00	11 30·0	11 31·9	10 58·6	0·0	0·0	6·0	4·7	12·0	9·3
01	11 30·3	11 32·1	10 58·8	0·1	0·1	6·1	4·7	12·1	9·4
02	11 30·5	11 32·4	10 59·0	0·2	0·2	6·2	4·8	12·2	9·5
03	11 30·8	11 32·6	10 59·3	0·3	0·2	6·3	4·9	12·3	9·5
04	11 31·0	11 32·9	10 59·5	0·4	0·3	6·4	5·0	12·4	9·6
05	11 31·3	11 33·1	10 59·8	0·5	0·4	6·5	5·0	12·5	9·7
06	11 31·5	11 33·4	11 00·0	0·6	0·5	6·6	5·1	12·6	9·8
07	11 31·8	11 33·6	11 00·2	0·7	0·5	6·7	5·2	12·7	9·8
08	11 32·0	11 33·9	11 00·5	0·8	0·6	6·8	5·3	12·8	9·9
09	11 32·3	11 34·1	11 00·7	0·9	0·7	6·9	5·3	12·9	10·0
10	11 32·5	11 34·4	11 01·0	1·0	0·8	7·0	5·4	13·0	10·1
11	11 32·8	11 34·6	11 01·2	1·1	0·9	7·1	5·5	13·1	10·2
12	11 33·0	11 34·9	11 01·4	1·2	0·9	7·2	5·6	13·2	10·2
13	11 33·3	11 35·1	11 01·7	1·3	1·0	7·3	5·7	13·3	10·3
14	11 33·5	11 35·4	11 01·9	1·4	1·1	7·4	5·7	13·4	10·4
15	11 33·8	11 35·6	11 02·1	1·5	1·2	7·5	5·8	13·5	10·5
16	11 34·0	11 35·9	11 02·4	1·6	1·2	7·6	5·9	13·6	10·5
17	11 34·3	11 36·2	11 02·6	1·7	1·3	7·7	6·0	13·7	10·6
18	11 34·5	11 36·4	11 02·9	1·8	1·4	7·8	6·0	13·8	10·7
19	11 34·8	11 36·7	11 03·1	1·9	1·5	7·9	6·1	13·9	10·8
20	11 35·0	11 36·9	11 03·3	2·0	1·6	8·0	6·2	14·0	10·9
21	11 35·3	11 37·2	11 03·6	2·1	1·6	8·1	6·3	14·1	10·9
22	11 35·5	11 37·4	11 03·8	2·2	1·7	8·2	6·4	14·2	11·0
23	11 35·8	11 37·7	11 04·1	2·3	1·8	8·3	6·4	14·3	11·1
24	11 36·0	11 37·9	11 04·3	2·4	1·9	8·4	6·5	14·4	11·2

Extract Number 2

March 7th
GHA sun 08h   297° 14′·4   297° 14′·4
increment 46m 03s   + 11° 30′·8   + 11° 30′·8

GHA 08h 46m 03s   308° 45′·2   308° 45′·2
long. W   − 85° 24′·7   long. E + 15° 07′·4

LHA sun 08h 46m 03s 223° 20′·5   323° 52′·6

The final figure should be between 0° and 360°. It may be necessary to add or subtract 360° to make it so, (see Fig 2.4a and 2.4b).

Example 3 (Use Extract Nos. 1 and 2)

Find the LHA of the sun on March 8th at 14h 46m 10s GMT, longitude 75° 04′·6W

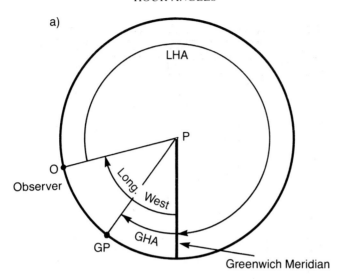

GHA + 360° − Longitude W = LHA

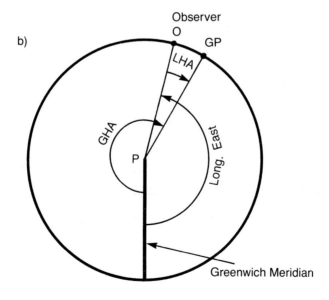

GHA + Longitude E −360° = LHA

Fig 2.4

March 8th	GHA sun 14h	27° 19'·0
	increment 46m 10s	+ 11° 32'·5
	GHA 14h 46m 10s	38° 51'·5
	add 360°	+ 360° 00'·0
		398° 51'·5
	long. W	− 75° 04'·6
	LHA sun 14h 46m 10s	323° 46'·9

Example 4 (Use Extract Nos. 1 and 2)

Find the LHA of the sun on March 8th at 01h 46m 15s GMT in longitude 165° 22'·7E

March 8th	GHA sun 01h	192° 17'·0
	increment 46m 15s	+ 11° 33'·8
	GHA sun 01h 46m 15s	203° 50'·8
	long. E	+ 165° 22'·7
		369° 13'·5
	subtract 360	− 360° 00'·0
	LHA sun 01h 46m 15s	9° 13'·5

GHA is not tabulated for stars. On the daily page under 'Aries', the GHA of Aries is tabulated. On the same page the SHA and declination of 57 selected stars is also tabulated. The GHA of a star can be found by adding the GHA of Aries to the SHA of the star, (see Fig. 2.5).

Example 5 (Use Extract Nos. 2 and 3)

Find the GHA of Altair on March 7th at 07h 46m 19s GMT.

SHA Altair	62° 33'·1+
GHA Aries 07h	270° 09'·1
increment 46m 19s	11° 36'·7
GHA Altair 07h 46m 19s	344° 18'·9

If the LHA is required, longitude is applied as in examples 2 and 4.

1980 MARCH 7, 8, 9 (FRI., SAT., SUN.)

G.M.T.	ARIES G.H.A.	VENUS −3.8 G.H.A.	Dec.	STARS Name	S.H.A.	Dec.
d h	° ′	° ′	° ′		° ′	° ′
7 00	164 51.8	137 08.3 N12	38.1	Acamar	315 37.8	S40 23.4
01	179 54.3	152 08.2	39.3	Achernar	335 46.1	S57 20.6
02	194 56.8	167 08.0	40.4	Acrux	173 36.9	S62 59.3
03	209 59.2	182 07.8 ··	41.6	Adhara	255 32.2	S28 57.0
04	225 01.7	197 07.7	42.8	Aldebaran	291 18.5	N16 28.1
05	240 04.2	212 07.5	43.9			
06	255 06.6	227 07.3 N12	45.1	Alioth	166 42.4	N56 03.9
07	270 09.1	242 07.1	46.3	Alkaid	153 18.5	N49 24.6
08	285 11.6	257 07.0	47.4	Al Na'ir	28 15.9	S47 03.5
F 09	300 14.0	272 06.8 ··	48.6	Alnilam	276 12.0	S 1 13.1
R 10	315 16.5	287 06.6	49.8	Alphard	218 20.6	S 8 34.5
I 11	330 18.9	302 06.5	50.9			
D 12	345 21.4	317 06.3 N12	52.1	Alphecca	126 32.3	N26 46.7
A 13	0 23.9	332 06.1	53.2	Alpheratz	358 10.0	N28 58.7
Y 14	15 26.3	347 05.9	54.4	Altair	62 33.1	N 8 48.8
15	30 28.8	2 05.8 ··	55.6	Ankaa	353 41.0	S42 25.1
				Antares	112 57.2	S26 23.2

	h m		
Mer. Pass.	12 54.5	v −0.2	d 1.2

Extract Number 3

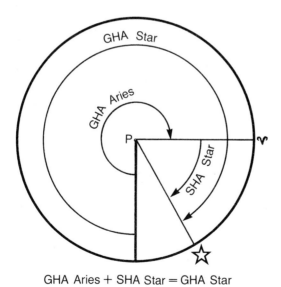

GHA Aries + SHA Star = GHA Star

Fig 2.5

'v' correction

Tabulations in the *Nautical Almanac* for GHA are based upon an assumed hourly rate of change which for Aries is 15° 02'·46, for the sun and the planets 15° 00'·0 and for the moon 14° 19'·0.

The actual hourly rates of change of the heavenly bodies differ from these tabulated values and so a quantity called 'v', which is the hourly difference between the tabulated and actual value, is included on the daily pages. For the planets quantity 'v' is tabulated tri-daily at the bottom of the appropriate GHA column; but for the moon, because its daily rate of change is significant, it is given hourly.

The correction applicable to quantity 'v' is found in the 'Increments and Corrections' table, corresponding to the extra minutes of GMT required. Quantity 'v' is tabulated under the heading 'v or d' and the correction (which is alongside it) under 'corrn'. It is added to the GHA except occasionally in the case of Venus (when it is prefixed by a minus sign).

No correction is given for the sun or stars as this is already incorporated in the tabulated figures.

Example 6 (Use Extract Nos. 2 and 3)

Find the GHA of Venus on March 7th at 09h 46m 01s GMT

The GHA of Venus for 09h is found on the daily page under the heading 'Venus'. Quantity 'v' is found at the bottom of the Venus column under GHA. The increment for 46m 01s is found in the 'Increments and Corrections' table for 46m. The 'v' correction for 46 minutes is found in the same table. Seconds are ignored.

March 7th GHA Venus 09h   272° 06'·8 +
           increment 46m 01s   11° 30'·3
                                   ─────────
                                   283° 37'·1 −
           quantity 'v' −0·2   0'·2 ('v' correction
                                   ─────────   for 46m)
           GHA Venus 09h 46m 01s 283° 36'·9

The 'v' correction is subtracted because quantity 'v' is prefixed by a minus sign.

Declination

Declination for the sun, moon and planets is tabulated hourly on the daily pages of the *Nautical Almanac*.

'd' correction

For extra minutes of GMT in excess of the tabulated hour, interpolation is necessary and a quantity called 'd', which is the mean hourly difference of declination, is given on each daily page for this purpose (tri-daily for the sun and planets, hourly for the moon).

The correction applicable to quantity 'd' is found in the 'Increments and Corrections' table for the appropriate number of minutes under the heading 'corrn', alongside quantity 'd' which is under the heading 'v or d'.

There is no correction for the stars.

Example 7 (Use Extract Nos. 2 and 3)

Find the declination of Venus on March 7th at 09h 46m 01s GMT.

Declination is found alongside the GHA in the Venus table. Quantity 'd' is found at the bottom of the declination column. The 'd' correction is found in the 'Increments and Corrections' table for 46 minutes. Seconds are ignored.

This correction is added if declination is increasing and subtracted if declination is decreasing.

March 7th
dec. Venus 09h   N12° 48'·6 + (increasing)
d 1·2   0'·9 (correction for 46m)

dec. Venus 09h 46m 01s   N12° 49'·5

The 'd' correction is added because declination is increasing.

QUESTION PAPER TWO

2.1   What is the GHA and declination of the sun on June 22nd at 09h 10m 0s GMT?

2.2   Find the GHA of Aries on March 7th at 14h 46m 10s GMT.

2.3   What is the LHA and declination of the moon on March 9th at 06h 10m 05s GMT, longitude 7° 24'·1W.

2.4   What is the LHA and declination of Spica on October 5th at 21h 36m 50s GMT, longitude 80° 16'·4E?

2.5   Find the LHA and declination of Jupiter on March 7th at 10h 36m 05s GMT, longitude 20° 16'·2W.

Answers on pages 154–5.

Chapter Three

Finding The Time

As the sun proceeds upon its daily journey across the sky, it provides us with a very convenient 24 hour clock. It does not keep perfect time but varies slightly throughout the year as it moves along the ecliptic. If we noted the time that the sun crossed our meridian every day, we would see that this varied slightly either side of 1200. Let us look at the extreme values: in October the sun would cross our meridian at approximately 1144; in February it would be later at about 1214. As it would be inconvenient for our timekeeping to have a constantly altering midday, we assume an imaginary mean sun which moves along the celestial equator and always keeps perfect time (called mean time). In this way the middle of the day will be at 1200 every day. The time difference between the mean sun and the true sun is called the Equation of Time. This is tabulated daily in the *Nautical Almanac* together with the time the true sun transits the Greenwich meridian.

Mean time could be measured from the time of the sun's passage across a local meridian (that time being 1200 local mean time (LMT)) but if everyone in the world kept their own local time there would be complete confusion. Neither is it practical for the whole world to keep the time of one meridian, such as the Greenwich meridian, although the Greenwich meridian is used for reference. Therefore, each country keeps a local standard time corresponding to a suitable local meridian. Places east of Greenwich will have local midday before that at Greenwich and in places west of Greenwich local midday will occur later.

By applying longitude converted to time (using the 'Conversion of Arc to Time' table) to LMT, the GMT (also known as Universal Time, UT) can be found:

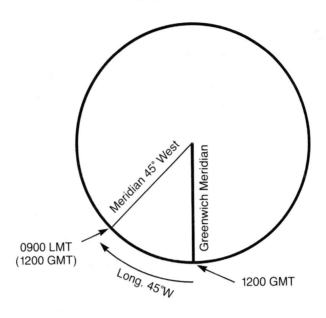

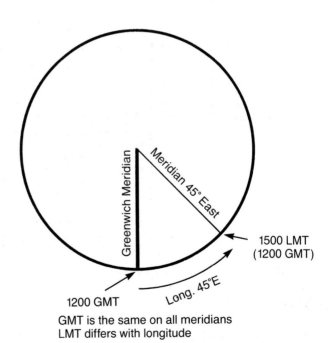

GMT is the same on all meridians
LMT differs with longitude

Fig 3.1 Local Mean Time.

The rule is:

$$GMT = LMT + long.\ W$$
(sun's passage AFTER Greenwich ADD)

$$GMT = LMT - long.\ E$$
(sun's passage SOONER than Greenwich SUBTRACT)

Example 8 (Use Extract No. 4)

	h m			h m	
	03 53	LMT		12 33	LMT
long. 60° 15'·0W+	04 01		long. 5° 15'·0E−	21	
	07 54	GMT		12 12	GMT

CONVERSION OF ARC TO TIME

0°–59°		60°–119°			0'·00	0'·25	0'·50	0'·75
°	h m	°	h m	'	m s	m s	m s	m s
0	0 00	60	4 00	0	0 00	0 01	0 02	0 03
1	0 04	61	4 04	1	0 04	0 05	0 06	0 07
2	0 08	62	4 08	2	0 08	0 09	0 10	0 11
3	0 12	63	4 12	3	0 12	0 13	0 14	0 15
4	0 16	64	4 16	4	0 16	0 17	0 18	0 19
5	0 20	65	4 20	5	0 20	0 21	0 22	0 23
6	0 24	66	4 24	6	0 24	0 25	0 26	0 27
7	0 28	67	4 28	7	0 28	0 29	0 30	0 31
8	0 32	68	4 32	8	0 32	0 33	0 34	0 35
9	0 36	69	4 36	9	0 36	0 37	0 38	0 39
				10	0 40	0 41	0 42	0 43
				11	0 44	0 45	0 46	0 47
				12	0 48	0 49	0 50	0 51
				13	0 52	0 53	0 54	0 55
				14	0 56	0 57	0 58	0 59
				15	1 00	1 01	1 02	1 03
				16	1 04	1 05	1 06	1 07
				17	1 08	1 09	1 10	1 11
				18	1 12	1 13	1 14	1 15
				19	1 16	1 17	1 18	1 19

Extract Number 4

Zone Time

For general convenience, particularly of travellers whose meridian is constantly changing, the world has been divided into time zones which differ from adjacent zones by 1 hour (see Fig. 3.2). The zones

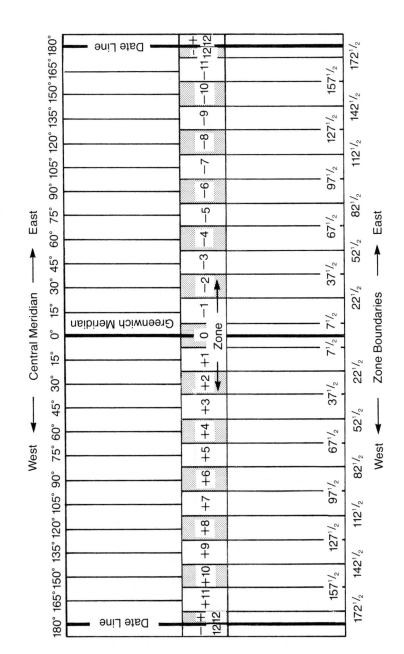

Fig 3.2 Time Zones.

are labelled from +1 to +12 west of Greenwich and −1 to −12 east of Greenwich, the +12 and −12 zones being, of course, synonymous. The time kept in each zone corresponds to the local standard time of its central meridian. To find GMT given zone time, obey the sign and add or subtract the number of hours indicated. When going from GMT to zone time reverse the sign.

Example 9

	h m			h m	
	05 31	+ zone time		17 16	− zone time
zone +4	04 00		zone −9	09 00	
	09 31	GMT		08 16	GMT

It is usual to keep a separate clock on the boat showing zone time which will be the boat's time for routine tasks such as changing watches. This clock is retarded one hour when travelling westward into another time zone and advanced one hour when travelling eastward. A record is kept in the boat's log book indicating the time zone to which the boat's clock is set.

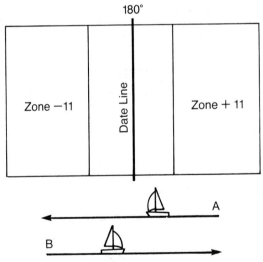

Boat A on a westerly course gains one day
Boat B on an easterly course loses one day

Fig 3.3 International Date Line.

International Date Line

The centre of time zone 12 (+ or −) is the 180th meridian. Crossing this meridian on a westerly course will gain one day and on an easterly course will lose one day (see Fig. 3.3).

The International Date Line to an extent corresponds with this meridian. However, it is conveniently sited around land masses and groups of islands that straddle the 180th meridian.

Greenwich date

Suppose it is 0200 in time zone −9 (in longitude east) on May 10th. The chronometer (showing GMT) indicates 5h 00m but it is not obvious whether it is 5h 00m in the morning or 5h 00m in the afternoon at Greenwich. When we correct the zone time to GMT (0200− 0900), it is seen to be 5h 00m in the afternoon (17h 00m) at Greenwich on the previous day. The correct Greenwich date is May 9th.

Example 10

	h m		
	02 00	− zone time 10d	(d = day)
zone −9	09 00		
	17 00	GMT 9d	

It is important to check the Greenwich date (GD) and time as these are used to enter the *Nautical Almanac*. Tabulations in the *Nautical Almanac* are in astronomical time (00–24 hours).

Chronometer

A chronometer is a very accurate timepiece which is kept at GMT. If it is mechanical, to minimise errors it should be wound every day at approximately the same time by the same person.

A quartz chronometer can be affected by temperature variation and so should be kept at as constant a temperature as possible. It is by far the best choice for a small boat, as a mechanical chronometer does not take kindly to the constant motion experienced in such a craft. Generally chronometers should be kept clear of magnetic fields and stowed in a safe dry place.

The time by chronometer should be compared regularly with

radio time signals. In this way any error can be recorded daily (in the deck log). The rate of change of the error can thus be observed and the daily errors can be estimated if no radio time check is available.

The Global Positioning System (GPS) uses very accurate time measurement, which can be accessed. In operation GPS time is corrected automatically but the onboard indication can drift without correction, producing an apparent difference with the radio time signal.

Example 11

On June 4th the chronometer which gains 3 seconds per day was 01m 06s fast. On June 7th the time shown on the same chronometer was 08h 10m 02s. What is the correct GMT?

Daily gain:	3 seconds
Total gain for 3 days:	9 seconds
Chronometer error on June 4th:	01m 06s fast
Chronometer error on June 7th:	01m 15s fast
	h m s
Chronometer time June 7th	08 10 01
Chronometer error June 7th	− 01 15
Correct GMT June 7th	08 08 46

Admiralty List of Radio Signals, Volume 2, gives the radio stations that broadcast regular time signals.

DECK WATCH

As it is not advisable to move the chronometer on deck when sights are taken, it is necessary to have a separate watch for this purpose. This can be a deck watch which is like a large pocket watch but kept in a padded box, or a reliable quartz watch. The error in deck watch time is obtained by comparison with the chronometer.

A deck watch also acts as a reserve for the chronometer.

QUESTION PAPER THREE

3.1 What is the GMT in the following time zones?

	zone time	zone
	h m	
a	04 36	−2
b	10 21	+5
c	06 40	+8
d	11 54	−7

3.2 Convert LMT to GMT. (Work to the nearest minute.)

	LMT	Long.
	h m	
a	12 40	5° 02'·0E
b	09 12	18° 07'·1W
c	22 45	3° 28'·0E
d	02 18	45° 15'·1W

3.3 Check the Greenwich Date.

local date	zone time	zone
	h m	
a June 12th	17 50	+9
b October 4th	05 20	−10

local date	LMT	Long.
	h m	
c July 6th	20 51	174° 14'·0W
d August 14th	11 43	169° 50'·0E

(Work to the nearest minute)

3.4 On July 14th a chronometer was 6 seconds slow. On July 18th it was 14 seconds slow. What was its error on July 21st?

3.5 On January 10th a chronometer was 30s fast. On January 12th it was 34s fast. On January 15th a sight was taken when the chronometer showed 05h 10m 15s. What was the correct GMT?

Answers on pages 155–6.

Chapter Four

Measuring The Angles

The sextant is a precision instrument used to measure an angle to an accuracy of one tenth of a minute. In celestial navigation this angle is between a heavenly body (such as the sun) and the horizon.

The sextant has two mirrors: one attached to a movable arm, called the index arm; and the other mirror (the horizon mirror) which is half silvered and half plain is level with the telescope on the body of the sextant. The index arm pivots on the sextant frame along an arc graduated in degrees called the index. There is a micrometer head for minutes and tenths of a minute.

When the index arm is moved to position the index mirror at the correct angle to the horizon mirror, an observer viewing the horizon directly under the sun through the sextant telescope would see the reflected image of the sun on the horizon (see Fig. 4.1).

The altitude of the sun, which is the angle at the observer between the sun and the horizon, would be indicated on the index by the index arm (see Fig. 4.2).

Taking a Sight

To take a sight of a star or planet the index arm is set to zero and the heavenly body viewed through the telescope. The clamp which secures the index arm is released and the sextant swivelled to bring the image of the heavenly body to the horizon. The micrometer head is used for final adjustment. The heavenly body should appear just to touch the horizon. To ensure that the sextant is vertical, it should be swung pendulum fashion from side to side so that the heavenly body touches the horizon at the bottom of the swing (see Fig. 4.3).

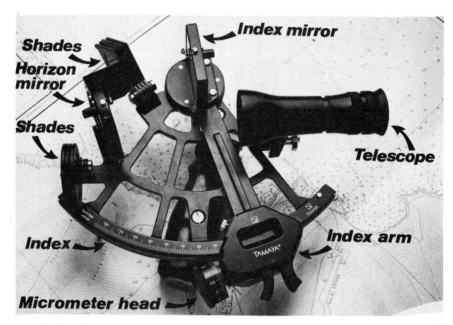

Plate 1 A modern yachtsman's sextant. This one is made by Tamaya, Japan. (*Photo courtesy of Telesonic Marine Ltd.*)

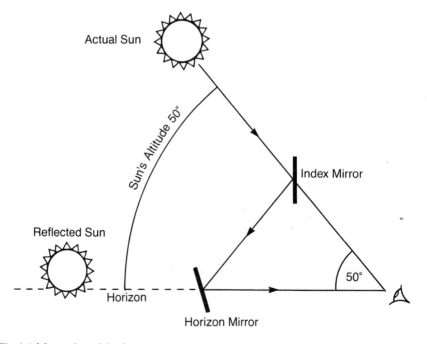

Fig 4.1 Measuring altitude.

Sometimes to find a star, its approximate altitude can be set on the sextant which is moved from side to side sweeping the horizon directly beneath the star. When the star's image appears in the telescope the micrometer head is turned to bring it to the horizon.

It is also possible to hold the sextant upside down in the left hand, aimed at the star, with the index arm set to zero. The index arm is moved until the horizon appears near the star. The sextant is then turned the correct way up and pointed at the horizon directly under the star. The micrometer head is used for the final adjustment and the sextant should be swung as before to ensure it is being held vertically.

For observations of the sun both the index and horizon shades should be used. The sextant is pointed at the horizon directly beneath the sun and by moving the index arm and the micrometer head the sun's image is brought to the horizon.

Sextant Errors

Like all instruments, the sextant is subject to errors, some of which can be corrected, some of which are inherent in the instrument and cannot be corrected.

The adjustable errors are all caused by incorrect alignment of the mirrors in relation to the instrument and to each other.

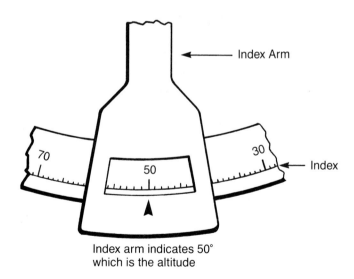

Index arm indicates 50°
which is the altitude

Fig 4.2 Reading the altitude.

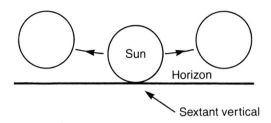

The sextant is vertical when
the sun is at the lowest point
of the arc.

Fig 4.3 Swinging the sextant to ensure that the instrument is vertical.

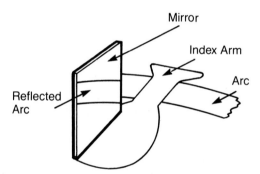

Fig 4.4 An error of perpendicularity. This can be seen clearly here. The index arc and its reflected image should make a perfect curve.

Fig 4.5 Checking for side error on your sextant.

ERROR OF PERPENDICULARITY

This error is caused when the index mirror is not perpendicular to the plane of the instrument. To check for this, you may need to take out the telescope. Set the index arm about halfway along the index, move the shades out of the way and hold the sextant horizontally, mirrors uppermost. Look obliquely into the index mirror. The actual index arc and its reflected image should make a continuous curve. If they do not there is an error of perpendicularity present (see Fig. 4.4). This is corrected by adjusting the screw behind the index mirror. This adjustment must be done first.

SIDE ERROR

To check for side error the index arm is set to zero and with the sextant held in the vertical position a star which has a fairly low altitude is sighted. When the micrometer screw is turned gently both ways, the reflected image of the star should pass directly over the actual star. If it does not and the image is horizontally displaced, the horizon mirror is not perpendicular to the plane of the instrument (see Fig. 4.5). During daylight, set the index arm to zero, hold the sextant in the vertical position and sight any distant clearly defined object that has a vertical edge, such as a chimney, flagstaff or building. If there is no side error the actual and reflected image will coincide.

The adjustment is done by turning the screw behind the horizon mirror that moves the mirror forwards or backwards (usually the screw furthest from the instrument).

INDEX ERROR

If the horizon mirror is not parallel with the index mirror, index error will occur. This can be found by one of the following methods:

1. USING THE HORIZON

The index arm is set to zero and with the sextant in the vertical position a distant horizon (about 5 miles away to avoid sextant parallax) is viewed through the telescope. The true horizon and its reflected image should appear as a continuous line. If they do not index error is present (see Fig. 4.6A).

To find the error the micrometer head is turned until true and reflected horizons coincide. The reading on the index is the error.

2. USING THE SUN

The sextant is held either vertically or horizontally and the index arm set to 32' *off* the arc (before the zero mark). Using the necessary shades the sun is sighted through the telescope. The true sun and its reflected image will be seen one above the other (or side by side) (see Fig. 4.6B). The micrometer head is turned until both suns coincide and the reading noted. The procedure is repeated but the index arm set to 32' *on* the arc (after the zero mark). The difference between the two readings is the index error. If the greater reading is *on* the arc the error is subtracted from any altitudes taken. If the greater reading is *off* the arc the error is added.

   If both readings are on the same side of the zero mark, the readings are added together and the total halved to give the index error which is added if the readings are *off* the arc and subtracted if they are *on* the arc.

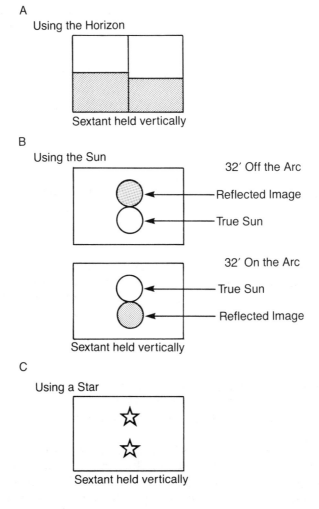

A
Using the Horizon

Sextant held vertically

B
Using the Sun

32' Off the Arc

Reflected Image

True Sun

32' On the Arc

True Sun

Reflected Image

Sextant held vertically

C
Using a Star

Sextant held vertically

Fig 4.6 Checking for index error.

The sum of the readings divided by four should agree with the semi-diameter tabulated in the *Nautical Almanac* for the day in question.

3. USING A STAR

The sextant is held in the vertical position and the index arm set to zero. A star is sighted. If any error is present the star and its reflected image will be seen vertically displaced (see Fig. 4.6C). The amount of error is found by bringing the star and its image into coincidence.

Adjustment for index error is made by turning the screw that swivels the horizon mirror, usually the one nearest the instrument.

Adjustments for side error and index error must be done in combination as the same mirror is involved and these errors interact.

When the necessary corrections have been made there is usually still a small amount of index error present which is left and allowed for. The sextant should be checked for index error every time before it is used because the screws behind the mirrors can work loose. Note that it is not good practice to adjust continually for small errors as this can cause the screws to become loose.

COLLIMATION ERROR

This is caused by the incorrect alignment of the axis of the telescope with the plane of the instrument. It should not occur on a reliable modern sextant, and many present day sextants do not have any means of adjusting this error.

NON-ADJUSTABLE ERRORS

Errors, such as bad optics, incorrect graduation of the index, index not on a common pivot with the index arm, cannot be corrected.

A good sextant will have a certificate tabulating its residual errors, which should be small, for various altitudes.

Care of the Sextant

The sextant is an essential and expensive instrument and should be treated with care. When removing from the case it should be lifted by the frame with the left hand and transferred to the right hand (holding the handle).

After use the mirrors, shades and scale should be wiped clean of spray or damp, using soft material such as a chamois leather, as abrasive material causes damage. It should be protected from knocks and always handled gently. When not in use it should be stowed in its box.

Practical considerations when taking a sight

1. Heavenly bodies with low altitudes, (less than 10°), especially the sun, should be avoided as refraction will give false readings.
2. Greenwich mean time of each sight to the exact second is essential (except for meridian altitude and Polaris sights, Chapters 8 and 9).
3. Sights should be taken in a position where the height of eye is known. (Height of eye is explained in Chapter 5.)
4. In rough weather the sight should be taken on the crest of a wave as this gives a better view of the horizon. Half the height of the wave should be added to the normal height of eye.
5. If time allows three sights of the same heavenly body should be taken. The average of the readings and times should be used, ignoring any suspect reading.
6. A series of sights leading up to the meridian passage of the sun will help to determine the time when the sun reaches its maximum altitude. The altitude will increase before meridian passage, reaching a maximum at the moment of passage.
7. Ex-meridian sights are useful if there is a possibility of meridian passage being missed. (Chapter 8)
8. The moon and the planets Venus and Jupiter can sometimes be observed in daylight. If planets are observed in daylight their approximate angle should be set on the sextant and the horizon directly beneath them swept to bring their image into view.
9. Sights can be taken after dark, using the horizon created by the moon. However, it is difficult to determine exactly where the horizon is even on a clear night, and the horizon directly under the moon can be deceptive.
10. Heavenly bodies due north or south give latitude, due east or west give longitude.
11. At evening twilight the eastern horizon disappears first. Similarly at morning twilight stars and planets over the eastern horizon will disappear first.
12. Observations of heavenly bodies due east or west are very sensitive to any errors in timing of the sights (1 second error is equivalent to 0.25 minutes of longitude).
13. In foggy weather, if the sea is calm, sights should be taken from as low a position as possible as the near horizon will be more clearly defined.
14. The sun and moon are usually observed by bringing their upper or lower limbs (the top or bottom) down to the horizon. Correction is made later for half their diameter (see Chapter 5).

QUESTION PAPER FOUR

4.1. What is a sextant?

4.2. How can you tell whether the sextant is being held vertically when taking a sight.

4.3. If a sextant has an index error of 2'·0 ON the arc and the sextant reading is 39° 05'·4, what is the correct sextant altitude?

4.4. A sextant with the index arm set to zero is showing a double image of a star horizontally disposed. What is the reason for this.

4.5. Why must adjustments for index error and side error be made in combination?

4.6. Why is it necessary to check the index error frequently?

Answers on page 156.

Chapter Five

Altitude

True altitude is the angle subtended at the earth's centre between the centre of a heavenly body and the celestial horizon. The altitude measured with the sextant is the angle subtended at the observer's eye between the heavenly body and the visible horizon.

Therefore, sextant altitude (SA) needs to be corrected before it becomes true altitude (TA). The corrections are as follows:

Index Error

Index error (IE) must be applied first.

Example 12

On March 10th a sight was taken of the sun's lower limb giving a sextant altitude of 35° 39'·4. Index error was 2'0 *on* the arc. What was the corrected sextant altitude?

The index error in this case will be SUBTRACTED because the error is ON the arc:

Sextant altitude	35° 39'·4
Index error	− 2'·0
Corrected sextant altitude	35° 37'·4

Height of Eye

Ideally a sextant altitude should be taken with the observer's eye at sea level. However, an observer's eye is always above sea level

when the sextant altitude is taken, which makes the altitude appear
to be greater than it is. The required angle is from the heavenly
body to a horizontal plane through the observer's eye called the
sensible horizon. The angle observed is from the heavenly body to
the visible horizon. The angle between the sensible horizon and the
visible horizon (called the angle of dip) is the correction for the
observer's height of eye above sea level and is applied to the
observed altitude (see Fig. 5.1).

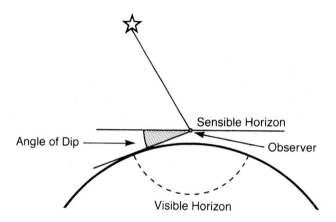

Fig 5.1 The angle of dip. This is the angle between the sensible horizon and the
visible horizon.

This correction is tabulated in the *Nautical Almanac* in the
'Altitude Correction Tables' under the heading of 'Dip'. It is always
subtracted. The higher the observer's eye above sea level the larger
the correction.

After corrections for index error and dip have been applied to the
sextant altitude, it is known as apparent altitude (AA).

Example 13

The corrected sextant altitude was 35° 37'·4, height of eye 3·2m,
what was the apparent altitude?

The dip table is entered with height of eye in metres (or feet).
The correction found (dip) is minutes of arc to be subtracted from
the sextant altitude (already corrected for index error):

A2 ALTITUDE CORRECTION TABLES 10°–90°—SUN, STARS, PLANETS

OCT.—MAR. SUN APR.—SEPT.

App. Alt.	Lower Limb	Upper Limb	App. Alt.	Lower Limb	Upper Limb
9 34	+10·8	−21·5	9 39	+10·6	−21·2
9 45	+10·9	−21·4	9 51	+10·7	−21·1
9 56	+11·0	−21·3	10 03	+10·8	−21·0
10 08	+11·1	−21·2	10 15	+10·9	−20·9
10 21	+11·2	−21·1	10 27	+11·0	−20·8
10 34	+11·3	−21·0	10 40	+11·1	−20·7
10 47	+11·4	−20·9	10 54	+11·2	−20·6
11 01	+11·5	−20·8	11 08	+11·3	−20·5
11 15	+11·6	−20·7	11 23	+11·4	−20·4
11 30	+11·7	−20·6	11 38	+11·5	−20·3
11 46	+11·8	−20·5	11 54	+11·6	−20·2
12 02	+11·9	−20·4	12 10	+11·7	−20·1
12 19	+12·0	−20·3	12 28	+11·8	−20·0
12 37	+12·1	−20·2	12 46	+11·9	−19·9
12 55	+12·2	−20·1	13 05	+12·0	−19·8
13 14	+12·3	−20·0	13 24	+12·1	−19·7
13 35	+12·4	−19·9	13 45	+12·2	−19·6
13 56	+12·5	−19·8	14 07	+12·3	−19·5
14 18	+12·6	−19·7	14 30	+12·4	−19·4
14 42	+12·7	−19·6	14 54	+12·5	−19·3
15 06	+12·8	−19·5	15 19	+12·6	−19·2
15 32	+12·9	−19·4	15 46	+12·7	−19·1
15 59	+13·0	−19·3	16 14	+12·8	−19·0
16 28	+13·1	−19·2	16 44	+12·9	−18·9
16 59	+13·2	−19·1	17 15	+13·0	−18·8
17 32	+13·3	−19·0	17 48	+13·1	−18·7
18 06	+13·4	−18·9	18 24	+13·2	−18·6
18 42	+13·5	−18·8	19 01	+13·3	−18·5
19 21	+13·6	−18·7	19 42	+13·4	−18·4
20 03	+13·7	−18·6	20 25	+13·5	−18·3
20 48	+13·8	−18·5	21 11	+13·6	−18·2
21 35	+13·9	−18·4	22 00	+13·7	−18·1
22 26	+14·0	−18·3	22 54	+13·8	−18·0
23 22	+14·1	−18·2	23 51	+13·9	−17·9
24 21	+14·2	−18·1	24 53	+14·0	−17·8
25 26	+14·3	−18·0	26 00	+14·1	−17·7
26 36	+14·4	−17·9	27 13	+14·2	−17·6
27 52	+14·5	−17·8	28 33	+14·3	−17·5
29 15	+14·6	−17·7	30 00	+14·4	−17·4
30 46	+14·7	−17·6	31 35	+14·5	−17·3
32 26	+14·8	−17·5	33 20	+14·6	−17·2
34 17	+14·9	−17·4	35 17	+14·7	−17·1
36 20	+15·0	−17·3	37 26	+14·8	−17·0
38 36	+15·1	−17·2	39 50	+14·9	−16·9
41 08	+15·2	−17·1	42 31	+15·0	−16·8
43 59	+15·3	−17·0	45 31	+15·1	−16·7
47 10	+15·4	−16·9	48 55	+15·2	−16·6
50 46	+15·5	−16·8	52 44	+15·3	−16·5
54 49	+15·6	−16·7	57 02	+15·4	−16·4
59 23	+15·7	−16·6	61 51	+15·5	−16·3
64 30	+15·8	−16·5	67 17	+15·6	−16·2
70 12	+15·9	−16·4	73 16	+15·7	−16·1
76 26	+16·0	−16·3	79 43	+15·8	−16·0
83 05	+16·1	−16·2	86 32	+15·9	−15·9
90 00			90 00		

STARS AND PLANETS

App. Alt.	Corrⁿ	App. Alt.	Additional Corrⁿ
			1980
9 56	−5·3		**VENUS**
10 08	−5·2	Jan. 1–Feb. 26	
10 20	−5·1	0	
10 33	−5·0	42	+ 0′·1
10 46	−4·9		
11 00	−4·8	Feb. 27–Apr. 13	
11 14	−4·7	0	
11 29	−4·6	47	+ 0′·2
11 45	−4·5		
12 01	−4·4	Apr. 14–May 9	
12 18	−4·3	0	
12 35	−4·2	46	+ 0′·3
12 54	−4·1		
13 13	−4·0	May 10–May 25	
13 33	−3·9	0	
13 54	−3·8	11	+ 0′·4
14 16	−3·7	41	+ 0·5
14 40	−3·6	May 26–June 3	
15 04	−3·5	0	
15 30	−3·4	6	+ 0′·5
15 57	−3·3	20	+ 0·7
16 26	−3·2	31	
16 56	−3·1	June 4–June 26	
17 28	−3·0	0	
18 02	−2·9	4	+ 0′·6
18 38	−2·8	12	+ 0·7
19 17	−2·7	22	+ 0·8
19 58	−2·6	June 27–July 6	
20 42	−2·5	0	
21 28	−2·4	6	+ 0′·5
22 19	−2·3	20	+ 0·6
23 13	−2·2	31	+ 0·7
24 11	−2·1	July 7–July 21	
25 14	−2·0	0	
26 22	−1·9	11	+ 0′·4
27 36	−1·8	41	+ 0·5
28 56	−1·7	July 22–Aug. 17	
30 24	−1·6	0	
32 00	−1·5	46	+ 0′·3
33 45	−1·4	Aug. 18–Oct. 2	
35 40	−1·3	0	
37 48	−1·2	47	+ 0′·2
40 08	−1·1	Oct. 3–Dec. 31	
42 44	−1·0	0	
45 36	−0·9	42	+ 0′·1
48 47	−0·8		
52 18	−0·7	**MARS**	
56 11	−0·6	Jan. 1–Apr. 28	
60 28	−0·5	0	
65 08	−0·4	41	+ 0′·2
70 11	−0·3	75	+ 0·1
75 34	−0·2	Apr. 29–Dec. 31	
81 13	−0·1	0	
87 03	0·0	60	+ 0′·1
90 00			

DIP

Ht. of Eye (m)	Corrⁿ	Ht. of Eye (ft.)	Ht. of Eye (m)	Corrⁿ
2·4	−2·8	8·0	1·0	− 1·8
2·6	−2·9	8·6	1·5	− 2·2
2·8	−3·0	9·2	2·0	− 2·5
3·0	−3·1	9·8	2·5	− 2·8
3·2	−3·2	10·5	3·0	− 3·0
3·4	−3·3	11·2		See table ←
3·6	−3·4	11·9		
3·8	−3·5	12·6	m	
4·0	−3·6	13·3	20	− 7·9
4·3	−3·7	14·1	22	− 8·3
4·5	−3·8	14·9	24	− 8·6
4·7	−3·9	15·7	26	− 9·0
5·0	−4·0	16·5	28	− 9·3
5·2	−4·1	17·4		
5·5	−4·2	18·3	30	− 9·6
5·8	−4·3	19·1	32	− 10·0
6·1	−4·4	20·1	34	− 10·3
6·3	−4·5	21·0	36	− 10·6
6·6	−4·6	22·0	38	− 10·8
6·9	−4·7	22·9		
7·2	−4·8	23·9	40	− 11·1
7·5	−4·9	24·9	42	− 11·4
7·9	−5·0	26·0	44	− 11·7
8·2	−5·1	27·1	46	− 11·9
8·5	−5·2	28·1	48	− 12·2
8·8	−5·3	29·2		
9·2	−5·4	30·4	ft.	
9·5	−5·5	31·5	2	− 1·4
9·9	−5·6	32·7	4	− 1·9
10·3	−5·7	33·9	6	− 2·4
10·6	−5·8	35·1	8	− 2·7
11·0	−5·9	36·3	10	− 3·1
11·4	−6·0	37·6		See table ←
11·8	−6·1	38·9		
12·2	−6·2	40·1	ft.	
12·6	−6·3	41·5	70	− 8·1
13·0	−6·4	42·8	75	− 8·4
13·4	−6·5	44·2	80	− 8·7
13·8	−6·6	45·5	85	− 8·9
14·2	−6·7	46·9	90	− 9·2
14·7	−6·8	48·4	95	− 9·5
15·1	−6·9	49·8		
15·5	−7·0	51·3	100	− 9·7
16·0	−7·1	52·8	105	− 9·9
16·5	−7·2	54·3	110	− 10·2
16·9	−7·3	55·8	115	− 10·4
17·4	−7·4	57·4	120	− 10·6
17·9	−7·5	58·9	125	− 10·8
18·4	−7·6	60·5		
18·8	−7·7	62·1	130	− 11·1
19·3	−7·8	63·8	135	− 11·3
19·8	−7·9	65·4	140	− 11·5
20·4	−8·0	67·1	145	− 11·7
20·9	−8·1	68·8	150	− 11·9
21·4		70·5	155	− 12·1

App. Alt. = Apparent altitude = Sextant altitude corrected for index error and dip.

Extract Number 5

Height of eye 3·2m = 3'·1

Sextant altitude	35° 39'·4
Index error	− 2'·0
Corrected sextant altitude	35° 37'·4
dip	− 3'·1
Apparent altitude	35° 34'·3

Index error and dip can be combined and applied together as one correction.

Example 14

Sextant altitude	35° 39'·4
Index error and dip	− 5'·1
Apparent altitude	35° 34'·3

When extracting information from the dip table for a height of eye of 3·2m there would appear to be a choice of corrections: 3'·1 (above) and 3'·2 (below). However the figure *above* (in this case 3'·1) always applies when the main left-hand column of the 'Dip' Table is used. The right-hand column contains separate small tables for quantities outside the main table and here the correction is alongside.

Refraction

As a ray of light emitted from a heavenly body enters the earth's atmosphere it passes through bands of air of different densities which cause it to bend (refract). This makes the heavenly body's altitude appear to be greater (see Fig. 5.2). Refraction is greatest at low altitudes.

The altitude correction tables are based upon mean values for normal conditions. Where abnormal atmospheric conditions occur, their values may differ. 'Table A4' in the *Nautical Almanac* gives additional corrections for temperatures and pressures which differ from the mean values, but if low altitudes (less than 10°) are avoided their use is not necessary.

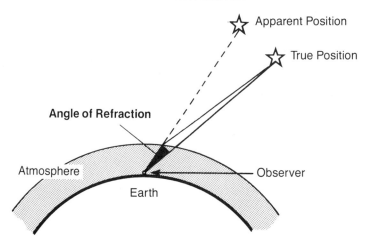

Fig 5.2 Refraction in the earth's atmosphere makes a heavenly body's altitude appear greater than it really is.

Semi-diameter

Compared with the stars and planets the sun and moon have appreciable visible diameters and when taking a sextant sight of these heavenly bodies it would not be sufficiently accurate to guess when the centre of their reflected image was on the horizon. Therefore, the image of either the upper or lower limb of the sun or the moon is brought down to the horizon and a correction for half the diameter applied (see Fig. 5.3).

The stars and planets are so distant that they appear as a point of light with no noticeable diameter and no correction is necessary.

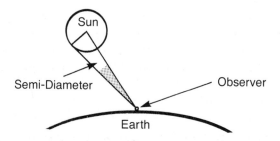

Fig 5.3 Semi-diameter. Because the sun and moon appear so large, the upper or lower limb (edge) is lined up on the horizon, instead of the centre which would be difficult to locate. A correction is then applied, using the tables.

Parallax in Altitude

Parallax in altitude occurs because a heavenly body is observed from the earth's surface and not its centre. It is the angle subtended at the heavenly body between the centre of the earth and the observer's position (see Fig. 5.4).

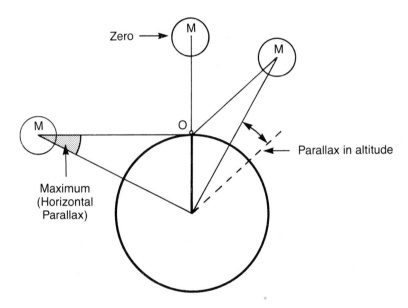

Fig 5.4 Parallax.

It varies with altitude, being zero when the heavenly body is overhead and maximum when it is on the horizon (called horizontal parallax). It also varies with distance and the nearer the heavenly body, the greater the parallax.

For the stars, because of their distance from the earth parallax is negligible. For the sun it is no more than $0' \cdot 15$ and for the planets small. The tabulations in the almanac incorporate parallax for the sun and the planets. For the moon, because of its proximity to the earth, parallax is significant and can be as much as $61'$. The moon's horizontal parallax (HP) is tabulated hourly, from which the parallax for any given altitude can be deduced using the formula:

parallax = horizontal parallax × cosine of altitude.

It is not, however, necessary to use this formula as the *Nautical Almanac* provides a table which gives the corrections to be applied to altitude.

Total Correction

Semi-diameter, refraction and parallax are all applied as a combined correction (with the exception of the moon) found in the 'Altitude Correction Tables'. Applying the total correction to apparent altitude gives true altitude (TA).

Sun

The altitude correction table for the sun consists of two tables for different months of the year and a correction for whichever limb (upper or lower), has been observed. The correction for the lower limb (LL) is added and for the upper limb (UL) subtracted. In example 15 14'·9 is between altitudes 34° 17' and 36° 20' and is the correction for any altitude between these figures; interpolation is not necessary.

Example 15 (SUN) (See Extract No. 5)

On March 10th a sight taken of the sun's lower limb gave an apparent altitude of 35° 34'·3. What was the true altitude?

Apparent altitude	35° 34'·3	
corrn.	+ 14'·9	(total corrn. for sun's
True altitude	35° 49'·2	lower limb for March.)

Stars and planets

Except for Venus and Mars where a small additional monthly correction is necessary, there is only one table for stars and planets.

Example 16 (STARS AND PLANETS) (See Extract No. 5)

The sextant altitude of Sirius was 36° 06'·4. Index error −1'·0. Height of eye 2·8m. What was the true altitude?

SA		36° 06'·4
IE	−	1'·0
		36° 05'·4
dip.	−	2'·9
AA		36° 02'·5
corrn.	−	1'·3
TA		36° 01'·2

Example 17 (VENUS AND MARS) (See Extract No. 5)

On August 9th, the sextant altitude of Venus was 15° 30'·7, index error −1'·5, height of eye 2·5m, what was the true altitude

SA		15° 30'·7
IE	−	1'·5
		15° 29'·2
dip	−	2'·8
AA		15° 26'·4
star corrn.	−	3'·5
		15° 22'·9
additional corrn.	+	0'·3
TA		15° 23'·2

Moon

'The Altitude Correction Tables' for the moon are in two parts, the upper part giving a correction to apparent altitude and the lower part giving a correction for parallax for either the moon's lower or upper limb. The top table is entered with the apparent altitude (degrees at the top and minutes on the left and right hand sides) interpolating as necessary. When the altitude correction has been found, the same column is followed down to the lower table until opposite the horizontal parallax (HP), (as obtained from the daily pages). The correction to be applied is found either under 'U' for upper limb or 'L' for lower limb whichever was used for the sight. Both corrections are *always* added but in the case of the upper limb 30' is subtracted from the answer.

Example 18 (MOON) (See Extract Nos. 5 and 6)

The sextant altitude of the moon's LL was 35° 24'·4. Index error −2'·0. Height of eye 3·4m. Horizontal parallax 54·6, (found on the daily pages of the *Nautical Almanac* in the moon table). What was the true altitude?

SA		35° 24'·4
IE	−	2'·0
		35° 22'·4
dip	−	3'·2
AA		35° 19'·2
corrn.	+	56'·3
HP	+	1'·7
TA		36° 17'·2

ALTITUDE CORRECTION TABLES 35°–90°—MOON

App. Alt.	35°–39° Corrⁿ	40°–44° Corrⁿ	45°–49° Corrⁿ
00	35 56·5	40 53·7	45 50·5
10	56·4	53·6	50·4
20	56·3	53·5	50·2
30	56·2	53·4	50·1
40	56·2	53·3	50·0
50	56·1	53·2	49·9
00	36 56·0	41 53·1	46 49·8
10	55·9	53·0	49·7
20	55·8	52·8	49·5
30	55·7	52·7	49·4
40	55·6	52·6	49·3
50	55·5	52·5	49·2
00	37 55·4	42 52·4	47 49·1
10	55·3	52·3	49·0
20	55·2	52·2	48·8
30	55·1	52·1	48·7
40	55·0	52·0	48·6
50	55·0	51·9	48·5
00	38 54·9	43 51·8	48 48·4
10	54·8	51·7	48·2
20	54·7	51·6	48·1
30	54·6	51·5	48·0
40	54·5	51·4	47·9
50	54·4	51·2	47·8
00	39 54·3	44 51·1	49 47·6
10	54·2	51·0	47·5
20	54·1	50·9	47·4
30	54·0	50·8	47·3
40	53·9	50·7	47·2
50	53·8	50·6	47·0

H.P.	L U	L U	L U
54·0	1·1 1·7	1·3 1·9	1·5 2·1
54·3	1·4 1·8	1·6 2·0	1·8 2·2
54·6	1·7 2·0	1·9 2·2	2·1 2·4
54·9	2·0 2·2	2·2 2·3	2·3 2·5
55·2	2·3 2·3	2·5 2·4	2·6 2·6
55·5	2·7 2·5	2·8 2·6	2·9 2·7
55·8	3·0 2·6	3·1 2·7	3·2 2·8
56·1	3·3 2·8	3·4 2·9	3·5 3·0
56·4	3·6 2·9	3·7 3·0	3·8 3·1
56·7	3·9 3·1	4·0 3·1	4·1 3·2

Extract Number 6

QUESTION PAPER FIVE

5.1.   On October 3rd Venus was observed giving sextant altitude of 31° 40'·2. Index error +2'·4. Height of eye 3·2m. What was the true altitude?.

5.2.   The sextant altitude of Arcturus was 45° 34'·2. Index error −1'·9. Height of eye 4·0m. What was the true altitude?

5.3.   On June 21st the sun's lower limb gave a sextant altitude of 55° 15'·2. Index error +1'·7. Height of eye 2·5m. What was the true altitude?

5.4.   The sextant altitude of the moon's upper limb was 59° 30'·0. Index error +1'·3. Height of eye 3·4m. Horizontal parallax 55·2. What was the true altitude?

5.5.   Find the true altitude of the sun's upper limb on March 14th. Sextant altitude 35° 29'·4. Index error −1'·7. Height of eye 3·8m.

Answers on pages 156–7.

Chapter Six

Sunrise – Sunset

Moon, star and planet sights can only be taken when both the horizon and the heavenly body are visible, which is normally during dawn or dusk twilight. Twilight is determined by the position of the sun and times of the visible rising and setting of the sun are tabulated tri-daily to the nearest minute on the daily pages of the *Nautical Almanac*. These times, given for latitudes north and south, are the Greenwich mean time on the Greenwich meridian, but can be regarded as the local mean time on any meridian.

To find GMT of sunrise or sunset at the DR position, longitude converted to time is applied.

Example 19

What is the GMT of sunset on June 23rd in DR position 50° 00'·0N, 25° 15'·0W?

	h m	
sunset 50° N	20 13	LMT 23d (from the daily pages)
long. 25° 15'·0W	1 41	(from the 'Conversion of Arc to Time table').
	21 54	GMT 23d at DR position

NOTE

As the LMT and the GMT may be on different days the date (23d) is always included in the calculations.

1980 JUNE 23, 24, 25 (MON., TUES., WED.)

Lat.	Twilight Naut.	Twilight Civil	Sunrise	Moonrise 23	24	25	26
°	h m	h m	h m	h m	h m	h m	h m
N 72	□	□	□	16 17	18 04	20 05	■■
N 70	□	□	□	16 03	17 39	19 21	21 08
68	□	□	□	15 51	17 20	18 52	20 23
66	□	□	□	15 41	17 05	18 31	19 54
64	////	////	01 32	15 33	16 53	18 13	19 32
62	////	////	02 10	15 26	16 43	17 59	19 14
60	////	00 51	02 37	15 20	16 34	17 48	19 00
N 58	////	01 41	02 57	15 15	16 26	17 37	18 47
56	////	02 11	03 14	15 10	16 19	17 29	18 36
54	00 47	02 34	03 28	15 06	16 13	17 21	18 27
52	01 33	02 52	03 41	15 02	16 08	17 14	18 19
50	02 01	03 07	03 51	14 59	16 03	17 07	18 11
45	02 47	03 37	04 14	14 51	15 52	16 54	17 55
N 40	03 17	03 59	04 32	14 45	15 43	16 42	17 42
35	03 41	04 17	04 47	14 40	15 36	16 33	17 31
30	03 59	04 33	05 00	14 35	15 29	16 25	17 21
20	04 28	04 58	05 22	14 27	15 18	16 10	17 04
N 10	04 51	05 18	05 41	14 20	15 08	15 58	16 50
0	05 10	05 36	05 59	14 14	14 59	15 46	16 36
S 10	05 27	05 53	06 16	14 07	14 50	15 35	16 23
20	05 43	06 11	06 35	14 01	14 40	15 22	16 08
30	06 00	06 30	06 56	13 53	14 29	15 08	15 52
35	06 08	06 40	07 08	13 48	14 23	15 00	15 43
40	06 18	06 52	07 22	13 43	14 15	14 51	15 32
45	06 28	07 05	07 39	13 38	14 07	14 40	15 19
S 50	06 40	07 22	08 00	13 31	13 57	14 28	15 04
52	06 45	07 29	08 10	13 28	13 52	14 22	14 57
54	06 51	07 37	08 21	13 24	13 47	14 15	14 49
56	06 57	07 46	08 34	13 20	13 42	14 08	14 40
58	07 04	07 57	08 48	13 16	13 36	13 59	14 30
S 60	07 11	08 08	09 06	13 11	13 29	13 50	14 18

Lat.	Sunset	Twilight Civil	Naut.	Moonset 23	24	25	26
°	h m	h m	h m	h m	h m	h m	h m
N 72	□	□	□	00 23	00 13	{ 00 01 / 23 40 }	■■
N 70	□	□	□	00 33	00 30	00 27	00 24
68	□	□	□	00 41	00 43	00 47	00 54
66	□	□	□	00 47	00 54	01 03	01 16
64	22 32	////	////	00 53	01 03	01 16	01 34
62	21 54	////	////	00 58	01 11	01 27	01 48
60	21 28	23 13	////	01 02	01 18	01 37	02 01
N 58	21 07	22 23	////	01 06	01 24	01 45	02 11
56	20 51	21 53	////	01 09	01 29	01 52	02 21
54	20 36	21 31	23 17	01 12	01 34	01 59	02 29
52	20 24	21 13	22 31	01 15	01 38	02 05	02 37
50	20 13	20 58	22 03	01 17	01 42	02 10	02 43
45	19 51	20 28	21 18	01 23	01 51	02 22	02 58
N 40	19 33	20 06	20 47	01 27	01 58	02 32	03 09
35	19 18	19 47	20 24	01 31	02 04	02 40	03 20
30	19 05	19 32	20 05	01 35	02 10	02 47	03 29
20	18 43	19 07	19 36	01 41	02 19	03 00	03 44
N 10	18 24	18 47	19 14	01 46	02 27	03 11	03 57
0	18 06	18 29	18 55	01 51	02 35	03 21	04 10

Extract Number 7

CONVERSION OF ARC TO TIME

0°–59°		60°–119°		120°–179°	
24	1 36	84	5 36	144	9 36
25	1 40	85	5 40	145	9 40
26	1 44	86	5 44	146	9 44
27	1 48	87	5 48	147	9 48
28	1 52	88	5 52	148	9 52
29	1 56	89	5 56	149	9 56
30	2 00	90	6 00	150	10 00
31	2 04	91	6 04	151	10 04
32	2 08	92	6 08	152	10 08
33	2 12	93	6 12	153	10 12
34	2 16	94	6 16	154	10 16
35	2 20	95	6 20	155	10 20
36	2 24	96	6 24	156	10 24
37	2 28	97	6 28	157	10 28
38	2 32	98	6 32	158	10 32
39	2 36	99	6 36	159	10 36
40	2 40	100	6 40	160	10 40
41	2 44	101	6 44	161	10 44
42	2 48	102	6 48	162	10 48
43	2 52	103	6 52	163	10 52
44	2 56	104	6 56	164	10 56
45	3 00	105	7 00	165	11 00
46	3 04	106	7 04	166	11 04
47	3 08	107	7 08	167	11 08
48	3 12	108	7 12	168	11 12
49	3 16	109	7 16	169	11 16

′	0′·00	0′·25	0′·50	0′·75
	m s	m s	m s	m s
0	0 00	0 01	0 02	0 03
1	0 04	0 05	0 06	0 07
2	0 08	0 09	0 10	0 11
3	0 12	0 13	0 14	0 15
4	0 16	0 17	0 18	0 19
5	0 20	0 21	0 22	0 23
6	0 24	0 25	0 26	0 27
7	0 28	0 29	0 30	0 31
8	0 32	0 33	0 34	0 35
9	0 36	0 37	0 38	0 39
10	0 40	0 41	0 42	0 43
11	0 44	0 45	0 46	0 47
12	0 48	0 49	0 50	0 51
13	0 52	0 53	0 54	0 55
14	0 56	0 57	0 58	0 59
15	1 00	1 01	1 02	1 03
16	1 04	1 05	1 06	1 07
17	1 08	1 09	1 10	1 11
18	1 12	1 13	1 14	1 15
19	1 16	1 17	1 18	1 19

Extract Number 8

Twilight

When the sun is below the horizon reflected light can still be seen which is the time called twilight. The form of twilight is dependent upon the angular distance of the sun below the horizon:

Civil twilight　　　　　　– sun's centre 6° below the horizon.
Nautical twilight　　　　– sun's centre 12° below the horizon.
Astronomical twilight　　– sun's centre 18° below the horizon.

Only the times of civil twilight and nautical twilight are tabulated in the *Nautical Almanac* and, of these two, civil twilight is normally used by navigators. At astronomical twilight the horizon cannot be clearly seen.

Any calculations in this book involving twilight refer to civil twilight.

As with sunrise and sunset, twilight times are tabulated tri-daily and are given as GMT on the Greenwich meridian, but they can be regarded as LMT on any meridian. Longitude converted to time is applied to find GMT at the DR position.

Example 20 (See Extract Nos. 7 and 8)

When is dawn twilight on June 24th in DR position 51° 06′·0N, 31° 15′·0W?

	h m	
dawn twilight	02 59LMT	24d (interpolation between 50°N and 52°N)
long. 31° 15′·0W	02 05	
	05 04GMT	24d at DR position

Moonrise and Moonset

This is tabulated daily. Tabulations for four days are on one daily page in the *Nautical Almanac*, giving the LMT on the Greenwich Meridian (which is GMT). The moon is relatively near to the earth and its movement is not constant so the tabulated times cannot be used as the LMT on other meridians without the following correction:

$$\frac{\text{longitude in degrees}}{360} \times \text{ daily difference}$$

The daily difference is taken between the day in question and the following day for westerly longitudes (the correction being added) or the preceding day for easterly longitudes (the correction being subtracted). Longitude converted to time is applied to the corrected LMT in the normal way to give GMT at the DR position.

Example 21 (See Extract Nos. 7 and 8)

Find the times of moonrise and moonset on June 24th, in DR position 30° 05′·3N, 165° 00′·1E.

	Moonrise	*Moonset*	
	h m	h m	
lat. 30° 05′·3N	15 29	02 10	24d ⎰ from the daily
	14 35	01 35	23d ⎱ pages
daily difference	54	35	

moonrise – $\dfrac{165}{360}$ × 54 = 24·7 (25 to the nearest minute)

moonset – $\dfrac{165}{360}$ × 35 = 16

	Moonrise	*Moonset*
	h m	h m
	15 29 LMT 24d	02 10 LMT 24d
long. corrn. –	25 at Greenwich	– 16 at Greenwich
	15 04 LMT at DR	01 54 LMT at DR
long. E	11 00	– 11 00
	04 04 GMT 24d at DR	14 54 GMT 23d at DR

Tri-daily Difference

Tabulations for sunrise, sunset and twilight are for the middle day of the page and if a very accurate time is required, one third of the tri-daily difference should be applied and an allowance made for longitude as for the moon. However, such precision is rarely needed as approximate times are normally used.

Amplitude of a Heavenly Body – Rising or Setting

The amplitude of a heavenly body is the arc of the horizon between that body and true east (when rising) or true west (when setting). Amplitude is only found when the heavenly body is rising or setting (see Fig. 6.1).

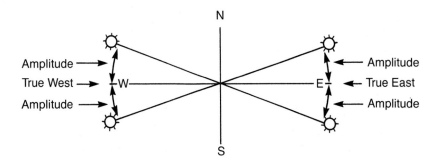

Fig 6.1 Amplitude of a heavenly body.

When a heavenly body such as the sun has a northerly declination
its azimuth on rising or setting will be north of east or west. When it
has a southerly declination its azimuth on rising or setting will be
south of east or west. 90° minus the amplitude equals the azimuth
which is named according to declination.

By taking a compass bearing of the sun (or other heavenly body)
when it is rising or setting and (after variation has been applied)
comparing the reading with the sun's true azimuth, the deviation of
the compass for the boat's heading at the time of the observation
can be determined.

Amplitude tables are available in *Norie's Nautical Tables* and
other nautical almanacs. A true azimuth can be calculated as
follows:

True Amplitudes (Norie's Nautical Tables) The co-ordinates
needed for the 'True Amplitudes' table are latitude (to the nearest
1°), which is down the left-hand side of the table, and declination
(to the nearest half degree), which is along the top.

The tabulated figure gives the amplitude (the angle from east
when the sun is rising and from west when the sun is setting, to
north or south dependent upon declination). (See Fig. 6.2a.)

*Sun's True Bearing At Sunrise and Sunset (Reed's Nautical
Almanac)* The co-ordinates needed for the 'Sun's True Bearing at
Sunrise and Sunset' table are latitude (to the nearest 1°), which is
down the left hand side of the table, and declination (to the nearest
half degree), which is along the top.

The tabulated figure gives a quadrantal azimuth (the angle from
north or south, determined by declination, to east when the sun is
rising and west when the sun is setting). (See Fig. 6.2b.)

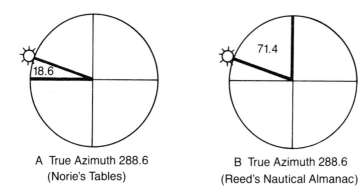

A True Azimuth 288.6   B True Azimuth 288.6
(Norie's Tables)   (Reed's Nautical Almanac)

Fig 6.2 The True Azimuth.

TRUE AZIMUTH

The figures tabulated in both *Norie's Nautical Tables* and *Reed's Nautical Almanac* can be converted to a true azimuth as follows:

NORIE'S NAUTICAL TABLES

If rising and declination is north *subtract* the figure in the tables from 090°.

If rising and declination is south *add* the figure in the tables to 090°.

If setting and declination is north *add* the figure in the tables to 270°.

If setting and declination is south *subtract* the figure in the tables from 270°.

REED'S NAUTICAL ALMANAC

If rising and declination is north *add* the figure in the tables to 000°.

If rising and declination is south *subtract* the figure in the tables from 180°.

If setting and declination is north *subtract* the figure in the tables from 360°.

If setting and declination is south *add* the figure in the tables to 180°.

Example 22 (See Extract Nos. 9 and 10)

What is the true azimuth of the sun at sunset in DR 30° N declination 16° N?

TRUE AMPLITUDES

Lat.	16°	17°	18°	19°	20°	20½°	21°	21½°	22°	22½°	23°	23½°	24°	24½°	25°
°	°	°	°	°	°	°	°	°	°	°	°	°	°	°	°
2	16·0	17·0	18·0	19·0	20·0	20·5	21·0	21·5	22·0	22·5	23·0	23·5	24·0	24·5	25·0
4	16·0	17·1	18·1	19·1	20·1	20·6	21·1	21·6	22·1	22·6	23·1	23·6	24·1	24·6	25·1
6	16·1	17·1	18·1	19·1	20·1	20·6	21·1	21·6	22·1	22·6	23·1	23·6	24·1	24·6	25·1
8	16·2	17·2	18·2	19·2	20·2	20·7	21·2	21·7	22·2	22·7	23·2	23·7	24·3	24·8	25·3
10	16·3	17·3	18·3	19·3	20·3	20·8	21·4	21·8	22·4	22·9	23·4	23·9	24·4	24·9	25·4
12	16·4	17·4	18·4	19·4	20·5	21·0	21·5	22·0	22·5	23·0	23·6	24·1	24·6	25·1	25·6
14	16·5	17·5	18·6	19·6	20·6	21·2	21·7	22·2	22·7	23·2	23·8	24·3	24·8	25·3	25·8
16	16·7	17·7	18·8	19·8	20·9	21·4	21·9	22·4	22·9	23·5	24·0	24·5	25·0	25·6	26·1
18	16·9	17·9	19·0	20·0	21·1	21·6	22·1	22·7	23·2	23·7	24·3	24·8	25·3	25·9	26·4
20	17·1	18·1	19·2	20·3	21·4	21·9	22·4	23·0	23·5	24·0	24·6	25·1	25·7	26·2	26·7
22	17·3	18·4	19·5	20·6	21·7	22·2	22·7	23·3	23·8	24·4	24·9	25·5	26·0	26·6	27·1
24	17·6	18·7	19·8	20·9	22·0	22·5	23·1	23·7	24·2	24·8	25·3	25·9	26·4	27·0	27·6
26	17·9	19·0	20·1	21·2	22·4	22·9	23·5	24·1	24·6	25·2	25·8	26·3	26·9	27·5	28·0
28	18·2	19·3	20·5	21·6	22·8	23·4	24·0	24·5	25·1	25·7	26·3	26·8	27·4	28·0	28·6
30	18·6	19·7	20·9	22·1	23·3	23·9	24·5	25·0	25·6	26·2	26·8	27·4	28·0	28·6	29·2
31	18·8	20·0	21·1	22·3	23·5	24·1	24·7	25·3	25·9	26·5	27·1	27·7	28·3	28·9	29·5

Extract Number 9

SUN'S TRUE BEARING AT SUNRISE AND SUNSET

LATITUDES 0° to 66°   DECLINATIONS 12° to 23°

LAT.	12°	13°	14°	15°	16°	17°	18°	19°	20°	21°	22°	23°
0° to 5°	77.9	76.9	75.9	74.9	73.9	72.9	71.9	70.9	69.9	68.9	67.9	66.9
6°	77.9	76.9	75.9	74.9	73.9	72.9	71.9	70.9	69.9	68.9	67.9	66.9
7°	77.9	76.9	75.9	74.9	73.9	72.9	71.9	70.8	69.8	68.8	67.8	66.8
8°	77.9	76.9	75.9	74.8	73.8	72.8	71.8	70.8	69.8	68.8	67.8	67.8
9°	77.8	76.8	75.8	74.8	73.8	72.8	71.8	70.7	69.7	68.7	67.7	66.7
10°	77.8	76.8	75.8	74.8	73.7	72.7	71.7	70.7	69.7	68.7	67.6	66.6
11°	77.8	76.8	75.7	74.7	73.7	72.7	71.6	70.6	69.6	68.6	67.6	66.5
12°	77.7	76.7	75.7	74.6	73.6	72.6	71.6	70.6	69.5	68.5	67.5	66.4
13°	77.7	76.6	75.6	74.6	73.6	72.5	71.5	70.5	69.4	68.4	67.4	66.4
14°	77.6	76.6	75.6	74.5	73.5	72.5	71.4	70.4	69.4	68.3	67.3	66.2
15°	77.6	76.5	75.5	74.4	73.4	72.4	71.3	70.3	69.3	68.2	67.2	66.1
16°	77.5	76.5	75.4	74.4	73.3	72.3	71.2	70.2	69.1	68.1	67.1	66.0
17°	77.4	76.4	75.3	74.3	73.3	72.2	71.1	70.1	69.0	68.0	66.9	65.9
18°	77.4	76.3	75.3	74.2	73.2	72.1	71.0	70.0	68.9	67.9	66.8	65.7
19°	77.4	76.2	75.2	74.1	73.0	72.0	70.9	69.9	68.8	67.7	66.7	65.6
20°	77.2	76.1	75.1	74.0	72.9	71.9	70.8	69.7	68.6	67.6	66.5	65.4
21°	77.1	76.0	75.0	73.9	72.8	71.7	70.7	69.6	68.5	67.4	66.3	65.2
22°	77.0	76.0	74.9	73.8	72.7	71.6	70.5	69.4	68.3	67.3	66.2	65.1
23°	76.9	75.9	74.8	73.7	72.6	71.5	70.4	69.3	68.2	67.1	66.0	64.9
24°	76.8	75.7	74.6	73.5	72.5	71.3	70.2	69.1	68.0	66.9	65.8	64.7
25°	76.7	75.6	74.5	73.4	72.3	71.2	70.1	68.9	67.8	66.7	65.6	64.5
26°	76.6	75.5	74.4	73.3	72.1	71.0	69.9	68.8	67.6	66.5	65.4	64.2
27°	76.5	75.4	74.3	73.1	72.0	70.8	69.7	68.6	67.4	66.3	65.1	64.0
28°	76.4	75.2	74.1	73.0	71.8	70.7	69.5	68.4	67.2	66.1	64.9	63.8
29°	76.2	75.1	73.9	72.8	71.6	70.5	69.3	68.2	67.0	65.8	64.6	63.5
30°	76.1	75.0	73.8	72.6	71.4	70.3	69.1	67.9	66.7	65.5	64.4	63.2
31°	76.0	74.8	73.6	72.4	71.2	70.0	68.9	67.6	66.5	65.3	64.1	62.9
32°	75.8	74.6	73.4	72.2	71.0	69.8	68.6	67.4	66.2	65.0	63.8	62.6
33°	75.7	74.4	73.2	72.0	70.8	69.6	68.4	67.1	65.9	64.7	63.5	62.2

Extract Number 10

Norie's Nautical Tables

W18·6N (west because the sun is
setting, north because dec is
north).

270 + 18·6 = 288° ·6T

Reed's Nautical Almanac

N71·4W (north because dec is north
west because it is setting)

360 − 71·4 = 288° ·6T

NOTE

Refraction makes the sun appear higher above the horizon than it actually is and compass bearings should be taken when the sun is about half a diameter above the horizon.

QUESTION PAPER SIX

Work to the nearest minute.

6.1   On March 8th, what is GMT of sunrise and sunset in DR position 25° 00'·4N, 19° 59'·3W?

6.2   What is the zone time of dawn twilight on June 23rd in DR position 31° 03'·4N, 35° 15'·1W?

6.3   What is the zone time of dusk twilight on October 4th, when in DR position 24° 59'·7S, 75° 30'·1E?

6.4   On March 7th what is the GMT of moonrise and moonset in DR position 20° 00'·3N, 42° 15'·1W?

6.5   Work out the following using *Norie's tables*:
On June 24th, in DR position 32° 59'·7N, 39° 58'·1W, the sun was sighted at sunrise using the steering compass azimuth mirror. The compass reading was 074° C. What is the compass error?

6.6   Work out the following using Extract A23:
At sunset on October 4th, in DR position 20° 03'·1N, 98° 15'·E the sun's compass bearing was 251° C. What is the compass error?

Answers on pages 157–9.

Chapter Seven

Calculated Altitude

Calculated altitude can be found from various sets of tables each of which has advantages and disadvantages. Some require more interpolation, some more calculation: whilst others are slightly more accurate. All methods require the Greenwich date and time together with a dead reckoning position (or a chosen position near the dead reckoning position) in order to determine the local hour angle (LHA) and declination of the heavenly body (except *AP 3270, Volume 1* which uses the LHA Aries). Further details of the tables will be found in Chapter 15.

Sight Reduction Tables for Air Navigation, AP 3270 Volume 1

This is undoubtedly the quickest and simplest method for finding the altitude and azimuth of several selected stars. Approximate altitude and azimuth can be found before the sights are taken by using the time of twilight so that the most suitable stars can be chosen. The approximate altitude of a star can be set on the sextant before the expected time of the sight and then the horizon beneath the star scanned thus saving time. *Volume 1* is entered with latitude and LHA Aries.

Chosen Position

Volume 1 is tabulated for whole degrees of latitude and LHA. To enter the table a chosen position (CP) is used which is as close as possible to the DR position. The chosen latitude is the nearest whole degree to the DR position. The chosen longitude is selected so that the LHA used will be a whole degree.

Example 23

Westerly longitude
        DR position 50° 10′·1N, 25° 12′·4W, GHA 341° 17′·3.

$$\begin{array}{rr} \text{GHA} & 341° \ 17'·3 \\ \text{chosen long.} - & 25° \ 17'·3 \\ \hline \text{LHA} & 316° \ 00'·0 \\ \hline \end{array}$$

Chosen position 50° N, 25° 17′·3W

Example 24

Easterly longitude.
        DR position 49° 50′·4N, 9° 35′·6E, GHA 142° 12′·8.

$$\begin{array}{rr} \text{GHA} & 142° \ 12'·8 \\ \text{chosen long.} + & 9° \ 47'·2 \\ \hline \text{LHA} & 152° \ 00'·0 \\ \hline \end{array}$$

Chosen position 50° N, 9° 47′·2E

Because the longitude chosen must be as near as possible to the DR longitude this may mean in some cases an alteration to degrees as well as minutes:

Example 25

Westerly longitude.
        DR position 48° 10′·4N, 19° 51′·7W, GHA 137° 20′·4.

$$\begin{array}{rr} \text{GHA} & 137° \ 20'·4 \\ \text{chosen long.} - & 20° \ 20'·4 \\ \hline \text{LHA} & 117° \ 00'·0 \\ \hline \end{array}$$

Chosen position 48° N, 20° 20′·4W

Easterly longitude.
        DR position 40° 15′·2S, 120° 48′·7E, GHA 18° 54′·3.

$$\begin{array}{rr} \text{GHA} & 18° \ 54'·3 \\ \text{chosen long.} + & 121° \ 05'·7 \\ \hline \text{LHA} & 140° \ 00'·0 \\ \hline \end{array}$$

Chosen position 40° S, 121° 05′·7E.

When calculating which stars are available for sights the DR longitude can be used and the LHA rounded off to the nearest degree.

Example 26 (See Extract No. 11)

On June 21st, at dawn twilight in DR position 50° 00′·0N 25° 16′·7W it is desired to know which stars are available for sights, together with their approximate altitudes and azimuths: GMT of twilight at the DR position is found first from the *Nautical Almanac* using the daily pages and the 'Conversion of Arc to Time' table:

		h	m		
twilight lat. 50° N		03	06	LMT	21d
long. 25° 16′·7W	+	01	41		
		04	47	GMT	21d at DR

(Note the Greenwich date has been automatically checked.)

The GHA of Aries for June 21st at 04h 47m 00s is found from the daily pages and the 'Increments and Corrections' table and longitude applied to find the LHA Aries:

GHA Aries 04h		329° 30′·4
increment 47m	+	11° 46′·9
GHA Aries 04h 47m		341° 17′·3
DR long. W	−	25° 16′·7
LHA Aries 04h 47m		316° 00′·6 (use 316)

Volume 1 is entered with nearest whole degree of latitude to the DR latitude (50° N) and LHA (316°).

Hc and Zn at the top of the table are altitude and azimuth respectively.

The 7 stars available are:

		Hc	Zn
	CAPELLA	17° 59′	038° T
◇	Hamal	26° 50′	085° T
	Alpheratz	49° 43′	104° T
	Enif	48° 58′	165° T
◇	ALTAIR	46° 01′	207° T
	VEGA	61° 40′	261° T
◇	Kochab	46° 39′	337° T

Capella Altair and Vega are printed in capital letters to show that they are the three brightest whilst Hamal, Altair and Kochab are marked with a diamond to show that their respective position lines give the best angle of cut.

These altitudes and azimuths are used for initial planning. When the actual sights are taken the time may differ from the planned time so the calculations must be worked using the *exact* time at which each sight is taken.

LAT 50°N

LHA ♈	Hc	Zn	Hc	Zn	Hc	Zn	Hc	Zn	Hc	Zn	Hc	Zn	Hc	Zn
	CAPELLA		♦Hamal		Alpheratz		Enif		♦ALTAIR		VEGA		♦Kochab	
315	17 36	037	26 12	084	49 06	103	48 48	164	46 18	206	62 18	260	46 54	337
316	17 59	038	26 50	085	49 43	104	48 58	165	46 01	207	61 40	261	46 39	337
317	18 23	038	27 29	086	50 21	105	49 08	167	45 43	208	61 02	262	46 24	337
318	18 47	039	28 07	086	50 58	106	49 16	168	45 25	210	60 24	263	46 09	337
319	19 12	040	28 46	087	51 35	107	49 23	170	45 05	211	59 46	264	45 54	337
320	19 37	040	29 24	088	52 12	108	49 30	171	44 45	212	59 07	265	45 39	337
321	20 02	041	30 03	089	52 48	109	49 35	173	44 24	214	58 29	265	45 24	337
322	20 27	041	30 41	089	53 25	110	49 40	174	44 02	215	57 50	266	45 09	338
323	20 53	042	31 20	090	54 01	111	49 43	176	43 40	216	57 12	267	44 55	338
324	21 19	043	31 59	091	54 37	112	49 45	177	43 17	217	56 33	268	44 40	338
325	21 45	043	32 37	092	55 12	113	49 47	179	42 53	219	55 55	269	44 26	338
326	22 12	044	33 16	093	55 48	114	49 47	180	42 29	220	55 16	269	44 11	338
327	22 38	044	33 54	093	56 22	116	49 46	182	42 04	221	54 38	270	43 57	339
328	23 06	045	34 33	094	56 57	117	49 44	183	41 38	222	53 59	271	43 43	339
329	23 33	045	35 11	095	57 31	118	49 42	185	41 12	223	53 21	272	43 29	339

Extract Number 11

PRECESSION AND NUTATION

The effect of the gravity of other heavenly bodies upon the earth (which is not a uniform sphere) cause the earth's axis to describe a small circle and also to wobble as it does so. These effects are called precession and nutation. We have until now regarded the stars' positions as being fixed in the heavens, with a constant SHA and declination, but over the years, due to precession and nutation, their SHA and declination change slightly. *AP 3270 Volume 1* has been computed for one particular year (called an Epoch) which is the middle year of a five year span. If any but the middle year is used a slight correction (found at the back of *Volume 1*), for precession and nutation is required.

If the tables are used within their 5 year span and this correction is ignored, the error caused will not amount to more than 2 miles.

AP 3270, Volumes 2 and 3, and NP 401 do not require any correction for precession and nutation, as they use an LHA and declination found from information in an almanac for the particular date of the sight.

Sight Reduction Tables for Air Navigation, AP 3270 Volumes 2 and 3

These require a little more calculation to be done than for *Volume 1*. They are not as simple to use but still provide a fairly quick method of finding altitude and azimuth.

Example 27

Find the altitude and azimuth of the sun at 08h 36m 06s GMT, on October 4th in DR position 50° 10'·4N, 6° 15'·3W

First we need to find the sun's LHA and declination from the *Nautical Alamanac* using the daily pages and the 'Increments and Corrections' table.

GHA sun 08h		302° 49'·6	dec.	S4° 26'·9
increment 36m 06s	+	9° 01'·5	d 1·0 +	0'·6
GHA sun 08h 36m 06s		311° 51'·1		S4° 27'·5
chosen long. W	−	5° 51'·1		
LHA sun 08h 36m 06s		306° 00'·0		

(a chosen longitude is used as for *Volume 1*)

Volume 3 is entered with chosen latitude 50° N, LHA 306° and declination 4°. (Extract No. 12). The table labelled CONTRARY is used as latitude (N) and declination (S) are contrary. Had they been both north for example the table labelled SAME would have been used. Hc at the top of the columns is altitude, d is altitude difference (used to find the correction for extra minutes of declination to apply to Hc), and Z is azimuth angle. There are rules for converting azimuth angle (Z) to azimuth (Zn), at the top left hand corner of the table for north latitudes and at the bottom left hand corner for south latitudes.

The tabulations for 50° N, LHA 306°, and declination 4° are:

Hc	d	Z
18° 52'	−50	122°

(The minus or plus sign for d is shown once every 5 tabulations). Table 5 (found inside the back cover), is entered with d along the top and the nearest minute of declination down the side, (seconds are ignored).

		Hc
		18° 52'
d −50 (for dec. 28') =	−	23'
Altitude		18° 29'

LAT 50°

DECLINATION (0°–14°) CONTRARY NAME TO LATITUDE

N. Lat. { LHA greater than 180° ...... Zn=Z
{ LHA less than 180° ...... Zn=360−Z

4° Hc	d	Z	5° Hc	d	Z	6° Hc	d	Z	7° Hc	d	Z	8° Hc	d	Z	9° Hc	d	Z	10° Hc	d	Z	11° Hc	d	Z	12° Hc	d	Z	13° Hc	d	Z	14° Hc	d	Z	LHA
10 10	48	109	09 22	48	110	08 34	47	110	07 47	48	111	06 59	48	111	06 11	48	112	05 23	48	113	04 35	48	113	03 47	48	114	02 59	48	114	02 11	48	115	291
10 46	48	110	09 58	48	110	09 10	47	111	08 23	48	112	07 35	48	112	06 47	48	113	05 59	48	113	05 11	49	114	04 22	48	115	03 34	48	115	02 46	48	116	292
11 22	48	111	10 34	48	111	09 46	48	112	08 58	48	112	08 10	48	113	07 22	48	114	06 34	48	114	05 46	49	115	04 57	48	115	04 09	48	115	03 21	49	117	293
11 58	48	112	11 10	48	112	10 22	48	113	09 34	48	113	08 46	49	114	07 57	48	114	07 09	48	115	06 21	49	116	05 32	48	116	04 44	49	116	03 55	48	117	294
12 34	−48	112	11 46	−48	113	10 58	−49	113	10 09	−48	114	09 21	−49	115	08 32	−48	115	07 44	−49	116	06 55	−48	116	06 07	−49	117	05 18	−49	117	04 29	−48	118	295
13 10	49	113	12 21	48	113	11 33	49	114	10 44	48	115	09 56	49	115	09 07	49	115	08 18	48	117	07 30	49	117	06 41	49	117	05 52	49	118	05 03	49	119	296
13 45	49	114	12 56	48	114	12 08	49	115	11 19	48	116	10 31	49	116	09 42	49	116	08 53	49	117	08 04	49	117	07 15	49	118	06 26	49	119	05 37	49	120	297
14 20	48	115	13 32	49	115	12 43	49	116	11 54	49	116	11 05	49	117	10 16	49	117	09 27	49	118	08 38	49	118	07 49	49	119	07 00	50	120	06 10	49	121	298
14 55	49	116	14 06	49	116	13 17	49	117	12 28	49	117	11 39	49	118	10 50	49	118	10 01	49	119	09 12	50	119	08 22	49	120	07 33	50	121	06 43	49	121	299
15 30	−49	116	14 41	−49	117	13 52	−50	118	13 02	−49	118	12 13	−49	119	11 24	−50	119	10 34	−49	120	09 45	−50	120	08 55	−49	120	08 06	−50	122	07 16	−50	122	300
16 04	49	117	15 15	49	118	14 26	50	118	13 36	49	119	12 47	50	120	11 57	49	120	11 08	50	121	10 18	50	121	09 28	49	122	08 39	50	122	07 49	50	123	301
16 38	49	118	15 49	49	119	15 00	50	119	14 10	50	120	13 20	49	120	12 31	50	121	11 41	50	122	10 51	50	122	10 01	50	123	09 11	50	123	08 21	50	124	302
17 12	49	119	16 23	50	119	15 33	50	120	14 43	50	121	13 53	49	121	13 04	50	122	12 14	51	122	11 23	50	123	10 33	50	123	09 43	50	124	08 53	50	125	303
17 46	50	120	16 56	50	120	16 06	50	121	15 16	50	121	14 26	50	122	13 36	50	123	12 46	50	123	11 56	50	124	11 05	50	124	10 15	51	125	09 24	50	125	304
18 19	−50	121	17 29	−50	121	16 39	−50	122	15 49	−50	122	14 59	−50	122	14 09	−51	124	13 18	−50	124	12 28	−51	125	11 37	−51	125	10 46	−50	126	09 56	−51	126	305
18 52	50	122	18 02	50	122	17 12	50	123	16 22	51	123	15 31	50	123	14 41	51	124	13 50	51	125	12 59	51	125	12 08	50	126	11 18	51	127	10 27	51	127	306
19 25	50	122	18 35	51	123	17 44	50	124	16 54	51	124	16 03	51	125	15 12	51	125	14 21	51	126	13 30	51	126	12 39	51	127	11 48	51	127	10 57	51	128	307
19 58	51	123	19 07	51	124	18 16	51	124	17 25	51	125	16 35	51	126	15 44	51	126	14 53	52	127	14 01	51	127	13 10	51	128	12 19	51	128	11 28	52	129	308
20 30	51	124	19 39	51	125	18 48	51	125	17 57	51	126	17 06	51	126	16 15	52	127	15 23	51	128	14 32	51	128	13 41	52	129	12 49	52	129	11 57	51	130	309
21 01	−51	125	20 10	−51	126	19 19	−51	126	18 28	−51	126	17 37	−52	127	16 45	−51	128	15 54	−52	128	15 02	−51	129	14 11	−52	129	13 19	−52	130	12 27	−52	130	310

Extract Number 12

TABLE 5.—Correction to Tabulated Altitude for Minutes of Declination

49	50	51	52	53	54	55	56	57	58	59	60	$\frac{d}{'}$
0	0	0	0	0	0	0	0	0	0	0	0	0
1	1	1	1	1	1	1	1	1	1	1	1	1
2	2	2	2	2	2	2	2	2	2	2	2	2
2	2	3	3	3	3	3	3	3	3	3	3	3
3	3	3	3	4	4	4	4	4	4	4	4	4
4	4	4	4	4	4	5	5	5	5	5	5	5
5	5	5	5	5	5	6	6	6	6	6	6	6
6	6	6	6	6	6	6	7	7	7	7	7	7
7	7	7	7	7	7	7	7	8	8	8	8	8
7	8	8	8	8	8	8	8	9	9	9	9	9
8	8	8	9	9	9	9	9	10	10	10	10	10
9	9	9	10	10	10	10	10	10	11	11	11	11
10	10	10	10	11	11	11	11	11	12	12	12	12
11	11	11	11	11	12	12	12	12	13	13	13	13
11	12	12	12	12	13	13	13	13	14	14	14	14
12	12	13	13	13	14	14	14	14	14	15	15	15
13	13	14	14	14	14	15	15	15	15	16	16	16
14	14	14	15	15	15	16	16	16	16	17	17	17
15	15	15	16	16	16	16	17	17	17	18	18	18
16	16	16	16	17	17	17	18	18	18	19	19	19
16	17	17	17	18	18	18	19	19	19	20	20	20
17	18	18	18	19	19	19	20	20	20	21	21	21
18	18	19	19	19	20	20	21	21	21	22	22	22
19	19	20	20	20	21	21	21	22	22	23	23	23
20	20	20	21	21	22	22	22	23	23	24	24	24
20	21	21	22	22	22	23	23	24	24	25	25	25
21	22	22	23	23	23	24	24	25	25	26	26	26
22	22	23	23	24	24	25	25	26	26	27	27	27
23	23	24	24	25	25	26	26	27	27	28	28	28
24	24	25	25	26	26	27	27	28	28	29	29	29

Extract Number 13

Z (azimuth angle) is converted to Zn (azimuth) by using the rules at the top or bottom of the table. In this case, latitude north, LHA greater than 180°, Zn = Z so the azimuth is 122° T.

Sight Reduction Tables for Marine Navigation, NP 401

These involve about the same amount of work as for *AP 3270, Volumes 2 and 3*.

Example 28

The same problem has been used as for example 27 (latitude 50° N, declination S4° 27'·5, LHA sun 306°).

NP 401 is entered with chosen latitude 50° N, LHA 306° and declination 4°. The table labelled CONTRARY is used as latitude (N) and declination (S) are contrary. Hc at the top of the columns is altitude, d is altitude difference (used to find the correction to apply to Hc for extra minutes of declination) and Z is azimuth angle. The rules for converting Z to Zn (azimuth) are at the top or bottom of the page (see the full extract in the appendix).

LATITUDE **CONTRARY** NAME TO DECLINATION   L.H.A. 54°, 306°

47°			48°			49°			50°			51°			52°			Dec.
Hc	d	Z	Hc	d	Z	Hc	d	Z	Hc	d	Z	Hc	d	Z	Hc	d	Z	
23 37.9	–47.9	118.0	23 09.6	–48.6	118.4	22 40.9	–49.1	118.7	22 11.9	–49.7	119.1	21 42.6	–50.3	119.5	21 12.9	–50.7	119.8	0
22 50.0	48.2	118.6	22 21.0	48.7	119.0	21 51.8	49.3	119.4	21 22.2	49.8	119.7	20 52.3	50.3	120.0	20 22.2	50.9	120.4	1
22 01.8	48.3	119.3	21 32.3	48.8	119.6	21 02.5	49.4	120.0	20 32.4	50.0	120.3	20 02.0	50.5	120.6	19 31.3	51.0	120.9	2
21 13.5	48.4	119.9	20 43.5	49.0	120.3	20 13.1	49.6	120.6	19 42.4	50.0	120.9	19 11.5	50.6	121.2	18 40.3	51.1	121.5	3
20 25.1	48.6	120.6	19 54.5	49.2	120.9	19 23.5	49.6	121.2	18 52.4	50.2	121.5	18 20.9	50.7	121.8	17 49.2	51.2	122.0	4
19 36.5	–48.6	121.2	19 05.3	–49.2	121.5	18 33.9	–49.8	121.8	18 02.2	–50.3	122.0	17 30.2	–50.8	122.3	16 58.0	–51.2	122.6	5
18 47.9	48.9	121.8	18 16.1	49.3	122.1	17 44.1	49.9	122.4	17 11.9	50.4	122.6	16 39.4	50.8	122.9	16 06.8	51.4	123.1	6
17 59.0	48.9	122.4	17 26.8	49.5	122.7	16 54.2	49.9	122.9	16 21.5	50.5	123.2	15 48.6	51.0	123.4	15 15.4	51.4	123.7	7
17 10.1	49.0	123.0	16 37.3	49.6	123.3	16 04.3	50.1	123.5	15 31.0	50.5	123.8	14 57.6	51.0	124.0	14 24.0	51.5	124.2	8
16 21.1	49.2	123.6	15 47.7	49.6	123.9	15 14.2	50.1	124.1	14 40.5	50.6	124.3	14 06.6	51.1	124.5	13 32.5	51.6	124.7	9

Extract Number 14

The tabulations for latitude 50° N, LHA 306° and declination 4° are:

Hc	d	Z
18° 52'·4−	−50'·2	121·5

(The minus or plus sign for d is shown once every 5 tabulations). The Interpolation Table (found inside both covers) is entered down the left hand side with the declination increment (27'·5) and along the top with altitude difference (d) (−50'·2). The first part of the table is for tens and the second part for units and decimals.

The correction found is applied to Hc:

	Hc
	18° 52'·4−
corrn. for 50'·0	22'·9
corrn. for 0'·2	00'·1
altitude	18° 29'·4

Z (azimuth angle) can be interpolated mentally between declinations 4° and 5° and then converted to Zn (azimuth). The azimuth, after interpolation is, 121° ·7 T.

Further calculations may be done if extra precision is desired but this increases the figure work involved which can always lead to error and is not necessary for normal use (unless d is printed in italic type and accompanied by a dot).

INTERPOLATION TABLE

Dec. Inc.	Tens 10'	20'	30'	40'	50'		Units 0'	1'	2'	3'	4'	5'	6'	7'	8'	9'	Double Second Diff. and Corr.
26.0	4.3	8.6	13.0	17.3	21.6	.0	0.0 0.4	0.9 1.3	1.8 2.2	2.6 3.1	3.5 4.0						0.8
26.1	4.3	8.7	13.0	17.4	21.7	.1	0.0 0.5	0.9 1.4	1.8 2.3	2.7 3.1	3.6 4.0						2.4
26.2	4.3	8.7	13.1	17.4	21.8	.2	0.1 0.5	1.0 1.4	1.9 2.3	2.7 3.2	3.6 4.1						4.0
26.3	4.4	8.8	13.1	17.5	21.9	.3	0.1 0.6	1.0 1.5	1.9 2.3	2.8 3.2	3.7 4.1						5.7
26.4	4.4	8.8	13.2	17.6	22.0	.4	0.2 0.6	1.1 1.5	1.9 2.4	2.8 3.3	3.7 4.2						7.3
26.5	4.4	8.8	13.3	17.7	22.1	.5	0.2 0.7	1.1 1.5	2.0 2.4	2.9 3.3	3.8 4.2						8.9
26.6	4.4	8.9	13.3	17.7	22.2	.6	0.3 0.7	1.1 1.6	2.0 2.5	2.9 3.4	3.8 4.2						10.5
26.7	4.5	8.9	13.4	17.8	22.3	.7	0.3 0.8	1.2 1.6	2.1 2.5	3.0 3.4	3.8 4.3						12.1
26.8	4.5	9.0	13.4	17.9	22.4	.8	0.4 0.8	1.2 1.7	2.1 2.6	3.0 3.4	3.9 4.3						13.7
26.9	4.5	9.0	13.5	18.0	22.5	.9	0.4 0.8	1.3 1.7	2.2 2.6	3.0 3.5	3.9 4.4						15.4
27.0	4.5	9.0	13.5	18.0	22.5	.0	0.0 0.5	0.9 1.4	1.8 2.3	2.7 3.2	3.7 4.1						17.0
27.1	4.5	9.0	13.5	18.0	22.6	.1	0.0 0.5	1.0 1.4	1.9 2.3	2.8 3.3	3.7 4.2						18.6
27.2	4.5	9.0	13.6	18.1	22.6	.2	0.1 0.5	1.0 1.5	1.9 2.4	2.8 3.3	3.8 4.2						20.2
27.3	4.5	9.1	13.6	18.2	22.7	.3	0.1 0.6	1.1 1.5	2.0 2.4	2.9 3.3	3.8 4.3						21.8
27.4	4.6	9.1	13.7	18.3	22.8	.4	0.2 0.6	1.1 1.6	2.0 2.5	2.9 3.4	3.8 4.3						23.4
27.5	4.6	9.2	13.8	18.3	22.9	.5	0.2 0.7	1.1 1.6	2.1 2.5	3.0 3.4	3.9 4.4						25.1
27.6	4.6	9.2	13.8	18.4	23.0	.6	0.3 0.7	1.2 1.6	2.1 2.6	3.0 3.5	3.9 4.4						26.7
27.7	4.6	9.3	13.9	18.5	23.1	.7	0.3 0.8	1.2 1.7	2.2 2.6	3.1 3.5	4.0 4.4						28.3
27.8	4.7	9.3	13.9	18.6	23.2	.8	0.4 0.8	1.3 1.7	2.2 2.7	3.1 3.6	4.0 4.5						29.9
27.9	4.7	9.3	14.0	18.6	23.3	.9	0.4 0.9	1.3 1.8	2.2 2.7	3.2 3.6	4.1 4.5						31.5

Double Second Diff. and Corr.: 0.8 (0.1), 2.4 (0.2), 4.0 (0.3), 5.7 (0.4), 7.3 (0.5), 8.9 (0.6), 10.5 (0.7), 12.1 (0.8), 13.7 (0.9), 15.4 (1.0), 17.0 (1.1), 18.6 (1.2), 20.2 (1.3), 21.8 (1.4), 23.4 (1.5), 25.1 (1.6), 26.7 (1.7), 28.3 (1.8), 29.9 (1.9), 31.5 (2.0), 33.1 (2.1), 34.7

Extract Number 15

Marc St Hilaire Haversine Method (Norie's Nautical Tables)

Although haversine and log tables are used for this method no special mathematical knowledge is required, only the ability to refer to tables. The method is a little longer than the previous methods with slightly more calculation but it is more accurate as the DR position is used. (A zenith distance and not an altitude is obtained from this method, which is subtracted from 90° to find the altitude.) The haversine formula is:

Haversine z = haversine (l ± d)* + haversine h cos l cos d

z = zenith distance.
l = latitude.
d = declination.
h = hour angle.

* *NOTE*
(1 + d) when latitude and declination have contrary names.
(1 − d) when latitude and declination have same names.

Example 29 (See Extract Nos. 16, 17, 18, 19 and 20)

(The same problem has been used as for Example 27.)
DR position, 50° 10'·4N, 6° 15'·3W, declination S4° 27'·5. GHA sun
311° 51'·1

GHA sun 08h 36m 06s	311° 51'·1
DR long. W	6° 15'·3
LHA sun 08h 36m 06s	305° 35'·8

LHA	305° 35'·8	9·32007+	log hav
l	50° 10'·4N	9·80650	log cos
d	4° 27'·5S	9·99869	log cos
		9·12526	log hav

0·13343+ nat hav

(l + d) 54° 37'·9   0·21059   nat hav

zenith distance 71° 49'·4   0·34402   nat hav

altitude 18° 10'·6

The first entry using LHA is in the 'Haversine' tables (Extract No.
16). The required degrees (305°) of LHA are at the bottom of the
table. The minutes, read from the bottom upwards, are on the
right-hand side. Tenths of a minute, are along the bottom and are
read from right to left. Arrows by the degrees indicate direction of
tabulation. (If the required degrees of LHA had been at the top of
the page the table would have been used from the top downwards
and across from left to right, tenths of a minute at the top of the
table.) The log haversine for LHA 305° 35'·8 (in heavy type) is
32007. At the top of the column above 32007 is another figure which
must preceed the log haversine, in this case 9 giving 9·32007.

The next entry for latitude is in the 'Logs of Trig Functions' table,
(Extract No. 17). Degrees are at the top left-hand corner of the
table, minutes down the left-hand side. (There is a 'parts' column
for tenths of a minute). The column required is headed 'cosine'.
Immediately opposite 10' is the figure 9·80656, the figure
immediately below this (for 11 minutes) is 9·80641. By looking in
the 'parts' column to the left of the 'cosine' column the correction
for 0'·4 will be seen to be 6 which is subtracted from 9·80656 (as the
figure for 11 minutes is less than that for 10 minutes) giving 9·80650.

In the same manner the log cosine for the declination is found:
this is 9·99869, (Extract No. 18). These three figures are added
together giving 29·12526. The 2 is discarded leaving 9·12526. This
figure is a log haversine. The natural haversine which corresponds to

54°	HAVERSINES											
→	.0		.2		.4		.6		.8			
	Log.	Nat.	Log.	Nat.	Log.	Nat.	Log.	Nat.	Log.	Nat.		
'	1.or(9.) 0.		1.or(9.) 0.		1.or(9.) 0.		1.or(9.) 0.		1.or(9.) 0.		'	
20	31903	20847	31908	20849	31913	20851	31918	20854	31923	20856	31928 20858	39
21	31928	20858	31933	20861	31938	20863	31943	20865	31948	20868	31953 20870	38
22	31953	20870	31958	20873	31962	20875	31967	20877	31972	20880	31977 20882	37
23	31977	20882	31982	20884	31987	20887	31992	20889	31997	20891	32002 20894	36
24	32002	20894	32007	20896	32012	20899	32017	20901	32021	20903	32026 20906	35
25	32026	20906	32031	20908	32036	20910	32041	20913	32046	20915	32051 20918	34
26	32051	20918	32056	20920	32061	20922	32066	20925	32071	20927	32076 20929	33
27	32076	20929	32081	20932	32085	20934	32090	20936	32095	20939	32100 20941	32
28	32100	20941	32105	20944	32110	20946	32115	20948	32120	20951	32125 20953	31
29	32125	20953	32130	20955	32134	20958	32139	20960	32144	20962	32149 20965	30
30	32149	20965	32154	20967	32159	20970	32164	20972	32169	20974	32174 20977	29
31	32174	20977	32179	20979	32184	20981	32188	20984	32193	20986	32198 20989	28
32	32198	20989	32203	20991	32208	20993	32213	20996	32218	20998	32223 21000	27
33	32223	21000	32228	21003	32233	21005	32237	21008	32242	21010	32247 21012	26
34	32247	21012	32252	21015	32257	21017	32262	21019	32267	21022	32272 21024	25
35	32272	21024	32277	21026	32282	21029	32286	21031	32291	21034	32296 21036	24
36	32296	21036	32301	21038	32306	21041	32311	21043	32316	21045	32321 21048	23
37	32321	21048	32326	21050	32330	21053	32335	21055	32340	21057	32345 21060	22
38	32345	21060	32350	21062	32355	21064	32360	21067	32365	21069	32370 21072	21
39	32370	21072	32374	21074	32379	21076	32384	21079	32389	21081	32394 21083	20

	.8	.6	.4	.2	.0 ←	
PARTS for 0'.1:		LOGS 2		NATURALS 1		305°

Extract Number 16

50° 230°	LOGS. OF TRIG. FUNCTIONS									
'	Sine	Parts	Cosec.	Tan.	Parts	Cotan.	Secant	Parts	Cosine	
00·0	1.(9) 88425		0.(10) 11575	0.(10) 07619		1.(9) 92381	0.(10) 19193		1.(9) 80807	60'
01·0	88436		11564	07644		92356	19208		80792	
02·0	88447	·1 1	11553	07670	·1 3	92330	19223	·1 2	80777	
03·0	88457		11543	07696		92304	19239		80762	
04·0	88468		11532	07721		92279	19254		80747	
05·0	88478	·2 2	11522	07747	·2 5	92253	19269	·2 3	80731	55'
06·0	88489		11511	07773		92227	19284		80716	
07·0	88499		11501	07798		92202	19299		80701	
08·0	88510	·3 3	11490	07824	·3 8	92176	19314	·3 5	80686	
09·0	88521		11479	07850		92150	19329		80671	50'
10·0	88531		11469	07875		92125	19344		80656	
11·0	88542	·4 4	11458	07901	·4 10	92099	19359	·4 6	80641	
12·0	88552		11448	07927		92073	19375		80625	
13·0	88563		11437	07952		92048	19390		80610	
14·0	88573	·5 5	11427	07978	·5 13	92022	19405	·5 8	80595	

Extract Number 17

4° 184°	LOGS. OF TRIG. FUNCTIONS									
'	Sine	Parts	Cosec.	Tan.	Parts	Cotan.	Secant	Parts	Cosine	
20·0	87829		12172	87953		12047	00124		99876	40'
21·0	87995	·1 16	12005	88120	·1 16	11880	00125		99875	
22·0	88161	·2 33	11839	88287	·2 33	11713	00126		99874	
23·0	88326	·3 49	11674	88453	·3 49	11547	00127		99873	
24·0	88490	·4 65	11510	88619	·4 66	11382	00128		99872	
25·0	88654	·5 82	11346	88783	·5 82	11217	00129		99871	35'
26·0	88817	·6 98	11183	88948	·6 99	11052	00130		99870	
27·0	88980	·7 114	11020	89111	·7 115	10889	00131		99869	
28·0	89142	·8 131	10858	89274	·8 132	10726	00132		99868	
29·0	89304	·9 147	10697	89437	·9 148	10563	00133		99867	

Extract Number 18

42°   HAVERSINES   317°

'	.0 Log.	Nat.	.2 Log.	Nat.	.4 Log.	Nat.	.6 Log.	Nat.	.8 Log.	Nat.	Log.	Nat.	'
	1̄.or.(9.)	0.	1̄.or(9.)	0.	1̄.or(9.)	0.	1̄.or(9.)	0.	1̄.or(9.)	0.	1̄.or(9.)	0.	
50	12494	13333	12500	13335	12506	13337	12513	13339	12519	13341	12526	13343	09
51	12526	13343	12532	13345	12539	13347	12545	13349	12552	13351	12558	13353	08
52	12558	13353	12564	13355	12571	13357	12577	13359	12584	13361	12590	13363	07
53	12590	13363	12597	13365	12603	13367	12610	13369	12616	13371	12622	13373	06
54	12622	13373	12629	13375	12635	13377	12642	13379	12648	13381	12655	13383	05
55	12655	13383	12661	13385	12667	13387	12674	13389	12680	13391	12687	13393	04
56	12687	13393	12693	13395	12699	13397	12706	13399	12712	13401	12719	13403	03
57	12719	13403	12725	13405	12732	13407	12738	13409	12745	13411	12751	13412	02
58	12751	13412	12757	13414	12764	13416	12770	13418	12777	13420	12783	13422	01
59	12783	13422	12789	13424	12796	13426	12802	13428	12809	13430	12815	13432	00
		.8		.6		.4		.2		.0	←		
	PARTS for 0'.1:		LOGS 3						NATURALS 1				

Extract Number 19

71°   HAVERSINES

'	.0 Log	Nat.	.2 Log	Nat.	.4 Log	Nat.	.6 Log	Nat.	.8 Log	Nat.	Log	Nat.	'
	1̄.or(9.)	0.	1̄.or(9.)	0.	1̄.or.(9.)	0.	1̄.ar(9.)	0.	1̄.or(9.)	0.	1̄.or(9.)	0.	
45	53582	34342	53586	34345	53589	34347	53593	34350	53596	34353	53600	34356	14
46	53600	34356	53603	34358	53607	34361	53610	34364	53614	34367	53617	34369	13
47	53617	34369	53621	34372	53624	34375	53628	34378	53631	34381	53635	34383	12
48	53635	34383	53638	34386	53642	34389	53645	34392	53649	34394	53652	34397	11
49	53652	34397	53656	34400	53659	34403	53663	34405	53666	34408	53670	34411	10
50	53670	34411	53673	34414	53677	34416	53680	34419	53684	34422	53687	34425	09
51	53687	34425	53690	34427	53694	34430	53697	34433	53701	34436	53704	34439	08
52	53704	34439	53708	34441	53711	34444	53715	34447	53718	34450	53722	34452	07
53	53722	34452	53725	34455	53729	34458	53732	34461	53736	34463	53739	34466	06
54	53739	34466	53743	34469	53746	34472	53750	34474	53753	34477	53757	34480	05

Extract Number 20

this log haversine is required and so the 'Haversine' tables (which are tabulated numerically) are entered with log haversine 9·12526 (in heavy type), (Extract No. 19). Next to this figure is found natural haversine 0·13343 (in light type). Sometimes slight interpolation may be necessary.

The sum of latitude and declination (54° 37′·9) is used to enter the 'Haversine' tables to find the natural haversine which is 0·21059 (Extract No. 16). (Interpolate between 21057 and 21060).

The two natural haversines are added together giving a natural haversine of 0·34402 which, from the 'Haversine' table corresponds to 71° 49′·4, (Extract No. 20). This is calculated zenith distance and has to be subtracted from 90° to give calculated altitude which is 18° 10′·6.

These tables do not give an azimuth angle or azimuth and a further calculation is required.

ABC Tables (Norie's Nautical Tables)

These are used to find the azimuth:
Table A is entered with LHA and latitude interpolating where necessary to obtain the A correction (A is named opposite to latitude except when the LHA is between 90° and 270°), Table B is entered with LHA and declination interpolating where necessary to obtain the B correction (B is always named the same as declination). A and B corrections are combined to give the C correction (C is named north or south according to A and B and west if the LHA is between 0° and 180° or east if the LHA is between 180° and 360°). The C Table is entered with the C correction to find a quadrantal azimuth, which is named according to C. This azimuth is converted to a three figure azimuth by using the following rules (see Fig. 7.1).

NE prefix by 0	(N40° E = 040°)
SE subtract from 180	(S25° E = 155°)
SW add to 180	(S60° W = 240°)
NW subtract from 360	(N15° W = 345°)

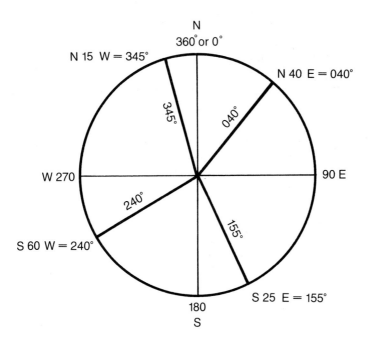

Fig 7.1 Converting a Quadrantal Azimuth to a Three Figure Azimuth.

Example 30 (See Extract Nos. 21, 22 and 23)

Latitude 50° 10'·4N, declination S4° 27'·5, LHA 305° 35'·8

$$A = 0·85 \text{ S}$$
$$B = 0·10 \text{ S}$$
$$C \quad \underline{0·95} \text{ S} \quad \text{Quadrantal Azimuth S58°·6E}$$

Three figure Azimuth 121°·4T

Lat. °	45° 315°	46° 314°	47° 313°	48° 312°	49° 311°	50° 310°	51° 309°	52° 308°	53° 307°	54° 306°	55° 305°	56° 304°	57° 303°	58° 302°	59° 301°	60° 300°	Lat. °
48	1·11	1·07	1·04	1·00	·97	·93	·90	·87	·84	·81	·78	·75	·72	·69	·67	·64	48
49	1·15	1·11	1·07	1·04	1·00	·97	·93	·90	·87	·84	·81	·78	·75	·72	·69	·66	49
50	1·19	1 15	1·11	1·07	1·04	1·00	·97	·93	·90	·87	·83	·80	·77	·75	·72	·69	50
51	1·23	1·19	1·15	1·11	1·07	1·04	1·00	·97	·93	·90	·86	·83	·80	·77	·74	71	51
52	1·28	1·24	1·19	1·15	1·11	1·07	1·04	1·00	·96	·93	·90	·86	·83	·80	·77	·74	52
53	1·33	1·28	1·24	1·19	1·15	1·11	1·07	1·04	1·00	·96	·93	·90	·86	·83	·80	·77	53
54	1·38	1·33	1·28	1·24	1·20	1·15	1·11	1·08	1·04	1·00	·96	·93	·89	·86	·83	·79	54
55	1·43	1·38	1·33	1·29	1·24	1·20	1·16	1·12	1·08	1·04	1·00	·96	·93	·89	·86	·82	55

TABLE A HOUR ANGLE

Extract Number 21

Dec. °	45° 315°	46° 314°	47° 313°	48° 312°	49° 311°	50° 310°	51° 309°	52° 308°	53° 307°	54° 306°	55° 305°	56° 304°	57° 303°	58° 302°	59° 301°	60° 300°	Dec. °
0	·00	·00	·00	·00	·00	·00	·00	·00	·00	·00	·00	·00	·00	·00	·00	·00	0
1	·02	·02	·02	·02	·02	·02	·02	·02	·02	·02	·02	·02	·02	·02	·02	·02	1
2	·05	·05	·05	·05	·05	·05	·04	·04	·04	·04	·04	·04	·04	·04	·04	·04	2
3	·07	·07	·07	·07	·07	·07	·07	·07	·07	·06	·06	·06	·06	·06	·06	·06	3
4	·10	·10	·10	·09	·09	·09	·09	·09	·09	·09	·09	·08	·08	·08	·08	·08	4
5	·12	·12	·12	·12	·12	·11	·11	·11	·11	·11	·11	·11	·10	·10	·10	·10	5
6	·15	·15	·14	·14	·14	·14	·14	·13	·13	·13	·13	·13	·13	·12	·12	·12	6
7	·17	·17	·17	·17	·16	·16	·16	·16	·15	·15	·15	·15	·15	·14	·14	·14	7
8	·20	·20	·19	·19	·19	·18	·18	·18	·18	·17	·17	·17	·17	·17	·16	·16	8
9	·22	·22	·22	·21	·21	·21	·20	·20	·20	·20	·19	·19	·19	·19	·18	·18	9
10	·25	·25	·24	·24	·23	·23	·23	·22	·22	·22	·22	·21	·21	·21	·21	·20	10
11	·27	·27	·27	·26	•26	·25	·25	·25	·24	·24	·24	·23	·23	·23	·23	·22	11
12	·30	·30	·29	·29	·28	·28	·27	·27	·27	·26	·26	·26	·25	·25	·25	·25	12

TABLE B HOUR ANGLE

Extract Number 22

Versine method (Reed's Nautical Almanac)

This method is similar to the haversine formula but more interpolation is required.

Example 31 (See Extract Nos. 24–28)

(This is the same problem as Example 29 which was done by the haversine formula.)

TABLE C

A & B CORRECTION.

AZIMUTHS

Lat.	·90'	·92'	·94'	·96'	·98'	1·00'	1·02'	1·04'	1·06'	1·08'	1·10'	1·12'	1·14'	1·16'	1·18'	1·20'	Lat.
45	57·5	57·0	56·4	55·8	55·3	54·7	54·2	53·7	53·1	52·6	52·1	51·6	51·1	50·6	50·2	49·7	45
46	58·0	57·4	56·9	56·3	55·8	55·2	54·7	54·2	53·6	53·1	52·6	52·1	51·6	51·1	50·7	50·2	46
47	58·5	57·9	57·3	56·8	56·2	55·7	55·2	54·7	54·1	53·6	53·1	52·6	52·1	51·7	51·2	50·7	47
48	58·9	58·4	57·8	57·3	56·7	56·2	55·7	55·2	54·7	54·1	53·6	53·2	52·7	52·2	51·7	51·2	48
49	59·4	58·9	58·3	57·8	57·3	56·7	56·2	55·7	55·2	54·7	54·2	53·7	53·2	52·7	52·3	51·8	49
50	60·0	59·4	58·9	58·3	57·8	57·3	56·7	56·2	55·7	55·2	54·7	54·2	53·8	53·3	52·8	52·4	50
51	60·5	59·9	59·4	58·9	58·3	57·8	57·3	56·8	56·3	55·8	55·3	54·8	54·3	53·9	53·4	52·9	51
52	61·0	60·5	59·9	59·4	58·9	58·4	57·9	57·4	56·9	56·4	55·9	55·4	54·9	54·5	54·0	53·5	52
53	61·6	61·0	60·5	60·0	59·5	59·0	58·5	58·0	57·5	57·0	56·5	56·0	55·5	55·1	54·6	54·2	53
54	62·1	61·6	61·1	60·6	60·1	59·6	59·1	58·6	58·1	57·6	57·1	56·6	56·2	55·7	55·3	54·8	54
55	62·7	62·2	61·7	61·2	60·7	60·2	59·7	59·2	58·7	58·2	57·8	57·3	56·8	56·4	55·9	55·5	55
56	63·3	62·8	62·3	61·8	61·3	60·8	60·3	59·8	59·3	58·9	58·4	57·9	57·5	57·0	56·6	56·1	56
57	63·9	63·4	62·9	62·4	61·9	61·4	60·9	60·5	60·0	59·5	59·1	58·6	58·2	57·7	57·3	56·8	57
58	64·5	64·0	63·5	63·0	62·6	62·1	61·6	61·1	60·7	60·2	59·8	59·3	58·9	58·4	58·0	57·5	58
59	65·1	64·6	64·2	63·7	63·2	62·7	62·3	61·8	61·4	60·9	60·5	60·0	59·6	59·1	58·7	58·3	59

A±B=·90' ·92' ·94' ·96' ·98' 1·00' 1·02' 1·04' 1·06' 1·08' 1·10' 1·12' 1·14' 1·16' 1·18' 1·20'=A±B

A & B **S**ame Names } RULE TO FIND { A & B **D**ifferent names
take **S**um, (add). } **C** CORRECTION { take **D**ifference (Sub.)
C CORRECTION, (A ± B) is named the same as the greater of these quantities.
AZIMUTH takes combined names of **C** Correction and Hour Angle

C

Extract Number 23

Latitude 50° 10'·4N, declination S4° 27'·5, LHA 305° 35'·8

LHA	305° 35'·8	9·6210 log ver
l	50° 10'·4	9·8065 log cos
dec.	4° 27'·5	9·9987 log cos
		9·4262 log ver

0·2669 nat ver

(1 + dec.) 54° 37'·9   0·4212 nat ver

zenith distance 71° 49'·5   0·6881 nat ver

altitude 18° 10'·5

Enter the 'Versine' (Extract No. 24) table with LHA. Interpolate where necessary. Next enter the 'cosine' table (Extract No. 25) with latitude, and similarly for declination (Extract No. 26). Add together the three figures found. In the 'Versine' table, find the resultant figure (in bold type), which is a log versine and extract the natural versine (in light type), (Extract No. 27).

Find the natural versine for the difference between latitude and declination in the same way as for the haversine method and add the two natural versines together. (Extract No. 24). This gives a natural versine which when found in the 'versine' table gives zenith distance. (Extract No. 28). Take this from 90° to find altitude.

A further calculation is necessary to find the azimuth:

VERSINES

	49° LOG.	49° NAT.	50° LOG.	50° NAT.	51° LOG.	51° NAT.	52° LOG.	52° NAT.	53° LOG.	53° NAT.	54° LOG.	54° NAT.	55° LOG.	55° NAT.	
21	9.5423	0.3486	5586	3619	9.5745	3754	5901	3892	9.6054	4031	6203	4172	9.6349	0.4314	39
22	9.5426	0.3488	5589	3621	9.5748	3757	5904	3894	9.6056	4033	6206	4174	9.6352	0.4317	38
23	9.5428	0.3490	5591	3624	9.5751	3759	5906	3896	9.6059	4035	6208	4176	9.6354	0.4319	37
24	9.5431	0.3492	5594	3626	9.5753	3761	5909	3899	9.6061	4038	6210	4179	9.6356	0.4322	36
25	9.5434	0.3494	5597	3628	9.5756	3763	5912	3901	9.6064	4040	6213	4181	9.6359	0.4324	35
26	9.5437	0.3497	5599	3630	9.5759	3766	5914	3903	9.6066	4042	6215	4184	9.6361	0.4326	34
27	9.5439	0.3499	5602	3632	9.5761	3768	5917	3905	9.6069	4045	6218	4186	9.6364	0.4329	33
28	9.5442	0.3501	5605	3635	9.5764	3770	5919	3908	9.6071	4047	6220	4188	9.6366	0.4331	32
29	9.5445	0.3503	5607	3637	9.5766	3773	5922	3910	9.6074	4049	6223	4191	9.6368	0.4334	31
30	9.5443	0.3506	5610	3639	9.5769	3775	5924	3912	9.6076	4052	6225	4193	9.6371	0.4336	30
31	9.5450	0.3508	5613	3641	9.5772	3777	5927	3915	9.6079	4054	6228	4195	9.6373	0.4338	29
32	9.5453	0.3510	5615	3644	9.5774	3779	5930	3917	9.6081	4056	6230	4198	9.6376	0.4341	28
33	9.5456	0.3512	5618	3646	9.5777	3782	5932	3919	9.6084	4059	6233	4200	9.6378	0.4343	27
34	9.5458	0.3514	5621	3648	9.5779	3784	5935	3922	9.6086	4061	6235	4202	9.6380	0.4346	26
35	9.5461	0.3517	5623	3650	9.5782	3786	5937	3924	9.6089	4063	6237	4205	9.6383	0.4348	25
36	9.5464	0.3519	5626	3653	9.5785	3789	5940	3926	9.6091	4066	6240	4207	9.6385	0.4350	24
37	9.5467	0.3521	5629	3655	9.5787	3791	5942	3929	9.6094	4068	6242	4210	9.6388	0.4353	23
38	9.5469	0.3523	5631	3657	9.5790	3793	5945	3931	9.6096	4070	6245	4212	9.6390	0.4355	22
39	9.5472	0.3525	5634	3659	9.5793	3795	5947	3933	9.6099	4073	6247	4214	9.6392	0.4358	21
40	9.5475	0.3528	5637	3662	9.5795	3798	5950	3935	9.6101	4075	6250	4217	9.6395	0.4360	20

LOG.	NAT.	LOG.	NAT.	LOG.	NAT.	LOG.	NAT.	LOG.	NAT.	LOG.	NAT.	LOG.	NAT.	
310°		309°		308°		307°		306°		305°		304°		

Extract Number 24

LOG COSINES

45° 46° 47° 48° 49° 50° 51° 52° 53° 54° 55° 56° 57° 58° 59°

	45°	46°	47°	48°	49°	50°	51°	52°	53°	54°	55°	56°	57°	58°	59°	
0	9.8495	8418	8338	8255	8169	9.8081	7989	7893	7795	9.7692	7586	7476	7361	7242	9.7118	60
1	9.8494	8416	8336	8254	8168	9.8079	7987	7892	7793	9.7690	7584	7474	7359	7240	9.7116	59
2	9.8492	8415	8335	8252	8167	9.8078	7986	7890	7791	9.7689	7582	7472	7357	7238	9.7114	58
3	9.8491	8414	8334	8251	8165	9.8076	7984	7889	7790	9.7687	7580	7470	7355	7236	9.7112	57
4	9.8490	8412	8332	8249	8164	9.8075	7982	7887	7788	9.7685	7579	7468	7353	7234	9.7110	56
5	9.8489	8411	8331	8248	8162	9.8073	7981	7885	7786	9.7683	7577	7466	7351	7232	9.7108	55
6	9.8487	8410	8330	8247	8161	9.8072	7979	7884	7785	9.7682	7575	7464	7349	7230	9.7106	54
7	9.8486	8409	8328	8245	8159	9.8070	7978	7882	7783	9.7680	7573	7462	7347	7228	9.7104	53
8	9.8485	8407	8327	8244	8158	9.8069	7976	7880	7781	9.7678	7571	7461	7345	7226	9.7102	52
9	9.8483	8406	8326	8242	8156	9.8067	7975	7879	7780	9.7676	7570	7459	7344	7224	9.7099	51
10	9.8482	8405	8324	8241	8155	9.8066	7973	7877	7778	9.7675	7568	7457	7342	7222	9.7097	50
11	9.8481	8403	8323	8240	8153	9.8064	7972	7876	7776	9.7673	7566	7455	7340	7220	9.7095	49
12	9.8480	8402	8322	8238	8152	9.8063	7970	7874	7774	9.7661	7564	7453	7338	7218	9.7093	48
13	9.8478	8401	8320	8237	8150	9.8061	7968	7872	7773	9.7669	7562	7451	7336	7216	9.7091	47
14	9.8477	8399	8319	8235	8149	9.8060	7967	7871	7771	9.7668	7561	7449	7334	7214	9.7089	46
15	9.8476	8398	8317	8234	8148	9.8058	7965	7869	7769	9.7666	7559	7447	7332	7212	9.7087	45

Extract Number 25

LOG COSINES

/	0°	1°	2°	3°	4°	5°	6°	7°	8°	9°	10°	11°	12°	13°	14°	
21	0.0000	9999	9996	9993	9987	9.9981	9973	9964	9954	9.9942	9929	9914	9898	9881	9.9862	39
22	0.0000	9999	9996	9992	9987	9.9981	9973	9954	9954	9.9942	9929	9914	9898	9881	9.9862	38
23	0.0000	9999	9996	9992	9987	9.9981	9973	9964	9953	9.9941	9928	9914	9898	9880	9.9862	37
24	0.0000	9999	9996	9992	9987	9.9981	9973	9964	9953	9.9941	9928	9913	9897	9880	9.9861	36
25	0.0000	9999	9996	9992	9987	9.9981	9973	9964	9953	9.9941	9928	9913	9897	9880	9.9861	35
26	0.0000	9999	9996	9992	9987	9.9980	9973	9963	9953	9.9941	9928	9913	9897	9879	9.9861	34
27	0.0000	9999	9996	9992	9987	9.9980	9972	9963	9953	9.9941	9927	9913	9897	9879	9.9860	33
28	0.0000	9999	9996	9992	9987	9.9980	9972	9963	9952	9.9940	9927	9912	9896	9879	9.9860	32
29	0.0000	9999	9996	9992	9987	9.9980	9972	9963	9952	9.9940	9927	9912	9896	9879	9.9860	31
30	0.0000	9999	9996	9992	9987	9.9980	9972	9963	9952	9.9940	9927	9912	9896	9878	9.9859	30

Extract Number 26

VERSINES

	LOG.	NAT.	LOG.	NAT.	LOG.	NAT.	LOG.	NAT.	LOG.	NAT.	LOG.	NAT.	LOG.	NAT.	
46	9.4247	0.2659	4438	2778	9.4624	2900	4806	3024	9.4984	3150	5157	3278	9.5326	0.3409	14
47	9.4250	0.2661	4441	2780	9.4627	2902	4809	3026	9.4986	3152	5160	3281	9.5329	0.3411	13
48	9.4253	0.2663	4444	2782	9.4630	2904	4812	3028	9.4989	3155	5162	3283	9.5331	0.3413	12
49	9.4256	0.2665	4447	2784	9.4633	2906	4815	3030	9.4992	3157	5165	3285	9.5334	0.3415	11
50	9.4260	0.2667	4450	2786	9.4637	2908	4818	3033	9.4995	3159	5168	3287	9.5337	0.3417	10
51	9.4263	0.2669	4454	2788	9.4640	2910	4821	3035	9.4998	3161	5171	3289	9.5340	0.3420	9
52	9.4266	0.2671	4457	2790	9.4643	2912	4824	3037	9.5001	3163	5174	3291	9.5343	0.3422	8
53	9.4269	0.2673	4460	2792	9.4646	2915	4827	3039	9.5004	3165	5177	3294	9.5345	0.3424	7
54	9.4273	0.2675	4463	2794	9.4649	2917	4830	3041	9.5007	3167	5180	3296	9.5348	0.3426	6
55	9.4276	0.2677	4466	2797	9.4652	2919	4833	3043	9.5010	3169	5182	3298	9.5351	0.3428	5
56	9.4279	0.2679	4469	2799	9.4655	2921	4836	3045	9.5013	3172	5185	3300	9.5354	0.3431	4
57	9.4282	0.2681	4472	2801	9.4658	2923	4839	3047	9.5016	3174	5188	3302	9.5357	0.3433	3
58	9.4285	0.2682	4476	2803	9.4661	2925	4842	3049	9.5018	3176	5191	3304	9.5359	0.3435	2
59	9.4289	0.2684	4479	2805	9.4664	2927	4845	3051	9.5021	3178	5194	3307	9.5362	0.3437	1
60	9.4292	0.2686	4482	2807	9.4667	2929	4848	3053	9.5024	3180	5197	3309	9.5365	0.3439	0
	LOG.	NAT.	LOG.	NAT.	LOG.	NAT.	LOG.	NAT.	LOG.	NAT.	LOG.	NAT.	LOG.	NAT.	/
	317°		316°		315°		314°		313°		312°		311°		

Extract Number 27

VERSINES

/	70°		71°		72°		73°		74°		75°		76°		
0	9.8182	0.6580	8289	6744	9.8395	6910	8498	7076	9.8600	7244	8699	7412	9.8797	0.7581	60
4	9.8189	0.6591	8296	6755	9.8402	6921	8505	7087	9.8606	7255	8706	7423	9.8804	0.7592	56
8	9.8197	0.6602	8304	6766	9.8409	6932	8512	7099	9.8613	7266	8712	7434	9.8810	0.7603	52
12	9.8204	0.6613	8311	6777	9.8416	6943	8519	7110	9.8620	7277	8719	7446	9.8817	0.7615	48
16	9.8211	0.6624	8318	6788	9.8422	6954	8525	7121	9.8626	7288	8726	7457	9.8823	0.7625	44
20	9.8218	0.6635	8325	6799	9.8429	6965	8532	7132	9.8633	7300	8732	7468	9.8829	0.7637	40
24	9.8225	0.6645	8332	6810	9.8436	6976	8539	7143	9.8640	7311	8739	7479	9.8836	0.7649	36
28	9.8232	0.6656	8339	6821	9.8443	6987	8546	7154	9.8646	7322	8745	7491	9.8842	0.7660	32
32	9.8240	0.6667	8346	6832	9.8450	6998	8552	7165	9.8653	7333	8752	7502	9.8849	0.7671	28
36	9.8247	0.6678	8353	6844	9.8457	7010	8559	7177	9.8660	7344	8758	7513	9.8855	0.7683	24
40	9.8254	0.6689	8360	6855	9.8464	7021	8566	7188	9.8666	7356	8765	7524	9.8861	0.7694	20
44	9.8261	0.6700	8367	6866	9.8471	7032	8573	7199	9.8673	7367	8771	7536	9.8868	0.7705	16
48	9.8268	0.6711	8374	6877	9.8478	7043	8579	7210	9.8679	7378	8778	7547	9.8874	0.7716	12
52	9.8275	0.6722	8381	6888	9.8484	7054	8586	7221	9.8686	7389	8784	7558	9.8881	0.7728	8
56	9.8282	0.6733	8388	6899	9.8491	7065	8593	7232	9.8693	7401	8791	7569	9.8887	0.7739	4
60	9.8289	0.6744	8395	6910	9.8498	7076	8600	7244	9.8699	7412	8797	7581	9.8893	0.7750	0

Extract Number 28

ABC TABLES (REED'S NAUTICAL ALMANAC)

These are used to find the azimuth.

Table A is entered with LHA and latitude (read the rule at the top of the table to indicate whether the quantity extracted is + or −). Table B is entered with LHA and declination (read the rule at the top of the table for + and −). The sum of these is used to enter Table C which gives a quadrantal azimuth labelled according to the rules on Table C. This can be converted to a three figure azimuth using the same rules as for the haversine method.

Example 32. (Use Extract Nos. 29 and 30)

Latitude 50° 10'·4N, declination S4° 27'·5, LHA 305° 35'·8

$$A = ·858+$$
$$B = ·096+ \quad \text{after interpolation}$$

$$C \quad ·954$$

Quadrantal Azimuth S58°·6E
Three figure Azimuth 121°·4T

A   HOUR ANGLE at top   +
           HOUR ANGLE at bottom   −

LAT	32° 328°	34° 326°	36° 324°	38° 322°	40° 320°	42° 318°	44° 316°	46° 314°	48° 312°	50° 310°	52° 308°	54° 306°	56° 304°	58° 302°	60° 300°
27	.815	.755	.701	.652	.607	.566	.528	.492	.459	.428	.398	.370	.344	.318	.294
30	.924	.856	.795	.739	.688	.641	.598	.558	.520	.484	.451	.419	.389	.361	.333
33	1.04	.963	.894	.831	.774	.721	.672	.627	.585	.545	.507	.472	.438	.406	.375
36	1.16	1.08	1.00	.930	.866	.807	.752	.702	.654	.610	.568	.528	.490	.454	.419
38	1.25	1.16	1.08	1.00	.931	.868	.809	.754	.703	.656	.610	.568	.527	.488	.451
40	1.34	1.24	1.15	1.07	1.00	.932	.869	.810	.756	.704	.656	.610	.566	.524	.484
42	1.44	1.33	1.24	1.15	1.07	1.00	.932	.870	.811	.756	.703	.654	.607	.563	.520
44	1.55	1.43	1.33	1.24	1.15	1.07	1.00	.933	.870	.810	.754	.702	.651	.603	.558
46	1.66	1.54	1.43	1.33	1.23	1.15	1.07	1.00	.932	.869	.809	.752	.698	.647	.598
48	1.78	1.65	1.53	1.42	1.32	1.23	1.15	1.07	1.00	.932	.868	.807	.749	.694	.641
50	1.91	1.77	1.64	1.53	1.42	1.32	1.23	1.15	1.07	1.00	.931	.866	.804	.745	.688
52	2.05	1.90	1.76	1.64	1.53	1.42	1.33	1.24	1.15	1.07	1.00	.930	.863	.800	.739
54	2.20	2.04	1.89	1.76	1.64	1.53	1.43	1.33	1.24	1.15	1.08	1.00	.928	.860	.795
56	2.37	2.20	2.04	1.90	1.77	1.65	1.54	1.43	1.33	1.24	1.16	1.08	1.00	.926	.856
58	2.56	2.37	2.20	2.05	1.91	1.78	1.66	1.55	1.44	1.34	1.25	1.16	1.08	1.00	.924
60	2.77	2.57	2.38	2.22	2.06	1.92	1.79	1.67	1.56	1.45	1.35	1.26	1.17	1.08	1.00
62	3.01	2.79	2.59	2.41	2.24	2.09	1.95	1.82	1.69	1.58	1.47	1.37	1.27	1.18	1.09
64	3.28	3.04	2.82	2.62	2.44	2.28	2.12	1.98	1.85	1.72	1.60	1.49	1.38	1.28	1.18
66	3.59	3.33	3.09	2.87	2.68	2.49	2.33	2.17	2.02	1.88	1.75	1.63	1.52	1.40	1.30
LAT	148° 212°	146° 214°	144° 216°	142° 218°	140° 220°	138° 222°	136° 224°	134° 226°	132° 228°	130° 230°	128° 232°	126° 234°	124° 236°	122° 238°	120° 240°

B   Lat. and Dec. SAME NAME   −
       Lat. and Dec. DIFFERENT NAMES   +

DEC.	32° 328°	34° 326°	36° 324°	38° 322°	40° 320°	42° 318°	44° 316°	46° 314°	48° 312°	50° 310°	52° 308°	54° 306°	56° 304°	58° 302°	60° 300°
0	.000	.000	.000	.000	.000	.000	.000	.000	.000	.000	.000	.000	.000	.000	.000
3	.099	.094	.089	.085	.082	.078	.075	.073	.071	.068	.067	.065	.063	.062	.061
6	.198	.188	.179	.171	.164	.157	.151	.146	.141	.137	.133	.130	.127	.124	.121
9	.299	.283	.269	.257	.246	.237	.228	.220	.213	.207	.201	.196	.191	.187	.183
12	.401	.380	.362	.345	.331	.318	.306	.295	.286	.277	.270	.263	.256	.251	.245
15	.506	.479	.456	.435	.417	.400	.386	.372	.361	.350	.340	.331	.323	.316	.309
18	.613	.581	.553	.528	.505	.486	.468	.452	.437	.424	.412	.402	.392	.383	.375
21	.724	.686	.653	.623	.597	.574	.553	.534	.517	.501	.487	.474	.463	.453	.443
24	.840	.796	.757	.723	.693	.665	.641	.619	.599	.581	.565	.550	.537	.525	.514
27	.962	.911	.867	.828	.793	.761	.733	.708	.686	.665	.647	.630	.615	.601	.588

Extract Number 29

C = A ± B

C

AZIMUTH

Lat.	.00	.05	.10	.15	.20	.25	.30	.35	.40	.45	.50	.55	.60	.70	.80	.90	1.00	1.10	1.20	1.40	1.60
0	90.0	87.1	84.3	81.5	78.7	76.0	73.3	70.7	68.2	65.8	63.4	61.2	59.0	55.0	51.3	48.0	45.0	42.3	39.8	35.5	32.0
10	90.0	87.2	84.4	81.6	78.9	76.2	73.5	71.0	68.5	66.1	63.8	61.6	59.4	55.4	51.8	48.4	45.4	42.7	40.2	36.0	32.4
20	90.0	87.3	84.6	82.0	79.4	76.8	74.3	71.8	69.4	67.1	64.8	62.7	60.6	56.7	53.1	49.8	46.8	44.1	41.6	37.2	33.6
24	90.0	87.4	84.8	82.2	79.6	77.1	74.7	72.3	69.9	67.7	65.5	63.3	61.3	57.4	53.8	50.6	47.6	44.9	42.4	38.0	34.4
28	90.0	87.5	85.0	82.5	80.0	77.6	75.2	72.8	70.5	68.3	66.2	64.1	62.1	58.3	54.8	51.5	48.6	45.8	43.3	39.0	35.3
30	90.0	87.5	85.1	82.6	80.2	77.8	75.4	73.1	70.9	68.7	66.6	64.5	62.5	58.8	55.3	52.1	49.1	46.4	43.9	39.5	35.8
32	90.0	87.6	85.2	82.8	80.4	78.0	75.7	73.5	71.3	69.1	67.0	65.0	63.0	59.3	55.8	52.7	49.7	47.0	44.5	40.1	36.4
34	90.0	87.6	85.4	82.9	80.6	78.3	76.0	73.8	71.7	69.5	67.5	65.5	63.6	59.9	56.4	53.3	50.3	47.6	45.1	40.7	37.0
36	90.0	87.7	85.5	83.1	80.8	78.6	76.4	74.2	72.1	70.0	68.0	66.0	64.2	60.5	57.1	53.9	51.0	48.3	45.8	41.4	37.7
38	90.0	87.7	85.5	83.3	81.0	78.9	76.7	74.6	72.5	70.5	68.5	66.6	64.7	61.1	57.8	54.7	51.8	49.1	46.6	42.2	38.4
40	90.0	87.8	85.6	83.4	81.3	79.2	77.1	75.0	73.0	71.0	69.0	67.2	65.3	61.8	58.5	55.4	52.5	49.9	47.4	43.0	39.2
42	90.0	87.9	85.7	83.6	81.5	79.5	77.4	75.4	73.4	71.5	69.6	67.8	66.0	62.5	59.3	56.2	53.4	50.7	48.3	43.9	40.0
44	90.0	87.9	85.9	83.8	81.8	79.8	77.8	75.9	73.9	72.1	70.2	68.4	66.7	63.3	60.1	57.1	54.3	51.6	49.2	44.8	41.0
46	90.0	88.0	86.0	84.1	82.1	80.1	78.2	76.3	74.5	72.6	70.8	69.1	67.4	64.1	60.9	58.0	55.2	52.6	50.2	45.8	42.0
48	90.0	88.1	86.2	84.3	82.4	80.5	78.6	76.8	75.0	73.2	71.5	69.8	68.1	64.9	61.8	58.9	56.2	53.6	51.2	46.9	43.0
50	90.0	88.2	86.3	84.5	82.7	80.9	79.1	77.3	75.6	73.9	72.2	70.5	68.9	65.8	62.8	60.0	57.3	54.7	52.4	48.0	44.2
52	90.0	88.3	86.5	84.7	83.0	81.2	79.5	77.8	76.2	74.5	72.9	71.3	69.7	66.7	63.8	61.0	58.4	55.9	53.5	49.2	45.4
54	90.0	88.4	86.6	85.0	83.3	81.6	80.0	78.4	76.8	75.2	73.6	72.1	70.6	67.6	64.8	62.1	59.6	57.1	54.8	50.6	46.8
56	90.0	88.5	86.8	85.2	83.6	82.0	80.5	78.9	77.4	75.9	74.4	72.9	71.5	68.6	65.9	63.3	60.8	58.4	56.1	51.9	48.2
58	90.0	88.5	87.0	85.5	84.0	82.5	81.0	79.5	78.0	76.6	75.2	73.8	72.4	69.6	67.0	64.5	62.1	59.8	57.5	53.4	49.7
60	90.0	88.6	87.1	85.7	84.3	82.9	81.5	80.1	78.7	77.3	76.0	74.6	73.3	70.7	68.2	65.8	63.4	61.2	59.0	55.0	51.3
62	90.0	88.7	87.3	86.0	84.6	83.3	82.0	80.7	79.4	78.1	76.8	75.5	74.3	71.8	69.4	67.1	64.9	62.7	60.6	56.7	53.1
64	90.0	88.7	87.5	86.2	85.0	83.7	82.5	81.3	80.1	78.8	77.6	76.4	75.3	72.9	70.7	68.5	66.3	64.3	62.3	58.5	55.0
66	90.0	88.8	87.7	86.5	85.3	84.2	83.0	81.9	80.8	79.6	78.5	77.4	76.3	74.1	72.0	69.9	67.9	65.9	64.0	60.3	56.9
68	90.0	88.9	87.9	86.8	85.7	84.6	83.6	82.5	81.5	80.4	79.4	78.4	77.3	75.3	73.3	71.4	69.5	67.6	65.8	62.3	59.1
Lat.	.00	.05	.10	.15	.20	.25	.30	.35	.40	.45	.50	.55	.60	.70	.80	.90	1.00	1.10	1.20	1.40	1.60

C CORRECTION

TO NAME AZIMUTH

+   SOUTH in N. Latitudes
    NORTH in S. Latitudes

−   NORTH in N. Latitudes
    SOUTH in S. Latitudes

Hour Angle LESS than 180° = WEST

Hour Angle GREATER than 180° = EAST

Extract Number 30

QUESTION PAPER SEVEN

7.1 What is the chosen position longitude and LHA for the following?

	GHA	DR long
a	26° 48'·1	14° 30'·4W
b	163° 14'·3	65° 32'·9E

7.2 On June 22nd at dawn twilight in DR position 49° 59'·7N, 24° 59'·9W which stars are available for observation? Which are the brightest? Select 3 for plotting. Give their altitudes and azimuths. State the reason for your choice.

7.3 On March 7th when in DR position 50° 02'·1N, 25° 00'·3W, it is desired to take a dawn sight of Altair. What is its approximate altitude and azimuth? (Use *AP 3270 Vol 3*).

7.4 On June 20th in DR position 49° 57'·8N, 17° 22'·4W a sight of the Sun was taken at 09h 36m 00s GMT. What was the calculated altitude and azimuth? (Use *NP 401*).

Answers on pages 159–60.

Chapter Eight

Latitude Made Easy

The sun's altitude as it crosses our meridian on its upper transit is at its greatest. At this time the LHA will be 0° and the sun's azimuth either due north or south. A position line obtained from a sight at this time will be at right angles to the azimuth, that is it will lie along a parallel of latitude. With very little calculation (and no plotting) the distance from the sun's geographical position and hence the true latitude can be found. This method of finding latitude is called latitude by meridian altitude. Early navigators would determine only their latitude and it was not until much later that the introduction of a reliable chronometer enabled longitude to be found.

Any heavenly body can be used to find latitude by observing meridian passage, but the most convenient one is the sun which is large and familiar. We know that the sun will cross any meridian around 1200 local time.

Let us see exactly how much work is involved for such a sight.

Example 33 (Use Extract No. 31)

On March 9th, in DR position 36° 30'·1N, 21° 14'·9W, the sextant altitude of the sun's lower limb was 48° 34'·4. Index error −3'·0. Height of eye 2·0m. What was the latitude?

First the LMT of the sun's meridian passage at Greenwich is found from the bottom right-hand corner of the daily page in the *Nautical Almanac*. This time can be regarded as LMT on any other meridian. The DR longitude is applied to this to give GMT of the sun's meridian passage at the DR position:

	h m
Meridian passage sun	12 11 LMT 9d
DR long. 21° 14'·9W	+01 25 ('Conversion of Arc To
	Time' table)
Meridian passage sun	13 36 GMT 9d at DR position.

Day	SUN Eqn. of Time 00ʰ	SUN Eqn. of Time 12ʰ	Mer. Pass.	MOON Mer. Pass. Upper	MOON Mer. Pass. Lower	Age	Phase
	m s	·m s	h m	h m	h m	d	
7	11 07	11 00	12 11	03 53	16 16	20	
8	10 53	10 45	12 11	04 39	17 03	21	
9	10 38	10 30	12 11	05 28	17 53	22	

Extract Number 31

This time is used to find the sun's declination at meridian passage (from the daily pages and the 'Increments and Corrections' table).

dec.	13h	S4° 18'·5
d 1·0 −	36m	0'·6
		S4° 17'·9

The sextant altitude at meridian passage is corrected to a true altitude (using the 'Altitude Correction Tables', and subtracted from 90° to find the true zenith distance:

SA		48° 34'·4
IE & dip		− 5'·5
AA		48° 28'·9
corrn. LL		+ 15'·4
TA		48° 44'·3
subtract from 90°		90° 00'·0
TZD		41° 15'·7

True zenith distance is compared with declination to find latitude:

TZD	41° 15'·7
dec.	− 4° 17'·9
	36° 57'·8N LATITUDE

In the above example the *difference* between true zenith distance and declination gave latitude. Figure 8.1 illustrates the rules for determining latitude given true zenith distance and declination.

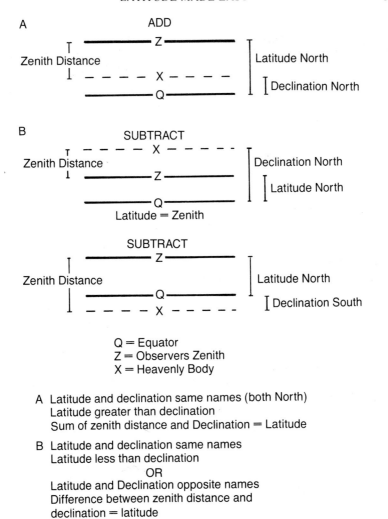

Q = Equator
Z = Observers Zenith
X = Heavenly Body

A Latitude and declination same names (both North)
   Latitude greater than declination
   Sum of zenith distance and Declination = Latitude

B Latitude and declination same names
   Latitude less than declination
                    OR
   Latitude and Declination opposite names
   Difference between zenith distance and
   declination = latitude

Fig 8.1 Zenith Distance, Declination and Latitude. This diagram gives the rules for determing latitude, given that you know true zenith distance and declination.

Example 34

1 DR latitude 59° 01′·5N.
     dec. 18° 03′·4N TZD 40° 46′·6 = LATITUDE 58° 50′·0N
2 DR latitude 15° 14′·1N.
     dec. 20° 59′·6N TZD 5° 23′·8 = LATITUDE 15° 35′·8N
3 DR latitude 21° 59′·45S.
     dec. 7° 18′·9N TZD 29° 34′·3 = LATITUDE 22° 15′·4S

The estimated time of meridian passage will depend on the accuracy of the DR longitude used to find it. As the sun's altitude changes slowly around the time of meridian passage, a small error (one minute) will not matter. Ideally the sun should be observed 10 minutes or so before the estimated time of meridian passage adjusting the sextant as the sun's altitude increases until maximum altitude is reached and the sun starts to 'dip'. This time is taken as the time of meridian passage. The maximum altitude (which must be recorded) is the sextant altitude of meridian passage.

Meridian Passage of the Moon.

Both upper and lower meridian passages of the moon are tabulated in the *Nautical Almanac*. The lower meridian passage of any heavenly body is only visible in high latitudes at certain times and is, therefore, normally of little practical use. The examples in this chapter for the moon and other heavenly bodies are for upper meridian passage.

The moon does not keep a 24 hour day like the sun but crosses the same meridian approximately 50 minutes later each day. Therefore, the LMT of meridian passage at Greenwich meridian cannot be regarded as the LMT on any other meridian as is possible with the sun. The exact daily difference must be found by comparing the time of meridian passage for the day in question (found in the *Nautical Almanac* next to the sun information) with the time of meridian passage for the preceding day for easterly longitude, or the following day for westerly longitude. The proportion of the daily difference applicable to the observer's longitude is then applied to the tabulated LMT of meridian passage at Greenwich to give LMT of meridian passage at the DR position. (Added if west, subtracted if east).

Example 35

DR longitude 90°W, daily difference 60 minutes.

When the moon transits the meridian 90°W of Greenwich it will have travelled a proportion of its daily orbit:

$$\frac{90}{360} \times 60 = 15\text{m (correction for longitude)}$$

The daily difference for 360° is 60 minutes of which a quarter, 15 minutes is required.

As longitude is west this correction is added to the LMT of meridian passage at Greenwich to give the LMT for a position 90°W.

Example 36 (Use Extract No. 31)

What is the GMT of meridian passage of the moon on March 8th, longitude 35° 30'·0W?

	h	m		
Meridian passage at Greenwich	04	39	LMT	8d
Meridian passage at Greenwich	05	28	LMT	9d
daily difference		49		

$$\frac{35 \cdot 5}{360} \times 49 = 4 \cdot 83 \text{ minutes (use 5 minutes)}$$

	h	m	
Meridian passage moon	04	39	LMT 8d Greenwich
long. corrn.	+	5	
Meridian passage moon	04	44	LMT 8d at DR

We must now apply longitude in the usual way to find the GMT of meridian passage at the DR longitude:

	h	m	
Meridian passage moon	04	44	LMT 8d at DR
long. 35° 30'·0W	+02	22	
Meridian passage moon	07	06	GMT 8d at DR

When GMT of meridian passage has been found procedure is the same as for the sun.

The moon's declination changes rapidly in comparison with the sun and it may be difficult to observe the exact time of its meridian passage. After dark there may be a false horizon under the moon caused by its reflection on the sea.

Planets

The occasions when planets can be used for a meridian altitude sight are limited as both planet and horizon must be visible. Meridian passage is tabulated in the *Nautical Almanac* for the four planets for the middle day of three days on the daily pages and a small interpolation is necessary if any but the middle day is used.

Once GMT of meridian passage at the DR position has been found, the procedure is the same as for the sun.

Stars

If stars are used, a little more calculation is necessary as a star's meridian passage is not tabulated. However, meridian passage of Aries is tabulated tri-daily and this can be used to find the time of the star's meridian passage:

Example 37 (Use Extract No. 32)

What is the LMT of meridian passage of Betelgeuse on June 22nd?

		h m	
Meridian passage Aries at Greenwich		06 01·6	LMT 21d
Meridian passage Aries at Greenwich		05 49·8	LMT 24d
	tri-daily difference	11·8	

	ARIES			ARIES
18	181 04.0		18	184 01.4
19	196 06.5		19	199 03.9
20	211 09.0		20	214 06.4
21	226 11.4		21	229 08.8
22	241 13.9		22	244 11.3
23	256 16.3		23	259 13.8
	h m			h m
21 d Mer. Pass.	6 01.6		24 d Mer. Pass.	5 49.8

Extract Number 32

One third of the tri-daily difference is 3·9m. LMT of meridian passage at Greenwich on June 22nd is therefore 5h 57·7m. (6h 01·6m less 3·9m).

We can regard this time as the LMT of meridian passage on the other meridians as we did with the sun.

If we now subtract from 360° the SHA of Betelgeuse (found on the daily pages), change it to time and apply it to the time of meridian passage of Aries, we will get the LMT of meridian passage of the star at the DR longitude:

$$360° \ 00'·0$$

SHA Betelgeuse − 271° 28'·8

$$88° \ 31'·2 \ = \ 5\text{h} \ 54\text{m}$$

	h m	
Meridian passage of Aries	5 58	LMT (to nearest minute)
	5 54	
Meridian passage of Betelgeuse	11 52	LMT at DR

It is now necessary to apply longitude to find the GMT of meridian passage at the DR position. Let us say the longitude is 12°W. Converted to time this would be 48 minutes. The rest of the calculation would be:

	h m	
Meridian passage of Betelgeuse	11 52	LMT 22d at DR
long. 12°W	48	
Meridian passage of Betelgeuse	12 40	GMT 22d at DR

We have also checked that the Greenwich date has not altered.

Declination of Betelgeuse which is N7° 24'·1 is tabulated next to its SHA on the daily pages and requires no correction.

Ex-meridian Sights

When a heavenly body is near the observer's meridian the rate of change in zenith distance (or altitude) is small and if, for some reason, it is not possible for an observation to be taken at the exact time of meridian passage, latitude can still be obtained by reducing the zenith distance at the time of the sight to the meridian zenith distance (MZD), and applying declination in the same way as for a meridian altitude sight.

This can be done by calculation, or by using Ex-meridian Tables such as those contained in *Norie's Nautical Tables*.

Example 38 (Use Extract Nos 33 and 34)

Ex-meridian Tables (Norie's Nautical Tables)
In DR position 36° 30'·1N, 21° 14'·5W a sight was taken of the sun near the time of meridian passage. The true altitude was 48° 40'·3. LHA 2° 30'·0. Declination 4° 17'·8S. What was the latitude?

Table 1, which gives the variation in altitude for one minute of time is entered with latitude and declination and quantity A extracted (in this case 2″·4). (The 'Different Name' table is used because latitude is north and declination south). Quantity A is used with the local hour angle to enter Table II. In the example, to save interpolation, Table II is entered for 2″0 giving 3′·3 and for 0″·4, giving 0′·67, making a total of 3′·97. (4′·0 can be used without any significant error). This quantity, called a reduction, is added to the true altitude at the upper transit of the body to give the true meridian altitude (TMA); the true zenith distance (TZD) is found by taking the true meridian altitude from 90°. Declination is then applied (the same as for a meridian altitude sight) to give latitude.

Table I   A = 2″·4
Table II   2″ = 3′·3
              0″·4+ = 0′·67

      Reduction   3′·97 (call it 4′0)

TA	48° 40′·3
Reduction	+ 4′·0
TMA	48° 44′·3
from 90	90° 00′·0
MZD	41° 15′·7
dec.	− S4° 17′·8
	36° 57′·9 LATITUDE

EX-MERIDIAN TABLE I
Latitude and Declination DIFFERENT NAME
Change of Altitude in one minute from Meridian Passage = A

Lat. °	DECLINATION															Lat. °
	0°″	1°″	2°″	3°″	4°″	5°″	6°″	7°″	8°″	9°″	10°″	11°″	12°″	13°″	14°″	
31	3.3	3.2	3.1	3.0	2.9	2.9	2.8	2.7	2.6	2.6	2.5	2.5	2.4	2.4	2.3	31
32	3.2	3.1	3.0	2.9	2.8	2.8	2.7	2.6	2.6	2.5	2.5	2.4	2.3	2.3	2.2	32
33	3.0	2.9	2.9	2.8	2.7	2.7	2.6	2.5	2.5	2.4	2.4	2.3	2.3	2.2	2.2	33
34	2.9	2.8	2.8	2.7	2.6	2.6	2.5	2.5	2.4	2.4	2.3	2.3	2.2	2.2	2.1	34
35	2.8	2.7	2.7	2.6	2.5	2.5	2.4	2.4	2.3	2.3	2.2	2.2	2.2	2.1	2.1	35
36	2.7	2.6	2.6	2.5	2.5	2.4	2.4	2.3	2.3	2.2	2.2	2.1	2.1	2.1	2.0	36
37	2.6	2.5	2.5	2.4	2.4	2.3	2.3	2.2	2.2	2.2	2.1	2.1	2.0	2.0	2.0	37
38	2.5	2.5	2.4	2.4	2.3	2.3	2.2	2.2	2.1	2.1	2.1	2.0	2.0	1.9	1.9	38
39	2.4	2.4	2.3	2.3	2.2	2.2	2.1	2.1	2.1	2.0	2.0	2.0	1.9	1.9	1.9	39
40	2.3	2.3	2.2	2.2	2.2	2.1	2.1	2.0	2.0	2.0	1.9	1.9	1.9	1.8	1.8	40

Extract Number 33

EX-MERIDIAN TABLE II

Reduction Plus to True Altitude at Upper Transit

HOUR ANGLE

A	2° 5′ 357°55′	2° 10′ 357°50′	2° 15′ 357°45′	2° 20′ 357°40′	2° 25′ 357°35′	2° 30′ 357°30′	2° 35′ 357°25′	2° 40′ 357°20′	2° 45′ 357°15′	2° 50′ 357°10′	2° 55′ 357° 5′	3° 0′ 357° 0′	A
1	1·2	1·3	1·4	1·5	1·6	1·7	1·8	1·9	2·0	2·1	2·3	2·4	1
2	2·3	2·5	2·7	2·9	3·1	3·3	3·5	3·8	4·0	4·2	4·5	4·8	2
3	3·5	3·8	4·1	4·4	4·7	5·0	5·3	5·7	6·1	6·5	6·9	7·2	3
4	4·7	5·0	5·4	5·8	6·2	6·7	7·1	7·6	8·1	8·6	9·1	9·6	4
5	5·8	6·3	6·8	7·3	7·8	8·3	8·9	9·5	10·1	10·7	11·4	12·0	5
6	6·9	7·5	8·1	8·7	9·3	10·0	10·7	11·4	12·1	12·8	13·6	14·4	6
7	8·1	8·8	9·5	10·2	10·9	11·7	12·5	13·3	14·1	14·9	15·8	16·8	7
8	9·2	10·0	10·8	11·6	12·5	13·3	14·2	15·1	16·1	17·1	18·1	19·2	8
9	10·4	11·3	12·2	13·1	14·1	15·0	16·0	17·1	18·2	19·3	20·5	21·6	9

Extract Number 34

The position line will not be exactly along a parallel of latitude as the heavenly body is not bearing exactly north or south. The azimuth and hence the position line which is plotted through the DR longitude can be found by using the ABC tables in *Norie's Nautical Tables*.

There is an additional table, Table III to be used when the amount of the main correction is considerable.

Table IV tabulates the limits of hour angle or time difference when ex-meridian sights can be taken and provided these limits are observed it is not necessary to use Table III.

Generally, if observations are within an hour of meridian passage satisfactory results can be obtained. High altitudes of above 75° should be avoided and there should be at least a 5° difference between latitude and declination.

QUESTION PAPER EIGHT

8.1   What is the GMT of the sun's meridian passage on June 21st in longitude 24° 30′·0W?

8.2   What is the GMT of the moon's meridian passage on June 22nd in longitude 5° 30′·0E?

8.3   On October 5th in DR position 56° 42′·1S 117° 01′·0W a meridian altitude sight was taken of the sun's lower limb, giving a sextant altitude of 38° 20′·0. Index error −1′·0. Height of eye 2·0m. What was the latitude?

8.4   On March 9th in DR position 42° 35′·4N, 21° 15′·0W the sun's upper limb was observed at meridian passage when the sextant altitude was 43° 02′·4, index error +2′·0, height of eye 2·8m. What was the latitude?

Answers on pages 160–62.

Chapter Nine

More About Latitude

As mentioned already in Chapter one we have a very conveniently situated star called Polaris (the Pole Star, or North Star), always bearing north, visible in the Northern Hemisphere.

If Polaris was exactly on the north celestial pole, we would find that its true altitude was equal to our latitude (see Fig. 9.1).

Polaris however, describes a small circle of radius up to 1° around the north celestial pole, and a small adjustment needs to be made to the altitude of Polaris to obtain our latitude.

The position of Polaris on this small circle corresponds to local hour angle and the altitude will vary according to this hour angle.

There is no SHA or declination tabulated for Polaris. This is not needed as special tables are available which have been compiled by using mean values for SHA and declination in conjunction with the Local Hour Angle of Aries and the altitude of Polaris.

The co-ordinates required for the Polaris table are LHA Aries, latitude, and the month of the year. The Greenwich date and time are, of course, needed to find the GHA Aries to which the longitude is applied to find the LHA.

The Polaris table consists of an upper section for apparent altitude (AA), with 10° divisions along the top and 1° intervals down the left-hand side. The correction extracted is called a_0. The same column is followed down into the next part of the table until level with latitude, giving a correction called a_1. Further down the same column in the third part of the table opposite the month of the year, is another correction a_2 (necessary because the SHA and declination used to compile the a_0 table were based on mean values). Corrections a_0, a_1 and a_2 are always added to the true altitude of Polaris but because small constants have been included in the table to make this so, the sum of these constants, which equals 1°, must be subtracted before true latitude can be found.

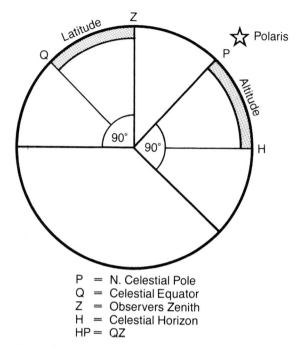

P = N. Celestial Pole
Q = Celestial Equator
Z = Observers Zenith
H = Celestial Horizon
HP = QZ

Fig 9.1 Altitude = Latitude.

Example 39 (Use Extract No. 35)

On March 9th, in DR position 58° 50′·4N, 40° 15′·1W, a sight was taken of Polaris at 08h 36m 01s GMT. Sextant altitude was 58° 02′·4. Index error −1′·0. Height of eye 2·0m. What was the latitude?

   First the LHA of Aries is found (from the daily pages and the 'Increments and Corrections' table):

GHA Aries 08h	287° 09′·8
increment 36m 01s	+ 9° 01′·7
GHA Aries 08h 36m 01s	296° 11′·5
DR long W	− 40° 15′·1
LHA Aries 08h 36m 01s	255° 56′·4

(The DR longitude is used, not a chosen longitude.)
The sextant altitude is corrected to a true altitude (using the 'Altitude Correction Tables'). The a_0, a_1 and a_2 corrections are added to the true altitude and 1° subtracted to give the latitude:

SA	58° 02'·4
IE & dip	− 3'·5
AA	57° 58'·9
corrn.	− 0'·6
TA	57° 58'·3
a_0	+ 1° 35'·4
a_1	0'·7
a_2	0'·4
	59° 34'·8
	− 1° 00'·0
	58° 34'·8 LATITUDE

For plotting purposes Polaris can be regarded as exactly north, since the small variation is of no consequence to the position line which is a parallel of latitude. The final part of the Polaris table gives an azimuth which can be used to check compass deviation.

It is a good plan to set the approximate altitude on the sextant beforehand and sweep the horizon in the vicinity of the star before its expected time as Polaris is not easily visible and there is only a short time to take the sight when both horizon and star can be seen. To do this the DR latitude could be used as an approximate altitude, but we can be a little more accurate than this if we find the LHA of Aries by using the time of twilight, extract the a_0 correction from the tables, subtract this from our DR position and add 1°. The result will leave only minor adjustments to be made to the sextant to bring the star on to the horizon.

Example 40 (Use Extract No. 35)

On March 9th, in DR position 58° 50'·4N, 40° 15'·1W, a morning sight is required of Polaris. What is the approximate time to take this sight and what is the approximate angle to set on the sextant?

	h m	
Dawn Twilight	05 56	LMT 9d
long. W	+02 41	
	08 37	GMT 9d at DR (use this time to
		find LHA Aries)

GHA Aries 08h   287° 09'·8
increment   37m   + 9° 16'·5

GHA Aries 08h 37m   296° 26'·3
DR long. W   − 40° 15'·1

LHA Aries 08h 37m   256° 11'·2
a_0 1° 35'·2

DR lat.   58° 50'·4N
a_0 − 1° 35'·2
                          57° 15'·2
                       + 1° 00'·0

                          58° 15'·2 (Approximate angle
                                      to set on sextant.)

POLARIS (POLE STAR) TABLES, 1980
FOR DETERMINING LATITUDE FROM SEXTANT ALTITUDE AND FOR AZIMUTH

Extract Number 35

L.H.A. ARIES	240°– 249°	250°– 259°	260°– 269°
	a_0	a_0	a_0
°	° ′	° ′	° ′
0	1 43·0	1 38·6	1 32·9
1	42·7	38·0	32·2
2	42·2	37·5	31·6
3	41·8	37·0	31·0
4	41·4	36·4	30·3
5	1 41·0	1 35·9	1 29·6
6	40·5	35·3	29·0
7	40·0	34·7	28·3
8	39·6	34·1	27·6
9	39·1	33·5	26·9
10	1 38·6	1 32·9	1 26·2
Lat.	a_1	a_1	a_1
°	′	′	′
0	0·5	0·4	0·3
10	·5	·4	·4
20	·5	·5	·4
30	·5	·5	·5
40	0·6	0·5	0·5
45	·6	·6	·6
50	·6	·6	·6
55	·6	·6	·7
60	·7	·7	·7
62	0·7	0·7	0·8
64	·7	·7	·8
66	·7	·8	·8
68	0·7	0·8	0·9
Month	a_2	a_2	a_2
	′	′	′
Jan.	0·5	0·5	0·5
Feb.	·4	·4	·4
Mar.	·4	·4	·4

QUESTION PAPER NINE

9.1   On March 7th, in DR position 51° 56'·4N, 35° 12'·4W, the sextant altitude of Polaris at 08h 36m 59s GMT was 51° 47'·3. Index error −1'·0. Height of eye 2·8m. What was the latitude?

9.2.   What is the approximate angle to set on the sextant for a dusk sight of Polaris on October 4th, in DR position 54° 12'·6N 23° 15'·0W?

9.3   On October 3rd, in DR position 53° 17'·9N, 37° 55'·1W, the sextant altitude of Polaris at 18h 04m 22s LMT time was 52° 30'·4. Index error +1'·5. Height of eye 3·0m. What was the latitude?

Answers on pages 162–4.

Chapter Ten

Plotting Position

Celestial sights can be plotted by several methods. As in coastal navigation a chart can be used, if a suitable large scale one is available. However, charts are normally produced where there is a coastline to be included, and the majority of an ocean passage is out of sight of land. An alternative to a chart, a special plotting sheet (published by the Hydrographic Office) can be used.

This is a large sheet of paper upon which is printed several latitude scales and a longitude scale. Plotting can also be done on squared or plain paper.

Three methods of plotting are shown below:

The Chart

Unlike coastal navigation where position lines are plotted from fixed landmarks, plotting is done from the dead reckoning (DR) position or from the chosen position (CP) used to find calculated altitude.

Example 41 (See Fig. 10.1)

Chosen position latitude 50° N, chosen position longitude 5° 03'·0W, intercept 1'·6 towards, 050° T (1·6T 050° T).

1. Use the latitude scale to plot the chosen position latitude 50° N.

2. Use the longitude scale to plot the chosen position longitude 5° 03'·0W, from the nearest meridian.

3. Use the latitude scale to plot the intercept (which is the line of azimuth), 1'·6 in the direction of 050° T because it is *towards* the heavenly body's GP.

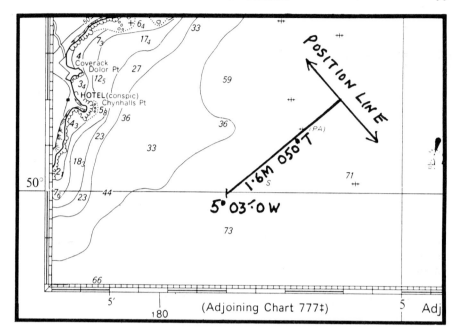

Fig 10.1   Plotting the sight.

Chosen lat.   50° N
Chosen long.   5° 03'W
Intercept   1·6T 050° T

4. The position thus found is the intercept terminal position (ITP). Through this plot the position line at right angles to the line of azimuth.

The observer's position is somewhere along this position line. To find the observed position at least two position lines are needed.

If several sights are taken, each is plotted from its own chosen position (see Fig. 10.2).

When more than two sights are taken the position lines do not usually exactly intersect and there will be a 'cocked hat' due to the time interval between sights. This can be reduced by allowing for the run of the boat between observations. The course and distance run from each chosen position (allowing for any set and drift) are plotted to give a position from which the intercept and position line are plotted (see Fig. 10.3).

In practice a small boat is not travelling fast enough to cause a large error between sights taken together.

If a DR position is used all intercepts will start from the same position unless it is necessary to allow for the run between sights (see Fig. 10.4).

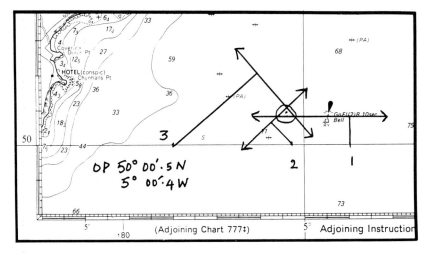

Fig 10.2   Simultaneous sights. *Chosen lat.* 50° N

Star	Chosen long.	Intercept	Azimuth
1	4° 59'·0W	0·4T	000° T
2	5° 00'·3W	0·4A	138° T
3	5° 03'·0W	1·6T	050° T
OP	50° 00'·5N		
	5° 00'·4W		

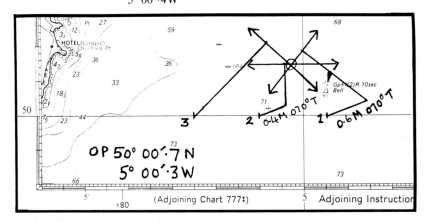

Fig 10.3 Allowing for Distance Run. *Chosen Lat.* 50° N

Star	Chosen Long.	Intercept	Azimuth
1	4° 59'·5W	1·2T	308° T
2	5° 01'·0W	0·6A	180° T
3	5° 02'·5W	1·4T	045° T

Distance run between sight 1 and sight 3 0·6M
Course 070° T
Distance run between sight 2 and sight 3 0·4M
Course 070°T
OP 50° 00'·7N
5° 00'·3W

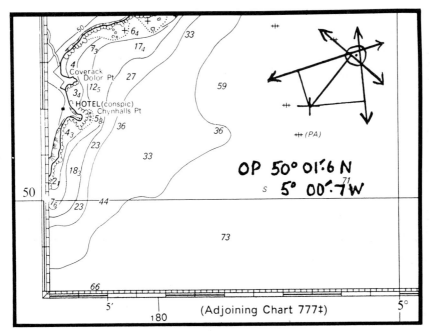

Fig 10.4 Plotting from a DR position.

> *DR position*   50° 01'·0N
>   05° 01'·5W

Star	Intercept	Azimuth
1	0·7T	040T
2	0·6T	085T
3	0·4A	163T

> *OP*   50° 01'·5N
>   05° 00'·7W

The Plotting Sheet

Plotting sheets are published by the Hydrographic Office to cover latitudes 0°–30° (5331); 30°–48° (5332); 48°–60° (5333). The plotting sheet needed for the examples and exercises in this book is *5333A*. Suffix 'A' denotes that a compass rose, meridians of longitude and a parallel of latitude are included in addition to the latitude and longitude scales.

Along the left-hand and right-hand margins of the sheet are latitude scales covering the range indicated. It is important to use *only* the scale for the latitude of the observation, as the sheet is mercator projection, and the length of a minute of latitude constantly increases as latitude increases. The longitude scale, which is constant, along the top and bottom margins is marked at 30' intervals with further 5' and 1' divisions.

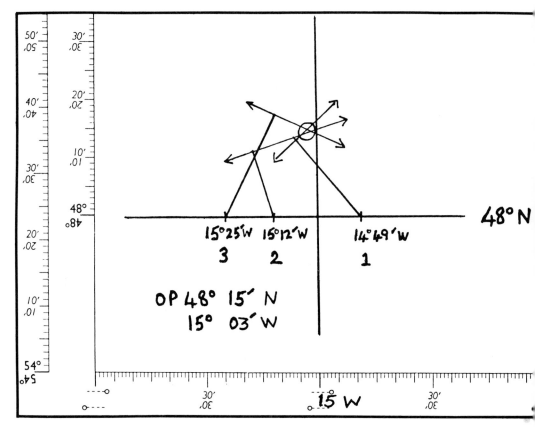

Fig 10.5 Plotting on a plotting sheet.

Example 42 (See Fig. 10.5)

Chosen position latitude 48°N

Star	CP long.	Intercept	Azimuth
1	14° 49'·0W	17'·0 Away from	140° T
2	15° 12'·0W	12'·0 Towards	343° T
3	15° 25'·0W	20'·0 Towards	026° T

1. Use latitude scale 48°. Draw in parallel of latitude 48°N (which is the chosen position latitude).

2. Label conveniently one of the meridians 15° W (which is the nearest whole degree of longitude to the chosen position longitudes).

3. Proceed as if plotting on a chart, using the 48° latitude scale for measuring distance.

Squared Paper (using Traverse Tables)

On the earth's surface meridians of longitude converge towards the poles. The angular difference between meridians, known as difference of longitude (d.long), remains the same whatever the latitude. The actual distance in miles, known as departure (dep), decreases as latitude increases. Along the equator d.long = dep, but at latitude 50° North or South 1'·0 of longitude = 0·6 miles of departure, (Fig. 10.6).

The relationship between d.long and dep is:

$$dep = d.\ long. \times cos\ lat.$$

or

$$d.long = \frac{dep}{cos\ lat.}$$

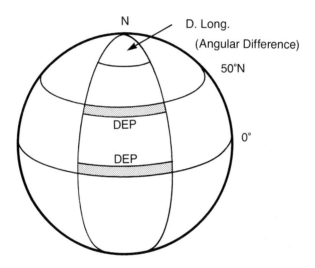

Departure = D. Long. Latitude 0°
Departure less than D. Long. Latitude 50°N

Fig 10.6 Longitude and Departure.

To avoid the distortion that would occur by representing a sphere on a flat surface such as a chart, when a mercator projection chart or plotting sheet is constructed, the meridians of longitude are projected as straight lines parallel to each other and the parallels of latitude are projected as straight parallel lines moved further apart as latitude increases. The longitude scale is constant for all latitudes,

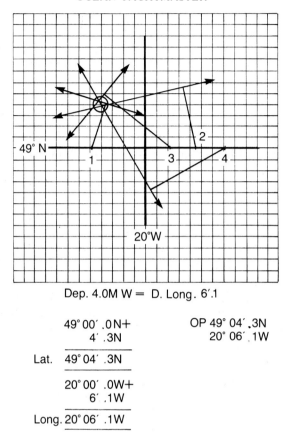

Dep. 4.0M W = D. Long. 6'.1

49° 00' .0 N+   OP 49° 04' .3N
    4' .3N   20° 06' .1W
       ——————
Lat. 49° 04' .3N
       ——————
20° 00' .0W+
    6' .1W
       ——————
Long. 20° 06' .1W

Fig 10.7 Plotting on squared paper.

but the length of one minute of arc on the latitude scale, on the same scale chart increases as latitude increases. Distance is always measured along the latitude scale opposite the area of the plot.

On squared paper, the squares can be taken to represent latitude, departure or distance, but not longitude. An adjustment has to be made when using squared paper for plotting. This is done by converting d.long to dep by using traverse tables:

Example 43 (See Fig. 10.7)

Using traverse tables (*Norie's Nautical Tables*), see Extract No. 36. Chosen latitude 49° N.

Star	CP long.	Intercept	Azimuth
1	20° 07'·5W	4'·2 Towards	017° T
2	19° 53'·3W	5'·7 Towards	350° T
3	19° 56'·7W	7'·7 Away from	130° T
4	19° 49'·0W	7'·6 Away from	060° T

1. Plot datum lines; latitude 49° N, longitude 20° W.

2. Enter the 'traverse tables' with latitude 49°. This is the large figure at the bottom of the page (Extract No. 36).

3. For 49° use only the figures above the headings, 'D.Lon' and 'Dep' which are in italic type *at the bottom* of the page. (If latitude had been 41° (at the top of the page), the tables would have been read from the top downwards).

4. Find the difference between longitude 20° W and the longitude of the star. For star 1 the difference is 7'·5. Enter the column of figures above 'D.Lon' and move upwards until the figure 7 is reached. 04·6 is found in the column above 'Dep.' which is the departure for a difference of longitude of 7'·0. The departure for a difference of longitude of 8'·0 is 05·2. As a departure is needed for a difference of longitude of 7'·5, which is not tabulated, an interpolation is necessary giving a departure of 04·9. This is labelled west because it is west of the datum line: 04·9W. Departure for the four stars is given below:

Star	d.long	dep
1	7'·5	4·9W
2	6'·7	4·4E
3	3'·3	2·2E
4	11'·0	7·2E

6. The chosen position longitude for each star is now plotted, using the departure found above (one square equals one mile of departure).

7. The intercept for each star is plotted. It is not necessary to use traverse tables for this as the side of one square equals one nautical mile.

8. The position line is drawn at right angles through the intercept terminal position.

The observed position is where the position lines intersect.

9. Latitude of the observed position is calculated by counting the number of squares from latitude 49° N (4·3) to the observed position, each square being equal to one minute of latitude.

10. The number of squares between longitude 20° W and the observed position is departure and the traverse tables must again be used to convert this to difference of longitude. Departure is 4·0W which for latitude 49° gives a difference of longitude of 6'·1.

41° | 319° / 221° | **TRAVERSE TABLE** — 41 Degrees | 041° / 139° — 2h 44m

D. Lon Dep. Dist.	D. Lat.	Dep.	Dist.	D. Lat.	Dep.	Dist.	D. Lat.	Dep.	Dist.	D. Lat.	Dep.	Dist.	D. Lat.	Dep.
1	00.8	00.7	61	46.0	40.0	121	91.3	79.4	181	136.6	118.7	241	181.9	158.1
2	01.5	01.3	62	46.8	40.7	122	92.1	80.0	182	137.4	119.4	242	182.6	158.8
3	02.3	02.0	63	47.5	41.3	123	92.8	80.7	183	138.1	120.1	243	183.4	159.4
4	03.0	02.6	64	48.3	42.0	124	93.6	81.4	184	138.9	120.7	244	184.1	160.1
5	03.8	03.3	65	49.1	42.6	125	94.3	82.0	185	139.6	121.4	245	184.9	160.7
6	04.5	03.9	66	49.8	43.3	126	95.1	82.7	186	140.4	122.0	246	185.7	161.4
7	05.3	04.6	67	50.6	44.0	127	95.8	83.3	187	141.1	122.7	247	186.4	162.0
8	06.0	05.2	68	51.3	44.6	128	96.6	84.0	188	141.9	123.3	248	187.2	162.7
9	06.8	05.9	69	52.1	45.3	129	97.4	84.6	189	142.6	124.0	249	187.9	163.4
10	07.5	06.6	70	52.8	45.9	130	98.1	85.3	190	143.4	124.7	250	188.7	164.0
11	08.3	07.2	71	53.6	46.6	131	98.9	85.9	191	144.1	125.3	251	189.4	164.7
12	09.1	07.9	72	54.3	47.2	132	99.6	86.6	192	144.9	126.0	252	190.2	165.3
13	09.8	08.5	73	55.1	47.9	133	100.4	87.3	193	145.7	126.6	253	190.9	166.0
14	10.6	09.2	74	55.8	48.5	134	101.1	87.9	194	146.4	127.3	254	191.7	166.6
51	38.5	33.5	111	83.8	72.8	171	129.1	112.2	231	174.3	151.5	291	219.6	190.9
52	39.2	34.1	112	84.5	73.5	172	129.8	112.8	232	175.1	152.2	292	220.4	191.6
53	40.0	34.8	113	85.3	74.1	173	130.6	113.5	233	175.8	152.9	293	221.1	192.2
54	40.8	35.4	114	86.0	74.8	174	131.3	114.2	234	176.6	153.5	294	221.9	192.9
55	41.5	36.1	115	86.8	75.4	175	132.1	114.8	235	177.4	154.2	295	222.6	193.5
56	42.3	36.7	116	87.5	76.1	176	132.8	115.5	236	178.1	154.8	296	223.4	194.2
57	43.0	37.4	117	88.3	76.8	177	133.6	116.1	237	178.9	155.5	297	224.1	194.8
58	43.8	38.1	118	89.1	77.4	178	134.3	116.8	238	179.6	156.1	298	224.9	195.5
59	44.5	38.7	119	89.8	78.1	179	135.1	117.4	239	180.4	156.8	299	225.7	196.2
60	45.3	39.4	120	90.6	78.7	180	135.8	118.1	240	181.1	157.5	300	226.4	196.8
Dist.	Dep.	D. Lat.	Dist.	Dep.	D. Lat.	Dist.	Dep.	D. Lat.	Dist.	Dep.	D. Lat.	Dist.	Dep.	D. Lat.
D. Lon		Dep.	D. Lon		Dep.	D. Lon		Dep.	D. Lon		Dep.	D. Lon		Dep.

49° | 311° / 229° | 49 Degrees | 049° / 131° — 3h 16m

Extract Number 36

Further use of the Traverse Tables

These can be used to find a dead reckoning position (DR) or estimated position (EP) after a day's run without the need for plotting in the following manner:

Example 44 (Use Extract Nos. 37, 38 and 39)

At 1200 GMT a boat is in DR position 48° 15′·4N, 12° 06′·8W on a course of 190° T, speed 5 kn. What is her DR position 10 hours later?

1. Use the figures tabulated at the top and bottom right and left hand corners of the table (ignore the larger degrees on the top and bottom outer margins which indicate latitude). These figures which are true courses are in boxes which correspond to the quadrants of the compass and they are placed either at the top or bottom of the page to indicate whether the headings to be used are at the top or bottom of the table. The headings in bold type are used and not the ones in italic type previously used. The course of 190° T in the example is at the top of the page in the south west quadrant and so the difference of latitude will be in a southerly direction and the difference of longitude will be in a westerly direction. The table is

entered at the top under the column labelled **'Dist'** with a distance of 50 miles (10 hours at 5 kn). The figures alongside 50 are 49·2 (under **'D.Lat.'**) which is difference of latitude and 08·7 (under **'Dep.'**) which is departure.

	'D.Lat.'		**'Dep.'**	
	N	S	E	W
	–	49'·2	–	08·7

TRAVERSE TABLE

10°

	350° / 190°				

D. Lon	Dep.		D. Lon	Dep.	
Dist.	D. Lat.	Dep.	Dist.	D. Lat.	Dep.
41	40·4	07·1	101	99·5	17·5
42	41·4	07·3	102	100·5	17·7
43	42·3	07·5	103	101·4	17·9
44	43·3	07·6	104	102·4	18·1
45	44·3	07·8	105	103·4	18·2
46	45·3	08·0	106	104·4	18·4
47	46·3	08·2	107	105·4	18·6
48	47·3	08·3	108	106·4	18·8
49	48·3	08·5	109	107·3	18·9
50	49·2	08·7	110	108·3	19·1
51	50·2	08·9	111	109·3	19·3
52	51·2	09·0	112	110·3	19·4
53	52·2	09·2	113	111·3	19·6
54	53·2	09·4	114	112·3	19·8
55	54·2	09·6	115	113·3	20·0
56	55·1	09·7	116	114·2	20·1
57	56·1	09·9	117	115·2	20·3
58	57·1	10·1	118	116·2	20·5
59	58·1	10·2	119	117·2	20·7
60	59·1	10·4	120	118·2	20·8

Extract Number 37

Difference of latitude can be applied directly:

At 1200	DR lat −48° 15'·4N
	d. lat − 49'·2S
At 2200	DR lat −47° 26'·2N

Departure has to be converted to difference of longitude before application. The latitude used to enter the tables corresponds to the mean or mid latitude between the original DR position and the new

DR position, which is 47° 50′·8. For absolute accuracy interpolation between latitudes 47° and 48° should be done:

	'Lat.'	'Dep.'	'D.Lon'
	47° 00′·0	8·7	12′·7
	48° 00′·0	8·7	13′·0
Interpolating:	47° 50′·8	8·7	12′·9

As departure is west, the new longitude is:

At 1200   DR long   +12° 06′·8W

d.long   +   12′·9W

At 2200   DR long   +12° 19′·7W

43°   317° / 223°   **TRAVERSE TABLE — 43 Degrees**   043° / 137°   2h 52m

Dist.	D. Lat.	Dep.	Dist.	D. Lat.	Dep.	Dist.	D. Lat.	Dep.	Dist.	D. Lat.	Dep.	Dist.	D. Lat.	Dep.
1	00·7	00·7	61	44·6	41·6	121	88·5	82·5	181	132·4	123·4	241	176·3	164·4
2	01·5	01·4	62	45·3	42·3	122	89·2	83·2	182	133·1	124·1	242	177·0	165·0
3	02·2	02·0	63	46·1	43·0	123	90·0	83·9	183	133·8	124·8	243	177·7	165·7
4	02·9	02·7	64	46·8	43·6	124	90·7	84·6	184	134·6	125·5	244	178·5	166·4
5	03·7	03·4	65	47·5	44·3	125	91·4	85·2	185	135·3	126·2	245	179·2	167·1
6	04·4	04·1	66	48·3	45·0	126	92·2	85·9	186	136·0	126·9	246	179·9	167·8
7	05·1	04·8	67	49·0	45·7	127	92·9	86·6	187	136·8	127·5	247	180·6	168·5
8	05·9	05·5	68	49·7	46·4	128	93·6	87·3	188	137·5	128·2	248	181·4	169·1
9	06·6	06·1	69	50·5	47·1	129	94·3	88·0	189	138·2	128·9	249	182·1	169·8
10	07·3	06·8	70	51·2	47·7	130	95·1	88·7	190	139·0	129·6	250	182·8	170·5
11	08·0	07·5	71	51·9	48·4	131	95·8	89·3	191	139·7	130·3	251	183·6	171·2
12	08·8	08·2	72	52·7	49·1	132	96·5	90·0	192	140·4	130·9	252	184·3	171·9
13	09·5	08·9	73	53·4	49·8	133	97·3	90·7	193	141·2	131·6	253	185·0	172·5
14	10·2	09·5	74	54·1	50·5	134	98·0	91·4	194	141·9	132·3	254	185·8	173·2
15	11·0	10·2	75	54·9	51·1	135	98·7	92·1	195	142·6	133·0	255	186·5	173·9
16	11·7	10·9	76	55·6	51·8	136	99·5	92·8	196	143·3	133·7	256	187·2	174·6
17	12·4	11·6	77	56·3	52·5	137	100·2	93·4	197	144·1	134·4	257	188·0	175·3
18	13·2	12·3	78	57·0	53·2	138	100·9	94·1	198	144·8	135·0	258	188·7	176·0
19	13·9	13·0	79	57·8	53·9	139	101·7	94·8	199	145·5	135·7	259	189·4	176·6
20	14·6	13·6	80	58·5	54·6	140	102·4	95·5	200	146·3	136·4	260	190·2	177·3

Dist.	D. Lat.	Dep.	Dist.	D. Lat.	Dep.	Dist.	D. Lat.	Dep.	Dist.	D. Lat.	Dep.	Dist.	D. Lat.	Dep.
51	37·3	34·8	111	81·2	75·7	171	125·1	116·6	231	168·9	157·5	291	212·8	198·5
52	38·0	35·5	112	81·9	76·4	172	125·8	117·3	232	169·7	158·2	292	213·6	199·1
53	38·8	36·1	113	82·6	77·1	173	126·5	118·0	233	170·4	158·9	293	214·3	199·8
54	39·5	36·8	114	83·4	77·7	174	127·3	118·7	234	171·1	159·6	294	215·0	200·5
55	40·2	37·5	115	84·1	78·4	175	128·0	119·3	235	171·9	160·3	295	215·7	201·2
56	41·0	38·2	116	84·8	79·1	176	128·7	120·0	236	172·6	161·0	296	216·5	201·9
57	41·7	38·9	117	85·6	79·8	177	129·4	120·7	237	173·3	161·6	297	217·2	202·6
58	42·4	39·6	118	86·3	80·5	178	130·2	121·4	238	174·1	162·3	298	217·9	203·2
59	43·1	40·2	119	87·0	81·2	179	130·9	122·1	239	174·8	163·0	299	218·7	203·9
60	43·9	40·9	120	87·8	81·8	180	131·6	122·8	240	175·5	163·7	300	219·4	204·6
Dist.	Dep.	D. Lat.	Dist.	Dep.	D. Lat.	Dist.	Dep.	D. Lat.	Dist.	Dep.	D. Lat.	Dist.	Dep.	D. Lat.
D. Lon		Dep.	D. Lon		Dep.	D. Lon		Dep.	D. Lon		Dep.	D. Lon		Dep.

47°   313° / 227°   **47 Degrees**   047° / 133°   3h 08m

Extract Number 38

Several courses can be calculated in this way. Tidal direction and rate (or ocean current set and drift) can be regarded as a course and distance and treated in the same manner. Leeway can be allowed for by entering the traverse tables with the water track instead of the course.

TRAVERSE TABLE
42 Degrees

318° / 222° 42° 042° / 138° 2h 48m

D. Lon	Dep.		D. Lon	Dep.		D. Lon	Dep.		D. Lon	Dep.		D. Lon	Dep.	
Dist.	D. Lat.	Dep.	Dist.	D. Lat.	Dep.	Dist.	D. Lat.	Dep.	Dist.	D. Lat.	Dep.	Dist.	D. Lat.	Dep.
1	00·7	00·7	61	45·3	40·8	121	89·9	81·0	181	134·5	121·1	241	179·1	161·3
2	01·5	01·3	62	46·1	41·5	122	90·7	81·6	182	135·3	121·8	242	179·8	161·9
3	02·2	02·0	63	46·8	42·2	123	91·4	82·3	183	136·0	122·5	243	180·6	162·6
4	03·0	02·7	64	47·6	42·8	124	92·1	83·0	184	136·7	123·1	244	181·3	163·3
5	03·7	03·3	65	48·3	43·5	125	92·9	83·6	185	137·5	123·8	245	182·1	163·9
6	04·5	04·0	66	49·0	44·2	126	93·6	84·3	186	138·2	124·5	246	182·8	164·6
7	05·2	04·7	67	49·8	44·8	127	94·4	85·0	187	139·0	125·1	247	183·6	165·3
8	05·9	05·4	68	50·5	45·5	128	95·1	85·6	188	139·7	125·8	248	184·3	165·9
9	06·7	06·0	69	51·3	46·2	129	95·9	86·3	189	140·5	126·5	249	185·0	166·6
10	07·4	06·7	70	52·0	46·8	130	96·6	87·0	190	141·2	127·1	250	185·8	167·3
11	08·2	07·4	71	52·8	47·5	131	97·4	87·7	191	141·9	127·8	251	186·5	168·0
12	08·9	08·0	72	53·5	48·2	132	98·1	88·3	192	142·7	128·5	252	187·3	168·6
13	09·7	08·7	73	54·2	48·8	133	98·8	89·0	193	143·4	129·1	253	188·0	169·3
14	10·4	09·4	74	55·0	49·5	134	99·6	89·7	194	144·2	129·8	254	188·8	170·0
15	11·1	10·0	75	55·7	50·2	135	100·3	90·3	195	144·9	130·5	255	189·5	170·6
16	11·9	10·7	76	56·5	50·9	136	101·1	91·0	196	145·7	131·1	256	190·2	171·3
17	12·6	11·4	77	57·2	51·5	137	101·8	91·7	197	146·4	131·8	257	191·0	172·0
18	13·4	12·0	78	58·0	52·2	138	102·6	92·3	198	147·1	132·5	258	191·7	172·6
19	14·1	12·7	79	58·7	52·9	139	103·3	93·0	199	147·9	133·2	259	192·5	173·3
20	14·9	13·4	80	59·5	53·5	140	104·0	93·7	200	148·6	133·8	260	193·2	174·0

51	37·9	34·1	111	82·5	74·3	171	127·1	114·4	231	171·7	154·6	291	216·3	194·7
52	38·6	34·8	112	83·2	74·9	172	127·8	115·1	232	172·4	155·2	292	217·0	195·4
53	39·4	35·5	113	84·0	75·6	173	128·6	115·8	233	173·2	155·9	293	217·7	196·1
54	40·1	36·1	114	84·7	76·3	174	129·3	116·4	234	173·9	156·6	294	218·5	196·7
55	40·9	36·8	115	85·5	77·0	175	130·1	117·1	235	174·6	157·2	295	219·2	197·4
56	41·6	37·5	116	86·2	77·6	176	130·8	117·8	236	175·4	157·9	296	220·0	198·1
57	42·4	38·1	117	86·9	78·3	177	131·5	118·4	237	176·1	158·6	297	220·7	198·7
58	43·1	38·8	118	87·7	79·0	178	132·3	119·1	238	176·9	159·3	298	221·5	199·4
59	43·8	39·5	119	88·4	79·6	179	133·0	119·8	239	177·6	159·9	299	222·2	200·1
60	44·6	40·1	120	89·2	80·3	180	133·8	120·4	240	178·4	160·6	300	222·9	200·7
Dist.	Dep.	D. Lat.	Dist.	Dep.	D. Lat.	Dist.	Dep.	D. Lat.	Dist.	Dep.	D. Lat.	Dist.	Dep.	D. Lat.
D. Lon		Dep.	D. Lon		Dep.	D. Lon		Dep.	D. Lon		Dep.	D. Lon		Dep.

48° 312° / 228° 48 Degrees 048° / 132° 3h 12m

Extract Number 39

Plotting on Squared Paper without Traverse Tables (see Fig. 10.8)

1. On squared paper draw the base line.

2. From the base line measure an angle equal to the latitude and draw the angle line.

3. Measure departure by counting squares along the base line and mark.

4. From this mark extend a perpendicular to intersect the angle line.

5. Place the point of a pencil compass on the left end of the base line and open out until the pencil is on the intersection of the perpendicular with the angle line.

6. Strike an arc across the base line.

7. The number of squares from the start of the base line to this arc represents minutes of longitude for the departure entered in 3 above.

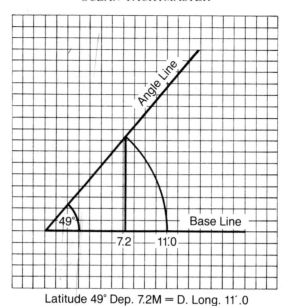

Latitude 49° Dep. 7.2M = D. Long. 11'.0

Fig 10.8 Plotting on squared paper without traverse tables.

Sun-run-Meridian Passage Sight

During daylight hours when usually only the sun is available for sights, an observed position can be obtained using a meridian altitude sight and a morning or afternoon sun sight. The time between sights should be sufficient to give a good angle of cut of the position lines. The principle is similar to a running fix or transferred position line in coastal navigation.

Example 45 (Fig. 10.9)

A boat in DR position 48° 58'·0N, 24° 19'·0W obtains a morning sun sight giving the following results:

Chosen position 49° N, 24° 15'·0W. Intercept 18'·0 Towards. Azimuth 099° T.

The boat ran on for 17·5M on a course of 202° T when a meridian altitude sight gave latitude 48° 37'·5N. Plot the observed position.

1. Plot the DR position.
2. Plot the chosen position.
3. Plot the intercept and position line from the chosen position.

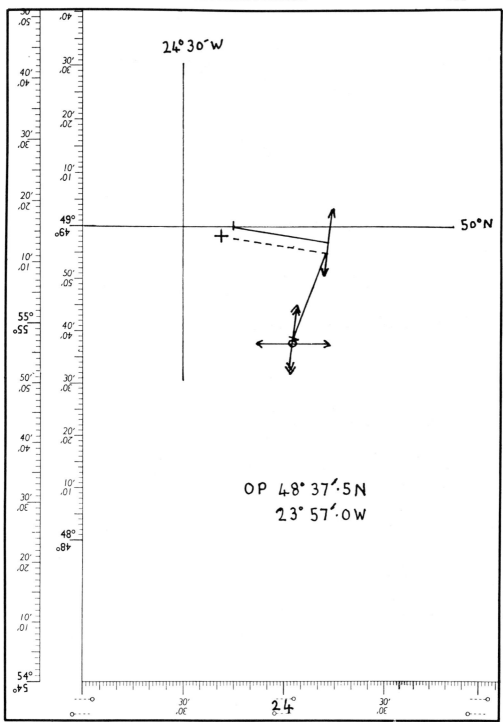

Fig 10.9 Plotting a Sun-Run-Sun sight.

4. Plot the course and distance run from this position line, starting at the point nearest to the DR position, to give the midday DR position. (The DR position longitude arrived at after the run is needed to find the time of the sun's meridian passage at Greenwich.)

5. Plot the latitude obtained by meridian altitude.

6. Transfer the first position line to the midday DR position plotted in 4 above.

The observed position is at the intersection of the transferred position line and the parallel of latitude.

Position Line Errors

When there is a run between two position lines, such as a sun-run-sun sight, the reliability of the resultant fix depends not only upon the correct assessment of the course steered, leeway, and current, but also upon the accuracy of the two position lines. When a latitude, which has been obtained by meridian altitude crosses a position line obtained after or before a run between sights, the accuracy of the longitude found will depend upon the accuracy of the latitude used.

In astronomical observations, the correct time is vitally important as even a small error will cause an incorrect LHA and declination and hence an incorrect calculated zenith distance (or altitude), which will affect the intercept and azimuth.

The tables and method used to find a calculated zenith distance or altitude may introduce small errors and the accuracy of any such tables used should be checked beforehand. The short method tables are slightly less accurate than those requiring more calculation.

When multiple sights are taken giving several position lines, there is a time difference between sights as the boat moves along her track, but this can be allowed for in the plot.

Due to cumulative errors, position lines will rarely if ever exactly intersect and a cocked hat is formed. Each position line may be subject to different errors and it is not possible to determine the boat's position exactly. For safety the boat's position should be assumed to be at the corner of the cocked hat nearest to any danger.

QUESTION PAPER TEN

10.1   Convert the following d. long to dep using traverse tables.

	lat.	*d. long*
a	41°	10'·5
b	49°	50'·7
c	41°	101'·6

10.2   Convert the following dep to d. long using traverse tables.

	lat.	*dep*
a	49°	32·9
b	41°	117·7
c	41°	70·2

10.3   Plot the following sights and find the observed position. Use squared paper. Assume no traverse tables are available.

Chosen latitude 45° N

Star	*Chosen long.*	*Intercept*	*Azimuth*
1	16° 05'·0W	04'·0 Away from	295° T
2	15° 56'·0W	10'·6 Towards	008° T
3	15° 52'·6W	08'·5 Towards	326° T
4	15° 44'·4W	11'·5 Towards	347° T

10.4   Plot on a plotting sheet the following sights and find the observed position.

Chosen latitude 48° S

Star	*Chosen long.*	*Intercept*	*Azimuth*
1	169° 28'·5E	7'·0 Towards	160° T
2	170° 03'·0E	3'·0 Towards	117° T
3	170° 00'·0E	8'·0 Away from	238° T
4	169° 42'·0E	7'·0 Towards	015° T

10.5   On June 21, a boat in DR position 49° 07'·0N, 14° 02'·0W, obtained a sun meridian altitude sight giving the latitude as 49° 10'·0N. The boat continued on a course of 233° T for 25 miles when an afternoon sun sight gave the following results:

Chosen position 49° N, 14° 04'·0W, intercept 14'·0 Towards, azimuth 254°T.

The estimated set and drift of the current was 075° T, 2·5 miles. Plot the observed position.

Answers on pages 165–6.

Chapter Eleven

Which Star Is It?

Stars need to be identified before they can be of use to the observer. This can be done by recognising a constellation such as the Plough, and either using the stars within the constellation or using the constellation to identify a neighbouring star. We have already seen an example of this when identifying Polaris which is in line with the two stars at the end of the Plough. The handle of the Plough points roughly in the direction of a bright star called Arcturus. Almanacs and the *Admiralty Manual of Navigation Vol II* contain identification charts. Star charts are also available separately.

During an ocean passage the stars chosen for dawn and dusk sights appear more or less in the same positions on succeeding days, and the observer can probably recognise them even in a partly clouded sky. However, should there be any doubt as to a star's identity, it can be verified by observing its altitude and azimuth and using these co-ordinates, together with the LHA of Aries at the time of the observation to find the stars approximate SHA and declination.

Selecting suitable stars for sights, or identifying an unknown star, can be done by using a star globe or a star finder or identifier:

1. Star Globe

A star globe is a globe on which all the stars positions are marked. It sits in a box and is free to move so that the observer's latitude and LHA Aries can be set up with the top half of the globe representing the sky above the observer. The altitude and azimuth of any particular star can then be used to identify that star. This method is quick and easy but it is not usual for a small boat to carry such an instrument, which is quite an expensive item. The position of planets can be marked (temporarily) on the star globe.

2. Star Finder or Identifier

This consists of a base disc upon which are printed stars for the northern and southern hemisphere, and the LHA of Aries together with a number of transparent discs for different latitudes printed with a graticule of curves which indicate altitude and azimuth. It is inexpensive, easy to use and stowage is no problem.

An unknown star can also be identified by one of the following methods:

1. Navigation Calculator/Computer. This is undoubtedly the quickest method, and a small programmed digital navigation computer like the one illustrated in Plate 2 requires only three inputs to provide the SHA and declination of the star observed. The inputs are altitude, azimuth and latitude. (See Example 48, below.)

2. Sight Reduction Tables for Marine Navigation NP 401. These tables, normally used for finding a calculated altitude and azimuth, can be entered with the observed altitude as declination, the true azimuth as LHA and the DR Latitude. The figures extracted under Hc represent declination, and under Z (after rules have been applied) LHA of the star. The LHA of the star is converted to the SHA of the star by subtracting the LHA of Aries at the time of the observation. An example is given below but, as the rule for converting Z to the LHA of the star varies according to latitude and observed altitude, the method should be studied in *NP 401* where a full explanation is given. The answer obtained is sufficiently accurate to identify a listed star, but the calculation required can lead to mathematical error.

Example 46 (See Extract No. 40)

When in DR position 45°01′·2N, 40° 00′·0W, a sight was taken of an unidentified star giving an approximate altitude of 46° and an azimuth of 247° T. The LHA Aries at this time was 256° 10′·6. Find the approximate SHA and declination to aid identification.

latitude = 45°
altitude = declination 46°
azimuth = LHA 247°

Hc	Z
18° 27′·9	42·4

Calculations to the nearest degree are sufficient, d can be ignored.

The altitude 18° represents the declination, named north because it was tabulated below the contrary same line on the right-hand page (see rules *NP 401*).

There is a special set of rules for converting the azimuth angle Z to azimuth Zn which represents the LHA of the star. In this case Z = Zn so the LHA of the star is 42°. The LHA of Aries is subtracted from the LHA of the star to give the SHA of the star which is 146°. (360° has been added to work the calculation).

By consulting the list of selected stars on the daily pages in the *Nautical Alamanc*, this SHA and declination are found to compare with Arcturus.

3. AP 3270 Volume 2 and Volume 3. These sight reduction tables can be used in the same way as *NP 401* but as tabulated declination is only between 0°–29° their usage is limited.

20	1 01.1 − 45.5 120.1	0 31.0 − 46.1 120.1
21	0 15.6 − 45.6 120.8	0 15.1 + 46.1 59.2
22	0 30.0 + 45.5 58.6	1 01.2 46.1 58.6
23	1 15.5 45.5 57.9	1 47.3 46.2 58.0
24	2 01.0 45.6 57.3	2 33.5 46.0 57.3
25	2 46.6 + 45.5 56.6	3 19.5 + 46.1 56.7
26	3 32.1 45.4 56.0	4 05.6 46.0 56.0
27	4 17.5 45.5 55.3	4 51.6 46.0 55.4
28	5 03.0 45.4 54.7	5 37.6 46.0 54.8
29	5 48.4 45.3 54.0	6 23.6 45.9 54.1
30	6 33.7 + 45.3 53.4	7 09.5 + 45.8 53.5
31	7 19.0 45.3 52.7	7 55.3 45.8 52.8
32	8 04.3 45.2 52.0	8 41.1 45.8 52.2
33	8 49.5 45.1 51.4	9 26.9 45.6 51.5
34	9 34.6 45.0 50.7	10 12.5 45.6 50.8
35	10 19.6 + 44.9 50.0	10 58.1 + 45.5 50.2
36	11 04.5 44.9 49.4	11 43.6 45.3 49.5
37	11 49.4 44.8 48.7	12 28.9 45.3 48.8
38	12 34.2 44.6 48.0	13 14.2 45.2 48.2
39	13 18.8 44.6 47.3	13 59.4 45.1 47.5
40	14 03.4 + 44.4 46.6	14 44.5 + 44.9 46.8
41	14 47.8 44.3 45.9	15 29.4 44.9 46.1
42	15 32.1 44.2 45.2	16 14.3 44.7 45.4
43	16 16.3 44.0 44.5	16 59.0 44.5 44.7
44	17 00.3 43.9 43.8	17 43.5 44.4 44.0
45	17 44.2 + 43.7 43.1	18 27.9 + 44.2 43.3
46	18 27.9 43.6 42.4	19 12.1 44.1 42.6
47	19 11.5 43.3 41.7	19 56.2 43.9 41.9
48	19 54.8 43.2 40.9	20 40.1 43.7 41.2
49	20 38.0 43.1 40.2	21 23.8 43.5 40.4

45°	**46°**

LATITUDE SAME NAME AS DECLINATION

L.H.A. 113°, 247°

Extract Number 40

Planets

The four navigational planets are easy to find because of their magnitude, but it may not always be obvious which one is being observed. A quick check can be done by measuring their altitude and azimuth and entering the sight reduction tables with these co-ordinates as for stars. The LHA and declination found are compared with the LHA's of the four planets at the time of the observation.

Choice of Stars

For multiple star sights a good angle of cut of the resultant position lines is necessary if a reliable observed position is to be obtained. It is also best to avoid an altitude of less than 10° as refraction affects the sight. Very high altitudes are also unsuitable and if used require special corrections when using *NP 401*.

If possible the brighter stars should be used as they are both easier to recognise and to observe with a sextant.

Magnitude

The brightness of a heavenly body, called its magnitude, is indicated in the *Nautical Almanac* by a number alongside the heavenly body's name. The lower the number, the brighter the heavenly body, the brightest being preceded by a minus sign. For example the sun's magnitude is −26·7, whereas that of Fomalhaut is 1·3. Although stars with very low magnitudes can be seen from earth, these would not be distinct enough for navigational purposes. 57 stars with magnitudes less than 3·0 are tabulated for normal usage.

QUESTION PAPER ELEVEN

11.1   List the following stars in order of brightness.

Star	Magnitude
Canopus	−0·9
Denebola	2·2
Sirius	−1·6
Capella	0·2
Rigel	0·3
Zuben'ubi	2·9

11.2   When choosing stars for a multiple sight, what would govern your choice.

11.3   What are the relative merits of the following for finding the approximate LHA and azimuth of a star or planet?

a.   The Star Globe.
b.   A Star Finder.
c.   A Star chart.

Answers on pages 165–6.

Chapter Twelve

Using A Calculator

Many celestial navigation problems involve the solution of the spherical triangle. As an alternative to using tables, several types of calculator are available which, given known angles or sides of a spherical triangle, will calculate the remaining angles or sides. The requirements for such a calculator are that it must have scientific notation, conversion for degrees and minutes to degrees and tenths of a degree, and at least two memory registers. There are, however, an increasing number of specialist calculators (or computers) which are designed specifically to solve problems of celestial navigation.

Celestial Navigation Calculators

Celestial navigation calculators can be grouped into those providing almanac information for the sun and Aries (hence suitable for stars) and those that include, in addition, the moon and the planets. The formulae covering the movements of the planets and the moon are more complex and require extra calculating power.

Calculations performed

The principal celestial calculation is to convert osbervations of clock time and sextant altitude into intercept and azimuth for plotting. Other celestial calculations that can be achieved include:

- identification of unknown star. Star coordinates (altitude, azimuth) are indicated; or LHA Aries for setting a star identifier.
- intercept adjustment for boat's track. For the twilight period, the DR positions are adjusted to a mean time.

Plate 2 The Tamaya NC 77 digital programmed navigation calculator. This is virtually a pocket computer and has proved a market winner. Once you are familiar with the keying procedures and the various formulae for celestial calculations, it can save the navigator a lot of time. (*Photo courtesy of Telesonic Marine Ltd.*)

- computation of fix from position lines. This does not allow the observer to make a judgement and it is preferable to plot the position lines anyway.
- great circle distance and initial track.

Data retention

Not all calculators retain data. The result of an earlier calculation may have to be re-entered. This can be annoying when the main cause of errors is the incorrect entry of data. A calculator with a 'data entry' program separate from the 'computation' program is highly desirable as it avoids the need to re-enter data. If the data from multiple sights can be retained then, by comparison, any misreading of the chronometer or sextant angle can become readily apparent. Indeed if three or more sights are taken and the time and sextant angle entered immediately, then an error will be apparent early enough for a sight to be retaken.

Data inputs

For every sight the observer enters the SEXTANT ALTITUDE and the TIME from the chronometer. On first switching on the calculator the Greenwich DATE and TIME are entered to enable the almanac function to work. On simpler calculators the star coordinates (SHA and DECLINATION) have to be entered. The LATITUDE and LONGITUDE of the observer's estimated position are required together with the HEIGHT OF EYE and sextant INDEX ERROR. In some calculators, the boat's COURSE and SPEED are entered.

Types of calculator

The first celestial navigation calculator suitable for small craft navigators was the *Tamaya NC77* (Plate 2). The programmed Sharp EL-512 calculator (*MERLIN*) and the programmed Sharp PC1246 pocket computer (*TERN*) include the sun and Aries almanacs. The *Tamaya NC88* together with the plug-in modules for the Sharp PC1500A and Hewlett Packard 41CV pocket computers provide the full sun, star, moon and planet almanacs.

Spherical Triangles

The basic formulae for solving a spherical triangle on a scientific calculator together with some examples are given below.

Basic Formulae

To find the third side of a spherical triangle (sides a, b, c and angles A, B, C) given two sides and an angle:

$$\cos a = \cos b \cos c + \sin b \sin c \cos A.$$

To find any angle of a spherical triangle given three sides:

$$\cos A = \frac{\cos a - \cos b \cos c}{\sin b \sin c}$$

(Note: side a is opposite angle A, etc.)

In the examples that follow, the sides a, b, c and angles A, B, C are different in each worked section.

Example 47

TO FIND LONGITUDE BY TIME
DR 49° 58'·1N 24° 11'·4W, GHA 326° 15'·1, declination 23° 26'·2N true altitude 38° 25'·8, heavenly body bearing approximately SE
a = 51° 34'·2 (true zenith distance)
b = 40° 01'·9 (co-latitude)
c = 66° 33'·8 (polar distance)
A = LHA (to be found)

$$\text{Formula: } \cos A = \frac{\cos a - \cos b \cos c}{\sin b \sin c}$$

$$A = 57° \ 30'·5$$

(The approximate bearing of the heavenly body shows that it is to the east. LHA is measured westwards, so it cannot be 57° 30'·5 but must be 360 − 57° 30'·5.)

correct for easterly bearing		360° 00'·0
		− 57° 30'·5
	LHA	302° 29'·5
to obtain longitude		
	GHA	326° 15'·1
	LHA	−302° 29'·5
	long. W	23° 45'·6

Example 48

IDENTIFYING AN UNKNOWN STAR
DR 45° 01'·2N 40° 00'·0W, approximate altitude of an unknown
star 46°, approximate azimuth 247° T, LHA Aries 256° 10'·6.

TO FIND DECLINATION:
b = 44° 58'·8 (co-latitude)
c = 44° 00'·0 (zenith distance)
A = 247° (azimuth)

Formula: cos a = cos b cos c + sin b sin c cos A
a = 71° 31'·3 (polar distance)

$$\text{corrn. for dec.:} \qquad \begin{array}{r} 90° \ 00'·0 \\ -71° \ 31'·3 \\ \hline N18° \ 28'·7 \ \text{dec.} \end{array}$$

TO FIND SHA
a = 44° 00'·0 (zenith distance)
b = 71° 31'·3 (polar distance)
c = 44° 58'·8 (co-latitude)

$$\text{Formula: } \cos A = \frac{\cos a - \cos b \cos c}{\sin b \sin c}$$

A = 42° 23'·4 (LHA)

$$\text{to obtain SHA:} \quad \begin{array}{lr} \text{LHA star} & 42° \ 23'·4 \\ \text{add } 360 & 360° \ 00'·0 \\ \hline & 402° \ 23'·4 \\ \text{LHA Aries} & -256° \ 10'·6 \\ \hline \text{SHA star} & 146° \ 12'·8 \end{array}$$

(Note: If the star bears east LHA = 360 − A; if it bears west LHA
= A.)
By consulting the list of selected stars in the almanac, the SHA and
declination correspond to ARCTURUS. (See Extract No. A10 in
the Appendix.)

Example 49

TO FIND CALCULATED ALTITUDE AND AZIMUTH
DR 50° 10'·4N 6° 15'·3W, LHA sun 305° 35'·8 declination S4° 27'·5

TO FIND ALTITUDE:
b = 94° 27'·5 (polar distance)
c = 39° 49'·6 (co-latitude)
A = 305° 35'·8 (LHA)

Formula: cos a = cos b cos c + sin b sin c cos A
a = 71° 49'·3 (zenith distance)

Calculated altitude = 90° − a
$$= 18° 10'·7$$

TO FIND AZIMUTH:
a = 71° 49'·3 (zenith distance)
b = 94° 27'·5 (polar distance)
c = 39° 49'·6 (co-latitude)

$$\text{Formula: cos B} = \frac{\cos b - \cos a \cos c}{\sin a \sin c}$$

B = 121° 25'·9 (calculated azimuth)

Example 50

GREAT CIRCLE DISTANCE AND INITIAL COURSE
To find the great circle distance and initial course from position A at Plymouth (50° 20'·0N 4° 09'·0W) and position B at Miami (25° 46'·0N 80° 12'·0W).

TO FIND DISTANCE:
A = 76° 03'·0 (d. long between A and B)
b = 64° 14'·0 (co-latitude B).
c = 39° 40'·0 (co-latitude A)

Formula: cos a = cos b cos c + sin b sin c cos A
a = 61° 45'·6 (great circle distance)

change degrees to minutes: great circle distance = 3705'·6
or 3705·6 nautical miles

TO FIND INITIAL COURSE
a = 64° 14'·0 (co-latitude B)
b = 39° 40'·0 (co-latitude A)
c = 61° 45'·6 (great circle distance)

$$\text{Formula: cos A} = \frac{\cos a - \cos b \cos c}{\sin b \sin c}$$

A = 82° 48'·0 or 277° (initial course)
(Note: d. long greater than 180, A = initial course; d. long less than 180, 360 − A = initial course.)

Plane Triangles

Traverse table problems can also be solved by using a calculator:

Example 51

TO FIND DEPARTURE
departure = d.long × cos lat.
latitude 49°, d.long 6'·7
   departure = 4'·4

TO FIND D.LONG

$$d.long = \frac{departure}{cos\ lat.}$$

latitude 49°, departure 2'·2
   d.long = 3'·4

TO FIND D. LAT (AFTER A RUN)
d. lat = distance × cos course
distance 50 miles, course 190° T
   d.lat = 49'·2

TO FIND DEPATURE (AFTER A RUN)
departure = distance × sin course
distance 50 miles, course 190° T
   departure = 8'·7

Chapter Thirteen

Satellite Navigation

In these days of modern technology using global satellite digital communications, data transfer is both simple and quick. Navigation warnings and weather forecasts can be rapidly updated, chart corrections are available the instant they are issued, and entire charts can be downloaded for instant use. The Global Maritime Distress and Safety System (GMDSS) co-ordinates any distress and urgency situation and the Global Positioning System (GPS) provides the boat position at all times.

Integrated Electronic Systems

If one is setting out on an ocean passage, it makes sense to have on board an integrated electronic system. With packet switching or time division multiplex, a local area network is created which accesses all the available sensors (GPS position, course, speed, depth, etc.) and into which a variety of computers and displays can be plugged. Whilst voice communication is usually kept separate, any associated data transmissions can be linked into the network. Thus all information is accessible at all times and the computers can process and display it as required. Almanacs, charts and pilotage information can be purchased on compact disks (CD ROMs) or downloaded as required. Electronic mail and the Internet are easily accessed. Even digital satellite mobile phones will be available.

Electronic Navigation Systems

Advanced technology enables small craft navigators to use an increasing number of sophisticated electronic aids to navigation. Systems based on radio waves transmitted from shore stations, known as hyperbolic systems, provide navigators with accurate present positions in all weather conditions but their range is limited. Systems based on radio waves transmitted from satellites give equivalent accuracy but with global coverage. These systems include computers to provide continuous outputs of navigational parameters such as: course and speed made good over the ground; range and bearing of other positions (waypoints); cross track error; estimated time of arrival.

Satallite datums

Satellite navigation systems use a slightly different datum reference to that used on charts. It is called the World Geodetic System 1984 datum. Positions given by satellite navigation systems could differ by up to 200m from those shown on a chart.

The Global Positioning System (GPS)

A network of 29 satellites orbits the earth at a height of 11,000 miles with their orbital plane at 55° to the equator. The satellites transmit continuously to earth on two frequencies in the D band (1 to 2 GHz) and supply users with their position, velocity and time. Time is obtained from three atomic clocks which are so accurate that they will gain or lose only one second in 50,000 years!

The satellites have an elaborate control system. There are five ground control monitor stations located round the earth to receive technical telemetered data from the satellites. The master control station sifts all the information it receives and transmits to the satellites their own true positions in space and the satellites in turn transmit their positions to the users.

A small craft will normally have a two-channel receiver. To use the receiver, switch it on and enter DR position, course and speed and ship's time. The receiver will search for available satellites, select the most suitable, and start tracking them. From each such satellite, it receives the satellite's position, its identity number and accurate time.

The receiver is able to calculate the satellite's range by measuring the time of receipt of the signal and multiplying the time taken for the signal to come from the satellite by the speed of radio waves in air. The receiver thus locates itself on a sphere of radius R_1, whose centre is the transmitting satellite. The receiver then measures the range of the second and third satellites to define spheres of radius R_2 and R_3. It can then work out where the spheres intersect and display this point as a latitude and longitude. More sophisticated receivers have five channels which makes the operation more efficient.

The accuracy of GPS is potentially extremely high (less than 16 metres) but for navigational purposes it is convenient to assume an accuracy of about 100 metres.

Glonass

The current status of the Russian Glonass satellite navigation system is 11 healthy satellites. However the condition of the service is not good, with major coverage gaps, data dropouts and ephemeris errors.

Galileo

Galileo will be the European alternative and complement to GPS. It is due to become operational in 2008.

Navigation Facilities

Latitude and Longitude

All modern receivers display the present position of the boat in latitude and longitude. This is appropriate for use with conventional marine charts. Be wary of the apparent authenticity caused by the coordinates of latitude and longitude being normally displayed to a resolution of 0.01 minutes:

$$50°31'.87N \quad 132°01'.56E$$

Waypoints

Almost every receiver has a waypoint facility. Waypoints are entered as a latitude and longitude. Each waypoint stored in the processor memory is assigned an identity number, so that by keying in that number the user obtains a display of the range and bearing of the waypoint (either as a Rhumb Line or a Great Circle). Because of the variety of functions that waypoints can perform there is a demand for large storage capacity and 1000 is not unusual. Some receivers have a 'man overboard' alarm button which automatically stores the current position (at the instant that the button is pressed) to enable a rapid return to that position to be made.

Course and Speed Made Good

The mean track (course made good) and speed made good are continuously assessed, though the sampling rate will affect the time of reaction to an alteration of course. If the boat's course and speed are input either directly or manually, a vector representing the mean set and drift of the tidal stream or current is obtained. The tidal stream information can be entered separately, enabling the Course to Steer and the Cross Track Error to be computed and displayed. All receivers have the facility to enter the date and time. Thus Time to Go to the next waypoint and the Estimated Time of Arrival (ETA) can be displayed. Some receivers allow automatic reversion to the Dead Reckoning (DR) mode if the received signal quality drops below a predetermined threshold level.

Plate 3 The Trimble NT 200D GPS receiver computes the ship's position every second to an accuracy of 5 metres. The position information is optionally overlaid on background charts which provide depth and hazard information to enable safe navigation. The sailing time between waypoints is automatically calculated based on velocity made good. The unit can store 500 waypoints and 50 routes for complex route navigation.

Chapter Fourteen

World Weather

The Atmosphere

The air around us is a mixture of various gases (mainly oxygen and nitrogen) and water vapour. These gases form a layer around the earth known as the atmosphere.

Air has mass which exerts a pressure at sea level on the earth's surface of about 15 lb/sq.in. This pressure of 15 lb/sq.in. is known as one atmosphere, one barometric pressure or one bar. A bar is divided into 1000 millibars (which is equivalent to standard atmospheric pressure).

Atmospheric pressure is varying at all times, but this variation is normally between 970 millibars and 1030 millibars, (with exceptional values of 925 millibars and 1050 millibars). Another measure of pressure is in inches of mercury, 29·5 inches (or 750 mm) of mercury being equivalent to 1000 millibars. The units normally used to measure pressure are millibars or inches of mercury.

Air Circulation

The earth's surface is warmed by radiation from the sun. Air in contact with this surface is warmed by conduction and convection. The sun's rays do not strike all parts of the earth's surface at the same angle. In equatorial regions, because its declination does not exceed 23° 27′ north or south of the equator, the sun is nearly overhead throughout the year and its rays are nearly perpendicular to the earth's surface. At the poles the sun's rays strike the earth's surface at an acute angle (see Fig. 14.1). This means that equatorial regions are subjected to stronger heating than the surrounding areas.

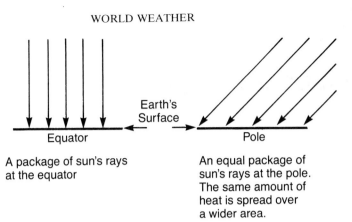

Earth's
Surface

Equator   Pole

A package of sun's rays   An equal package of
at the equator   sun's rays at the pole.
                                 The same amount of
                                 heat is spread over
                                 a wider area.

Fig 14.1 Unequal heating on the earth's surface.

As air warms over equatorial regions, it rises, causing low
pressure on the earth's surface and high pressure in the upper
atmosphere. Over polar regions, cold air descends causing high
pressure on the earth's surface and low pressure in the upper
atmosphere.

Air tries to move from an area of high pressure to an area of
lower pressure and so, in the upper atmosphere, it flows away from
the equator. On the earth's surface it flows away from the poles. It
does not, however, follow a straight path but is modified by the
earth's rotation.

Coriolis Force

Let us consider a ring of air around the surface of the earth at the
equator. This ring of air will be drawn by surface friction in the
same direction and at the same speed as the surface of the earth
rotates. If this ring of air is displaced towards the poles its radius
decreases. By the laws of physics, the momentum of air will remain
constant and so its velocity will increase. This increase of velocity
will appear to an observer on the earth's surface as a westerly wind.

Conversely, if this ring of air is displaced towards the equator, its
radius will increase and its velocity decrease. It will, therefore,
appear to an observer on the earth's surface as an easterly wind.
This phenomenon is known as coriolis force.

Pressure Distribution

Air in the upper atmosphere flowing away from the equatorial high
pressure area both cools and piles up in the vicinity of latitudes 30°

north and 30° south. It then descends, forming a band of high pressure on the earth's surface, where it spreads out towards the equator becoming a band of easterly wind (NE and SE trades) and towards the poles becoming a band of westerly wind (westerlies).

On the earth's surface, air moving from polar high pressure areas towards the equator becomes an easterly wind.

The warmer polewards flowing air meets the colder polar air and ascends over it causing the surface pressure to fall and creating a band of low pressure in temperate latitudes.

Assuming no intervening effects, the prevailing winds caused by these pressure areas would be as shown in Fig. 14.2.

Seasonal Changes

The bands of pressure move in phase with the change of declination of the sun.

Differential Heating of Land and Sea

Land tends to heat up and cool down more rapidly than adjacent sea areas. The sea warms relatively slowly but tends to retain that heat such that over the oceans the pressure distribution remains relatively constant. Over land masses, low pressure develops in summer and high pressure in winter. This differential heating has a major effect on the pressure bands shown in Fig. 14.2, especially in the northern hemisphere where there is a large proportion of land.

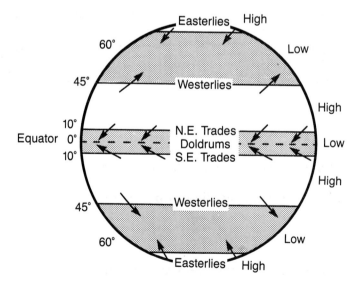

Fig 14.2 Pressure distribution and associated winds.

Buys Ballot's Law

Air flowing from a high pressure area on the earth's surface is deflected by coriolis force such that, in the northern hemisphere, northward travelling air is deflected to the east and southward travelling air to the west. This sets up a clockwise circulation around the area of high pressure. The converse is true for a low pressure area. In the southern hemisphere this effect is reversed.

The relationship between wind direction and pressure gradient was summarised by a Dutchman named Buys Ballot thus:

> Face the wind, and the centre of low pressure will be on your right hand in the northern hemisphere, and on your left hand in the southern hemisphere.

Winds and Weather

Polar Winds

Position – Polar side of the Westerlies.
Direction – Mainly easterly.
Weather – Frequent gales in winter, usually cloudy in summer.

Westerlies

Position – Between the polar winds and the variables.
Direction – Westerly but modified by frequent depressions and anticyclones.
Weather – Frequent gales especially in winter, weather changeable. Often fog in spring and summer. In the Southern Hemisphere south of latitude 40° gales are so frequent that the winds are known as the roaring forties.

Variables

Position – In between the westerlies and the trades.
Direction – Variable.
Weather – Light winds generally fine with little rain.

Trades

Position – Between the variables and the doldrums.
Direction – Easterly.

Weather – Generally fair, winds blow steadily throughout the year with an average speed of 14 knots except when tropical revolving storms are present. On the eastern side of the oceans there is little cloud or rain. On the western side more cloud and frequent rain.

Doldrums

Position – Straddling the equator between the trades.
Direction – Variable.
Weather – Winds vary from light to squally and rain can be either a few scattered showers or heavy rain and thunderstorms.

The Monsoons

The strong summer heating over Asia causes an area of extreme low pressure to develop over the land mass. Moist air is drawn in from over the sea. The SE trade wind is also drawn into the circulation, crossing the equator to become a SW wind. This wind, known as the SW monsoon is experienced in the Arabian Sea, Bay of Bengal, and the China Sea (see Fig. 14.3). It occurs from May to September, causing intense rainfall in many areas such as India, SE Asia and the NW Pacific. Gale force winds can occur in the Indian Ocean. Cyclones can occur in the Bay of Bengal and the Indian Ocean.

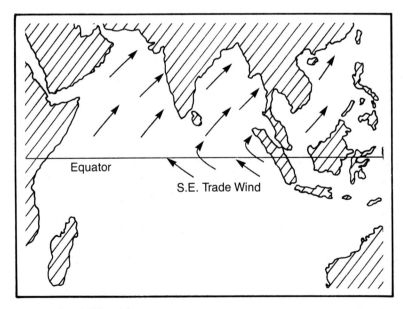

Fig 14.3 The South West Monsoon.

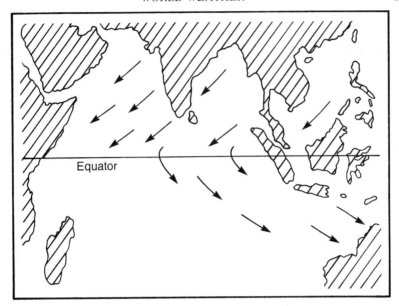

Fig 14.4 The North East and North West Monsoons.

During October to March, when the land mass of Asia has
cooled, an extensive high pressure system develops over Siberia
causing a strong NE wind, (known as the NE monsoon) (see Fig.
14.4). However, this wind is not as strong as the wind of the SW
monsoon nor the weather as wet. The NE wind crosses the equator
and changes direction, moving towards Australia as the NW
monsoon. The NW monsoon occurs about November to March.

Generally in the north Indian Ocean the weather is fine and dry
but in some places such as the south coast of China, fog and drizzle
can occur.

Hurricanes and Such

Hurricane is one of the regional names used for a Tropical Revolving
Storm (TRS) which is a cyclonic system of great intensity. (Other
names are: Cyclone, Typhoon, and Willy-willy.) The pressure at the
centre may be similar to that in a depression encountered in
temperate regions but the pressure gradient is extremely steep
causing hurricane force winds. In the centre, the winds may be
variable light to moderate with a fairly clear sky but the sea can be
very confused with heavy swell. Around the centre spray and heavy
rain reduces visibility to zero. The area covered by a tropical
revolving storm varies, but it is smaller than that covered by the

average depression in temperate regions. Its diameter increases as the storm ages. It cannot form at latitudes less than 5° as the deflective force due to the earth's rotation is insufficient to develop the cyclonic circulation needed, and usually begins its life towards the western sides of the ocean between latitudes 7° and 20° north or south. After formation the general tendency is for it to move slowly westerly and polewards, at a speed of 10 knots to 15 knots until it reaches latitude 25° where it curves round, speeds up and follows a northeasterly or southeasterly track to higher latitudes. It may then die out completely or turn into, or join, a temperate depression. Sometimes it does not curve, but follows the alternate track shown in Fig. 14.5.

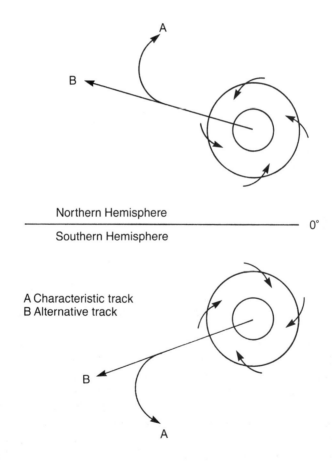

Fig 14.5 The track of a typical Tropical Revolving Storm.

Warning of Approach

Apart from listening to the various world radio warning services, the following practical observations are useful.

1. Check the barometer regularly when in tropical regions during the hurricane season. The pressure normally varies little in these areas except for a slight diurnal change and any fall outside the normal for that time of year should be viewed with suspicion. Pressure falls more rapidly as the storm approaches but a fall of 5 millibars or more below the normal reading is a good indication that a tropical revolving storm is approaching.

2. The cloud formations will be similar to a depression in higher latitudes, starting with cirrus probably in vivid bands pointing towards the storm centre. This is followed by heavy stratus type cloud.

3. Wind direction alters and the wind strengthens.

4. Swell may be felt several hundred miles ahead of an approaching storm.

Keeping Clear

These storms occur only at certain times, which is usually the summer or early autumn for the hemisphere concerned. In the north Atlantic this is from June to November with September being the worst month. Figure 14.6 gives a general indication for other parts of the world.

Having confirmed that a tropical revolving storm is in the vicinity it is important to try to establish the position of the centre and the probable track to determine whether the boat is in a dangerous position.

Buys Ballot's law can be used to determine the approximate bearing of the centre. The angle between the true wind direction and the centre increases in proportion with the boat's distance away. This angle will be about 90° when close to the centre and about 110° at a distance of 200 miles.

Repeated hourly observations, preferably with the boat stopped, should be taken to try to ascertain the storm's track.

If the boat is found to be in its direct path it is necessary to find out in which quadrant the boat is likely to enter in order to determine the correct action to take. As before it is best to stop the boat to get an accurate idea of the true wind direction. Refer to Fig. 14.7a, which is for the northern hemisphere, where the storm field has been divided into quadrants. (Avoiding action should be as shown in the diagram.)

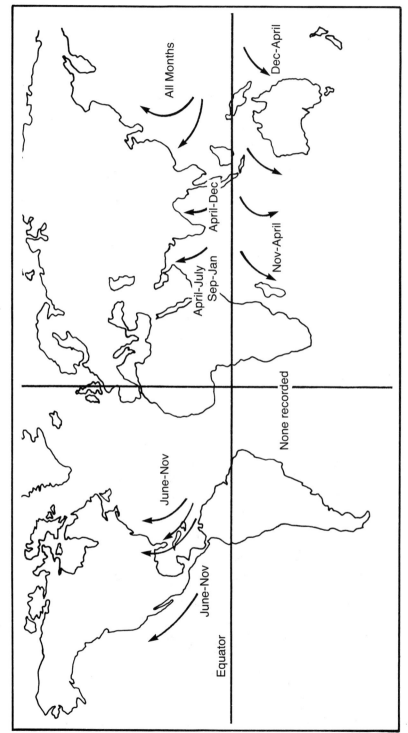

Fig 14.6 Seasons when Tropical Revolving Storms occur.

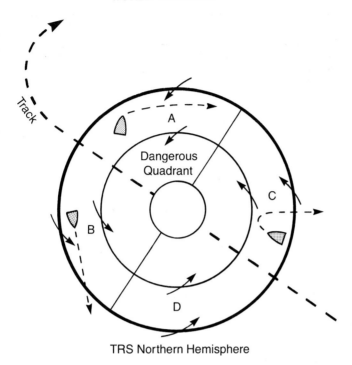

Fig 14.7a Avoiding action: Northern Hemisphere.

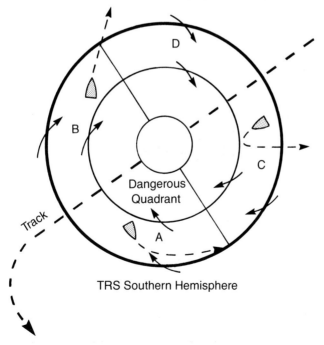

Fig 14.7b Avoiding action: Southern Hemisphere.

A. If the boat is in this quadrant as the storm progresses, the wind will change in a clockwise direction and the barometer fall. This is a dangerous position to be in as the storm can curve bringing the centre over the boat or the boat can be blown towards the centre by the strong winds.

B. In this quadrant the pressure will also fall but the wind will change in an anti-clockwise direction.

C. Provided the boat is stopped the pressure will rise and the wind will change direction clockwise. It is, however, possible to overtake the storm when the wind will change direction anti-clockwise and the pressure fall as it does in quadrant B giving the false impression that the boat may be in this quadrant which, if recommended action for quadrant B is applied, could put the boat in a very dangerous position in the storms centre.

D. In quadrant D the wind alters direction anti-clockwise and the pressure rises, no alteration of course is needed in this case as the storm has passed.

Should the wind remain steady and the barometer fall the boat is in the direct path of the storm and course should be altered towards the equator.

In the southern hemisphere the wind will alter direction anti-clockwise in quadrants A and C, and clockwise in quadrants B and D. The pressure will behave the same as it does in the northern hemisphere, falling in quadrants A and B and rising in quadrants C and D (see Fig. 14.7b). Avoiding action should be as shown in the diagram.

Ocean Currents

Currents can be caused through several reasons such as; an unequal water density (a density current), a slope on the surface of the sea (gradient current), or wind blowing along the sea surface (drift current).

In the open ocean the surface currents are wind driven and follow the general circulation of the wind in the pressure systems. Figure 14.8 shows the main ocean currents.

In monsoon areas the currents change with the seasons as the wind changes.

When a warm current such as the Gulf Stream meets a cold current such as the Labrador current, fog banks can form.

Detailed information on ocean currents and prevailing winds is found on routeing or pilot charts. More local information for coastal areas may be found in sailing directions (pilots).

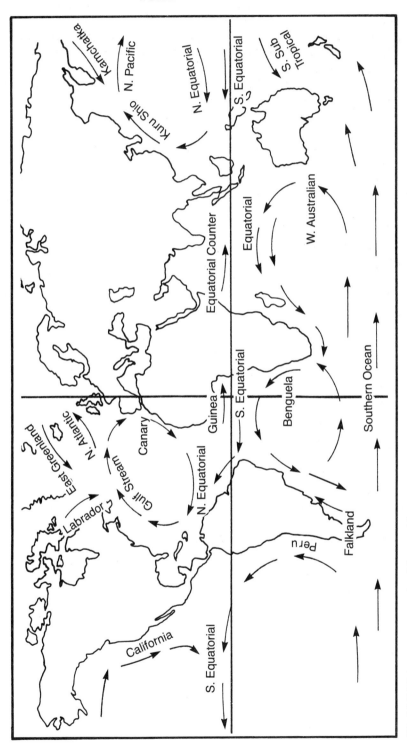

Fig 14.8 Main ocean currents of the world.

QUESTION PAPER FOURTEEN

The page number upon which the answer is found is in brackets after the question.

14.1. Draw a diagram showing the pressure distribution on the earth's surface. Show the prevailing winds and their approximate latitudes. (p. 132.)

14.2. Give reasons for monsoon weather and draw a simple sketch showing the NE and SW monsoons. (p. 135.)

14.3. In what areas and between what latitudes do tropical revolving storms occur? (p. 136.)

14.4. What signs would indicate a tropical revolving storm was in the locality? (p. 137.)

14.5. What track does a tropical revolving storm normally follow? (p. 136.)

14.6. Look at Figs. 14.7a and 14.7b. How can the boat's position in the storm field be determined. Give examples for all 4 quadrants. (p. 140.)

14.7. In Fig. 14.7a why is it advisable for boat C to heave-to before deciding upon what action to take? (p. 140.)

14.8. Draw a simple diagram showing the principle drift currents throughout the world. (p. 141.)

Chapter Fifteen

Preparing For An Ocean Passage

World (cruising) Routes — Jimmy Cornell

Before undertaking an ocean passage much thought and pre-planning is necessary.

References (not necessarily needed on the passage)
1. *Ocean Passages for the World* (NP 136).
2. *The Mariner's Handbook* (NP 100).
3. *Routeing Charts* (known as *Pilot Charts* in the United States).
4. Gnomonic (or Great Circle) Charts.
5. Admiralty Sailing Directions.
6. *Admiralty List of Radio Signals.*
7. *Catalogue of Admiralty Charts and Publications* (NP 131).
8. *World Cruising Routes* by Jimmy Cornell.
9. *World Cruising Handbook* by Jimmy Cornell.
10. *Heavy Weather Sailing* by Adlard Coles revised by Peter Bruce.
11. *The American Practical Navigator* by Nathaniel Bowditch.
12. *Weather Predicting Simplified* by Michael Carr.
13. *Boatowner's Mechanical and Electrical Manual* by Nigel Calder.
14. *Boatowner's Practical & Technical Cruising Manual* by Nigel Calder.
15. *Marine Diesel Engines* by Nigel Calder.
Nautical Almanac published by HM Stationery Office and the US Government Printing Office.
Websites:
Weather: www.hffax.de, www.xaxero.com, www.ocens.com, www.meteo.fr/marine/naviweb/.
Chart details and corrections: www.hydro.gov.uk, www.chartco.com.

The following points need to be considered:
1. Likelihood of fog and ice.
2. Likelihood of storms.
3. Electronic navigation aids available.

4. Rescue organisations available.
5. Where fresh water, food and fuel can be obtained.
6. Port services including engineering facilities.
7. Where replacement charts or extra charts can be purchased.
8. Immigration controls at ports likely to be visited.

The following publications will be needed on the passage:

1. Nautical Almanac

2003 Commercial Edition

There are several choices available, some of which are listed below:

THE NAUTICAL ALMANAC NP 314

This comprehensive almanac is published in the United Kingdom by HM Stationery Office and in the United States of America by the US Government Printing Office. It is very easy to use as little interpolation is needed, and a full explanation of the tables is given in the back section. Information includes: GHA of Aries, GHA and declination of the sun, moon and the 4 navigational planets (tabulated hourly for each day with an 'Increment and Correction' table for minutes and seconds), tri-daily tabulations for sunrise, sunset and twilight, daily tabulations for moonrise and moonset, meridian passage of the sun and moon, equation of time, SHA and declination of 57 stars and their magnitudes, 'Polaris (Pole Star) Tables', 'Conversion of Arc to Time' table, 'Apparent Altitude Tables', star charts, eclipse diagrams and much other information.

BROWN'S NAUTICAL ALMANAC

This is published by Brown, Son & Ferguson, Ltd, Glasgow. It is a worldwide almanac which reprints directly pages of the *Nautical Almanac, NP 314*, and contains extensive information on ports and ocean passages.

2. Nautical Tables

Nautical almanacs are used in conjunction with nautical tables which tabulate an altitude or zenith distance and an azimuth or azimuth angle.

SIGHT REDUCTION TABLES for Air Nav. Vol 1 - Epoch 2005
Vol 2 - Lat 0-40° Dec. 0-29°
AP 3270 Volumes 1, 2 and 3. Published in the United Kingdom by HM Stationery Office. *Volume 1* provides a very quick method for obtaining an altitude and azimuth, but can only be used for 41

selected stars, 7 of which are tabulated at any one time. All latitudes north and south are covered, declination is not needed, the LHA Aries and latitude are the only values required.

Volume 2 covers latitudes 0°–39°, *Volume 3* latitudes 40°–89°. Both cover declinations 0°–29°. They can be used for any heavenly body with a declination of 29° or less and are entered with LHA and declination, giving an altitude and an azimuth angle.

These tables are published in the United States by the Defense Mapping Agency Hydrographic Centre. *AP 3270 Volume 1* is equivalent to *No. 249 Star Tables for Air Navigation*; *AP 3270 Volumes 2 and 3* to *No. 249 Sight Reduction Tables for Air Navigation.*

Sight Reduction Tables for Marine Navigation NP 401.   Published in the United Kingdom by the Hydrographic Office, and in the United States of America as *HO 229* by U.S. Naval Oceanographic Office. These tables are in 6 volumes each covering 15 degrees of latitude, all declinations are covered. They can be used for any heavenly body and require for entry LHA and declination. They give an altitude and azimuth angle.

NORIE'S NAUTICAL TABLES
Published by Imray Norie Laurie and Wilson Ltd. This is a set of nautical tables for general use. They comprise many tables some of which are: 'Traverse Tables', 'Haversine Tables', 'Logs of Trig Functions' and 'Ex-Meridian Tables'. Zenith distances and quadrantal azimuths can be found from these tables for any latitude and declination.

Other publications are: *Burton's Tables* and *Inman's Tables* similar to *Norie's Nautical Tables,*

Charts and Plotting Sheets

Charts corrected to date will be required for coastal parts of the ocean passage. In mid-ocean, plotting sheets are used where a larger scale than an ocean chart is required.

ADMIRALTY AND LOCAL SAILING DIRECTIONS (PILOTS)
These give navigational information such as port entry, leading

Reeds Nautical Almanac 2013

Atlantic Spain + Portugal

lights, transits, tidal streams, canal transit instructions, descriptions of coastlines etc.

ADMIRALTY LIST OF LIGHTS
These give detailed information of light positions and characteristics, plus details of light structures. It should be noted that there are very few lights in many parts of the world.

ADMIRALTY LIST OF RADIO SIGNALS
These are published in 7 volumes: *Volume 1* – Coast Radio Stations; *Volume 2* – Radio Navigational Aids, Electronic Position Fixing Systems and Radio Time Signals; *Volume 3* – Maritime Safety Information Services; *Volume 4* – Meteorological Observation Stations; *Volume 5* – Global Maritime Distress and Safety System (GMDSS); *Volume 6* – Pilot Services, Vessel Traffic Services and Port Operations; *Volume 7* – Satellite Navigation Systems.

ADMIRALTY NOTICES TO MARINERS
The latest edition of this will be required to correct all Hydrographic Office Publications including charts and sailing directions, Admiralty charts, List of Lights and Radio Signals.

Navigational Instruments

Celestial navigation is an absolute method of navigation which makes sophisticated instruments unnecessary. The following is a minimum suggested list:

1. Plotting instruments.
2. A reliable sextant.
3. An accurate chronometer. (Correct GMT is very important to accuracy of observed positions).
4. A good steering compass which has been swung for deviation and a good hand bearing compass.
5. A log, preferably a towed one which is more reliable. (It is essential to have an accurate record of distance run.) A spare rotator if a towed log is used.
6. Radio Direction Finder. There are few radiobeacons in some parts of the world, but many radio stations on various islands. Radio direction finding equipment should, therefore, include the frequency range of these as well as the normal marine radio beacons.
7. A satellite navigator is ideal (but not essential).
8. A portable digital navigation calculator/computer is extremely useful, but again not essential.
9. A facsimile receiver (see Plate 4 on page 152).

Organisations to Contact before Sailing

    1. Lloyds of London operate a deep sea yacht surveillance scheme.

    2. HM Coastguard offer surveillance whilst in European waters, and are in contact with US Coastguard AMVER organisation.

    3. HM Customs and Excise to arrange authority to export duty free stores.

Log Book (Deck Log)

The boat's logbook must be adequate and it must be kept up to date. There is no legal requirement for small boats to do this but in principle it should include sufficient navigational records to reconstruct the whole voyage at a later date. In the event of an insurance claim a properly kept log is significant. It is a legal document (for registered merchant vessels) when used in investigations regarding collision or loss of life. Pencil entries can be used but they should never be erased, only crossed through if an error is made. An accurate time signal should be received and recorded daily. Barometric pressure should be recorded every 4 hours (barometric trend is one of the first indications of approaching bad weather).

Best Route

The shortest route may not necessarily be the most comfortable one. A careful study of the relevant routeing chart (or pilot chart) should be made. These charts are available for all the oceans for every month of the year and contain the following information:

    1. Prevailing winds.

    2. Ocean currents.

    3. Ice and fog areas.

    4. Tracks of tropical revolving storms.

    5. Shipping routes.

  There is also much other information which mainly concerns commercial shipping.

Great Circle Sailing

On the surface of a sphere such as the earth, an arc of a great circle is the shortest distance between two points. (A great circle is a circle whose plane passes through the centre of the sphere.) On a great circle chart (which is gnomonic projection), an arc of a great circle

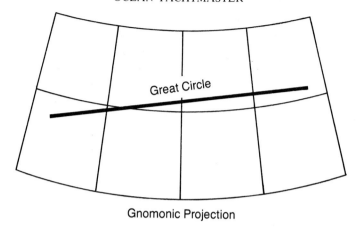

Gnomonic Projection

Fig 15.1 A Great Circle appears as a straight line when plotted onto a gnomonic projection chart.

appears as a straight line (see Fig. 15.1). If a boat followed a great circle track her course, being relative to true north would be constantly altering. For this reason, distances of 600 nautical miles or less are plotted on a mercator projection chart as a rhumb line track. However, a rhumb line track would be significantly longer than a great circle track over larger distances:

Example 52

Distances are in miles

	Gt. Circle	Rhumb Line	Difference
Plymouth to Miami	3705·4	3839·6	134·2
Capetown to Freemantle	4685·4	4922·5	237·1
San Francisco to Brisbane	6146·7	6188·4	41·7

On a mercator projection chart the only great circles to appear as straight lines are the meridians and the equator. All other great circles appear as a curve (see Fig. 15.2).

In practice a near great circle track is sailed which is found by plotting the track on a great circle chart, or on *Admiralty Great Circle Chart diagram No 5029* (full instructions given on this diagram), and then selecting points along the track about 5° apart. These points are transferred to a mercator projection chart (using latitude and longitude) and form a track made up of a series of rhumb lines (see Fig. 15.3).

Sometimes the desired great circle track may take the boat into

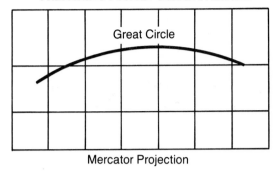

Fig 15.2 A Great Circle appears as a curve when plotted onto a Mercator projection chart.

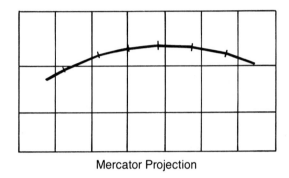

Fig 15.3 A Great Circle Track divided into Rhumb lines (Mercator projection).

unsuitable areas such as fog banks or ice boundaries and it is not desirable to sail above a certain latitude. To avoid this a composite track is plotted by drawing in a limiting danger line, plotting the great circle track from the starting point to make a tangent at this line and the great circle track from the finishing point to make a tangent at this line. A composite track is thus formed from portions of two great circles with a line of latitude between them.

Great Circle Distance

Distance along a great circle track and the initial course can be found by various methods:

TABLES
Tables which solve a spherical triangle such as the PZX triangle can be used to solve this problem. ZX which is normally the zenith distance will be the great circle distance.

Example 53

The great circle distance and initial track is required between A Plymouth, 50° 20'·0N 4° 09'·0W and B Miami 25° 46'·0N 80° 12'·0W.

Using NP 401

Use exactly as for finding an altitude and azimuth but enter as follows (full instructions given in *NP 401* which should be studied carefully):

Difference of longitude between A and B = LHA
Latitude A = latitude
Latitude B = declination

If latitude A and B are the same names use the *same* tables.
If latitude A and B are different names use the *contrary* tables.

LHA 76° Latitude A 50° N Declination 25° 46'N

	Hc	d	Z
	27° 41'·4+	+42'·4	82·7 = 277° ·3
corrn. for 40'·0	30'·6		
corrn. for 02'·4	1'·9		

28° 13'·9− (subtract from 90°)

AB = 61° 46'·1 = 3706·1 miles

Great circle distance is 3706·1 miles.
Great circle initial track is 277° ·3.

76°, 284° L.H.A. LATITUDE SAME NAME AS DECLINATION

49°			50°			51°			52°			
Hc	d	Z	Hc	d	Z	Hc	d	Z	Hc	d	Z	Dec.
° '	'	°	° '	'	°	° '	'	°	° '	'	°	°
24 02.0 +42.9		86.7	24 05.2 +43.7		87.1	24 08.0 +44.5		87.6	24 10.3 +45.3		88.0	20
24 44.9	42.7	85.9	24 48.9	43.5	86.4	24 52.5	44.3	86.8	24 55.6	45.0	87.3	21
25 27.6	42.4	85.1	25 32.4	43.3	85.6	25 36.8	44.0	86.1	25 40.6	44.8	86.6	22
26 10.0	42.2	84.4	26 15.7	42.9	84.8	26 20.8	43.8	85.3	26 25.4	44.6	85.8	23
26 52.2	41.9	83.6	26 58.6	42.8	84.1	27 04.6	43.5	84.6	27 10.0	44.3	85.1	24
27 34.1 +41.6		82.8	27 41.4 +42.4		83.3	27 48.1 +43.3		83.8	27 54.3 +44.1		84.3	25
28 15.7	41.3	81.9	28 23.8	42.2	82.5	28 31.4	43.0	83.0	28 38.4	43.8	83.6	26
28 57.0	41.0	81.1	29 06.0	41.9	81.7	29 14.4	42.7	82.2	29 22.2	43.6	82.8	27
29 38.0	40.7	80.3	29 47.9	41.5	80.8	29 57.1	42.4	81.4	30 05.8	43.2	82.0	28
30 18.7	40.4	79.4	30 29.4	41.3	80.0	30 39.5	42.1	80.6	30 49.0	43.0	81.2	29

Extract Number 41

INTERPOLATION TABLE

Dec. Inc.	Tens					Decimals	Units										Double Second Diff. and Corr.
	10'	20'	30'	40'	50'		0'	1'	2'	3'	4'	5'	6'	7'	8'	9'	
44.0	7.3	14.6	22.0	29.3	36.6	.0	0.0 0.7	1.5 2.2	3.0 3.7	4.4 5.2	5.9 6.7						
44.1	7.3	14.7	22.0	29.4	36.7	.1	0.1 0.8	1.6 2.3	3.0 3.8	4.5 5.3	6.0 6.7						
44.2	7.3	14.7	22.1	29.4	36.8	.2	0.1 0.9	1.6 2.4	3.1 3.9	4.6 5.3	6.1 6.8						1.1
44.3	7.4	14.8	22.1	29.5	36.9	.3	0.2 1.0	1.7 2.4	3.2 3.9	4.7 5.4	6.2 6.9						3.2 0.1
44.4	7.4	14.8	22.2	29.6	37.0	.4	0.3 1.0	1.8 2.5	3.3 4.0	4.7 5.5	6.2 7.0						5.3 0.2
44.5	7.4	14.8	22.3	29.7	37.1	.5	0.4 1.1	1.9 2.6	3.3 4.1	4.8 5.6	6.3 7.0						7.5 0.3
44.6	7.4	14.9	22.3	29.7	37.2	.6	0.4 1.2	1.9 2.7	3.4 4.2	4.9 5.6	6.4 7.1						9.6 0.4
44.7	7.5	14.9	22.4	29.8	37.3	.7	0.5 1.3	2.0 2.7	3.5 4.2	5.0 5.7	6.5 7.2						11.7 0.5
44.8	7.5	15.0	22.4	29.9	37.4	.8	0.6 1.3	2.1 2.8	3.6 4.3	5.0 5.8	6.5 7.3						13.9 0.6
44.9	7.5	15.0	22.5	30.0	37.5	.9	0.7 1.4	2.2 2.9	3.6 4.4	5.1 5.9	6.6 7.3						16.0 0.7
																	18.1 0.8
45.0	7.5	15.0	22.5	30.0	37.5	.0	0.0 0.8	1.5 2.3	3.0 3.8	4.5 5.3	6.1 6.8						20.3 0.9
45.1	7.5	15.0	22.5	30.0	37.6	.1	0.1 0.8	1.6 2.4	3.1 3.9	4.6 5.4	6.1 6.9						22.4 1.0
45.2	7.5	15.0	22.6	30.1	37.6	.2	0.2 0.9	1.7 2.4	3.2 3.9	4.7 5.5	6.2 7.0						24.5 1.1
45.3	7.5	15.1	22.6	30.2	37.7	.3	0.2 1.0	1.7 2.5	3.3 4.0	4.8 5.5	6.3 7.1						26.7 1.2
45.4	7.6	15.1	22.7	30.3	37.8	.4	0.3 1.1	1.8 2.6	3.3 4.1	4.9 5.6	6.4 7.1						28.8 1.3
45.5	7.6	15.2	22.8	30.3	37.9	.5	0.4 1.1	1.9 2.7	3.4 4.2	4.9 5.7	6.4 7.2						30.9 1.4
45.6	7.6	15.2	22.8	30.4	38.0	.6	0.5 1.2	2.0 2.7	3.5 4.2	5.0 5.8	6.5 7.3						33.1 1.5
45.7	7.6	15.3	22.9	30.5	38.1	.7	0.5 1.3	2.0 2.8	3.6 4.3	5.1 5.8	6.6 7.4						35.2 1.6
45.8	7.7	15.3	22.9	30.6	38.2	.8	0.6 1.4	2.1 2.9	3.6 4.4	5.2 5.9	6.7 7.4						
45.9	7.7	15.3	23.0	30.6	38.3	.9	0.7 1.4	2.2 3.0	3.7 4.5	5.2 6.0	6.7 7.5						
46.0	7.6	15.3	23.0	30.6	38.3	.0	0.0 0.8	1.5 2.3	3.1 3.9	4.6 5.4	6.2 7.0						1.2
46.1	7.7	15.3	23.0	30.7	38.4	.1	0.1 0.9	1.6 2.4	3.2 4.0	4.7 5.5	6.3 7.1						3.5 0.1
46.2	7.7	15.4	23.1	30.8	38.5	.2	0.2 0.9	1.7 2.5	3.3 4.0	4.8 5.6	6.4 7.1						5.8 0.2
46.3	7.7	15.4	23.1	30.9	38.6	.3	0.2 1.0	1.8 2.6	3.3 4.1	4.9 5.7	6.4 7.2						8.1 0.3
46.4	7.7	15.5	23.2	30.9	38.7	.4	0.3 1.1	1.9 2.6	3.4 4.2	5.0 5.7	6.5 7.3						10.5 0.4

Extract Number 42

In the example latitude and LHA have been taken to the nearest degree but these can be interpolated more accurately by using the special diagrams in *NP 401*. The great circle distance in this case is less than 5400 miles (90° angle). If it had been greater the rules given are slightly modified.

QUESTION PAPER FIFTEEN

15.1.   Why is a composite track sometimes preferable to a great circle track?

15.2.   What navigational publications would you include on an ocean passage?

15.3.   What information is on a routeing chart (Pilot chart)?

15.4.   When planning an ocean passage what considerations would you give to:
   a. Time of year.
   b. Route.

15.5.   On a small boat with a limited budget, what instruments, apart from plotting instruments would you consider essential?

Answers on page 167.

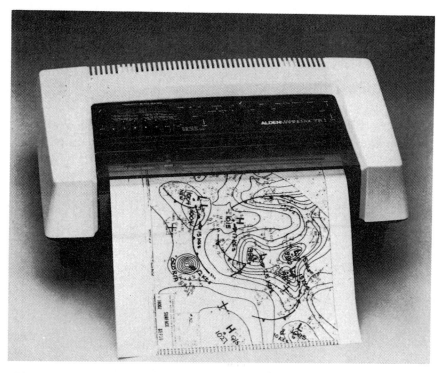

Plate 4 A facsimile receiver.

Test Paper

A. At 0510 on October 4th (zone + 0100) sights were taken of the following stars:

Star	GMT	SA
Dubhe	06h 10m 00s	51° 31'·3
Sirius	06h 10m 45s	23° 04'·8
Mirfak	06h 11m 25s	61° 07'·0

DR position 50° 11'·0N, 9° 30'·0W. Log reading 115·5. Index error +1'·5. Height of eye 3·0m.
Plot the observed position at 0510.

B. From the 0510 observed position the boat continued on a course of 268° T. At 0736 (log reading 127·0) a sight of the sun's lower limb was taken as follows:

GMT	SA
08h 36m 00s	15° 57'·7

At 0736 the boat altered course to 207° T.
Assuming a boat's speed of 4 knots and a current of 080° T, 0·5 knots, what will be the time of the sun's meridian passage?

C. At 1130 (log reading 143·0), the sextant altitude of the sun's lower limb was 35° 20'·3.
Plot the observed position at 1130.

D. At 1130 course was altered to 222° T. Assuming a boat's speed of 5 knots and a current of 080° T, 0·5k, at what time can evening star sights be obtained?

E. At 1746 (log reading 174·0) sights were taken of the following stars:

Star	GMT	SA
Mirfak	18h 46m 00s	19° 37'·7
Altair	18h 46m 35s	47° 54'·4
Arcturus	18h 47m 00s	26° 43'·9
Polaris	18h 47m 50s	49° 20'·7

Plot the observed position at 1746

F. What has been the current set and drift experienced between 0510 and 1746?

Answers on pages 167–72.

Answers to Exercises

Chapter One

1.1. The Ecliptic is the **apparent path of the sun around the celestial sphere over a period of one year.**
The plane of the ecliptic is inclined at an angle of 23° 27′ to the plane of the celestial equator.
1.2. The First Point of Aries is **the position on the celestial sphere where the ecliptic intersects the celestial equator at the Vernal Equinox.** This occurs on about March 21st. This position used to be in constellation of Aries but due to a slow backward movement in the last 2000 years it is currently in the constellation of Pisces.
1.3. a. Declination is **the angular distance of the heavenly body north or south of the celestial equator.**
b. Sidereal hour angle is **the angle subtended at the celestial pole between the meridian passing through the First Point of Aries and that passing through the heavenly body.** It is always measured westwards.
1.4. a. **10′·7 away** from, b. **12′·2 away** from, c. **6′·5 towards**, d. **16′·1 towards**, e. **9′·1 away** from, f. **10′·3 towards**.

Chapter Two.

2.1.
June 22nd

GHA sun 09h		314° 31′·0	dec.	**N23° 26′·1**	d 0·0
increment	10m	+ 2° 30′·0			
GHA sun 09h 10m		**317° 01′·0**			

2.2.
March 7th

GHA Aries 14h	15° 26′·3
increment 46m 10s	+11° 34′·4
GHA Aries 14h 46m 10s	**27° 00′·7**

2.3.
March 9th

GHA moon 06h	7° 49′·8	v 10·9	dec. S16° 50′·9	d 5·0
increment 10m 05s	+ 2° 24′·4		d corrn. + 0′·9	
v corrn.	+ 1′·9		**S16° 51′·8**	
GHA moon 06h 10m 05s	10° 16′·1			
long. W	− 7° 24′·1			
LHA moon 06h 10m 05s	**02° 52′·0**			

2.4.
October 5th

SHA Spica	158° 57′·8	dec. **S11° 03′·4**
GHA Aries 21h	+329° 41′·0	
increment 36m 50s	+ 9° 14′·0	
GHA Spica 21h 36m 50s	497° 52′·8	
long. E	+080° 16′·4	
	578° 09′·2	
	−360° 00′·0	
LHA Spica 21h 36m 50s	**218° 09′·2**	

2.5.
March 7th

GHA Jupiter 10h	159° 06′·2	v 2·8	dec. N11° 21′·1	d 0·1
increment 36m 05s	+ 9° 01′·3		d corrn. + 0′·1	
v corrn.	+ 01′·7		**N11° 21′·2**	
GHA Jupiter 10h 36m 05s	168° 09′·2			
long. W	− 20° 16′·2			
LHA Jupiter 10h 36m 05s	**147° 53′·0**			

Chapter Three

All times GMT
3.1. a. **02h 36m**, b. **15h 21m**, c. **14h 40m**, d. **04h 54m**.
3.2. a. **12h 20m**, b. **10h 24m**, c. **22h 31m**, d. **05h 19m**.

3.3. a. **02h 50m 13d**, b. **19h 20m 3d**. c. **08h 28m 7d**, d. **00h 24m 14d**.
3.4. **20s slow.**
3.5. **05h 09m 35s.**

Chapter Four

4.1. A sextant is **a precision instrument used to measure angles.**
4.2. **Gently swing the sextant from side to side using a pendulum motion**. The heavenly body will appear to describe an arc. The sextant is vertical when the heavenly body is at the lowest point of the arc.
4.3. **39° 03′·4**.
4.4. **There is side error present** caused by incorrect adjustment of the horizon mirror (which is not absolutely perpendicular to the plane of the instrument).
4.5. **The horizon mirror is responsible for both errors** and so the adjustment to correct one error may affect the other.
4.6. **The screws behind the mirrors can work loose** directly affecting the adjustment of the mirrors. The index error affects the accuracy of the sextant reading; other errors have much the same effect.

Chapter Five

5.1	SA		31° 40′·2
	IE	+	2′·4
			31° 42′·6
	dip	−	3′·1
	AA		31° 39′·5
	corrn.	−	1′·6
			31° 37′·9
	additional corrn.	+	0′·1
	TA		**31° 38′·0**
5.2.	SA		45° 34′·2
	IE	−	1′·9
			45° 32′·3
	dip	−	3′·5
	AA		45° 28′·8
	corrn.	−	1′·0
	TA		**45° 27′·8**

5.3	SA		55° 15'·2
	IE	+	1'·7
			55° 16'·9
	dip	−	2'·8
	AA		55° 14'·1
	corrn. LL.	+	15'·3
	TA		**55° 29'·4**

5.4.	SA		59° 30'·0
	IE	+	1'·3
			59° 31'·3
	dip	−	3'·2
	AA		59° 28'·1
	corrn.UL.	+	39'·4
	HP	+	2'·9
			60° 10'·4
		−	30'·0
	TA		**59° 40'·4**

5.5.	SA		35° 29'·4
	IE	−	1'·7
			35° 27'·7
	dip	−	03'·4
			35° 24'·3
	corrn.	−	17'·4
	TA		**35° 06'·9**

Chapter Six

6.1.

	Sunrise	*Sunset*
	h m	h m
	06 16 LMT 8d	18 06 LMT 8d
long. W	+01 20	+01 20
	07 36 GMT 8d at DR	**19 26** GMT 8d at DR

6.2.   *Dawn twilight*
                         h   m
                         04 30+ LMT 23d
long. W   +02 21
                         ─────────
                         06 51 GMT 23d
zone + 2   −02 00
                         ─────────
                         04 51 zone time 23d

6.3.   *Dusk twilight*
                         h   m
                         18 24 LMT 4d
long. E   −05 02
                         ─────────
                         13 22 GMT 4d
zone −5   +05 00
                         ─────────
                         18 22 zone time 4d

6.4.   *Moonrise*   *Moonset*
            h   m   h   m
            23 41 LMT 8d   10 28 LMT 8d
            −22 49 LMT 7d   −09 46 LMT 7d
            ─────────   ─────────
                52   42

$$\frac{42 \cdot 25}{360} \times 52 = 6m \qquad \frac{42 \cdot 25}{360} \times 42 = 5m$$

                    h   m   h   m
                    22 49 LMT 7d   09 46 LMT 7d
corrn. for long.   +   6   +   5
                    ─────────   ─────────
                    22 55   09 51
long. W   +02 49   +02 49
                    ─────────   ─────────
                    01 44 GMT 8d   **12 40** GMT 7d

6.5.   *Sunrise*
                         h   m
                         04 52 LMT 24d
long. W   +02 40
                         ─────────
                         07 32 GMT 24d at DR

Declination sun N23° 24'·5
Amplitude E28·4N
True Azimuth 061·6   074
Compass error **12°·4 W**

6.6.   *Sunset*
                    h   m
                    17 45 LMT 4d
                    − 6 33
                    ─────────
                    11 12 GMT 4d at DR

Declination sun S4° 29′·8
Quadrantal azimuth S85·2W
True azimuth 265·2   25 1
Compass error **14°·3E**

Chapter Seven

7.1.   a.GHA   26° 48′·1   b. GHA   163° 14′·3
        chosen long. −14° 48′·1   chosen long. + 65° 45′·7
                      ─────────   ─────────
        LHA   **12° 00′·0**   LHA   **229° 00′·0**

7.2   *Dawn twilight*
                                h   m
                                03 06 LMT 22d
        long. W   +01 40
                               ─────────
                                04 46 GMT 22d at DR

        GHA Aries 04h   330° 29′·5
        increment 46m   + 11° 31′·9
                               ─────────
        GHA Aries 04h 46m   342° 01′·4
        DR long.   − 24° 59′·9
                               ─────────
                                317° 01′·5 (use 317).

Available:
Capella, Hamal, Alpheratz, Enif, Altair, Vega, Kochab.

Brightest:
Capella, Altair, Vega.

Those chosen:

	Hc	*Zn*
Hamal	27° 29	086° T
Altair	45° 43	208° T
Kochab	46° 24	337° T

Chosen because **the resultant position lines will give the best angle of cut.**

7.3.

	h m
Dawn twilight	05 56 LMT 7d
long. W	+01 40
	07 36 GMT 7d at DR

SHA Altair	62° 33'·1	dec. N8° 48'·8
GHA Aries 7h	+270° 09'·1	
increment 36m	+ 9° 01'·5	
GHA Altair 7h 36m	341° 43'·7	
chosen long. W	− 24° 43'·7	
LHA Altair 7h 36m	317° 00'·0	

Hc	d	Z	Zn
34° 54'	+51	125°	125°
+ 42'			
35° 36'			

Altitude 35° 36'   **Azimuth 125° T**

7.4.

GHA sun 09h	314° 37'·6	dec. N23° 26'·2 d 0·0
increment 36m	+ 9° 00'·0	
GHA sun 09h 36m	323° 37'·6	
chosen long. W	− 17° 37'·6	
LHA sun 09h 36m	306° 00'·0	

	Hc	d	Z	Zn
	40° 19'·4	+43·7	102°	102°
dec. incre. 40·0 +	17'·4			
3·0 +	01'·4			
0·7 +	00'·3			
	40° 38'·5			

Altitude 40° 38'·5   **Azimuth 102° T**

Chapter Eight

8.1.

	h m
	12 02 LMT MP 21d at DR
long. W+01 38	
	13 40 GMT MP 21d at DR

8.2.

```
                      h   m
                     19  41 LMT MP 22d at Greenwich
                     18  59 LMT MP 21d at Greenwich
daily difference         42
```

$$\frac{5\cdot5}{360} \times 42 = 0\cdot64 \text{ minutes (call it 1 minute)}.$$

```
                      h   m
                     19  41 LMT MP 22d at Greenwich
long. corrn.         −    1
                     19  40 LMT MP 22d at DR
long. E              −   22
                     19  18 GMT MP 22d at DR
```

8.3.

```
                      h   m
                     11  48 LMT MP 5d at DR
long. W              + 7  48
                     19  36 GMT MP 5d at DR
```

```
dec. sun         S5° 00'·6        d 1·0
d corrn.      +      0'·6
              S5° 01'·2
        SA    38° 20'·0
        IE  −      1'·0
              38° 19'·0
       dip  −      2'·5
        AA    38° 16'·5
 corrn. LL  +     15'·0
        TA    38° 31'·5
       TZD    51° 28'·5
       dec. +  5° 01'·2
              56° 29'·7S LATITUDE
```

8.4.

```
                      h   m
                     12  11 LMT MP 9d at DR
long. W           +01  25
                     13  36 GMT MP 9d at DR
```

dec. sun 13h	S4° 18'·5	d 1·0−
d corrn.	− 0'·6	
	S4° 17'·9	

SA	43° 02'·4
IE	+ 2'·0
	43° 04'·4
dip	− 2'·9
AA	43° 01'·5
corrn. UL	− 17'·1
TA	42° 44'·4
TZD	47° 15'·6(TA − 90)
dec.	− 4° 17'·9
	42° 57'·7N LATITUDE

Chapter Nine.

9.1.

GHA Aries 08h	285° 11'·6
increment 36m 59s	+ 9° 16'·3
GHA Aries 08h 36m 59s	294° 27'·9
long. W	− 35° 12'·4
LHA Aries 08h 36m 59s	259° 15'·5

SA	51° 47'·3
IE	− 1'·0
	51° 46'·3
dip	− 2'·9
AA	51° 43'·4
corrn.	− 0'·8
TA	51° 42'·6
a_0	+ 1° 33'·3
a_1	+ 0'·6
a_2	+ 0'·4
	53° 16'·9
	− ,1° 00'·0
	52° 16'·9 LATITUDE

9.2.

	h m	
Dusk twilight	18 04	LMT 4d at DR
long. W +	1 33	
	19 37	GMT 4d at DR

GHA Aries 19h	298° 36′·9
increment 37m	+ 9° 16′·5
GHA Aries 19h 37m	307° 53′·4
long. W	− 23° 15′·0
LHA Aries 19h 37m	284° 38′·4

$$a_0 \quad = \quad 1° \ 14′·9$$

DR Lat	54° 12′·6
a_0	− 1° 14′·9
	52° 57′·7
	+ 1° 00′·0

53° 57′·7 Angle to set on sextant.

9.3.

	h m s	
	18 04 22	LMT 3d at DR
long. W +	2 31 40	
	20 36 02	GMT 3d at DR

GHA Aries 20h	312° 40′·2
increment 36m 02s	+ 9° 02′·0
GHA Aries 20h 36m 02s	321° 42′·2
long. W	− 37° 55′·1
LHA Aries 20h 36m 02s	283° 47′·1

SA	52° 30'·4
IE	+ 1'·5
	52° 31'·9
dip	− 3'·0
AA	52° 28'·9
corrn.	− 0·7
TA	52° 28'·2
a_0	+ 1° 15'·6
a_1	+ 0'·7
a_2	+ 0'·9
	53° 45'·4
	− 1° 00'·0
	52° 45'·4 LATITUDE

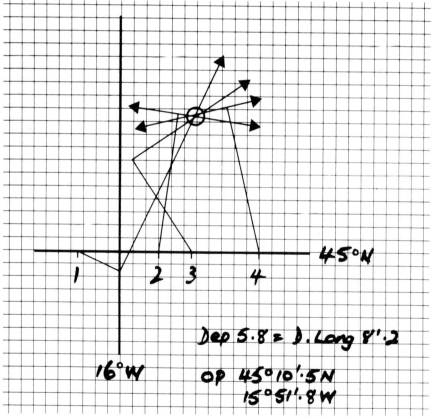

45°N

1 2 3 4

Dep 5.8 = D. Long 8'·2

OP 45°10'·5N
15°51'·8W

16°W

Fig A10.3 Answer 10.3: Plot.

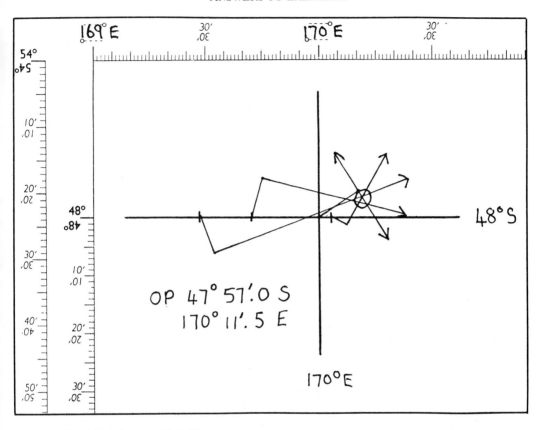

Fig A10.4 Answer 10.4: Plot.

Chapter Ten

10.1. a. **7.9**, b. **33.3**, c. **76.7.**

10.2. a. **50′·1**, b. **156′0**, c. **93′0**

10.3. **See plot.** To convert d.long. to dep. a graph similar to the one shown in Fig. 10.8 can be used or it can be done by calculation.

10.4. **See plot.**

10.5. **See plot.**

Chapter Eleven.

11.1. **Sirius, Canopus, Capella, Rigel, Denebola, Zuben'ubi.**

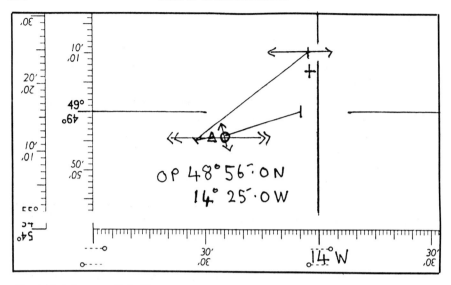

Fig A10.5 Answer 10.5: Plot.

11.2. Angle of cut of position lines, brightness, and altitude. By taking a sight on the beam of the boat and another dead ahead or astern, the two position lines obtained will approximate to the course steered and the distance run. Similarly a sight taken due north or south (for example Polaris) and one due east or west will give position lines corresponding to latitude and longitude direct. Both these methods are used by ocean navigators but such sights are not always easy to obtain and are no substitute for three or more sights giving a good angle of cut of the position lines.

11.3.

a. A star globe is **easy to use, but difficult to stow** on a small boat. It is also expensive.

b. A star finder is **fairly easy to use and stow** on a small boat and **relatively inexpensive**. It **has a limited life**, scratches easily and tends to warp in hot climates.

c. A star chart **can only be sensibly used to identify relative positions of stars**.

In all these cases, the positions of the planets have to be marked in separately.

Chapter Fourteen

The page number upon which these answers are to be found is printed in brackets after the questions.

Chapter Fifteen

15.1. A great circle track may pass through an unsuitable area (such as one containing icebergs) whereas **a composite track can be shaped to stay in safe water or in favourable winds.**

15.2. *Nautical Almanac*, **Sight Reduction Tables** (or an almanac which contains both), **mathematical tables** (*Norie's Nautical Tables*), **Admiralty List of Lights*, *Admiralty List of Radio Signals*, *Sailing **Directions (Pilot)**, **Charts*, **Routeing* **Charts (Pilot Charts)**, ***Plotting sheets**, *Admiralty Notices to Mariners*.
* As appropriate to the voyage.

15.3. **Prevailing winds, ocean currents, ice and fog areas, tracks of tropical revolving storms, shipping routes.** Routeing charts are published for each ocean for each month of the year.

15.4.
  a. The passage should be planned **to avoid contrary winds and currents, fog and poor visibility; winter gales** in higher latitudes and **tropical revolving storms** in lower latitudes.
  b. The route should be planned **to avoid areas where there are icebergs, fog and poor visibility, with consideration given to favourable ocean currents and winds.**
  Various publications such as *Ocean Passages of the World* give details of the best routes for sailing boats which vary throughout the year.

15.5. **Steering compass, hand bearing compass, towed log** with spare rotator, **radio direction finder, sextant, chronometer, echo sounder.**

Test Paper

A.	*Dubhe*		*Sirius*		*Mirfak*
October 4th					
GHA Aries 06h	103° 04'·9		103° 04'·9		103° 04'·9
increment 10m	2° 30'·4	10m 45s	2° 41'·7	11m 25s	2° 51'·7
GHA Aries	105° 35'·3		105° 46'·6		105° 56'·6
Chosen long. W	9° 35'·3		9° 46'·6		9° 56'·6
ARIES	96° 00'·0		96° 00'·0		96° 00'·0

A.	Dubhe	Sirius	Mirfak
Chosen lat. 50° N			
Hc	51° 21'·0	23° 10'·0	61° 17'·0
Zn	045° T	175° T	287° T
SA	51° 31'·3	23° 04'·8	61° 07'·0
IE	+1'·5	+1'·5	+1'·5
	51° 32'·8	23° 06'·3	61° 08'·5
dip	−3'·0	−3'·0	−3'·0
AA	51° 29'·8	23° 03'·3	61° 05'·5
corrn.	−0'·8	−2'·3	−0'·5
TA	51° 29'·0	23° 01'·0	61° 05°·0
CA	51° 21'·0	23° 10'·0	61° 17'·0
intercept	8'·0 Towards	9'·0 Away from	12'·0 Away from

0510 OP 50° 10'·0N, 9° 32'·5W

See plot.

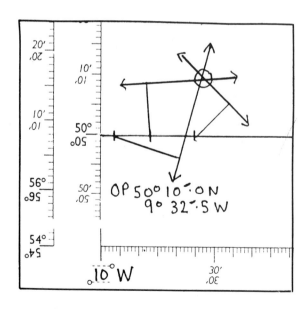

Fig TA Answer A: Plot.

B.

0736 EP 50° 09′·8N, 9° 48′·5W.

GHA sun 08h	302° 49′·6	dec.	S4° 26′·9
increment 36m	+ 9° 00′·0	d 1·0 +	0′·6
GHA sun	311° 49′·6		S4° 27′·5
Chosen long. W	− 9° 49′·6		
LHA sun	302° 00′·0		

Chosen lat. 50° N
Chosen dec. S4° 28′

Hc	d	Z	Zn
16° 38′	−49	118	**118°T**
− 23′			
16° 15′			

SA	15° 57′·7	
IE & dip	− 1′·5	
AA	15° 56′·2	
corrn. LL	+ 12′·9	
TA	16° 09′·1	
CA	16° 15′·0	
intercept	**5′·9** Away from	

	h m	
MP	11 49	LMT
long. W	+ 40	
	12 29−	GMT at DR
zone + 1	01 00	
	11 29	zone time

C.

dec. 12h	S4° 30′·8+	
29m	+ 0′·5	(no increment table available:
	S4° 31′·3	interpolate between 12h and 13h)

SA		35° 20′·3
IE & dip	−	1′·5
AA		35° 18′·8
corrn. LL	+	14′·9
TA		35° 33′·7
from 90°		90° 00′·0
TZD		54° 26′·3
dec.		4° 31′·3
		49° 55′·0 N LATITUDE

1130 OP 49° 55′·0N, 10° 02′·0W
See plot below.

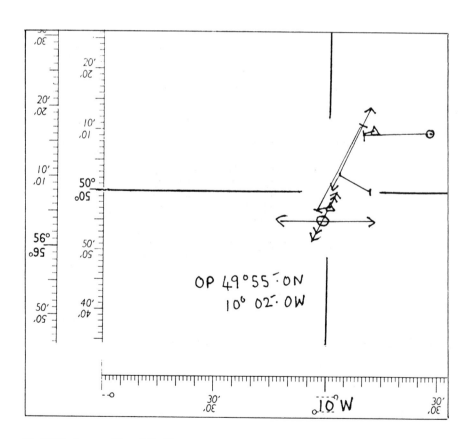

Fig TBC Answer B and C: Plot.

D.

Zone Time Civil Twilight   1746.
The stars and the horizon should be visible between 1746 and 1806.
See plot opposite.

E.

1746 EP 49° 32'·5N, 10° 29'·5W.

	Mirfak	*Altair*	*Arcturus*	*Polaris*
	(18h 46m 00s)	*(18h 46m 35s)*	*(18h 47m 00s)*	*(18h 47m 50s)*

GHA

	Mirfak	Altair	Arcturus	Polaris
Aries 18h	283° 34'·4	283° 34'·4	283° 34'·4	283° 34'·4
increment	11° 31'·9	11° 40'·7	11° 46'·9	11° 59'·5
	295° 06'·3	295° 15'·1	295° 21'·3	295° 33'·9
chosen long.W	10° 06'·3	10° 15'·1	10° 21'·3	10° 29'·5 (EP long)
	285° 00'·0	285° 00'·0	285° 00'·0	285° 04'·4
Hc	20° 03'·0	47° 32'·0	26° 35'·0	
Zn	034° T	162° T	269° T	
SA	19° 37'·7	47° 54'·4	26° 43'·9	49° 20'·7
IE & dip	− 1'·5	− 1'·5	− 1'·5	− 1'·5
	19° 36'·2	47° 52'·9	26° 42'·4	49° 19'·2
corrn.	− 2'·7	− 0'·9	− 1'·9	− 0'·8
TA	19° 33'·5	47° 52'·0	26° 40'·5	49° 18'·4
CA	20° 03'·0	47° 32'·0	26° 35'·0	a_0 +1° 14'·6
intercept	29'·5	20'·0	5'·5	a_1 + 0'·6
	Away from	Towards	Towards	a_2 + 0'·9
				50° 34'·5

less 1° −1° 00'·0

LATITUDE 49° 34'·5N

1746 OP 49° 34'·5N, 10° 31'·0W. See plot opposite.

F.

041° T, 2·9M

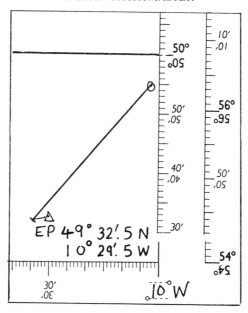

Fig TD Answer D: Plot.

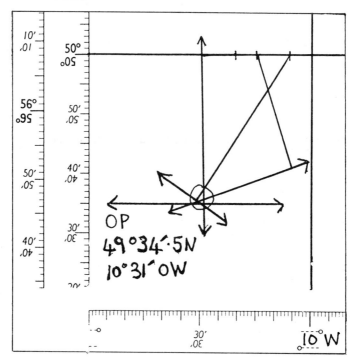

Fig TE Answer E: Plot.

Appendices

A Extracts from the *Nautical Almanac NP 314*

B Extracts from *AP 3270 Volumes 1 and 3*

C Extracts from *NP 401 Volume 4*

D Extracts from *Reed's Nautical Almanac* **and** *Norie's Nautical Tables*

E Sight Reduction Forms

F Shorebased Syllabus of RYA/DTp Yachtmaster Ocean Certificate

Appendix A

Extracts from the *Nautical Almanac NP 314*

CONVERSION OF ARC TO TIME

0°–59°		60°–119°		120°–179°		180°–239°		240°–299°		300°–359°			0'·00	0'·25	0'·50	0'·75
°	h m	°	h m	°	h m	°	h m	°	h m	°	h m	'	m s	m s	m s	m s
0	0 00	60	4 00	120	8 00	180	12 00	240	16 00	300	20 00	0	0 00	0 01	0 02	0 03
1	0 04	61	4 04	121	8 04	181	12 04	241	16 04	301	20 04	1	0 04	0 05	0 06	0 07
2	0 08	62	4 08	122	8 08	182	12 08	242	16 08	302	20 08	2	0 08	0 09	0 10	0 11
3	0 12	63	4 12	123	8 12	183	12 12	243	16 12	303	20 12	3	0 12	0 13	0 14	0 15
4	0 16	64	4 16	124	8 16	184	12 16	244	16 16	304	20 16	4	0 16	0 17	0 18	0 19
5	0 20	65	4 20	125	8 20	185	12 20	245	16 20	305	20 20	5	0 20	0 21	0 22	0 23
6	0 24	66	4 24	126	8 24	186	12 24	246	16 24	306	20 24	6	0 24	0 25	0 26	0 27
7	0 28	67	4 28	127	8 28	187	12 28	247	16 28	307	20 28	7	0 28	0 29	0 30	0 31
8	0 32	68	4 32	128	8 32	188	12 32	248	16 32	308	20 32	8	0 32	0 33	0 34	0 35
9	0 36	69	4 36	129	8 36	189	12 36	249	16 36	309	20 36	9	0 36	0 37	0 38	0 39
10	0 40	70	4 40	130	8 40	190	12 40	250	16 40	310	20 40	10	0 40	0 41	0 42	0 43
11	0 44	71	4 44	131	8 44	191	12 44	251	16 44	311	20 44	11	0 44	0 45	0 46	0 47
12	0 48	72	4 48	132	8 48	192	12 48	252	16 48	312	20 48	12	0 48	0 49	0 50	0 51
13	0 52	73	4 52	133	8 52	193	12 52	253	16 52	313	20 52	13	0 52	0 53	0 54	0 55
14	0 56	74	4 56	134	8 56	194	12 56	254	16 56	314	20 56	14	0 56	0 57	0 58	0 59
15	1 00	75	5 00	135	9 00	195	13 00	255	17 00	315	21 00	15	1 00	1 01	1 02	1 03
16	1 04	76	5 04	136	9 04	196	13 04	256	17 04	316	21 04	16	1 04	1 05	1 06	1 07
17	1 08	77	5 08	137	9 08	197	13 08	257	17 08	317	21 08	17	1 08	1 09	1 10	1 11
18	1 12	78	5 12	138	9 12	198	13 12	258	17 12	318	21 12	18	1 12	1 13	1 14	1 15
19	1 16	79	5 16	139	9 16	199	13 16	259	17 16	319	21 16	19	1 16	1 17	1 18	1 19
20	1 20	80	5 20	140	9 20	200	13 20	260	17 20	320	21 20	20	1 20	1 21	1 22	1 23
21	1 24	81	5 24	141	9 24	201	13 24	261	17 24	321	21 24	21	1 24	1 25	1 26	1 27
22	1 28	82	5 28	142	9 28	202	13 28	262	17 28	322	21 28	22	1 28	1 29	1 30	1 31
23	1 32	83	5 32	143	9 32	203	13 32	263	17 32	323	21 32	23	1 32	1 33	1 34	1 35
24	1 36	84	5 36	144	9 36	204	13 36	264	17 36	324	21 36	24	1 36	1 37	1 38	1 39
25	1 40	85	5 40	145	9 40	205	13 40	265	17 40	325	21 40	25	1 40	1 41	1 42	1 43
26	1 44	86	5 44	146	9 44	206	13 44	266	17 44	326	21 44	26	1 44	1 45	1 46	1 47
27	1 48	87	5 48	147	9 48	207	13 48	267	17 48	327	21 48	27	1 48	1 49	1 50	1 51
28	1 52	88	5 52	148	9 52	208	13 52	268	17 52	328	21 52	28	1 52	1 53	1 54	1 55
29	1 56	89	5 56	149	9 56	209	13 56	269	17 56	329	21 56	29	1 56	1 57	1 58	1 59
30	2 00	90	6 00	150	10 00	210	14 00	270	18 00	330	22 00	30	2 00	2 01	2 02	2 03
31	2 04	91	6 04	151	10 04	211	14 04	271	18 04	331	22 04	31	2 04	2 05	2 06	2 07
32	2 08	92	6 08	152	10 08	212	14 08	272	18 08	332	22 08	32	2 08	2 09	2 10	2 11
33	2 12	93	6 12	153	10 12	213	14 12	273	18 12	333	22 12	33	2 12	2 13	2 14	2 15
34	2 16	94	6 16	154	10 16	214	14 16	274	18 16	334	22 16	34	2 16	2 17	2 18	2 19
35	2 20	95	6 20	155	10 20	215	14 20	275	18 20	335	22 20	35	2 20	2 21	2 22	2 23
36	2 24	96	6 24	156	10 24	216	14 24	276	18 24	336	22 24	36	2 24	2 25	2 26	2 27
37	2 28	97	6 28	157	10 28	217	14 28	277	18 28	337	22 28	37	2 28	2 29	2 30	2 31
38	2 32	98	6 32	158	10 32	218	14 32	278	18 32	338	22 32	38	2 32	2 33	2 34	2 35
39	2 36	99	6 36	159	10 36	219	14 36	279	18 36	339	22 36	39	2 36	2 37	2 38	2 39
40	2 40	100	6 40	160	10 40	220	14 40	280	18 40	340	22 40	40	2 40	2 41	2 42	2 43
41	2 44	101	6 44	161	10 44	221	14 44	281	18 44	341	22 44	41	2 44	2 45	2 46	2 47
42	2 48	102	6 48	162	10 48	222	14 48	282	18 48	342	22 48	42	2 48	2 49	2 50	2 51
43	2 52	103	6 52	163	10 52	223	14 52	283	18 52	343	22 52	43	2 52	2 53	2 54	2 55
44	2 56	104	6 56	164	10 56	224	14 56	284	18 56	344	22 56	44	2 56	2 57	2 58	2 59
45	3 00	105	7 00	165	11 00	225	15 00	285	19 00	345	23 00	45	3 00	3 01	3 02	3 03
46	3 04	106	7 04	166	11 04	226	15 04	286	19 04	346	23 04	46	3 04	3 05	3 06	3 07
47	3 08	107	7 08	167	11 08	227	15 08	287	19 08	347	23 08	47	3 08	3 09	3 10	3 11
48	3 12	108	7 12	168	11 12	228	15 12	288	19 12	348	23 12	48	3 12	3 13	3 14	3 15
49	3 16	109	7 16	169	11 16	229	15 16	289	19 16	349	23 16	49	3 16	3 17	3 18	3 19
50	3 20	110	7 20	170	11 20	230	15 20	290	19 20	350	23 20	50	3 20	3 21	3 22	3 23
51	3 24	111	7 24	171	11 24	231	15 24	291	19 24	351	23 24	51	3 24	3 25	3 26	3 27
52	3 28	112	7 28	172	11 28	232	15 28	292	19 28	352	23 28	52	3 28	3 29	3 30	3 31
53	3 32	113	7 32	173	11 32	233	15 32	293	19 32	353	23 32	53	3 32	3 33	3 34	3 35
54	3 36	114	7 36	174	11 36	234	15 36	294	19 36	354	23 36	54	3 36	3 37	3 38	3 39
55	3 40	115	7 40	175	11 40	235	15 40	295	19 40	355	23 40	55	3 40	3 41	3 42	3 43
56	3 44	116	7 44	176	11 44	236	15 44	296	19 44	356	23 44	56	3 44	3 45	3 46	3 47
57	3 48	117	7 48	177	11 48	237	15 48	297	19 48	357	23 48	57	3 48	3 49	3 50	3 51
58	3 52	118	7 52	178	11 52	238	15 52	298	19 52	358	23 52	58	3 52	3 53	3 54	3 55
59	3 56	119	7 56	179	11 56	239	15 56	299	19 56	359	23 56	59	3 56	3 57	3 58	3 59

The above table is for converting expressions in arc to their equivalent in time ; its main use in this Almanac is for the conversion of longitude for application to L.M.T. (*added* if *west*, *subtracted* if *east*) to give G.M.T. or vice versa, particularly in the case of sunrise, sunset, etc.

Extract Number A1

ALTITUDE CORRECTION TABLES 10°-90°—SUN, STARS, PLANETS

SUN

OCT.—MAR. App. Alt.	Lower Limb	Upper Limb	APR.—SEPT. App. Alt.	Lower Limb	Upper Limb
° ′	′	′	° ′	′	′
9 34			9 39		
	+10·8	−21·5		+10·6	−21·2
9 45			9 51		
	+10·9	−21·4		+10·7	−21·1
9 56			10 03		
	+11·0	−21·3		+10·8	−21·0
10 08			10 15		
	+11·1	−21·2		+10·9	−20·9
10 21			10 27		
	+11·2	−21·1		+11·0	−20·8
10 34			10 40		
	+11·3	−21·0		+11·1	−20·7
10 47			10 54		
	+11·4	−20·9		+11·2	−20·6
11 01			11 08		
	+11·5	−20·8		+11·3	−20·5
11 15			11 23		
	+11·6	−20·7		+11·4	−20·4
11 30			11 38		
	+11·7	−20·6		+11·5	−20·3
11 46			11 54		
	+11·8	−20·5		+11·6	−20·2
12 02			12 10		
	+11·9	−20·4		+11·7	−20·1
12 19			12 28		
	+12·0	−20·3		+11·8	−20·0
12 37			12 46		
	+12·1	−20·2		+11·9	−19·9
12 55			13 05		
	+12·2	−20·1		+12·0	−19·8
13 14			13 24		
	+12·3	−20·0		+12·1	−19·7
13 35			13 45		
	+12·4	−19·9		+12·2	−19·6
13 56			14 07		
	+12·5	−19·8		+12·3	−19·5
14 18			14 30		
	+12·6	−19·7		+12·4	−19·4
14 42			14 54		
	+12·7	−19·6		+12·5	−19·3
15 06			15 19		
	+12·8	−19·5		+12·6	−19·2
15 32			15 46		
	+12·9	−19·4		+12·7	−19·1
15 59			16 14		
	+13·0	−19·3		+12·8	−19·0
16 28			16 44		
	+13·1	−19·2		+12·9	−18·9
16 59			17 15		
	+13·2	−19·1		+13·0	−18·8
17 32			17 48		
	+13·3	−19·0		+13·1	−18·7
18 06			18 24		
	+13·4	−18·9		+13·2	−18·6
18 42			19 01		
	+13·5	−18·8		+13·3	−18·5
19 21			19 42		
	+13·6	−18·7		+13·4	−18·4
20 03			20 25		
	+13·7	−18·6		+13·5	−18·3
20 48			21 11		
	+13·8	−18·5		+13·6	−18·2
21 35			22 00		
	+13·9	−18·4		+13·7	−18·1
22 26			22 54		
	+14·0	−18·3		+13·8	−18·0
23 22			23 51		
	+14·1	−18·2		+13·9	−17·9
24 21			24 53		
	+14·2	−18·1		+14·0	−17·8
25 26			26 00		
	+14·3	−18·0		+14·1	−17·7
26 36			27 13		
	+14·4	−17·9		+14·2	−17·6
27 52			28 33		
	+14·5	−17·8		+14·3	−17·5
29 15			30 00		
	+14·6	−17·7		+14·4	−17·4
30 46			31 35		
	+14·7	−17·6		+14·5	−17·3
32 26			33 20		
	+14·8	−17·5		+14·6	−17·2
34 17			35 17		
	+14·9	−17·4		+14·7	−17·1
36 20			37 26		
	+15·0	−17·3		+14·8	−17·0
38 36			39 50		
	+15·1	−17·2		+14·9	−16·9
41 08			42 31		
	+15·2	−17·1		+15·0	−16·8
43 59			45 31		
	+15·3	−17·0		+15·1	−16·7
47 10			48 55		
	+15·4	−16·9		+15·2	−16·6
50 46			52 44		
	+15·5	−16·8		+15·3	−16·5
54 49			57 02		
	+15·6	−16·7		+15·4	−16·4
59 23			61 51		
	+15·7	−16·6		+15·5	−16·3
64 30			67 17		
	+15·8	−16·5		+15·6	−16·2
70 12			73 16		
	+15·9	−16·4		+15·7	−16·1
76 26			79 43		
	+16·0	−16·3		+15·8	−16·0
83 05			86 32		
	+16·1	−16·2		+15·9	−15·9
90 00			90 00		

STARS AND PLANETS

App. Alt.	Corrⁿ
° ′	′
9 56	
	−5·3
10 08	
	−5·2
10 20	
	−5·1
10 33	
	−5·0
10 46	
	−4·9
11 00	
	−4·8
11 14	
	−4·7
11 29	
	−4·6
11 45	
	−4·5
12 01	
	−4·4
12 18	
	−4·3
12 35	
	−4·2
12 54	
	−4·1
13 13	
	−4·0
13 33	
	−3·9
13 54	
	−3·8
14 16	
	−3·7
14 40	
	−3·6
15 04	
	−3·5
15 30	
	−3·4
15 57	
	−3·3
16 26	
	−3·2
16 56	
	−3·1
17 28	
	−3·0
18 02	
	−2·9
18 38	
	−2·8
19 17	
	−2·7
19 58	
	−2·6
20 42	
	−2·5
21 28	
	−2·4
22 19	
	−2·3
23 13	
	−2·2
24 11	
	−2·1
25 14	
	−2·0
26 22	
	−1·9
27 36	
	−1·8
28 56	
	−1·7
30 24	
	−1·6
32 00	
	−1·5
33 45	
	−1·4
35 40	
	−1·3
37 48	
	−1·2
40 08	
	−1·1
42 44	
	−1·0
45 36	
	−0·9
48 47	
	−0·8
52 18	
	−0·7
56 11	
	−0·6
60 28	
	−0·5
65 08	
	−0·4
70 11	
	−0·3
75 34	
	−0·2
81 13	
	−0·1
87 03	
	0·0
90 00	

Additional Corrⁿ (App. Alt. / Additional Corrⁿ)

1980

VENUS

Period	App. Alt.	Additional Corrⁿ
Jan. 1–Feb. 26	0°	
		+0′·1
	42	
Feb. 27–Apr. 13	0°	
		+0′·2
	47	
Apr. 14–May 9	0°	
		+0′·3
	46	
May 10–May 25	0°	
		+0′·4
	11	
		+0·5
	41	
May 26–June 3	0°	
		+0′·5
	6	
		+0·6
	20	
		+0·7
	31	
June 4–June 26	0°	
		+0′·6
	4	
		+0·7
	12	
		+0·8
	22	
June 27–July 6	0°	
		+0′·5
	6	
		+0·6
	20	
		+0·7
	31	
July 7–July 21	0°	
		+0′·4
	11	
		+0·5
	41	
July 22–Aug. 17	0°	
		+0′·3
	46	
Aug. 18–Oct. 2	0°	
		+0′·2
	47	
Oct. 3–Dec. 31	0°	
		+0′·1
	42	

MARS

Period	App. Alt.	Additional Corrⁿ
Jan. 1–Apr. 28	0°	
		+0′·2
	41	
		+0·1
	75	
Apr. 29–Dec. 31	0°	
		+0′·1
	60	

DIP

Ht. of Eye (m)	Corrⁿ	Ht. of Eye (ft.)
2·4		8·0
	−2′·8	
2·6		8·6
	−2·9	
2·8		9·2
	−3·0	
3·0		9·8
	−3·1	
3·2		10·5
	−3·2	
3·4		11·2
	−3·3	
3·6		11·9
	−3·4	
3·8		12·6
	−3·5	
4·0		13·3
	−3·6	
4·3		14·1
	−3·7	
4·5		14·9
	−3·8	
4·7		15·7
	−3·9	
5·0		16·5
	−4·0	
5·2		17·4
	−4·1	
5·5		18·3
	−4·2	
5·8		19·1
	−4·3	
6·1		20·1
	−4·4	
6·3		21·0
	−4·5	
6·6		22·0
	−4·6	
6·9		22·9
	−4·7	
7·2		23·9
	−4·8	
7·5		24·9
	−4·9	
7·9		26·0
	−5·0	
8·2		27·1
	−5·1	
8·5		28·1
	−5·2	
8·8		29·2
	−5·3	
9·2		30·4
	−5·4	
9·5		31·5
	−5·5	
9·9		32·7
	−5·6	
10·3		33·9
	−5·7	
10·6		35·1
	−5·8	
11·0		36·3
	−5·9	
11·4		37·6
	−6·0	
11·8		38·9
	−6·1	
12·2		40·1
	−6·2	
12·6		41·5
	−6·3	
13·0		42·8
	−6·4	
13·4		44·2
	−6·5	
13·8		45·5
	−6·6	
14·2		46·9
	−6·7	
14·7		48·4
	−6·8	
15·1		49·8
	−6·9	
15·5		51·3
	−7·0	
16·0		52·8
	−7·1	
16·5		54·3
	−7·2	
16·9		55·8
	−7·3	
17·4		57·4
	−7·4	
17·9		58·9
	−7·5	
18·4		60·5
	−7·6	
18·8		62·1
	−7·7	
19·3		63·8
	−7·8	
19·8		65·4
	−7·9	
20·4		67·1
	−8·0	
20·9		68·8
	−8·1	
21·4		70·5

Ht. of Eye	Corrⁿ
m	′
1·0	−1·8
1·5	−2·2
2·0	−2·5
2·5	−2·8
3·0	−3·0
See table ←	
m	′
20	−7·9
22	−8·3
24	−8·6
26	−9·0
28	−9·3
30	−9·6
32	−10·0
34	−10·3
36	−10·6
38	−10·8
40	−11·1
42	−11·4
44	−11·7
46	−11·9
48	−12·2
ft.	′
2	−1·4
4	−1·9
6	−2·4
8	−2·7
10	−3·1
See table ←	
ft.	′
70	−8·1
75	−8·4
80	−8·7
85	−8·9
90	−9·2
95	−9·5
100	−9·7
105	−9·9
110	−10·2
115	−10·4
120	−10·6
125	−10·8
130	−11·1
135	−11·3
140	−11·5
145	−11·7
150	−11·9
155	−12·1

App. Alt. = Apparent altitude = Sextant altitude corrected for index error and dip.

Extract Number A2

ALTITUDE CORRECTION TABLES 35°-90°—MOON

App. Alt.	35°-39° Corrⁿ	40°-44° Corrⁿ	45°-49° Corrⁿ	50°-54° Corrⁿ	55°-59° Corrⁿ	60°-64° Corrⁿ	65°-69° Corrⁿ	70°-74° Corrⁿ	75°-79° Corrⁿ	80°-84° Corrⁿ	85°-89° Corrⁿ	App. Alt.
00	35 56·5	40 53·7	45 50·5	50 46·9	55 43·1	60 38·9	65 34·6	70 30·1	75 25·3	80 20·5	85 15·6	00
10	56·4	53·6	50·4	46·8	42·9	38·8	34·4	29·9	25·2	20·4	15·5	10
20	56·3	53·5	50·2	46·7	42·8	38·7	34·3	29·7	25·0	20·2	15·3	20
30	56·2	53·4	50·1	46·5	42·7	38·5	34·1	29·6	24·9	20·0	15·1	30
40	56·2	53·3	50·0	46·4	42·5	38·4	34·0	29·4	24·7	19·9	15·0	40
50	56·1	53·2	49·9	46·3	42·4	38·2	33·8	29·3	24·5	19·7	14·8	50
00	36 56·0	41 53·1	46 49·8	51 46·2	56 42·3	61 38·1	66 33·7	71 29·1	76 24·4	81 19·6	86 14·6	00
10	55·9	53·0	49·7	46·0	42·1	37·9	33·5	29·0	24·2	19·4	14·5	10
20	55·8	52·8	49·5	45·9	42·0	37·8	33·4	28·8	24·1	19·2	14·3	20
30	55·7	52·7	49·4	45·8	41·8	37·7	33·2	28·7	23·9	19·1	14·1	30
40	55·6	52·6	49·3	45·7	41·7	37·5	33·1	28·5	23·8	18·9	14·0	40
50	55·5	52·5	49·2	45·5	41·6	37·4	32·9	28·3	23·6	18·7	13·8	50
00	37 55·4	42 52·4	47 49·1	52 45·4	57 41·4	62 37·2	67 32·8	72 28·2	77 23·4	82 18·6	87 13·7	00
10	55·3	52·3	49·0	45·3	41·3	37·1	32·6	28·0	23·3	18·4	13·5	10
20	55·2	52·2	48·8	45·2	41·2	36·9	32·5	27·9	23·1	18·2	13·3	20
30	55·1	52·1	48·7	45·0	41·0	36·8	32·3	27·7	22·9	18·1	13·2	30
40	55·0	52·0	48·6	44·9	40·9	36·6	32·2	27·6	22·8	17·9	13·0	40
50	55·0	51·9	48·5	44·8	40·8	36·5	32·0	27·4	22·6	17·8	12·8	50
00	38 54·9	43 51·8	48 48·4	53 44·6	58 40·6	63 36·4	68 31·9	73 27·2	78 22·5	83 17·6	88 12·7	00
10	54·8	51·7	48·2	44·5	40·5	36·2	31·7	27·1	22·3	17·4	12·5	10
20	54·7	51·6	48·1	44·4	40·3	36·1	31·6	26·9	22·1	17·3	12·3	20
30	54·6	51·5	48·0	44·2	40·2	35·9	31·4	26·8	22·0	17·1	12·2	30
40	54·5	51·4	47·9	44·1	40·1	35·8	31·3	26·6	21·8	16·9	12·0	40
50	54·4	51·2	47·8	44·0	39·9	35·6	31·1	26·5	21·7	16·8	11·8	50
00	39 54·3	44 51·1	49 47·6	54 43·9	59 39·8	64 35·5	69 31·0	74 26·3	79 21·5	84 16·6	89 11·7	00
10	54·2	51·0	47·5	43·7	39·6	35·3	30·8	26·1	21·3	16·5	11·5	10
20	54·1	50·9	47·4	43·6	39·5	35·2	30·7	26·0	21·2	16·3	11·4	20
30	54·0	50·8	47·3	43·5	39·4	35·0	30·5	25·8	21·0	16·1	11·2	30
40	53·9	50·7	47·2	43·3	39·2	34·9	30·4	25·7	20·9	16·0	11·0	40
50	53·8	50·6	47·0	43·2	39·1	34·7	30·2	25·5	20·7	15·8	10·9	50

H.P.	L U	L U	L U	L U	L U	L U	L U	L U	L U	L U	L U	H.P.
54·0	1·1 1·7	1·3 1·9	1·5 2·1	1·7 2·4	2·0 2·6	2·3 2·9	2·6 3·2	2·9 3·5	3·2 3·8	3·5 4·1	3·8 4·5	54·0
54·3	1·4 1·8	1·6 2·0	1·8 2·2	2·0 2·5	2·3 2·7	2·5 3·0	2·8 3·2	3·0 3·5	3·3 3·8	3·6 4·1	3·9 4·4	54·3
54·6	1·7 2·0	1·9 2·2	2·1 2·4	2·3 2·6	2·5 2·8	2·7 3·0	3·0 3·3	3·2 3·5	3·5 3·8	3·7 4·1	4·0 4·3	54·6
54·9	2·0 2·2	2·2 2·3	2·3 2·5	2·5 2·7	2·7 2·9	2·9 3·1	3·2 3·3	3·4 3·5	3·6 3·8	3·9 4·0	4·1 4·3	54·9
55·2	2·3 2·3	2·5 2·4	2·6 2·6	2·8 2·8	3·0 2·9	3·2 3·1	3·4 3·3	3·6 3·5	3·8 3·7	4·0 4·0	4·2 4·2	55·2
55·5	2·7 2·5	2·8 2·6	2·9 2·7	3·1 2·9	3·2 3·0	3·4 3·2	3·6 3·4	3·7 3·5	3·9 3·7	4·1 3·9	4·3 4·1	55·5
55·8	3·0 2·6	3·1 2·7	3·2 2·8	3·3 3·0	3·5 3·1	3·6 3·3	3·8 3·4	3·9 3·6	4·1 3·7	4·2 3·9	4·4 4·0	55·8
56·1	3·3 2·8	3·4 2·9	3·5 3·0	3·6 3·1	3·7 3·2	3·8 3·3	4·0 3·4	4·1 3·6	4·2 3·7	4·4 3·8	4·5 4·0	56·1
56·4	3·6 2·9	3·7 3·0	3·8 3·1	3·9 3·2	3·9 3·3	4·0 3·4	4·1 3·5	4·3 3·6	4·4 3·7	4·5 3·8	4·6 3·9	56·4
56·7	3·9 3·1	4·0 3·1	4·1 3·2	4·1 3·3	4·2 3·3	4·3 3·4	4·3 3·5	4·4 3·6	4·5 3·7	4·6 3·8	4·7 3·8	56·7
57·0	4·3 3·2	4·3 3·3	4·3 3·3	4·4 3·4	4·4 3·4	4·5 3·5	4·5 3·5	4·6 3·6	4·7 3·6	4·7 3·7	4·8 3·8	57·0
57·3	4·6 3·4	4·6 3·4	4·6 3·4	4·6 3·5	4·7 3·5	4·7 3·5	4·7 3·6	4·8 3·6	4·8 3·6	4·8 3·7	4·9 3·7	57·3
57·6	4·9 3·6	4·9 3·6	4·9 3·6	4·9 3·6	4·9 3·6	4·9 3·6	4·9 3·6	5·0 3·6	5·0 3·6	5·0 3·6	5·0 3·6	57·6
57·9	5·2 3·7	5·2 3·7	5·2 3·7	5·2 3·7	5·2 3·7	5·1 3·6	5·1 3·6	5·1 3·6	5·1 3·6	5·1 3·6	5·1 3·6	57·9
58·2	5·5 3·9	5·5 3·8	5·5 3·8	5·4 3·8	5·4 3·7	5·4 3·7	5·3 3·7	5·3 3·6	5·2 3·6	5·2 3·5	5·2 3·5	58·2
58·5	5·9 4·0	5·8 4·0	5·8 3·9	5·7 3·9	5·6 3·8	5·6 3·8	5·5 3·7	5·5 3·6	5·4 3·6	5·3 3·5	5·3 3·4	58·5
58·8	6·2 4·2	6·1 4·1	6·0 4·1	6·0 4·0	5·9 3·9	5·8 3·8	5·7 3·7	5·6 3·6	5·5 3·5	5·4 3·5	5·3 3·4	58·8
59·1	6·5 4·3	6·4 4·3	6·3 4·2	6·2 4·1	6·1 4·0	6·0 3·9	5·9 3·8	5·8 3·6	5·7 3·5	5·6 3·4	5·4 3·3	59·1
59·4	6·8 4·5	6·7 4·4	6·6 4·3	6·5 4·2	6·4 4·1	6·2 3·9	6·1 3·8	6·0 3·7	5·8 3·5	5·7 3·4	5·5 3·2	59·4
59·7	7·1 4·6	7·0 4·5	6·9 4·4	6·8 4·3	6·6 4·1	6·5 4·0	6·3 3·8	6·2 3·7	6·0 3·5	5·8 3·3	5·6 3·2	59·7
60·0	7·5 4·8	7·3 4·7	7·2 4·5	7·0 4·4	6·9 4·2	6·7 4·0	6·5 3·9	6·3 3·7	6·1 3·5	5·9 3·3	5·7 3·1	60·0
60·3	7·8 5·0	7·6 4·8	7·5 4·7	7·3 4·5	7·1 4·3	6·9 4·1	6·7 3·9	6·5 3·7	6·3 3·5	6·0 3·2	5·8 3·0	60·3
60·6	8·1 5·1	7·9 5·0	7·7 4·8	7·6 4·6	7·3 4·4	7·1 4·2	6·9 3·9	6·7 3·7	6·4 3·4	6·2 3·2	5·9 2·9	60·6
60·9	8·4 5·3	8·2 5·1	8·0 4·9	7·8 4·7	7·6 4·5	7·3 4·2	7·1 4·0	6·8 3·7	6·6 3·4	6·3 3·2	6·0 2·9	60·9
61·2	8·7 5·4	8·5 5·2	8·3 5·0	8·1 4·8	7·8 4·5	7·6 4·3	7·3 4·0	7·0 3·7	6·7 3·4	6·4 3·1	6·1 2·8	61·2
61·5	9·1 5·6	8·8 5·4	8·6 5·1	8·3 4·9	8·1 4·6	7·8 4·3	7·5 4·0	7·2 3·7	6·9 3·4	6·5 3·1	6·2 2·7	61·5

Extract Number A3

POLARIS (POLE STAR) TABLES, 1980
FOR DETERMINING LATITUDE FROM SEXTANT ALTITUDE AND FOR AZIMUTH

L.H.A. ARIES	240°– 249°	250°– 259°	260°– 269°	270°– 279°	280°– 289°
	a_0	a_0	a_0	a_0	a_0
°	° ′	° ′	° ′	° ′	° ′
0	1 43·0	1 38·6	1 32·9	1 26·2	1 18·6
1	42·7	38·0	32·2	25·4	17·8
2	42·2	37·5	31·6	24·7	17·0
3	41·8	37·0	31·0	24·0	16·2
4	41·4	36·4	30·3	23·2	15·4
5	1 41·0	1 35·9	1 29·6	1 22·5	1 14·6
6	40·5	35·3	29·0	21·7	13·8
7	40·0	34·7	28·3	20·9	12·9
8	39·6	34·1	27·6	20·2	12·1
9	39·1	33·5	26·9	19·4	11·3
10	1 38·6	1 32·9	1 26·2	1 18·6	1 10·5
Lat.	a_1	a_1	a_1	a_1	a_1
°	′	′	′	′	′
0	0·5	0·4	0·3	0·3	0·2
10	·5	·4	·4	·3	·3
20	·5	·5	·4	·4	·3
30	·5	·5	·5	·4	·4
40	0·6	0·5	0·5	0·5	0·5
45	·6	·6	·6	·5	·5
50	·6	·6	·6	·6	·6
55	·6	·6	·7	·7	·7
60	·7	·7	·7	·7	·8
62	0·7	0·7	0·8	0·8	0·8
64	·7	·7	·8	·8	·9
66	·7	·8	·8	0·9	0·9
68	0·7	0·8	0·9	1·0	1·0
Month	a_2	a_2	a_2	a_2	a_2
	′	′	′	′	′
Jan.	0·5	0·5	0·5	0·5	0·6
Feb.	·4	·4	·4	·4	·4
Mar.	·4	·4	·4	·3	·3
Apr.	0·5	0·5	0·4	0·3	0·3
May	·7	·6	·5	·4	·4
June	·8	·7	·7	·6	·5
July	0·9	0·9	0·8	0·7	0·7
Aug.	·9	·9	·9	·9	·8
Sept.	·9	·9	·9	·9	·9
Oct.	0·8	0·9	0·9	0·9	0·9
Nov.	·7	·7	·8	·8	·9
Dec.	0·5	0·6	0·6	0·7	0·8
Lat.					
°	°	°	°	°	°
0	0·4	0·6	0·6	0·7	0·8
20	0·5	0·6	0·7	0·8	0·8
40	0·6	0·7	0·8	0·9	1·0
50	0·7	0·8	1·0	1·1	1·2
55	0·7	0·9	1·1	1·3	1·4
60	0·9	1·1	1·3	1·4	1·6
65	1·0	1·3	1·5	1·7	1·8

Extract Number A4

1980 MARCH 7, 8, 9 (FRI., SAT., SUN.)

G.M.T.	ARIES G.H.A.	VENUS −3.8 G.H.A.	Dec.	MARS −0.8 G.H.A.	Dec.	JUPITER −2.0 G.H.A.	Dec.	SATURN +0.8 G.H.A.	Dec.	STARS Name	S.H.A.	Dec.
7 00	164 51.8	137 08.3 N12	38.1	9 40.0 N14	47.6	8 38.6 N11	19.9	349 13.7 N 4	30.4	Acamar	315 37.8	S40 23.4
01	179 54.3	152 08.2	39.3	24 43.3	47.9	23 41.3	20.1	4 16.3	30.4	Achernar	335 46.1	S57 20.6
02	194 56.8	167 08.0	40.4	39 46.7	48.1	38 44.1	20.2	19 18.9	30.5	Acrux	173 36.9	S62 59.3
03	209 59.2	182 07.8 ··	41.6	54 50.0 ··	48.4	53 46.8 ··	20.3	34 21.6 ··	30.6	Adhara	255 32.2	S28 57.0
04	225 01.7	197 07.7	42.8	69 53.4	48.6	68 49.6	20.4	49 24.2	30.7	Aldebaran	291 18.5	N16 28.1
05	240 04.2	212 07.5	43.9	84 56.7	48.9	83 52.4	20.5	64 26.9	30.8			
06	255 06.6	227 07.3 N12	45.1	100 00.1 N14	49.2	98 55.1 N11	20.6	79 29.5 N 4	30.9	Alioth	166 42.4	N56 03.9
07	270 09.1	242 07.1	46.3	115 03.4	49.4	113 57.9	20.7	94 32.2	30.9	Alkaid	153 18.5	N49 24.6
08	285 11.6	257 07.0	47.4	130 06.7	49.7	129 00.6	20.9	109 34.8	31.0	Al Na'ir	28 15.9	S47 03.5
F 09	300 14.0	272 06.8 ··	48.6	145 10.1 ··	49.9	144 03.4 ··	21.0	124 37.4 ··	31.1	Alnilam	276 12.0	S 1 13.1
R 10	315 16.5	287 06.6	49.8	160 13.4	50.2	159 06.2	21.1	139 40.1	31.2	Alphard	218 20.6	S 8 34.5
I 11	330 18.9	302 06.5	50.9	175 16.8	50.5	174 08.9	21.2	154 42.7	31.3			
D 12	345 21.4	317 06.3 N12	52.1	190 20.1 N14	50.7	189 11.7 N11	21.3	169 45.4 N 4	31.3	Alphecca	126 32.3	N26 46.7
A 13	0 23.9	332 06.1	53.2	205 23.5	51.0	204 14.4	21.4	184 48.0	31.4	Alpheratz	358 10.0	N28 58.7
Y 14	15 26.3	347 05.9	54.4	220 26.8	51.2	219 17.2	21.5	199 50.7	31.5	Altair	62 33.1	N 8 48.8
15	30 28.8	2 05.8 ··	55.6	235 30.1 ··	51.5	234 20.0 ··	21.7	214 53.3 ··	31.6	Ankaa	353 41.0	S42 25.1
16	45 31.3	17 05.6	56.7	250 33.5	51.7	249 22.7	21.8	229 55.9	31.7	Antares	112 57.2	S26 23.2
17	60 33.7	32 05.4	57.9	265 36.8	52.0	264 25.5	21.9	244 58.6	31.7			
18	75 36.2	47 05.3 N12	59.0	280 40.1 N14	52.3	279 28.3 N11	22.0	260 01.2 N 4	31.8	Arcturus	146 18.6	N19 17.0
19	90 38.7	62 05.1 13	00.2	295 43.5	52.5	294 31.0	22.1	275 03.9	31.9	Atria	108 21.8	S68 59.2
20	105 41.1	77 04.9	01.4	310 46.8	52.8	309 33.8	22.2	290 06.5	32.0	Avior	234 27.8	S59 27.0
21	120 43.6	92 04.7 ··	02.5	325 50.1 ··	53.0	324 36.5 ··	22.3	305 09.1 ··	32.1	Bellatrix	278 59.1	N 6 19.7
22	135 46.1	107 04.6	03.7	340 53.5	53.3	339 39.3	22.4	320 11.8	32.1	Betelgeuse	271 28.6	N 7 24.0
23	150 48.5	122 04.4	04.8	355 56.8	53.5	354 42.0	22.6	335 14.4	32.2			
8 00	165 51.0	137 04.2 N13	06.0	11 00.1 N14	53.8	9 44.8 N11	22.7	350 17.1 N 4	32.3	Canopus	264 07.2	S52 41.5
01	180 53.4	152 04.0	07.1	26 03.5	54.0	24 47.6	22.8	5 19.7	32.4	Capella	281 11.8	N45 58.8
02	195 55.9	167 03.9	08.3	41 06.8	54.3	39 50.3	22.9	20 22.4	32.5	Deneb	49 49.0	N45 12.4
03	210 58.4	182 03.7 ··	09.5	56 10.1 ··	54.5	54 53.1 ··	23.0	35 25.0 ··	32.5	Denebola	182 59.1	N14 40.9
04	226 00.8	197 03.5	10.6	71 13.5	54.8	69 55.8	23.1	50 27.7	32.6	Diphda	349 21.6	S18 06.0
05	241 03.3	212 03.4	11.8	86 16.8	55.0	84 58.6	23.2	65 30.3	32.7			
06	256 05.8	227 03.2 N13	12.9	101 20.1 N14	55.3	100 01.4 N11	23.4	80 32.9 N 4	32.8	Dubhe	194 22.0	N61 51.5
07	271 08.2	242 03.0	14.1	116 23.5	55.5	115 04.1	23.5	95 35.6	32.9	Elnath	278 44.6	N28 35.4
S 08	286 10.7	257 02.8	15.2	131 26.8	55.8	130 06.9	23.6	110 38.2	33.0	Eltanin	90 58.0	N51 29.2
A 09	301 13.2	272 02.7 ··	16.4	146 30.1 ··	56.0	145 09.6 ··	23.7	125 40.9 ··	33.0	Enif	34 12.2	N 9 46.9
T 10	316 15.6	287 02.5	17.5	161 33.4	56.3	160 12.4	23.8	140 43.5	33.1	Fomalhaut	15 52.2	S29 43.8
U 11	331 18.1	302 02.3	18.7	176 36.8	56.5	175 15.2	23.9	155 46.2	33.2			
R 12	346 20.6	317 02.1 N13	19.8	191 40.1 N14	56.8	190 17.9 N11	24.0	170 48.8 N 4	33.3	Gacrux	172 28.5	S57 00.0
D 13	1 23.0	332 02.0	21.0	206 43.4	57.0	205 20.7	24.1	185 51.4	33.4	Gienah	176 18.0	S17 26.0
A 14	16 25.5	347 01.8	22.1	221 46.7	57.3	220 23.4	24.3	200 54.1	33.4	Hadar	149 23.3	S60 16.4
Y 15	31 27.9	2 01.6 ··	23.3	236 50.0 ··	57.5	235 26.2 ··	24.4	215 56.7 ··	33.5	Hamal	328 29.6	N23 22.0
16	46 30.4	17 01.5	24.4	251 53.4	57.8	250 28.9	24.5	230 59.4	33.6	Kaus Aust.	84 17.5	S34 23.5
17	61 32.9	32 01.3	25.6	266 56.7	58.0	265 31.7	24.6	246 02.0	33.7			
18	76 35.3	47 01.1 N13	26.7	282 00.0 N14	58.3	280 34.5 N11	24.7	261 04.7 N 4	33.8	Kochab	137 18.4	N74 14.0
19	91 37.8	62 00.9	27.9	297 03.3	58.5	295 37.2	24.8	276 07.3	33.8	Markab	14 03.8	N15 05.7
20	106 40.3	77 00.8	29.0	312 06.6	58.7	310 40.0	24.9	291 09.9	33.9	Menkar	314 41.7	N 4 00.5
21	121 42.7	92 00.6 ··	30.2	327 10.0 ··	59.0	325 42.7 ··	25.0	306 12.6 ··	34.0	Menkent	148 37.1	S36 16.2
22	136 45.2	107 00.4	31.3	342 13.3	59.2	340 45.5	25.2	321 15.2	34.1	Miaplacidus	221 44.1	S69 38.4
23	151 47.7	122 00.2	32.5	357 16.6	59.5	355 48.2	25.3	336 17.9	34.2			
9 00	166 50.1	137 00.1 N13	33.6	12 19.9 N14	59.7	10 51.0 N11	25.4	351 20.5 N 4	34.2	Mirfak	309 16.8	N49 47.5
01	181 52.6	151 59.9	34.7	27 23.2 15	00.0	25 53.8	25.5	6 23.2	34.3	Nunki	76 29.8	S26 19.2
02	196 55.0	166 59.7	35.9	42 26.5	00.2	40 56.5	25.6	21 25.8	34.4	Peacock	53 59.4	S56 47.8
03	211 57.5	181 59.5 ··	37.0	57 29.8 ··	00.4	55 59.3 ··	25.7	36 28.4 ··	34.5	Pollux	243 58.4	N28 04.4
04	227 00.0	196 59.4	38.2	72 33.2	00.7	71 02.0	25.8	51 31.1	34.6	Procyon	245 26.0	N 5 16.4
05	242 02.4	211 59.2	39.3	87 36.5	00.9	86 04.8	25.9	66 33.7	34.7			
06	257 04.9	226 59.0 N13	40.5	102 39.8 N15	01.2	101 07.5 N11	26.1	81 36.4 N 4	34.7	Rasalhague	96 30.0	N12 34.3
07	272 07.4	241 58.8	41.6	117 43.1	01.4	116 10.3	26.2	96 39.0	34.8	Regulus	208 10.1	N12 03.8
08	287 09.8	256 58.7	42.7	132 46.4	01.6	131 13.1	26.3	111 41.7	34.9	Rigel	281 36.4	S 8 13.7
S 09	302 12.3	271 58.5 ··	43.9	147 49.7 ··	01.9	146 15.8 ··	26.4	126 44.3 ··	35.0	Rigil Kent.	140 25.9	S60 44.9
U 10	317 14.8	286 58.3	45.0	162 53.0	02.1	161 18.6	26.5	141 47.0	35.1	Sabik	102 41.6	S15 42.0
N 11	332 17.2	301 58.1	46.2	177 56.3	02.3	176 21.3	26.6	156 49.6	35.1			
D 12	347 19.7	316 58.0 N13	47.3	192 59.6 N15	02.5	191 24.1 N11	26.7	171 52.2 N 4	35.2	Schedar	350 09.9	N56 25.7
A 13	2 22.2	331 57.8	48.4	208 02.9	02.8	206 26.8	26.8	186 54.9	35.3	Shaula	96 56.3	S37 05.2
Y 14	17 24.6	346 57.6	49.6	223 06.2	03.0	221 29.6	26.9	201 57.5	35.4	Sirius	258 55.9	S16 41.6
15	32 27.1	1 57.4 ··	50.7	238 09.5 ··	03.3	236 32.3 ··	27.1	217 00.2 ··	35.5	Spica	158 57.7	S11 03.5
16	47 29.5	16 57.3	51.8	253 12.8	03.5	251 35.1	27.2	232 02.8	35.5	Suhail	223 10.6	S43 21.4
17	62 32.0	31 57.1	53.0	268 16.1	03.7	266 37.9	27.3	247 05.5	35.6			
18	77 34.5	46 56.9 N13	54.1	283 19.4 N15	04.0	281 40.6 N11	27.4	262 08.1 N 4	35.7	Vega	80 56.2	N38 45.7
19	92 36.9	61 56.7	55.2	298 22.7	04.2	296 43.4	27.5	277 10.7	35.8	Zuben'ubi	137 33.3	S15 57.5
20	107 39.4	76 56.6	56.4	313 26.0	04.4	311 46.1	27.6	292 13.4	35.9		S.H.A.	Mer. Pass.
21	122 41.9	91 56.4 ··	57.5	328 29.3 ··	04.7	326 48.9 ··	27.7	307 16.0 ··	35.9		° '	h m
22	137 44.3	106 56.2	58.6	343 32.6	04.9	341 51.6	27.8	322 18.7	36.0	Venus	331 13.2	14 52
23	152 46.8	121 56.0	59.8	358 35.9	05.1	356 54.4	27.9	337 21.3	36.1	Mars	205 09.2	23 11
	h m									Jupiter	203 53.8	23 17
Mer. Pass.	12 54.5	v −0.2 d 1.2		v 3.3 d 0.2		v 2.8 d 0.1		v 2.6 d 0.1		Saturn	184 26.1	0 39

Extract Number A5

1980 MARCH 7, 8, 9 (FRI., SAT., SUN.)

SUN / MOON

G.M.T.	SUN G.H.A.	SUN Dec.	MOON G.H.A.	v	MOON Dec.	d	H.P.
7 00	177 13.2	S 5 18.0	303 24.6	14.0	S10 43.9	8.3	54.7
01	192 13.4	17.0	317 57.6	13.9	10 52.2	8.2	54.7
02	207 13.5	16.0	332 30.5	13.8	11 00.4	8.1	54.7
03	222 13.7	·· 15.1	347 03.3	13.8	11 08.5	8.1	54.7
04	237 13.8	14.1	1 36.1	13.8	11 16.6	8.1	54.7
05	252 14.0	13.1	16 08.9	13.7	11 24.7	8.0	54.7
06	267 14.1	S 5 12.1	30 41.6	13.7	S11 32.7	8.0	54.8
07	282 14.3	11.2	45 14.3	13.6	11 40.7	7.9	54.8
08	297 14.4	10.2	59 46.9	13.6	11 48.6	7.8	54.8
F 09	312 14.6	·· 09.2	74 19.5	13.5	11 56.4	7.9	54.8
R 10	327 14.7	08.2	88 52.0	13.5	12 04.3	7.8	54.8
I 11	342 14.9	07.3	103 24.5	13.5	12 12.1	7.7	54.9
D 12	357 15.0	S 5 06.3	117 57.0	13.4	S12 19.8	7.7	54.9
A 13	12 15.2	05.3	132 29.4	13.3	12 27.5	7.6	54.9
Y 14	27 15.3	04.4	147 01.7	13.3	12 35.1	7.6	54.9
15	42 15.5	·· 03.4	161 34.0	13.2	12 42.7	7.5	54.9
16	57 15.6	02.4	176 06.2	13.2	12 50.2	7.5	55.0
17	72 15.8	01.4	190 38.4	13.1	12 57.7	7.4	55.0
18	87 15.9	S 5 00.5	205 10.5	13.1	S13 05.1	7.4	55.0
19	102 16.1	4 59.5	219 42.6	13.0	13 12.5	7.3	55.0
20	117 16.2	58.5	234 14.6	13.0	13 19.8	7.2	55.0
21	132 16.4	·· 57.5	248 46.6	12.9	13 27.0	7.2	55.1
22	147 16.6	56.6	263 18.5	12.9	13 34.2	7.2	55.1
23	162 16.7	55.6	277 50.4	12.8	13 41.4	7.1	55.1
8 00	177 16.9	S 4 54.6	292 22.2	12.8	S13 48.5	7.0	55.1
01	192 17.0	53.6	306 54.0	12.7	13 55.5	7.0	55.2
02	207 17.2	52.7	321 25.7	12.7	14 02.5	6.9	55.2
03	222 17.3	·· 51.7	335 57.4	12.5	14 09.4	6.8	55.2
04	237 17.5	50.7	350 28.9	12.6	14 16.2	6.8	55.2
05	252 17.6	49.7	5 00.5	12.5	14 23.0	6.7	55.3
06	267 17.8	S 4 48.8	19 32.0	12.4	S14 29.7	6.7	55.3
07	282 17.9	47.8	34 03.4	12.4	14 36.4	6.6	55.3
S 08	297 18.1	46.8	48 34.8	12.3	14 43.0	6.6	55.3
A 09	312 18.2	·· 45.8	63 06.1	12.2	14 49.6	6.4	55.4
T 10	327 18.4	44.9	77 37.3	12.2	14 56.0	6.4	55.4
U 11	342 18.6	43.9	92 08.5	12.2	15 02.4	6.4	55.4
R 12	357 18.7	S 4 42.9	106 39.7	12.0	S15 08.8	6.3	55.4
D 13	12 18.9	41.9	121 10.7	12.0	15 15.1	6.2	55.5
A 14	27 19.0	41.0	135 41.7	12.0	15 21.3	6.1	55.5
Y 15	42 19.2	·· 40.0	150 12.7	11.9	15 27.4	6.1	55.5
16	57 19.3	39.0	164 43.6	11.8	15 33.5	6.0	55.5
17	72 19.5	38.0	179 14.4	11.8	15 39.5	5.9	55.6
18	87 19.6	S 4 37.1	193 45.2	11.7	S15 45.4	5.9	55.6
19	102 19.8	36.1	208 15.9	11.7	15 51.3	5.8	55.6
20	117 20.0	35.1	222 46.6	11.6	15 57.1	5.7	55.6
21	132 20.1	·· 34.1	237 17.2	11.5	16 02.8	5.7	55.7
22	147 20.3	33.1	251 47.7	11.5	16 08.5	5.5	55.7
23	162 20.4	32.2	266 18.2	11.4	16 14.0	5.5	55.7
9 00	177 20.6	S 4 31.2	280 48.6	11.3	S16 19.5	5.5	55.8
01	192 20.7	30.2	295 18.9	11.3	16 25.0	5.3	55.8
02	207 20.9	29.2	309 49.2	11.3	16 30.3	5.3	55.8
03	222 21.1	·· 28.3	324 19.5	11.1	16 35.6	5.2	55.8
04	237 21.2	27.3	338 49.6	11.1	16 40.8	5.1	55.9
05	252 21.4	26.3	353 19.7	11.1	16 45.9	5.0	55.9
06	267 21.5	S 4 25.3	7 49.8	10.9	S16 50.9	5.0	56.0
07	282 21.7	24.3	22 19.7	10.9	16 55.9	4.9	56.0
08	297 21.8	23.4	36 49.6	10.9	17 00.8	4.8	56.0
S 09	312 22.0	·· 22.4	51 19.5	10.8	17 05.6	4.7	56.0
U 10	327 22.2	21.4	65 49.3	10.7	17 10.3	4.6	56.1
N 11	342 22.3	20.4	80 19.0	10.6	17 14.9	4.6	56.1
D 12	357 22.5	S 4 19.5	94 48.6	10.6	S17 19.5	4.4	56.1
A 13	12 22.6	18.5	109 18.2	10.6	17 23.9	4.4	56.2
Y 14	27 22.8	17.5	123 47.8	10.4	17 28.3	4.3	56.2
15	42 23.0	·· 16.5	138 17.2	10.4	17 32.6	4.2	56.2
16	57 23.1	15.5	152 46.6	10.4	17 36.8	4.1	56.3
17	72 23.3	14.6	167 16.0	10.3	17 40.9	4.0	56.3
18	87 23.4	S 4 13.6	181 45.3	10.2	S17 44.9	4.0	56.3
19	102 23.6	12.6	196 14.5	10.1	17 48.9	3.8	56.3
20	117 23.7	11.6	210 43.6	10.1	17 52.7	3.8	56.4
21	132 23.9	·· 10.6	225 12.7	10.1	17 56.5	3.7	56.4
22	147 24.1	09.7	239 41.8	9.9	18 00.2	3.6	56.4
23	162 24.2	08.7	254 10.7	9.9	18 03.8	3.4	56.5
	S.D. 16.1	d 1.0	S.D. 15.0		15.1		15.3

Twilight / Moonrise

Lat.	Naut.	Civil	Sunrise	7	8	9	10
N 72	04 33	05 52	07 00	00 11	01 58	03 57	■
N 70	04 42	05 54	06 54	25 28	01 28	03 05	04 42
68	04 49	05 54	06 50	25 06	01 06	02 33	03 56
66	04 55	05 55	06 46	24 48	00 48	02 10	03 26
64	05 00	05 56	06 43	24 34	00 34	01 51	03 04
62	05 04	05 56	06 40	24 23	00 23	01 36	02 46
60	05 08	05 56	06 38	24 13	00 13	01 24	02 31
N 58	05 11	05 56	06 35	24 04	00 04	01 13	02 19
56	05 13	05 56	06 33	23 57	25 03	01 03	02 08
54	05 16	05 56	06 32	23 50	24 55	00 55	01 58
52	05 17	05 56	06 30	23 44	24 48	00 48	01 50
50	05 19	05 56	06 29	23 38	24 41	00 41	01 42
45	05 22	05 56	06 25	23 27	24 27	00 27	01 26
N 40	05 24	05 56	06 23	23 17	24 15	00 15	01 13
35	05 26	05 55	06 20	23 09	24 05	00 05	01 01
30	05 26	05 54	06 18	23 02	23 56	24 51	00 51
20	05 27	05 52	06 14	22 49	23 41	24 35	00 35
N 10	05 25	05 50	06 11	22 38	23 28	24 20	00 20
0	05 23	05 47	06 07	22 28	23 16	24 06	00 06
S 10	05 18	05 43	06 04	22 18	23 04	23 52	24 45
20	05 12	05 38	06 00	22 07	22 51	23 38	24 29
30	05 03	05 32	05 56	21 55	22 36	23 21	24 11
35	04 58	05 28	05 53	21 48	22 27	23 11	24 01
40	04 51	05 23	05 50	21 40	22 18	23 00	23 49
45	04 42	05 17	05 47	21 31	22 06	22 48	23 36
S 50	04 30	05 10	05 43	21 20	21 53	22 32	23 19
52	04 25	05 06	05 41	21 15	21 46	22 24	23 11
54	04 18	05 02	05 38	21 09	21 39	22 16	23 02
56	04 11	04 58	05 36	21 03	21 31	22 07	22 52
58	04 03	04 53	05 33	20 56	21 23	21 57	22 41
S 60	03 53	04 47	05 30	20 48	21 13	21 45	22 28

Twilight / Moonset

Lat.	Sunset	Civil	Naut.	7	8	9	10
N 72	17 24	18 32	19 52	07 19	07 08	06 48	■
N 70	17 29	18 30	19 42	07 39	07 39	07 41	07 50
68	17 34	18 29	19 35	07 55	08 02	08 14	08 36
66	17 37	18 28	19 28	08 08	08 20	08 38	09 06
64	17 40	18 28	19 23	08 19	08 35	08 57	09 29
62	17 43	18 27	19 19	08 28	08 47	09 12	09 49
60	17 45	18 27	19 15	08 36	08 57	09 25	10 02
N 58	17 47	18 26	19 12	08 43	09 07	09 37	10 15
56	17 49	18 26	19 09	08 49	09 15	09 46	10 26
54	17 51	18 26	19 07	08 54	09 22	09 55	10 36
52	17 52	18 26	19 05	08 59	09 28	10 03	10 45
50	17 54	18 26	19 04	09 04	09 34	10 10	10 52
45	17 57	18 26	19 00	09 14	09 47	10 25	11 09
N 40	18 00	18 27	18 58	09 22	09 57	10 37	11 23
35	18 02	18 27	18 56	09 29	10 06	10 48	11 34
30	18 04	18 28	18 56	09 35	10 14	10 57	11 44
20	18 08	18 30	18 55	09 46	10 28	11 13	12 02
N 10	18 11	18 32	18 56	09 55	10 39	11 27	12 17
0	18 14	18 35	18 59	10 04	10 51	11 40	12 31
S 10	18 17	18 38	19 03	10 13	11 02	11 53	12 45
20	18 21	18 43	19 09	10 23	11 14	12 07	13 00
30	18 25	18 49	19 17	10 34	11 28	12 23	13 18
35	18 28	18 53	19 23	10 40	11 36	12 32	13 28
40	18 31	18 58	19 30	10 47	11 45	12 42	13 40
45	18 34	19 04	19 39	10 56	11 55	12 55	13 53
S 50	18 38	19 11	19 50	11 06	12 08	13 10	14 10
52	18 40	19 14	19 55	11 10	12 14	13 17	14 18
54	18 42	19 18	20 02	11 16	12 21	13 25	14 26
56	18 44	19 22	20 09	11 22	12 28	13 35	14 36
58	18 47	19 27	20 16	11 28	12 37	13 44	14 47
S 60	18 50	19 32	20 26	11 35	12 47	13 56	15 00

SUN / MOON

Day	SUN Eqn. of Time 00ʰ	SUN Eqn. of Time 12ʰ	Mer. Pass.	MOON Mer. Pass. Upper	MOON Mer. Pass. Lower	Age	Phase
7	11 07	11 00	12 11	03 53	16 16	20	
8	10 53	10 45	12 11	04 39	17 03	21	
9	10 38	10 30	12 11	05 28	17 53	22	◗

Extract Number A6

1980 JUNE 20, 21, 22 (FRI., SAT., SUN.)

G.M.T.	ARIES G.H.A.	VENUS −3.2 G.H.A.	Dec.	MARS +1.1 G.H.A.	Dec.	JUPITER −1.5 G.H.A.	Dec.	SATURN +1.3 G.H.A.	Dec.	STARS Name	S.H.A.	Dec.
20 00	268 21.4	187 29.4 N20	56.8	98 10.4 N 5	03.9	111 41.1 N10	55.7	95 51.9 N 5	38.5	Acamar	315 37.7	S40 22.9
01	283 23.9	202 33.4	56.2	113 11.7	03.4	126 43.2	55.6	110 54.2	38.4	Achernar	335 45.7	S57 20.0
02	298 26.3	217 37.4	55.6	128 13.0	02.9	141 45.4	55.4	125 56.6	38.4	Acrux	173 37.3	S62 59.7
03	313 28.8	232 41.3 ··	55.0	143 14.4 ··	02.3	156 47.5 ··	55.3	140 58.9 ··	38.3	Adhara	255 32.6	S28 56.8
04	328 31.3	247 45.3	54.3	158 15.7	01.8	171 49.6	55.2	156 01.3	38.3	Aldebaran	291 18.5	N16 28.1
05	343 33.7	262 49.3	53.7	173 17.0	01.2	186 51.7	55.0	171 03.6	38.2			
06	358 36.2	277 53.3 N20	53.1	188 18.3 N 5	00.7	201 53.9 N10	54.9	186 06.0 N 5	38.2	Alioth	166 42.6	N56 04.3
07	13 38.6	292 57.2	52.5	203 19.7 5	00.2	216 56.0	54.8	201 08.4	38.1	Alkaid	153 18.5	N49 25.0
08	28 41.1	308 01.2	51.8	218 21.0 4	59.6	231 58.1	54.6	216 10.7	38.1	Al Na'ir	28 15.0	S47 03.2
F 09	43 43.6	323 05.2 ··	51.2	233 22.3 ··	59.1	247 00.3 ··	54.5	231 13.1 ··	38.0	Alnilam	276 12.2	S 1 12.9
R 10	58 46.0	338 09.1	50.6	248 23.6	58.5	262 02.4	54.4	246 15.4	38.0	Alphard	218 21.0	S 8 34.5
I 11	73 48.5	353 13.1	50.0	263 24.9	58.0	277 04.5	54.2	261 17.8	37.9			
D 12	88 51.0	8 17.1 N20	49.4	278 26.3 N 4	57.5	292 06.7 N10	54.1	276 20.1 N 5	37.9	Alphecca	126 32.0	N26 47.0
A 13	103 53.4	23 21.0	48.7	293 27.6	56.9	307 08.8	54.0	291 22.5	37.8	Alpheratz	358 09.5	N28 58.7
Y 14	118 55.9	38 25.0	48.1	308 28.9	56.4	322 10.9	53.8	306 24.9	37.7	Altair	62 32.4	N 8 49.0
15	133 58.4	53 28.9 ··	47.5	323 30.2 ··	55.8	337 13.1 ··	53.7	321 27.2 ··	37.7	Ankaa	353 40.5	S42 24.6
16	149 00.8	68 32.9	46.9	338 31.6	55.3	352 15.2	53.5	336 29.6	37.6	Antares	112 56.7	S26 23.3
17	164 03.3	83 36.8	46.3	353 32.9	54.8	7 17.3	53.4	351 31.9	37.6			
18	179 05.7	98 40.8 N20	45.6	8 34.2 N 4	54.2	22 19.5 N10	53.3	6 34.3 N 5	37.5	Arcturus	146 18.5	N19 17.2
19	194 08.2	113 44.7	45.0	23 35.5	53.7	37 21.6	53.1	21 36.6	37.5	Atria	108 20.5	S68 59.6
20	209 10.7	128 48.7	44.4	38 36.8	53.1	52 23.7	53.0	36 39.0	37.4	Avior	234 28.8	S59 27.0
21	224 13.1	143 52.6 ··	43.8	53 38.2 ··	52.6	67 25.8 ··	52.9	51 41.3 ··	37.4	Bellatrix	278 59.3	N 6 19.8
22	239 15.6	158 56.5	43.2	68 39.5	52.0	82 28.0	52.7	66 43.7	37.3	Betelgeuse	271 28.8	N 7 24.1
23	254 18.1	174 00.5	42.6	83 40.8	51.5	97 30.1	52.6	81 46.0	37.3			
21 00	269 20.5	189 04.4 N20	42.0	98 42.1 N 4	51.0	112 32.2 N10	52.5	96 48.4 N 5	37.2	Canopus	264 07.8	S52 41.2
01	284 23.0	204 08.3	41.3	113 43.4	50.4	127 34.4	52.3	111 50.8	37.1	Capella	281 12.0	N45 58.6
02	299 25.5	219 12.3	40.7	128 44.7	49.9	142 36.5	52.2	126 53.1	37.1	Deneb	49 48.2	N45 12.5
03	314 27.9	234 16.2 ··	40.1	143 46.1 ··	49.3	157 38.6 ··	52.1	141 55.5 ··	37.0	Denebola	182 59.3	N14 41.0
04	329 30.4	249 20.1	39.5	158 47.4	48.8	172 40.7	51.9	156 57.8	37.0	Diphda	349 21.1	S18 05.6
05	344 32.9	264 24.0	38.9	173 48.7	48.2	187 42.9	51.8	172 00.2	36.9			
06	359 35.3	279 27.9 N20	38.3	188 50.0 N 4	47.7	202 45.0 N10	51.7	187 02.5 N 5	36.9	Dubhe	194 22.6	N61 51.7
07	14 37.8	294 31.9	37.7	203 51.3	47.2	217 47.1	51.5	202 04.9	36.8	Elnath	278 44.7	N28 35.4
S 08	29 40.2	309 35.8	37.1	218 52.7	46.6	232 49.2	51.4	217 07.2	36.8	Eltanin	90 57.3	N51 29.6
A 09	44 42.7	324 39.7 ··	36.5	233 54.0 ··	46.1	247 51.4 ··	51.3	232 09.6 ··	36.7	Enif	34 11.6	N 9 47.1
T 10	59 45.2	339 43.6	35.9	248 55.3	45.5	262 53.5	51.1	247 11.9	36.6	Fomalhaut	15 51.5	S29 43.4
U 11	74 47.6	354 47.5	35.3	263 56.6	45.0	277 55.6	51.0	262 14.3	36.6			
R 12	89 50.1	9 51.4 N20	34.6	278 57.9 N 4	44.4	292 57.8 N10	50.8	277 16.6 N 5	36.5	Gacrux	172 28.8	S57 00.4
D 13	104 52.6	24 55.3	34.0	293 59.2	43.9	307 59.9	50.7	292 19.0	36.5	Gienah	176 18.1	S17 26.0
A 14	119 55.0	39 59.2	33.4	309 00.5	43.3	323 02.0	50.6	307 21.4	36.4	Hadar	149 23.2	S60 16.9
Y 15	134 57.5	55 03.1 ··	32.8	324 01.9 ··	42.8	338 04.1 ··	50.4	322 23.7 ··	36.4	Hamal	328 29.3	N23 22.0
16	150 00.0	70 07.0	32.2	339 03.2	42.3	353 06.3	50.3	337 26.1	36.3	Kaus Aust.	84 16.7	S34 23.6
17	165 02.4	85 10.8	31.6	354 04.5	41.7	8 08.4	50.2	352 28.4	36.3			
18	180 04.9	100 14.7 N20	31.0	9 05.8 N 4	41.2	23 10.5 N10	50.0	7 30.8 N 5	36.2	Kochab	137 18.3	N74 14.5
19	195 07.4	115 18.6	30.4	24 07.1	40.6	38 12.6	49.9	22 33.1	36.1	Markab	14 03.2	N15 05.9
20	210 09.8	130 22.5	29.8	39 08.4	40.1	53 14.8	49.8	37 35.5	36.1	Menkar	314 41.6	N 4 00.7
21	225 12.3	145 26.4 ··	29.2	54 09.7 ··	39.5	68 16.9 ··	49.6	52 37.8 ··	36.0	Menkent	148 37.0	S36 16.5
22	240 14.7	160 30.2	28.6	69 11.0	39.0	83 19.0	49.5	67 40.2	36.0	Miaplacidus	221 45.5	S69 38.5
23	255 17.2	175 34.1	28.0	84 12.4	38.4	98 21.1	49.3	82 42.5	35.9			
22 00	270 19.7	190 38.0 N20	27.4	99 13.7 N 4	37.9	113 23.3 N10	49.2	97 44.9 N 5	35.9	Mirfak	309 16.7	N49 47.3
01	285 22.1	205 41.8	26.8	114 15.0	37.4	128 25.4	49.1	112 47.2	35.8	Nunki	76 29.0	S26 19.2
02	300 24.6	220 45.7	26.2	129 16.3	36.8	143 27.5	49.0	127 49.6	35.7	Peacock	53 58.2	S56 47.7
03	315 27.1	235 49.6 ··	25.6	144 17.6 ··	36.3	158 29.6 ··	48.8	142 51.9 ··	35.7	Pollux	243 58.7	N28 04.4
04	330 29.5	250 53.4	25.0	159 18.9	35.7	173 31.8	48.7	157 54.3	35.6	Procyon	245 26.3	N 5 16.5
05	345 32.0	265 57.3	24.4	174 20.2	35.2	188 33.9	48.5	172 56.6	35.6			
06	0 34.5	281 01.1 N20	23.9	189 21.6 N 4	34.6	203 36.0 N10	48.4	187 59.0 N 5	35.5	Rasalhague	96 29.4	N12 34.5
07	15 36.9	296 05.0	23.3	204 22.9	34.1	218 38.1	48.3	203 01.3	35.5	Regulus	208 10.4	N12 03.9
08	30 39.4	311 08.8	22.7	219 24.2	33.5	233 40.3	48.1	218 03.7	35.4	Rigel	281 36.5	S 8 13.5
S 09	45 41.8	326 12.7 ··	22.1	234 25.5 ··	33.0	248 42.4 ··	48.0	233 06.0 ··	35.3	Rigil Kent.	140 25.6	S60 45.4
U 10	60 44.3	341 16.5	21.5	249 26.8	32.4	263 44.5	47.9	248 08.4	35.3	Sabik	102 41.0	S15 42.0
N 11	75 46.8	356 20.3	20.9	264 28.1	31.9	278 46.6	47.7	263 10.7	35.2			
D 12	90 49.2	11 24.2 N20	20.3	279 29.4 N 4	31.3	293 48.7 N10	47.6	278 13.1 N 5	35.2	Schedar	350 09.2	N56 25.5
A 13	105 51.7	26 28.0	19.7	294 30.7	30.8	308 50.9	47.5	293 15.4	35.1	Shaula	96 55.6	S37 05.3
Y 14	120 54.2	41 31.8	19.2	309 32.0	30.3	323 53.0	47.3	308 17.8	35.1	Sirius	258 56.2	S16 41.5
15	135 56.6	56 35.6 ··	18.6	324 33.3 ··	29.7	338 55.1 ··	47.2	323 20.1 ··	35.0	Spica	158 57.6	S11 03.5
16	150 59.1	71 39.5	18.0	339 34.7	29.2	353 57.2	47.0	338 22.5	34.9	Suhail	223 11.2	S43 21.4
17	166 01.6	86 43.3	17.4	354 36.0	28.6	8 59.4	46.9	353 24.8	34.9			
18	181 04.0	101 47.1 N20	16.8	9 37.3 N 4	28.1	24 01.5 N10	46.8	8 27.2 N 5	34.8	Vega	80 55.5	N38 46.0
19	196 06.5	116 50.9	16.2	24 38.6	27.5	39 03.6	46.6	23 29.5	34.8	Zuben'ubi	137 33.0	S15 57.6
20	211 09.0	131 54.7	15.7	39 39.9	27.0	54 05.7	46.5	38 31.9	34.7		S.H.A.	Mer. Pass.
21	226 11.4	146 58.5 ··	15.1	54 41.2 ··	26.4	69 07.8 ··	46.3	53 34.2 ··	34.7		° '	h m
22	241 13.9	162 02.3	14.5	69 42.5	25.9	84 10.0	46.2	68 36.6	34.6	Venus	279 43.9	11 21
23	256 16.3	177 06.1	13.9	84 43.8	25.3	99 12.1	46.1	83 38.9	34.5	Mars	189 21.6	17 24
Mer. Pass.	6 01.6	v 3.9	d 0.6	v 1.3	d 0.5	v 2.1	d 0.1	v 2.4	d 0.1	Jupiter	203 11.7	16 28
										Saturn	187 27.9	17 30

Extract Number A7

1980 JUNE 20, 21, 22 (FRI., SAT., SUN.)

G.M.T.	SUN G.H.A.	SUN Dec.	MOON G.H.A.	MOON v	MOON Dec.	MOON d	MOON H.P.
	° '	° '	° '	'	° '	'	'
20 00	179 38.8	N23 26.1	93 36.3	15.2	N 5 12.0	9.7	54.4
01	194 38.6	26.1	108 10.5	15.2	5 02.3	9.7	54.4
02	209 38.5	26.1	122 44.7	15.3	4 52.6	9.7	54.4
03	224 38.4 ··	26.1	137 19.0	15.3	4 42.9	9.8	54.4
04	239 38.2	26.1	151 53.3	15.3	4 33.1	9.7	54.3
05	254 38.1	26.2	166 27.6	15.4	4 23.4	9.8	54.3
06	269 38.0	N23 26.2	181 02.0	15.3	N 4 13.6	9.8	54.3
07	284 37.8	26.2	195 36.3	15.4	4 03.8	9.8	54.3
08	299 37.7	26.2	210 10.7	15.4	3 54.0	9.8	54.3
F 09	314 37.6 ··	26.2	224 45.1	15.4	3 44.2	9.8	54.3
R 10	329 37.4	26.2	239 19.5	15.5	3 34.4	9.8	54.3
I 11	344 37.3	26.3	253 54.0	15.4	3 24.6	9.9	54.3
D 12	359 37.1	N23 26.3	268 28.4	15.5	N 3 14.7	9.8	54.3
A 13	14 37.0	26.3	283 02.9	15.4	3 04.9	9.9	54.3
Y 14	29 36.9	26.3	297 37.3	15.5	2 55.0	9.9	54.3
15	44 36.7 ··	26.3	312 11.8	15.5	2 45.1	9.8	54.3
16	59 36.6	26.3	326 46.3	15.5	2 35.3	9.9	54.3
17	74 36.5	26.3	341 20.8	15.5	2 25.4	9.9	54.3
18	89 36.3	N23 26.3	355 55.3	15.6	N 2 15.5	9.9	54.3
19	104 36.2	26.3	10 29.9	15.5	2 05.6	10.0	54.3
20	119 36.1	26.4	25 04.4	15.5	1 55.6	9.9	54.3
21	134 35.9 ··	26.4	39 38.9	15.6	1 45.7	9.9	54.3
22	149 35.8	26.4	54 13.5	15.6	1 35.8	10.0	54.3
23	164 35.7	26.4	68 48.1	15.5	1 25.8	9.9	54.3
21 00	179 35.5	N23 26.4	83 22.6	15.6	N 1 15.9	9.9	54.3
01	194 35.4	26.4	97 57.2	15.6	1 06.0	10.0	54.3
02	209 35.2	26.4	112 31.8	15.5	0 56.0	9.9	54.3
03	224 35.1 ··	26.4	127 06.3	15.6	0 46.1	10.0	54.3
04	239 35.0	26.4	141 40.9	15.6	0 36.1	10.0	54.3
05	254 34.8	26.4	156 15.5	15.6	0 26.1	9.9	54.3
06	269 34.7	N23 26.4	170 50.1	15.6	N 0 16.2	10.0	54.3
07	284 34.6	26.4	185 24.7	15.6	N 0 06.2	9.9	54.3
S 08	299 34.4	26.4	199 59.3	15.5	S 0 03.7	10.0	54.3
A 09	314 34.3 ··	26.4	214 33.8	15.6	0 13.7	10.0	54.3
T 10	329 34.2	26.4	229 08.4	15.6	0 23.7	9.9	54.3
U 11	344 34.0	26.4	243 43.0	15.6	0 33.6	10.0	54.3
R 12	359 33.9	N23 26.4	258 17.6	15.5	S 0 43.6	9.9	54.3
D 13	14 33.7	26.4	272 52.1	15.6	0 53.5	10.0	54.3
A 14	29 33.6	26.4	287 26.7	15.5	1 03.5	9.9	54.3
Y 15	44 33.5 ··	26.4	302 01.2	15.6	1 13.5	9.9	54.3
16	59 33.3	26.3	316 35.8	15.5	1 23.4	10.0	54.3
17	74 33.2	26.3	331 10.3	15.5	1 33.4	9.9	54.3
18	89 33.1	N23 26.3	345 44.8	15.6	S 1 43.3	9.9	54.3
19	104 32.9	26.3	0 19.4	15.5	1 53.2	10.0	54.3
20	119 32.8	26.3	14 53.9	15.5	2 03.2	9.9	54.3
21	134 32.6 ··	26.3	29 28.4	15.5	2 13.1	9.9	54.3
22	149 32.5	26.3	44 02.9	15.4	2 23.0	9.9	54.3
23	164 32.4	26.3	58 37.3	15.5	2 32.9	9.8	54.3
22 00	179 32.2	N23 26.3	73 11.8	15.4	S 2 42.8	9.9	54.3
01	194 32.1	26.3	87 46.2	15.5	2 52.7	9.9	54.3
02	209 32.0	26.2	102 20.7	15.4	3 02.6	9.9	54.3
03	224 31.8 ··	26.2	116 55.1	15.4	3 12.5	9.8	54.3
04	239 31.7	26.2	131 29.5	15.3	3 22.3	9.9	54.3
05	254 31.6	26.2	146 03.8	15.4	3 32.2	9.8	54.3
06	269 31.4	N23 26.2	160 38.2	15.3	S 3 42.0	9.9	54.3
07	284 31.3	26.2	175 12.5	15.4	3 51.9	9.8	54.3
08	299 31.2	26.1	189 46.9	15.3	4 01.7	9.8	54.3
S 09	314 31.0 ··	26.1	204 21.2	15.2	4 11.5	9.8	54.3
U 10	329 30.9	26.1	218 55.4	15.3	4 21.3	9.8	54.3
N 11	344 30.8	26.1	233 29.7	15.2	4 31.1	9.8	54.3
D 12	359 30.6	N23 26.1	248 03.9	15.2	S 4 40.9	9.7	54.3
A 13	14 30.5	26.0	262 38.1	15.2	4 50.6	9.7	54.3
Y 14	29 30.4	26.0	277 12.3	15.2	5 00.3	9.8	54.3
15	44 30.2 ··	26.0	291 46.5	15.1	5 10.1	9.7	54.3
16	59 30.1	26.0	306 20.6	15.1	5 19.8	9.7	54.4
17	74 30.0	25.9	320 54.7	15.1	5 29.5	9.6	54.4
18	89 29.8	N23 25.9	335 28.8	15.1	S 5 39.1	9.7	54.4
19	104 29.7	25.9	350 02.9	15.0	5 48.8	9.6	54.5
20	119 29.6	25.9	4 36.9	15.0	5 58.4	9.6	54.5
21	134 29.4 ··	25.8	19 10.9	14.9	6 08.0	9.6	54.5
22	149 29.3	25.8	33 44.8	15.0	6 17.6	9.6	54.5
23	164 29.2	25.8	48 18.8	14.9	6 27.2	9.5	54.5
	S.D. 15.8	d 0.0	S.D. 14.8		14.8		14.8

Twilight / Sunrise / Moonrise

Lat.	Twilight Naut.	Twilight Civil	Sunrise	Moonrise 20	21	22	23
°	h m	h m	h m	h m	h m	h m	h m
N 72	☐	☐	☐	11 25	13 01	14 37	16 17
N 70	☐	☐	☐	11 30	12 59	14 30	16 03
68	☐	☐	☐	11 33	12 58	14 24	15 51
66	☐	☐	☐	11 36	12 57	14 18	15 41
64	////	////	01 31	11 39	12 57	14 14	15 33
62	////	////	02 09	11 41	12 56	14 10	15 26
60	////	00 49	02 36	11 44	12 55	14 07	15 20
N 58	////	01 40	02 56	11 45	12 55	14 04	15 15
56	////	02 10	03 13	11 47	12 54	14 02	15 10
54	00 45	02 33	03 27	11 48	12 54	13 59	15 06
52	01 32	02 51	03 40	11 50	12 53	13 57	15 02
50	02 00	03 06	03 51	11 51	12 53	13 56	14 59
45	02 46	03 36	04 13	11 53	12 52	13 51	14 51
N 40	03 17	03 58	04 31	11 56	12 52	13 48	14 45
35	03 40	04 17	04 46	11 57	12 51	13 45	14 40
30	03 58	04 32	04 59	11 59	12 51	13 43	14 35
20	04 28	04 57	05 21	12 02	12 50	13 38	14 27
N 10	04 50	05 17	05 40	12 04	12 49	13 34	14 20
0	05 09	05 36	05 58	12 07	12 49	13 31	14 14
S 10	05 26	05 53	06 16	12 09	12 48	13 27	14 07
20	05 43	06 10	06 34	12 12	12 47	13 23	14 01
30	05 59	06 29	06 55	12 14	12 47	13 19	13 53
35	06 08	06 40	07 08	12 16	12 46	13 17	13 48
40	06 17	06 51	07 22	12 18	12 46	13 14	13 43
45	06 28	07 05	07 39	12 20	12 45	13 11	13 38
S 50	06 39	07 21	08 00	12 23	12 45	13 07	13 31
52	06 45	07 29	08 10	12 24	12 44	13 05	13 28
54	06 50	07 37	08 21	12 25	12 44	13 03	13 24
56	06 57	07 46	08 33	12 26	12 44	13 01	13 20
58	07 03	07 56	08 48	12 28	12 43	12 59	13 16
S 60	07 11	08 08	09 06	12 30	12 43	12 56	13 11

Sunset / Twilight / Moonset

Lat.	Sunset	Twilight Civil	Twilight Naut.	Moonset 20	21	22	23
°	h m	h m	h m	h m	h m	h m	h m
N 72	☐	☐	☐	00 49	00 41	00 32	00 23
N 70	☐	☐	☐	00 42	00 39	00 36	00 33
68	☐	☐	☐	00 37	00 38	00 39	00 41
66	☐	☐	☐	00 32	00 37	00 42	00 47
64	22 33	////	////	00 28	00 36	00 44	00 53
62	21 54	////	////	00 24	00 36	00 46	00 58
60	21 28	23 15	////	00 21	00 35	00 48	01 02
N 58	21 07	22 23	////	00 19	00 34	00 50	01 06
56	20 50	21 53	////	00 16	00 34	00 51	01 09
54	20 36	21 31	23 19	00 14	00 33	00 52	01 12
52	20 24	21 13	22 31	00 12	00 33	00 53	01 15
50	20 13	20 58	22 03	00 10	00 32	00 55	01 17
45	19 50	20 28	21 18	00 06	00 32	00 57	01 23
N 40	19 32	20 05	20 47	00 03	00 31	00 59	01 27
35	19 17	19 47	20 24	00 00	00 31	01 00	01 31
30	19 04	19 32	20 05	24 30	00 30	01 02	01 35
20	18 42	19 07	19 36	24 29	00 29	01 04	01 41
N 10	18 23	18 46	19 13	24 28	00 28	01 07	01 46
0	18 05	18 28	18 54	24 27	00 27	01 09	01 51
S 10	17 48	18 11	18 37	24 26	00 26	01 11	01 56
20	17 29	17 53	18 21	24 25	00 25	01 13	02 02
30	17 08	17 35	18 04	24 24	00 24	01 16	02 08
35	16 56	17 24	17 56	24 23	00 23	01 17	02 11
40	16 42	17 12	17 46	24 23	00 23	01 19	02 15
45	16 25	16 59	17 36	24 22	00 22	01 21	02 20
S 50	16 04	16 42	17 24	24 21	00 21	01 23	02 26
52	15 54	16 35	17 19	24 20	00 20	01 24	02 28
54	15 43	16 27	17 13	24 20	00 20	01 25	02 31
56	15 30	16 18	17 07	24 19	00 19	01 27	02 34
58	15 15	16 07	17 00	24 19	00 19	01 28	02 38
S 60	14 58	15 56	16 53	24 18	00 18	01 30	02 42

SUN / MOON

Day	SUN Eqn. of Time 00ʰ	SUN Eqn. of Time 12ʰ	SUN Mer. Pass.	MOON Mer. Pass. Upper	MOON Mer. Pass. Lower	Age	Phase
	m s	m s	h m	h m	h m	d	
20	01 25	01 31	12 02	18 17	05 56	08	
21	01 38	01 44	12 02	18 59	06 38	09	
22	01 51	01 57	12 02	19 41	07 20	10	◗

Extract Number A8

1980 JUNE 23, 24, 25 (MON., TUES., WED.)

G.M.T.	ARIES G.H.A.	VENUS −3.4 G.H.A.	Dec.	MARS +1.1 G.H.A.	Dec.	JUPITER −1.4 G.H.A.	Dec.	SATURN +1.3 G.H.A.	Dec.	STARS Name	S.H.A.	Dec.
23 00	271 18.8	192 09.9 N20	13.4	99 45.1 N 4	24.8	114 14.2 N10	45.9	98 41.2 N 5	34.5	Acamar	315 37.7	S40 22.9
01	286 21.3	207 13.7	12.8	114 46.4	24.2	129 16.3	45.8	113 43.6	34.4	Achernar	335 45.7	S57 20.0
02	301 23.7	222 17.5	12.2	129 47.7	23.7	144 18.4	45.7	128 45.9	34.4	Acrux	173 37.3	S62 59.7
03	316 26.2	237 21.3 ··	11.6	144 49.0 ··	23.1	159 20.6 ··	45.5	143 48.3 ··	34.3	Adhara	255 32.6	S28 56.8
04	331 28.7	252 25.1	11.1	159 50.3	22.6	174 22.7	45.4	158 50.6	34.2	Aldebaran	291 18.5	N16 28.1
05	346 31.1	267 28.8	10.5	174 51.6	22.0	189 24.8	45.2	173 53.0	34.2			
06	1 33.6	282 32.6 N20	09.9	189 52.9 N 4	21.5	204 26.9 N10	45.1	188 55.3 N 5	34.1	Alioth	166 42.6	N56 04.3
07	16 36.1	297 36.4	09.3	204 54.2	20.9	219 29.0	45.0	203 57.7	34.1	Alkaid	153 18.5	N49 25.0
08	31 38.5	312 40.2	08.8	219 55.5	20.4	234 31.2	44.8	219 00.0	34.0	Al Na'ir	28 14.9	S47 03.2
M 09	46 41.0	327 43.9 ··	08.2	234 56.9 ··	19.8	249 33.3 ··	44.7	234 02.4 ··	34.0	Alnilam	276 12.2	S 1 12.9
O 10	61 43.5	342 47.7	07.6	249 58.2	19.3	264 35.4	44.5	249 04.7	33.9	Alphard	218 21.0	S 8 34.5
N 11	76 45.9	357 51.5	07.1	264 59.5	18.7	279 37.5	44.4	264 07.1	33.8			
D 12	91 48.4	12 55.2 N20	06.5	280 00.8 N 4	18.2	294 39.6 N10	44.3	279 09.4 N 5	33.8	Alphecca	126 32.0	N26 47.0
A 13	106 50.8	27 59.0	05.9	295 02.1	17.6	309 41.8	44.1	294 11.8	33.7	Alpheratz	358 09.5	N28 58.7
Y 14	121 53.3	43 02.7	05.4	310 03.4	17.1	324 43.9	44.0	309 14.1	33.7	Altair	62 32.4	N 8 49.0
15	136 55.8	58 06.5 ··	04.8	325 04.7 ··	16.5	339 46.0 ··	43.9	324 16.5 ··	33.6	Ankaa	353 40.5	S42 24.6
16	151 58.2	73 10.2	04.2	340 06.0	16.0	354 48.1	43.7	339 18.8	33.5	Antares	112 56.7	S26 23.3
17	167 00.7	88 14.0	03.7	355 07.3	15.4	9 50.2	43.6	354 21.1	33.5			
18	182 03.2	103 17.7 N20	03.1	10 08.6 N 4	14.9	24 52.4 N10	43.4	9 23.5 N 5	33.4	Arcturus	146 18.5	N19 17.2
19	197 05.6	118 21.4	02.5	25 09.9	14.3	39 54.5	43.3	24 25.8	33.4	Atria	108 20.6	S68 59.6
20	212 08.1	133 25.2	02.0	40 11.2	13.8	54 56.6	43.2	39 28.2	33.3	Avior	234 28.8	S59 27.0
21	227 10.6	148 28.9 ··	01.4	55 12.5 ··	13.2	69 58.7 ··	43.0	54 30.5 ··	33.2	Bellatrix	278 59.3	N 6 19.8
22	242 13.0	163 32.6	00.9	70 13.8	12.7	85 00.8	42.9	69 32.9	33.2	Betelgeuse	271 28.8	N 7 24.1
23	257 15.5	178 36.3 20	00.3	85 15.1	12.1	100 02.9	42.7	84 35.2	33.1			
24 00	272 17.9	193 40.0 N19	59.7	100 16.4 N 4	11.6	115 05.1 N10	42.6	99 37.6 N 5	33.1	Canopus	264 07.8	S52 41.2
01	287 20.4	208 43.8	59.2	115 17.7	11.0	130 07.2	42.5	114 39.9	33.0	Capella	281 12.0	N45 58.6
02	302 22.9	223 47.5	58.6	130 19.0	10.5	145 09.3	42.3	129 42.2	33.0	Deneb	49 48.2	N45 12.5
03	317 25.3	238 51.2 ··	58.1	145 20.3 ··	09.9	160 11.4 ··	42.2	144 44.6 ··	32.9	Denebola	182 59.3	N14 41.0
04	332 27.8	253 54.9	57.5	160 21.6	09.4	175 13.5	42.0	159 46.9	32.8	Diphda	349 21.1	S18 05.6
05	347 30.3	268 58.6	57.0	175 22.9	08.8	190 15.6	41.9	174 49.3	32.8			
06	2 32.7	284 02.3 N19	56.4	190 24.2 N 4	08.3	205 17.8 N10	41.8	189 51.6 N 5	32.7	Dubhe	194 22.6	N61 51.7
07	17 35.2	299 06.0	55.9	205 25.5	07.7	220 19.9	41.6	204 54.0	32.7	Elnath	278 44.7	N28 35.4
08	32 37.7	314 09.7	55.3	220 26.8	07.2	235 22.0	41.5	219 56.3	32.6	Eltanin	90 57.3	N51 29.6
T 09	47 40.1	329 13.3 ··	54.8	235 28.1 ··	06.6	250 24.1 ··	41.3	234 58.7 ··	32.5	Enif	34 11.5	N 9 47.1
U 10	62 42.6	344 17.0	54.2	250 29.4	06.1	265 26.2	41.2	250 01.0	32.5	Fomalhaut	15 51.5	S29 43.4
E 11	77 45.1	359 20.7	53.7	265 30.7	05.5	280 28.3	41.1	265 03.3	32.4			
S D 12	92 47.5	14 24.4 N19	53.1	280 32.0 N 4	05.0	295 30.4 N10	40.9	280 05.7 N 5	32.4	Gacrux	172 28.8	S57 00.4
A 13	107 50.0	29 28.1	52.6	295 33.3	04.4	310 32.6	40.8	295 08.0	32.3	Gienah	176 18.1	S17 26.0
Y 14	122 52.4	44 31.7	52.0	310 34.6	03.8	325 34.7	40.6	310 10.4	32.2	Hadar	149 23.2	S60 16.9
15	137 54.9	59 35.4 ··	51.5	325 35.9 ··	03.3	340 36.8 ··	40.5	325 12.7 ··	32.2	Hamal	328 29.3	N23 22.0
16	152 57.4	74 39.0	51.0	340 37.1	02.7	355 38.9	40.4	340 15.0	32.1	Kaus Aust.	84 16.7	S34 23.6
17	167 59.8	89 42.7	50.4	355 38.4	02.2	10 41.0	40.2	355 17.4	32.1			
18	183 02.3	104 46.4 N19	49.9	10 39.7 N 4	01.6	25 43.1 N10	40.1	10 19.7 N 5	32.0	Kochab	137 18.3	N74 14.5
19	198 04.8	119 50.0	49.3	25 41.0	01.1	40 45.2	39.9	25 22.1	31.9	Markab	14 03.2	N15 05.9
20	213 07.2	134 53.7	48.8	40 42.3	00.5	55 47.4	39.8	40 24.4	31.9	Menkar	314 41.5	N 4 00.7
21	228 09.7	149 57.3 ··	48.3	55 43.6 4	00.0	70 49.5 ··	39.6	55 26.8 ··	31.8	Menkent	148 37.0	S36 16.5
22	243 12.2	165 00.9	47.7	70 44.9 3	59.4	85 51.6	39.5	70 29.1	31.7	Miaplacidus	221 45.6	S69 38.5
23	258 14.6	180 04.6	47.2	85 46.2	58.9	100 53.7	39.4	85 31.4	31.7			
25 00	273 17.1	195 08.2 N19	46.7	100 47.5 N 3	58.3	115 55.8 N 5	39.2	100 33.8 N 5	31.6	Mirfak	309 16.7	N49 47.3
01	288 19.6	210 11.8	46.1	115 48.8	57.8	130 57.9	39.1	115 36.1	31.6	Nunki	76 29.0	S26 19.2
02	303 22.0	225 15.5	45.6	130 50.1	57.2	146 00.0	38.9	130 38.5	31.5	Peacock	53 58.2	S56 47.7
03	318 24.5	240 19.1 ··	45.1	145 51.4 ··	56.6	161 02.1 ··	38.8	145 40.8 ··	31.4	Pollux	243 58.7	N28 04.4
04	333 26.9	255 22.7	44.5	160 52.7	56.1	176 04.3	38.7	160 43.1	31.4	Procyon	245 26.3	N 5 16.5
05	348 29.4	270 26.3	44.0	175 54.0	55.5	191 06.4	38.5	175 45.5	31.3			
06	3 31.9	285 29.9 N19	43.5	190 55.3 N 3	55.0	206 08.5 N10	38.4	190 47.8 N 5	31.3	Rasalhague	96 29.4	N12 34.6
07	18 34.3	300 33.5	43.0	205 56.6	54.4	221 10.6	38.2	205 50.2	31.2	Regulus	208 10.4	N12 03.9
W 08	33 36.8	315 37.1	42.4	220 57.8	53.9	236 12.7	38.1	220 52.5	31.1	Rigel	281 36.5	S 8 13.5
E 09	48 39.3	330 40.7 ··	41.9	235 59.1 ··	53.3	251 14.8 ··	37.9	235 54.8 ··	31.1	Rigil Kent.	140 25.6	S60 45.4
D 10	63 41.7	345 44.3	41.4	251 00.4	52.8	266 16.9	37.8	250 57.2	31.0	Sabik	102 41.0	S15 42.0
N 11	78 44.2	0 47.9	40.9	266 01.7	52.2	281 19.0	37.7	265 59.5	31.0			
E S 12	93 46.7	15 51.5 N19	40.3	281 03.0 N 3	51.6	296 21.1 N10	37.5	281 01.9 N 5	30.9	Schedar	350 09.2	N56 25.5
D 13	108 49.1	30 55.1	39.8	296 04.3	51.1	311 23.3	37.4	296 04.2	30.8	Shaula	96 55.6	S37 05.3
A 14	123 51.6	45 58.7	39.3	311 05.6	50.5	326 25.4	37.2	311 06.5	30.8	Sirius	258 56.2	S16 41.5
Y 15	138 54.0	61 02.3 ··	38.8	326 06.9 ··	50.0	341 27.5 ··	37.1	326 08.9 ··	30.7	Spica	158 57.6	S11 03.5
16	153 56.5	76 05.8	38.3	341 08.2	49.4	356 29.6	36.9	341 11.2	30.6	Suhail	223 11.2	S43 21.4
17	168 59.0	91 09.4	37.7	356 09.5	48.9	11 31.7	36.8	356 13.6	30.6			
18	184 01.4	106 13.0 N19	37.2	11 10.8 N 3	48.3	26 33.8 N10	36.7	11 15.9 N 5	30.5	Vega	80 55.5	N38 46.0
19	199 03.9	121 16.5	36.7	26 12.0	47.8	41 35.9	36.5	26 18.2	30.5	Zuben'ubi	137 33.0	S15 57.6
20	214 06.4	136 20.1	36.2	41 13.3	47.2	56 38.0	36.4	41 20.6	30.4		S.H.A.	Mer. Pass.
21	229 08.8	151 23.7 ··	35.7	56 14.6 ··	46.6	71 40.1 ··	36.2	56 22.9 ··	30.3	Venus	281 22.1	11 03
22	244 11.3	166 27.2	35.2	71 15.9	46.1	86 42.2	36.1	71 25.2	30.3	Mars	187 58.4	17 17
23	259 13.8	181 30.8	34.7	86 17.2	45.5	101 44.3	35.9	86 27.6	30.2	Jupiter	202 47.1	16 17
Mer. Pass. 5 49.8		v 3.7 d 0.5		v 1.3 d 0.6		v 2.1 d 0.1		v 2.3 d 0.1		Saturn	187 19.6	17 19

Extract Number A9

1980 JUNE 23, 24, 25 (MON., TUES., WED.)

G.M.T.	SUN G.H.A.	Dec.	MOON G.H.A.	v	Dec.	d	H.P.
23 00	179 29.0	N23 25.7	62 52.7	14.8	S 6 36.7	9.5	54.5
01	194 28.9	25.7	77 26.5	14.9	6 46.2	9.5	54.5
02	209 28.8	25.7	92 00.4	14.8	6 55.7	9.5	54.5
03	224 28.6 ··	25.7	106 34.2	14.7	7 05.2	9.5	54.5
04	239 28.5	25.6	121 07.9	14.8	7 14.7	9.4	54.6
05	254 28.4	25.6	135 41.7	14.6	7 24.1	9.4	54.6
06	269 28.2	N23 25.6	150 15.3	14.7	S 7 33.5	9.4	54.6
07	284 28.1	25.5	164 49.0	14.6	7 42.9	9.3	54.6
08	299 28.0	25.5	179 22.6	14.6	7 52.2	9.4	54.6
M 09	314 27.8 ··	25.4	193 56.2	14.5	8 01.6	9.3	54.6
O 10	329 27.7	25.4	208 29.7	14.5	8 10.9	9.2	54.6
N 11	344 27.6	25.4	223 03.2	14.5	8 20.1	9.3	54.7
D 12	359 27.4	N23 25.3	237 36.7	14.4	S 8 29.4	9.2	54.7
A 13	14 27.3	25.3	252 10.1	14.4	8 38.6	9.2	54.7
Y 14	29 27.2	25.3	266 43.5	14.3	8 47.8	9.1	54.7
15	44 27.0 ··	25.2	281 16.8	14.3	8 56.9	9.1	54.7
16	59 26.9	25.2	295 50.1	14.2	9 06.0	9.1	54.7
17	74 26.8	25.1	310 23.3	14.2	9 15.1	9.1	54.7
18	89 26.6	N23 25.1	324 56.5	14.2	S 9 24.2	9.0	54.8
19	104 26.5	25.0	339 29.7	14.1	9 33.2	9.0	54.8
20	119 26.4	25.0	354 02.8	14.1	9 42.2	8.9	54.8
21	134 26.2 ··	25.0	8 35.9	14.0	9 51.1	8.9	54.8
22	149 26.1	24.9	23 08.9	13.9	10 00.0	8.9	54.8
23	164 25.9	24.9	37 41.8	14.0	10 08.9	8.8	54.9
24 00	179 25.8	N23 24.8	52 14.8	13.8	S10 17.7	8.8	54.9
01	194 25.7	24.8	66 47.6	13.9	10 26.5	8.8	54.9
02	209 25.5	24.7	81 20.5	13.7	10 35.3	8.7	54.9
03	224 25.4 ··	24.7	95 53.2	13.7	10 44.0	8.7	54.9
04	239 25.3	24.6	110 25.9	13.7	10 52.7	8.6	54.9
05	254 25.1	24.6	124 58.6	13.6	11 01.3	8.6	55.0
06	269 25.0	N23 24.5	139 31.2	13.6	S11 09.9	8.6	55.0
07	284 24.9	24.5	154 03.8	13.5	11 18.5	8.5	55.0
08	299 24.8	24.4	168 36.3	13.5	11 27.0	8.4	55.0
T 09	314 24.6 ··	24.4	183 08.8	13.4	11 35.4	8.5	55.0
U 10	329 24.5	24.3	197 41.2	13.3	11 43.9	8.3	55.1
E 11	344 24.4	24.3	212 13.5	13.3	11 52.2	8.4	55.1
S 12	359 24.2	N23 24.2	226 45.8	13.3	S12 00.6	8.3	55.1
D 13	14 24.1	24.1	241 18.1	13.2	12 08.9	8.2	55.1
A 14	29 24.0	24.1	255 50.3	13.1	12 17.1	8.2	55.1
Y 15	44 23.8 ··	24.0	270 22.4	13.1	12 25.3	8.1	55.2
16	59 23.7	24.0	284 54.5	13.0	12 33.4	8.1	55.2
17	74 23.6	23.9	299 26.5	12.9	12 41.5	8.0	55.2
18	89 23.4	N23 23.8	313 58.4	12.9	S12 49.5	8.0	55.2
19	104 23.3	23.8	328 30.3	12.9	12 57.5	8.0	55.2
20	119 23.2	23.7	343 02.2	12.8	13 05.5	7.8	55.3
21	134 23.0 ··	23.7	357 34.0	12.7	13 13.3	7.9	55.3
22	149 22.9	23.6	12 05.7	12.6	13 21.2	7.7	55.3
23	164 22.8	23.5	26 37.3	12.6	13 28.9	7.7	55.3
25 00	179 22.6	N23 23.5	41 08.9	12.6	S13 36.6	7.7	55.3
01	194 22.5	23.4	55 40.5	12.5	13 44.3	7.6	55.4
02	209 22.4	23.3	70 12.0	12.4	13 51.9	7.5	55.4
03	224 22.2 ··	23.3	84 43.4	12.3	13 59.4	7.5	55.4
04	239 22.1	23.2	99 14.7	12.3	14 06.9	7.4	55.4
05	254 22.0	23.1	113 46.0	12.3	14 14.3	7.4	55.5
06	269 21.8	N23 23.0	128 17.3	12.1	S14 21.7	7.3	55.5
W 07	284 21.7	23.0	142 48.4	12.2	14 29.0	7.2	55.5
E 08	299 21.6	22.9	157 19.6	12.0	14 36.2	7.2	55.5
D 09	314 21.4 ··	22.9	171 50.6	12.0	14 43.4	7.1	55.6
N 10	329 21.3	22.8	186 21.6	11.9	14 50.5	7.1	55.6
E 11	344 21.2	22.7	200 52.5	11.9	14 57.6	7.0	55.6
S 12	359 21.0	N23 22.6	215 23.4	11.8	S15 04.6	6.9	55.6
D 13	14 20.9	22.6	229 54.2	11.7	15 11.5	6.8	55.7
A 14	29 20.8	22.5	244 24.9	11.7	15 18.3	6.8	55.7
Y 15	44 20.7 ··	22.4	258 55.6	11.6	15 25.1	6.7	55.7
16	59 20.5	22.3	273 26.2	11.5	15 31.8	6.7	55.7
17	74 20.4	22.3	287 56.7	11.5	15 38.5	6.5	55.7
18	89 20.3	N23 22.2	302 27.2	11.4	S15 45.0	6.5	55.8
19	104 20.1	22.1	316 57.6	11.3	15 51.5	6.5	55.8
20	119 20.0	22.0	331 27.9	11.3	15 58.0	6.3	55.8
21	134 19.9 ··	22.0	345 58.2	11.2	16 04.3	6.3	55.8
22	149 19.7	21.9	0 28.4	11.2	16 10.6	6.2	55.9
23	164 19.6	21.8	14 58.6	11.1	16 16.8	6.1	55.9
	S.D. 15.8	d 0.1	S.D. 14.9		15.0		15.2

Moonrise

Lat.	Twilight Naut.	Civil	Sunrise	23	24	25	26
N 72	□	□	□	16 17	18 04	20 05	■
N 70	□	□	□	16 03	17 39	19 21	21 08
68	□	□	□	15 51	17 20	18 52	20 23
66	□	□	□	15 41	17 05	18 31	19 54
64	////	////	01 32	15 33	16 53	18 13	19 32
62	////	////	02 10	15 26	16 43	17 59	19 14
60	////	00 51	02 37	15 20	16 34	17 48	19 00
N 58	////	01 41	02 57	15 15	16 26	17 37	18 47
56	////	02 11	03 14	15 10	16 19	17 29	18 36
54	00 47	02 34	03 28	15 06	16 13	17 21	18 27
52	01 33	02 52	03 41	15 02	16 08	17 14	18 19
50	02 01	03 07	03 51	14 59	16 03	17 07	18 11
45	02 47	03 37	04 14	14 51	15 52	16 54	17 55
N 40	03 17	03 59	04 32	14 45	15 43	16 42	17 42
35	03 41	04 17	04 47	14 40	15 36	16 33	17 31
30	03 59	04 33	05 00	14 35	15 29	16 25	17 21
20	04 28	04 58	05 22	14 27	15 18	16 10	17 04
N 10	04 51	05 18	05 41	14 20	15 08	15 58	16 50
0	05 10	05 36	05 59	14 14	14 59	15 46	16 36
S 10	05 27	05 53	06 16	14 07	14 50	15 35	16 23
20	05 43	06 11	06 35	14 01	14 40	15 22	16 08
30	06 00	06 30	06 56	13 53	14 29	15 08	15 52
35	06 08	06 40	07 08	13 48	14 23	15 00	15 43
40	06 18	06 52	07 22	13 43	14 15	14 51	15 32
45	06 28	07 05	07 39	13 38	14 07	14 40	15 19
S 50	06 40	07 22	08 00	13 31	13 57	14 28	15 04
52	06 45	07 29	08 10	13 28	13 52	14 22	14 57
54	06 51	07 37	08 21	13 24	13 47	14 15	14 49
56	06 57	07 46	08 34	13 20	13 42	14 08	14 40
58	07 04	07 57	08 48	13 16	13 36	13 59	14 30
S 60	07 11	08 08	09 06	13 11	13 29	13 50	14 18

Moonset

Lat.	Sunset	Twilight Civil	Naut.	23	24	25	26
N 72	□	□	□	00 23	00 13	{ 00 06 / 23 40 }	■
N 70	□	□	□	00 33	00 30	00 27	00 24
68	□	□	□	00 41	00 43	00 47	00 54
66	□	□	□	00 47	00 54	01 03	01 16
64	22 32	////	////	00 53	01 03	01 16	01 34
62	21 54	////	////	00 58	01 11	01 27	01 48
60	21 28	23 13	////	01 02	01 18	01 37	02 01
N 58	21 07	22 23	////	01 06	01 24	01 45	02 11
56	20 51	21 53	////	01 09	01 29	01 52	02 21
54	20 36	21 31	23 17	01 12	01 34	01 59	02 29
52	20 24	21 13	22 31	01 15	01 38	02 05	02 37
50	20 13	20 58	22 03	01 17	01 42	02 10	02 43
45	19 51	20 28	21 18	01 23	01 51	02 22	02 58
N 40	19 33	20 06	20 47	01 27	01 58	02 32	03 09
35	19 18	19 47	20 24	01 31	02 04	02 40	03 20
30	19 05	19 32	20 05	01 35	02 10	02 47	03 29
20	18 43	19 07	19 36	01 41	02 19	03 00	03 44
N 10	18 24	18 47	19 14	01 46	02 27	03 11	03 57
0	18 06	18 29	18 55	01 51	02 35	03 21	04 10
S 10	17 49	18 13	18 38	01 56	02 43	03 32	04 23
20	17 30	17 54	18 22	02 02	02 52	03 43	04 36
30	17 09	17 35	18 05	02 08	03 01	03 56	04 52
35	16 57	17 25	17 56	02 11	03 07	04 03	05 01
40	16 42	17 13	17 47	02 15	03 13	04 12	05 11
45	16 26	16 59	17 37	02 20	03 20	04 22	05 23
S 50	16 05	16 43	17 25	02 26	03 29	04 33	05 38
52	15 55	16 36	17 20	02 28	03 33	04 39	05 45
54	15 44	16 28	17 14	02 31	03 38	04 45	05 52
56	15 16	16 19	17 08	02 34	03 43	04 52	06 01
58	15 16	16 08	17 01	02 38	03 49	05 00	06 11
S 60	14 59	15 57	16 53	02 42	03 55	05 09	06 22

Day	SUN Eqn. of Time 00h	12h	Mer. Pass.	MOON Mer. Pass. Upper	Lower	Age	Phase
23	02 04	02 10	12 02	20 25	08 03	11	☽
24	02 16	02 23	12 02	21 10	08 47	12	
25	02 29	02 36	12 03	21 58	09 34	13	

Extract Number A10

1980 OCTOBER 3, 4, 5 (FRI., SAT., SUN.)

G.M.T.	ARIES G.H.A.	VENUS −3.7 G.H.A.	Dec.	MARS +1.5 G.H.A.	Dec.	JUPITER −1.2 G.H.A.	Dec.	SATURN +1.2 G.H.A.	Dec.
3 00	11 50.9	221 52.7 N12	21.0	140 57.9 S19	19.7	196 02.6 N 2	57.9	189 42.7 N 1	20.0
01	26 53.4	236 52.4	20.2	155 58.5	20.1	211 04.5	57.7	204 44.9	19.9
02	41 55.9	251 52.0	19.4	170 59.2	20.6	226 06.5	57.5	219 47.1	19.8
03	56 58.3	266 51.7 ··	18.6	185 59.9 ··	21.1	241 08.5 ··	57.3	234 49.2 ··	19.7
04	72 00.8	281 51.3	17.7	201 00.6	21.5	256 10.5	57.1	249 51.4	19.5
05	87 03.3	296 51.0	16.9	216 01.2	22.0	271 12.4	56.9	264 53.6	19.4
06	102 05.7	311 50.6 N12	16.1	231 01.9 S19	22.4	286 14.4 N 2	56.7	279 55.8 N 1	19.3
07	117 08.2	326 50.3	15.3	246 02.6	22.9	301 16.4	56.5	294 58.0	19.2
08	132 10.7	341 50.0	14.4	261 03.3	23.4	316 18.4	56.3	310 00.1	19.1
F 09	147 13.1	356 49.6 ··	13.6	276 03.9 ··	23.8	331 20.3 ··	56.1	325 02.3 ··	18.9
R 10	162 15.6	11 49.3	12.8	291 04.6	24.3	346 22.3	55.9	340 04.5	18.8
I 11	177 18.0	26 48.9	11.9	306 05.3	24.7	1 24.3	55.7	355 06.7	18.7
D 12	192 20.5	41 48.6 N12	11.1	321 06.0 S19	25.2	16 26.3 N 2	55.4	10 08.9 N 1	18.6
A 13	207 23.0	56 48.3	10.3	336 06.6	25.6	31 28.2	55.2	25 11.1	18.5
Y 14	222 25.4	71 47.9	09.4	351 07.3	26.1	46 30.2	55.0	40 13.2	18.3
15	237 27.9	86 47.6 ··	08.6	6 08.0 ··	26.6	61 32.2 ··	54.8	55 15.4 ··	18.2
16	252 30.4	101 47.2	07.8	21 08.7	27.0	76 34.2	54.6	70 17.6	18.1
17	267 32.8	116 46.9	06.9	36 09.3	27.5	91 36.1	54.4	85 19.8	18.0
18	282 35.3	131 46.6 N12	06.1	51 10.0 S19	27.9	106 38.1 N 2	54.2	100 22.0 N 1	17.9
19	297 37.8	146 46.2	05.3	66 10.7	28.4	121 40.1	54.0	115 24.1	17.7
20	312 40.2	161 45.9	04.4	81 11.3	28.8	136 42.1	53.8	130 26.3	17.6
21	327 42.7	176 45.5 ··	03.6	96 12.0 ··	29.3	151 44.0 ··	53.6	145 28.5 ··	17.5
22	342 45.2	191 45.2	02.7	111 12.7	29.8	166 46.0	53.4	160 30.7	17.4
23	357 47.6	206 44.8	01.9	126 13.4	30.2	181 48.0	53.2	175 32.9	17.3
4 00	12 50.1	221 44.5 N12	01.1	141 14.0 S19	30.7	196 50.0 N 2	52.9	190 35.0 N 1	17.2
01	27 52.5	236 44.2 12	00.2	156 14.7	31.1	211 51.9	52.7	205 37.2	17.0
02	42 55.0	251 43.8 11	59.4	171 15.4	31.6	226 53.9	52.5	220 39.4	16.9
03	57 57.5	266 43.5 ··	58.5	186 16.0 ··	32.0	241 55.9 ··	52.3	235 41.6 ··	16.8
04	72 59.9	281 43.1	57.7	201 16.7	32.5	256 57.9	52.1	250 43.8	16.7
05	88 02.4	296 42.8	56.9	216 17.4	32.9	271 59.8	51.9	265 45.9	16.6
06	103 04.9	311 42.5 N11	56.0	231 18.0 S19	33.4	287 01.8 N 2	51.7	280 48.1 N 1	16.4
07	118 07.3	326 42.1	55.2	246 18.7	33.8	302 03.8	51.5	295 50.3	16.3
S 08	133 09.8	341 41.8	54.3	261 19.4	34.3	317 05.8	51.3	310 52.5	16.2
A 09	148 12.3	356 41.4 ··	53.5	276 20.0 ··	34.7	332 07.7 ··	51.1	325 54.7 ··	16.1
T 10	163 14.7	11 41.1	52.6	291 20.7	35.2	347 09.7	50.9	340 56.8	16.0
U 11	178 17.2	26 40.8	51.8	306 21.4	35.7	2 11.7	50.7	355 59.0	15.8
R 12	193 19.7	41 40.4 N11	50.9	321 22.0 S19	36.1	17 13.7 N 2	50.5	11 01.2 N 1	15.7
D 13	208 22.1	56 40.1	50.1	336 22.7	36.6	32 15.6	50.2	26 03.4	15.6
A 14	223 24.6	71 39.7	49.2	351 23.4	37.0	47 17.6	50.0	41 05.6	15.5
Y 15	238 27.0	86 39.4 ··	48.4	6 24.0 ··	37.5	62 19.6 ··	49.8	56 07.8 ··	15.4
16	253 29.5	101 39.1	47.5	21 24.7	37.9	77 21.6	49.6	71 09.9	15.3
17	268 32.0	116 38.7	46.7	36 25.4	38.4	92 23.5	49.4	86 12.1	15.1
18	283 34.4	131 38.4 N11	45.8	51 26.0 S19	38.8	107 25.5 N 2	49.2	101 14.3 N 1	15.0
19	298 36.9	146 38.0	45.0	66 26.7	39.3	122 27.5	49.0	116 16.5	14.9
20	313 39.4	161 37.7	44.1	81 27.4	39.7	137 29.5	48.8	131 18.7	14.8
21	328 41.8	176 37.4 ··	43.3	96 28.0 ··	40.2	152 31.4 ··	48.6	146 20.8 ··	14.6
22	343 44.3	191 37.0	42.4	111 28.7	40.6	167 33.4	48.4	161 23.0	14.5
23	358 46.8	206 36.7	41.6	126 29.3	41.1	182 35.4	48.2	176 25.2	14.4
5 00	13 49.2	221 36.3 N11	40.7	141 30.0 S19	41.5	197 37.4 N 2	48.0	191 27.4 N 1	14.3
01	28 51.7	236 36.0	39.8	156 30.7	42.0	212 39.3	47.8	206 29.6	14.2
02	43 54.1	251 35.7	39.0	171 31.3	42.4	227 41.3	47.6	221 31.7	14.0
03	58 56.6	266 35.3 ··	38.1	186 32.0 ··	42.9	242 43.3 ··	47.3	236 33.9 ··	13.9
04	73 59.1	281 35.0	37.3	201 32.7	43.3	257 45.3	47.1	251 36.1	13.8
05	89 01.5	296 34.6	36.4	216 33.3	43.7	272 47.2	46.9	266 38.3	13.7
06	104 04.0	311 34.3 N11	35.6	231 34.0 S19	44.2	287 49.2 N 2	46.7	281 40.5 N 1	13.6
07	119 06.5	326 34.0	34.7	246 34.6	44.6	302 51.2	46.5	296 42.6	13.4
08	134 08.9	341 33.6	33.8	261 35.3	45.1	317 53.2	46.3	311 44.8	13.3
S 09	149 11.4	356 33.3 ··	33.0	276 36.0 ··	45.5	332 55.1 ··	46.1	326 47.0 ··	13.2
U 10	164 13.9	11 32.9	32.1	291 36.6	46.0	347 57.1	45.9	341 49.2	13.1
N 11	179 16.3	26 32.6	31.2	306 37.3	46.4	2 59.1	45.7	356 51.4	13.0
D 12	194 18.8	41 32.3 N11	30.4	321 37.9 S19	46.9	18 01.1 N 2	45.5	11 53.6 N 1	12.9
A 13	209 21.3	56 31.9	29.5	336 38.6	47.3	33 03.0	45.3	26 55.7	12.7
Y 14	224 23.7	71 31.6	28.7	351 39.2	47.8	48 05.0	45.1	41 57.9	12.6
15	239 26.2	86 31.2 ··	27.8	6 39.9 ··	48.2	63 07.0 ··	44.9	57 00.1 ··	12.5
16	254 28.6	101 30.9	26.9	21 40.6	48.6	78 09.0	44.7	72 02.3	12.4
17	269 31.1	116 30.6	26.1	36 41.2	49.1	93 11.0	44.4	87 04.5	12.3
18	284 33.6	131 30.2 N11	25.2	51 41.9 S19	49.5	108 12.9 N 2	44.2	102 06.6 N 1	12.1
19	299 36.0	146 29.9	24.3	66 42.5	50.0	123 14.9	44.0	117 08.8	12.0
20	314 38.5	161 29.6	23.5	81 43.2	50.4	138 16.9	43.8	132 11.0	11.9
21	329 41.0	176 29.2 ··	22.6	96 43.8 ··	50.9	153 18.9 ··	43.6	147 13.2 ··	11.8
22	344 43.4	191 28.9	21.7	111 44.5	51.3	168 20.8	43.4	162 15.4	11.7
23	359 45.9	206 28.5	20.8	126 45.1	51.8	183 22.8	43.2	177 17.6	11.5
Mer. Pass.	23 04.9	v −0.3	d 0.8	v 0.7	d 0.5	v 2.0	d 0.2	v 2.2	d 0.1

STARS

Name	S.H.A.	Dec.
Acamar	315 36.9	S40 22.8
Achernar	335 44.7	S57 20.0
Acrux	173 37.9	S62 59.4
Adhara	255 32.1	S28 56.5
Aldebaran	291 17.8	N16 28.2
Alioth	166 43.1	N56 04.0
Alkaid	153 19.0	N49 24.8
Al Na'ir	28 14.6	S47 03.4
Alnilam	276 11.6	S 1 12.8
Alphard	218 20.8	S 8 34.3
Alphecca	126 32.4	N26 47.1
Alpheratz	358 08.9	N28 59.1
Altair	62 32.4	N 8 49.2
Ankaa	353 39.8	S42 24.6
Antares	112 57.0	S26 23.3
Arcturus	146 18.8	N19 17.2
Atria	108 21.5	S68 59.7
Avior	234 28.4	S59 26.6
Bellatrix	278 58.6	N 6 20.0
Betelgeuse	271 28.2	N 7 24.3
Canopus	264 07.1	S52 40.8
Capella	281 11.1	N45 58.6
Deneb	49 48.2	N45 13.0
Denebola	182 59.4	N14 41.0
Diphda	349 20.5	S18 05.5
Dubhe	194 22.8	N61 51.3
Elnath	278 44.0	N28 35.4
Eltanin	90 57.8	N51 29.9
Enif	34 11.4	N 9 47.3
Fomalhaut	15 51.1	S29 43.5
Gacrux	172 29.3	S57 00.1
Gienah	176 18.3	S17 25.9
Hadar	149 23.9	S60 16.7
Hamal	328 28.6	N23 22.3
Kaus Aust.	84 16.9	S34 23.7
Kochab	137 20.1	N74 14.4
Markab	14 02.9	N15 06.2
Menkar	314 40.9	N 4 00.9
Menkent	148 37.4	S36 16.4
Miaplacidus	221 45.4	S69 38.0
Mirfak	309 15.7	N49 47.4
Nunki	76 29.2	S26 19.2
Peacock	53 58.2	S56 48.0
Pollux	243 58.2	N28 04.3
Procyon	245 25.8	N 5 16.6
Rasalhague	96 29.7	N12 34.7
Regulus	208 10.2	N12 03.0
Rigel	281 35.9	S 8 13.3
Rigil Kent.	140 26.4	S60 45.3
Sabik	102 41.3	S15 42.0
Schedar	350 08.4	N56 25.9
Shaula	96 55.9	S37 05.4
Sirius	258 55.7	S16 41.2
Spica	158 57.8	S11 03.4
Suhail	223 11.0	S43 21.0
Vega	80 55.9	N38 46.3
Zuben'ubi	137 33.3	S15 57.5

	S.H.A.	Mer. Pass.
Venus	208 54.4	9 13
Mars	128 23.9	14 34
Jupiter	183 59.9	10 51
Saturn	177 45.0	11 16

Extract Number A11

1980 OCTOBER 3, 4, 5 (FRI., SAT., SUN.)

G.M.T.	SUN G.H.A.	Dec.	MOON G.H.A.	v	Dec.	d	H.P.	Lat.	Twilight Naut.	Civil	Sunrise	Moonrise 3	4	5	6
d h	o ′	o ′	o ′	′	o ′	′	′	o	h m	h m	h m	h m	h m	h m	h m
3 00	182 43.4	S 3 56.0	247 48.7	10.5	N18 13.3	4.4	56.0	N 72	04 05	05 25	06 33	22 00	23 58	25 45	01 45
01	197 43.6	57.0	262 18.2	10.7	18 08.9	4.5	56.0	N 70	04 15	05 27	06 28	22 44	24 24	00 24	02 00
02	212 43.8	58.0	276 47.9	10.7	18 04.4	4.6	55.9	68	04 23	05 28	06 24	23 13	24 43	00 43	02 12
03	227 44.0	·· 58.9	291 17.6	10.7	17 59.8	4.7	55.9	66	04 29	05 29	06 20	23 35	24 59	00 59	02 22
04	242 44.2	3 59.9	305 47.3	10.8	17 55.1	4.8	55.9	64	04 39	05 31	06 18	23 52	25 11	01 11	02 31
05	257 44.4	4 00.9	320 17.1	10.9	17 50.3	4.8	55.9	62	04 39	05 31	06 15	24 07	00 07	01 22	02 38
06	272 44.6	S 4 01.8	334 47.0	10.9	N17 45.5	4.9	55.8	60	04 43	05 31	06 13	24 19	00 19	01 31	02 44
07	287 44.8	02.8	349 16.9	11.0	17 40.6	5.1	55.8	N 58	04 46	05 32	06 11	24 29	00 29	01 39	02 49
08	302 45.0	03.8	3 46.9	11.0	17 35.5	5.1	55.8	56	04 49	05 32	06 09	24 38	00 38	01 46	02 54
F 09	317 45.2	·· 04.7	18 16.9	11.1	17 30.4	5.2	55.7	54	04 51	05 32	06 07	24 46	00 46	01 52	02 59
R 10	332 45.4	05.7	32 47.0	11.1	17 25.2	5.2	55.7	52	04 53	05 32	06 06	24 53	00 53	01 58	03 02
I 11	347 45.6	06.7	47 17.1	11.2	17 20.0	5.4	55.7	50	04 55	05 32	06 05	24 59	00 59	02 03	03 06
D 12	2 45.8	S 4 07.6	61 47.3	11.3	N17 14.6	5.4	55.7	45	04 58	05 32	06 02	00 13	01 13	02 13	03 14
A 13	17 46.0	08.6	76 17.6	11.3	17 09.2	5.5	55.6	N 40	05 01	05 32	05 59	00 26	01 24	02 22	03 20
Y 14	32 46.2	09.6	90 47.9	11.4	17 03.7	5.6	55.6	35	05 02	05 32	05 57	00 37	01 34	02 30	03 25
15	47 46.3	·· 10.5	105 18.3	11.5	16 58.1	5.7	55.6	30	05 03	05 31	05 55	00 47	01 42	02 37	03 30
16	62 46.5	11.5	119 48.8	11.5	16 52.4	5.8	55.6	20	05 04	05 30	05 52	01 04	01 57	02 48	03 39
17	77 46.7	12.5	134 19.3	11.5	16 46.6	5.8	55.5	N 10	05 03	05 27	05 48	01 19	02 10	02 59	03 46
18	92 46.9	S 4 13.4	148 49.8	11.7	N16 40.8	5.9	55.5	0	05 01	05 25	05 45	01 32	02 21	03 08	03 53
19	107 47.1	14.4	163 20.5	11.6	16 34.9	6.0	55.5	S 10	04 57	05 21	05 42	01 46	02 33	03 17	03 59
20	122 47.3	15.4	177 51.1	11.8	16 28.9	6.0	55.5	20	04 51	05 17	05 39	02 01	02 46	03 28	04 07
21	137 47.5	·· 16.3	192 21.9	11.8	16 22.9	6.2	55.5	30	04 42	05 11	05 35	02 17	03 00	03 39	04 15
22	152 47.7	17.3	206 52.7	11.8	16 16.7	6.2	55.4	35	04 37	05 07	05 32	02 27	03 08	03 46	04 20
23	167 47.9	18.3	221 23.5	11.9	16 10.5	6.2	55.4	40	04 30	05 02	05 30	02 38	03 18	03 53	04 25
4 00	182 48.1	S 4 19.2	235 54.4	12.0	N16 04.3	6.4	55.4	45	04 21	04 57	05 26	02 51	03 29	04 02	04 31
01	197 48.3	20.2	250 25.4	12.0	15 57.9	6.4	55.4	S 50	04 10	04 50	05 22	03 07	03 42	04 12	04 38
02	212 48.5	21.2	264 56.4	12.1	15 51.5	6.5	55.3	52	04 05	04 46	05 21	03 14	03 49	04 17	04 42
03	227 48.7	·· 22.1	279 27.5	12.1	15 45.0	6.6	55.3	54	03 59	04 43	05 19	03 23	03 55	04 23	04 46
04	242 48.8	23.1	293 58.6	12.2	15 38.4	6.6	55.3	56	03 52	04 39	05 16	03 32	04 03	04 28	04 50
05	257 49.0	24.1	308 29.8	12.3	15 31.8	6.7	55.3	58	03 44	04 34	05 14	03 42	04 12	04 35	04 54
06	272 49.2	S 4 25.0	323 01.1	12.3	N15 25.1	6.8	55.2	S 60	03 35	04 29	05 11	03 54	04 21	04 42	04 59

G.M.T.	SUN G.H.A.	Dec.	MOON G.H.A.	v	Dec.	d	H.P.	Lat.	Sunset	Twilight Civil	Naut.	Moonset 3	4	5	6
07	287 49.4	26.0	337 32.4	12.3	15 18.3	6.8	55.2								
S 08	302 49.6	26.9	352 03.7	12.4	15 11.5	6.9	55.2	o	h m	h m	h m	h m	h m	h m	h m
A 09	317 49.8	·· 27.9	6 35.1	12.5	15 04.6	7.0	55.2	N 72	17 02	18 09	19 29	18 29	18 09	17 56	17 46
T 10	332 50.0	28.9	21 06.6	12.5	14 57.6	7.0	55.2	N 70	17 08	18 08	19 20	17 44	17 42	17 39	17 36
U 11	347 50.2	29.8	35 38.1	12.6	14 50.6	7.1	55.1	68	17 12	18 07	19 12	17 14	17 21	17 25	17 27
R 12	2 50.4	S 4 30.8	50 09.7	12.6	N14 43.5	7.2	55.1	66	17 15	18 06	19 06	16 52	17 05	17 14	17 21
D 13	17 50.6	31.8	64 41.3	12.7	14 36.3	7.2	55.1	64	17 18	18 06	19 01	16 34	16 52	17 05	17 15
A 14	32 50.7	32.7	79 13.0	12.8	14 29.1	7.3	55.1	62	17 21	18 05	18 57	16 19	16 40	16 57	17 10
Y 15	47 50.9	·· 33.7	93 44.8	12.8	14 21.8	7.4	55.1	60	17 23	18 05	18 53	16 07	16 31	16 50	17 05
16	62 51.1	34.7	108 16.6	12.8	14 14.4	7.4	55.0	N 58	17 25	18 04	18 50	15 56	16 22	16 43	17 01
17	77 51.3	35.6	122 48.4	12.9	14 07.0	7.4	55.0	56	17 27	18 04	18 47	15 46	16 15	16 38	16 58
18	92 51.5	S 4 36.6	137 20.3	12.9	N13 59.6	7.6	55.0	54	17 29	18 04	18 45	15 38	16 08	16 33	16 55
19	107 51.7	37.5	151 52.2	13.1	13 52.0	7.6	55.0	52	17 30	18 04	18 43	15 31	16 02	16 29	16 52
20	122 51.9	38.5	166 24.3	13.0	13 44.4	7.6	55.0	50	17 32	18 04	18 41	15 24	15 57	16 25	16 49
21	137 52.1	·· 39.5	180 56.3	13.1	13 36.8	7.7	54.9	45	17 35	18 04	18 38	15 09	15 45	16 16	16 44
22	152 52.3	40.4	195 28.4	13.2	13 29.1	7.8	54.9	N 40	17 37	18 04	18 36	14 57	15 35	16 08	16 39
23	167 52.4	41.4	210 00.6	13.2	13 21.3	7.8	54.9	35	17 40	18 05	18 34	14 47	15 26	16 02	16 35
5 00	182 52.6	S 4 42.4	224 32.8	13.2	N13 13.5	7.8	54.9	30	17 42	18 06	18 33	14 38	15 19	15 56	16 31
01	197 52.8	43.3	239 05.0	13.3	13 05.7	8.0	54.9	20	17 45	18 07	18 33	14 23	15 06	15 47	16 25
02	212 53.0	44.3	253 37.3	13.4	12 57.7	8.0	54.8	N 10	17 49	18 10	18 34	14 09	14 55	15 38	16 19
03	227 53.2	·· 45.2	268 09.7	13.4	12 49.7	8.0	54.8	0	17 52	18 13	18 37	13 56	14 44	15 30	16 14
04	242 53.4	46.2	282 42.1	13.4	12 41.7	8.1	54.8	S 10	17 55	18 16	18 41	13 43	14 33	15 22	16 08
05	257 53.6	47.2	297 14.5	13.5	12 33.6	8.1	54.8	20	17 59	18 21	18 47	13 30	14 22	15 13	16 02
06	272 53.7	S 4 48.1	311 47.0	13.6	N12 25.5	8.2	54.8	30	18 03	18 27	18 55	13 14	14 09	15 03	15 56
07	287 53.9	49.1	326 19.6	13.6	12 17.3	8.2	54.8	35	18 06	18 31	19 01	13 05	14 01	14 57	15 52
08	302 54.1	50.1	340 52.2	13.6	12 09.1	8.3	54.7	40	18 08	18 36	19 08	12 54	13 52	14 50	15 48
S 09	317 54.3	·· 51.0	355 24.8	13.7	12 00.8	8.3	54.7	45	18 12	18 42	19 17	12 41	13 42	14 42	15 42
U 10	332 54.5	52.0	9 57.5	13.7	11 52.5	8.4	54.7	S 50	18 16	18 49	19 28	12 26	13 29	14 33	15 36
N 11	347 54.7	52.9	24 30.2	13.8	11 44.1	8.4	54.7	52	18 18	18 52	19 34	12 19	13 24	14 29	15 34
D 12	2 54.9	S 4 53.9	39 03.0	13.8	N11 35.7	8.5	54.7	54	18 20	18 56	19 40	12 11	13 17	14 24	15 30
A 13	17 55.1	54.9	53 35.8	13.9	11 27.2	8.5	54.7	56	18 22	19 00	19 47	12 02	13 10	14 19	15 27
Y 14	32 55.2	55.8	68 08.7	13.9	11 18.7	8.6	54.7	58	18 25	19 05	19 55	11 52	13 02	14 13	15 23
15	47 55.4	·· 56.8	82 41.6	14.0	11 10.1	8.6	54.6	S 60	18 27	19 10	20 04	11 41	12 53	14 06	15 19
16	62 55.6	57.8	97 14.6	14.0	11 01.5	8.7	54.6								
17	77 55.8	58.7	111 47.6	14.0	10 52.8	8.7	54.6								
18	92 56.0	S 4 59.7	126 20.6	14.1	N10 44.1	8.7	54.6			SUN			MOON		
19	107 56.2	5 00.6	140 53.7	14.1	10 35.4	8.8	54.6	Day	Eqn. of Time 00ʰ	12ʰ	Mer. Pass.	Mer. Pass. Upper	Lower	Age	Phase
20	122 56.3	01.6	155 26.8	14.2	10 26.6	8.8	54.6		m s	m s	h m	h m	h m	d	
21	137 56.5	·· 02.6	170 00.0	14.2	10 17.8	8.9	54.5	3	10 53	11 03	11 49	07 44	20 09	24	
22	152 56.7	03.5	184 33.2	14.2	10 08.9	8.9	54.5	4	11 12	11 21	11 49	08 33	20 56	25	
23	167 56.9	04.5	199 06.4	14.3	10 00.0	8.9	54.5	5	11 30	11 39	11 48	09 19	21 41	26	
	S.D. 16.0	d 1.0	S.D. 15.2		15.0		14.9									

Extract Number A12

10ᵐ INCREMENTS AND CORRECTIONS **11ᵐ**

10	SUN PLANETS	ARIES	MOON	v or Corrn d	v or Corrn d	v or Corrn d
00	2 30·0	2 30·4	2 23·2	0·0 0·0	6·0 1·1	12·0 2·1
01	2 30·3	2 30·7	2 23·4	0·1 0·0	6·1 1·1	12·1 2·1
02	2 30·5	2 30·9	2 23·6	0·2 0·0	6·2 1·1	12·2 2·1
03	2 30·8	2 31·2	2 23·9	0·3 0·1	6·3 1·1	12·3 2·2
04	2 31·0	2 31·4	2 24·1	0·4 0·1	6·4 1·1	12·4 2·2
05	2 31·3	2 31·7	2 24·4	0·5 0·1	6·5 1·1	12·5 2·2
06	2 31·5	2 31·9	2 24·6	0·6 0·1	6·6 1·2	12·6 2·2
07	2 31·8	2 32·2	2 24·8	0·7 0·1	6·7 1·2	12·7 2·2
08	2 32·0	2 32·4	2 25·1	0·8 0·1	6·8 1·2	12·8 2·2
09	2 32·3	2 32·7	2 25·3	0·9 0·2	6·9 1·2	12·9 2·3
10	2 32·5	2 32·9	2 25·6	1·0 0·2	7·0 1·2	13·0 2·3
11	2 32·8	2 33·2	2 25·8	1·1 0·2	7·1 1·2	13·1 2·3
12	2 33·0	2 33·4	2 26·0	1·2 0·2	7·2 1·3	13·2 2·3
13	2 33·3	2 33·7	2 26·3	1·3 0·2	7·3 1·3	13·3 2·3
14	2 33·5	2 33·9	2 26·5	1·4 0·2	7·4 1·3	13·4 2·3
15	2 33·8	2 34·2	2 26·7	1·5 0·3	7·5 1·3	13·5 2·4
16	2 34·0	2 34·4	2 27·0	1·6 0·3	7·6 1·3	13·6 2·4
17	2 34·3	2 34·7	2 27·2	1·7 0·3	7·7 1·3	13·7 2·4
18	2 34·5	2 34·9	2 27·5	1·8 0·3	7·8 1·4	13·8 2·4
19	2 34·8	2 35·2	2 27·7	1·9 0·3	7·9 1·4	13·9 2·4
20	2 35·0	2 35·4	2 27·9	2·0 0·4	8·0 1·4	14·0 2·5
21	2 35·3	2 35·7	2 28·2	2·1 0·4	8·1 1·4	14·1 2·5
22	2 35·5	2 35·9	2 28·4	2·2 0·4	8·2 1·4	14·2 2·5
23	2 35·8	2 36·2	2 28·7	2·3 0·4	8·3 1·5	14·3 2·5
24	2 36·0	2 36·4	2 28·9	2·4 0·4	8·4 1·5	14·4 2·5
25	2 36·3	2 36·7	2 29·1	2·5 0·4	8·5 1·5	14·5 2·5
26	2 36·5	2 36·9	2 29·4	2·6 0·5	8·6 1·5	14·6 2·6
27	2 36·8	2 37·2	2 29·6	2·7 0·5	8·7 1·5	14·7 2·6
28	2 37·0	2 37·4	2 29·8	2·8 0·5	8·8 1·5	14·8 2·6
29	2 37·3	2 37·7	2 30·1	2·9 0·5	8·9 1·6	14·9 2·6
30	2 37·5	2 37·9	2 30·3	3·0 0·5	9·0 1·6	15·0 2·6
31	2 37·8	2 38·2	2 30·6	3·1 0·5	9·1 1·6	15·1 2·6
32	2 38·0	2 38·4	2 30·8	3·2 0·6	9·2 1·6	15·2 2·7
33	2 38·3	2 38·7	2 31·0	3·3 0·6	9·3 1·6	15·3 2·7
34	2 38·5	2 38·9	2 31·3	3·4 0·6	9·4 1·6	15·4 2·7
35	2 38·8	2 39·2	2 31·5	3·5 0·6	9·5 1·7	15·5 2·7
36	2 39·0	2 39·4	2 31·8	3·6 0·6	9·6 1·7	15·6 2·7
37	2 39·3	2 39·7	2 32·0	3·7 0·6	9·7 1·7	15·7 2·7
38	2 39·5	2 39·9	2 32·2	3·8 0·7	9·8 1·7	15·8 2·8
39	2 39·8	2 40·2	2 32·5	3·9 0·7	9·9 1·7	15·9 2·8
40	2 40·0	2 40·4	2 32·7	4·0 0·7	10·0 1·8	16·0 2·8
41	2 40·3	2 40·7	2 32·9	4·1 0·7	10·1 1·8	16·1 2·8
42	2 40·5	2 40·9	2 33·2	4·2 0·7	10·2 1·8	16·2 2·8
43	2 40·8	2 41·2	2 33·4	4·3 0·8	10·3 1·8	16·3 2·9
44	2 41·0	2 41·4	2 33·7	4·4 0·8	10·4 1·8	16·4 2·9
45	2 41·3	2 41·7	2 33·9	4·5 0·8	10·5 1·8	16·5 2·9
46	2 41·5	2 41·9	2 34·1	4·6 0·8	10·6 1·9	16·6 2·9
47	2 41·8	2 42·2	2 34·4	4·7 0·8	10·7 1·9	16·7 2·9
48	2 42·0	2 42·4	2 34·6	4·8 0·8	10·8 1·9	16·8 2·9
49	2 42·3	2 42·7	2 34·9	4·9 0·9	10·9 1·9	16·9 3·0
50	2 42·5	2 42·9	2 35·1	5·0 0·9	11·0 1·9	17·0 3·0
51	2 42·8	2 43·2	2 35·3	5·1 0·9	11·1 1·9	17·1 3·0
52	2 43·0	2 43·4	2 35·6	5·2 0·9	11·2 2·0	17·2 3·0
53	2 43·3	2 43·7	2 35·8	5·3 0·9	11·3 2·0	17·3 3·0
54	2 43·5	2 43·9	2 36·1	5·4 0·9	11·4 2·0	17·4 3·0
55	2 43·8	2 44·2	2 36·3	5·5 1·0	11·5 2·0	17·5 3·1
56	2 44·0	2 44·4	2 36·5	5·6 1·0	11·6 2·0	17·6 3·1
57	2 44·3	2 44·7	2 36·8	5·7 1·0	11·7 2·0	17·7 3·1
58	2 44·5	2 45·0	2 37·0	5·8 1·0	11·8 2·1	17·8 3·1
59	2 44·8	2 45·2	2 37·2	5·9 1·0	11·9 2·1	17·9 3·1
60	2 45·0	2 45·5	2 37·5	6·0 1·1	12·0 2·1	18·0 3·2

11	SUN PLANETS	ARIES	MOON	v or Corrn d	v or Corrn d	v or Corrn d
00	2 45·0	2 45·5	2 37·5	0·0 0·0	6·0 1·2	12·0 2·3
01	2 45·3	2 45·7	2 37·7	0·1 0·0	6·1 1·2	12·1 2·3
02	2 45·5	2 46·0	2 38·0	0·2 0·0	6·2 1·2	12·2 2·3
03	2 45·8	2 46·2	2 38·2	0·3 0·1	6·3 1·2	12·3 2·4
04	2 46·0	2 46·5	2 38·4	0·4 0·1	6·4 1·2	12·4 2·4
05	2 46·3	2 46·7	2 38·7	0·5 0·1	6·5 1·2	12·5 2·4
06	2 46·5	2 47·0	2 38·9	0·6 0·1	6·6 1·3	12·6 2·4
07	2 46·8	2 47·2	2 39·2	0·7 0·1	6·7 1·3	12·7 2·4
08	2 47·0	2 47·5	2 39·4	0·8 0·2	6·8 1·3	12·8 2·5
09	2 47·3	2 47·7	2 39·6	0·9 0·2	6·9 1·3	12·9 2·5
10	2 47·5	2 48·0	2 39·9	1·0 0·2	7·0 1·3	13·0 2·5
11	2 47·8	2 48·2	2 40·1	1·1 0·2	7·1 1·4	13·1 2·5
12	2 48·0	2 48·5	2 40·3	1·2 0·2	7·2 1·4	13·2 2·5
13	2 48·3	2 48·7	2 40·6	1·3 0·2	7·3 1·4	13·3 2·5
14	2 48·5	2 49·0	2 40·8	1·4 0·3	7·4 1·4	13·4 2·6
15	2 48·8	2 49·2	2 41·1	1·5 0·3	7·5 1·4	13·5 2·6
16	2 49·0	2 49·5	2 41·3	1·6 0·3	7·6 1·5	13·6 2·6
17	2 49·3	2 49·7	2 41·5	1·7 0·3	7·7 1·5	13·7 2·6
18	2 49·5	2 50·0	2 41·8	1·8 0·3	7·8 1·5	13·8 2·6
19	2 49·8	2 50·2	2 42·0	1·9 0·4	7·9 1·5	13·9 2·7
20	2 50·0	2 50·5	2 42·3	2·0 0·4	8·0 1·5	14·0 2·7
21	2 50·3	2 50·7	2 42·5	2·1 0·4	8·1 1·6	14·1 2·7
22	2 50·5	2 51·0	2 42·7	2·2 0·4	8·2 1·6	14·2 2·7
23	2 50·8	2 51·2	2 43·0	2·3 0·4	8·3 1·6	14·3 2·7
24	2 51·0	2 51·5	2 43·2	2·4 0·5	8·4 1·6	14·4 2·8
25	2 51·3	2 51·7	2 43·4	2·5 0·5	8·5 1·6	14·5 2·8
26	2 51·5	2 52·0	2 43·7	2·6 0·5	8·6 1·6	14·6 2·8
27	2 51·8	2 52·2	2 43·9	2·7 0·5	8·7 1·7	14·7 2·8
28	2 52·0	2 52·5	2 44·2	2·8 0·5	8·8 1·7	14·8 2·8
29	2 52·3	2 52·7	2 44·4	2·9 0·6	8·9 1·7	14·9 2·9
30	2 52·5	2 53·0	2 44·6	3·0 0·6	9·0 1·7	15·0 2·9
31	2 52·8	2 53·2	2 44·9	3·1 0·6	9·1 1·7	15·1 2·9
32	2 53·0	2 53·5	2 45·1	3·2 0·6	9·2 1·8	15·2 2·9
33	2 53·3	2 53·7	2 45·4	3·3 0·6	9·3 1·8	15·3 2·9
34	2 53·5	2 54·0	2 45·6	3·4 0·7	9·4 1·8	15·4 3·0
35	2 53·8	2 54·2	2 45·8	3·5 0·7	9·5 1·8	15·5 3·0
36	2 54·0	2 54·5	2 46·1	3·6 0·7	9·6 1·8	15·6 3·0
37	2 54·3	2 54·7	2 46·3	3·7 0·7	9·7 1·9	15·7 3·0
38	2 54·5	2 55·0	2 46·6	3·8 0·7	9·8 1·9	15·8 3·0
39	2 54·8	2 55·2	2 46·8	3·9 0·7	9·9 1·9	15·9 3·0
40	2 55·0	2 55·5	2 47·0	4·0 0·8	10·0 1·9	16·0 3·1
41	2 55·3	2 55·7	2 47·3	4·1 0·8	10·1 1·9	16·1 3·1
42	2 55·5	2 56·0	2 47·5	4·2 0·8	10·2 2·0	16·2 3·1
43	2 55·8	2 56·2	2 47·7	4·3 0·8	10·3 2·0	16·3 3·1
44	2 56·0	2 56·5	2 48·0	4·4 0·8	10·4 2·0	16·4 3·1
45	2 56·3	2 56·7	2 48·2	4·5 0·9	10·5 2·0	16·5 3·2
46	2 56·5	2 57·0	2 48·5	4·6 0·9	10·6 2·0	16·6 3·2
47	2 56·8	2 57·2	2 48·7	4·7 0·9	10·7 2·1	16·7 3·2
48	2 57·0	2 57·5	2 48·9	4·8 0·9	10·8 2·1	16·8 3·2
49	2 57·3	2 57·7	2 49·2	4·9 0·9	10·9 2·1	16·9 3·2
50	2 57·5	2 58·0	2 49·4	5·0 1·0	11·0 2·1	17·0 3·3
51	2 57·8	2 58·2	2 49·7	5·1 1·0	11·1 2·1	17·1 3·3
52	2 58·0	2 58·5	2 49·9	5·2 1·0	11·2 2·1	17·2 3·3
53	2 58·3	2 58·7	2 50·1	5·3 1·0	11·3 2·2	17·3 3·3
54	2 58·5	2 59·0	2 50·4	5·4 1·0	11·4 2·2	17·4 3·3
55	2 58·8	2 59·2	2 50·6	5·5 1·1	11·5 2·2	17·5 3·4
56	2 59·0	2 59·5	2 50·8	5·6 1·1	11·6 2·2	17·6 3·4
57	2 59·3	2 59·7	2 51·1	5·7 1·1	11·7 2·2	17·7 3·4
58	2 59·5	3 00·0	2 51·3	5·8 1·1	11·8 2·3	17·8 3·4
59	2 59·8	3 00·2	2 51·6	5·9 1·1	11·9 2·3	17·9 3·4
60	3 00·0	3 00·5	2 51·8	6·0 1·2	12·0 2·3	18·0 3·5

Extract Number A13

36ᵐ — INCREMENTS AND CORRECTIONS — 37ᵐ

36ᵐ

36	SUN PLANETS	ARIES	MOON	v or d	Corrⁿ	v or d	Corrⁿ	v or d	Corrⁿ
s	° ′	° ′	° ′	′	′	′	′	′	′
00	9 00·0	9 01·5	8 35·4	0·0	0·0	6·0	3·7	12·0	7·3
01	9 00·3	9 01·7	8 35·6	0·1	0·1	6·1	3·7	12·1	7·4
02	9 00·5	9 02·0	8 35·9	0·2	0·1	6·2	3·8	12·2	7·4
03	9 00·8	9 02·2	8 36·1	0·3	0·2	6·3	3·8	12·3	7·5
04	9 01·0	9 02·5	8 36·4	0·4	0·2	6·4	3·9	12·4	7·5
05	9 01·3	9 02·7	8 36·6	0·5	0·3	6·5	4·0	12·5	7·6
06	9 01·5	9 03·0	8 36·8	0·6	0·4	6·6	4·0	12·6	7·7
07	9 01·8	9 03·2	8 37·1	0·7	0·4	6·7	4·1	12·7	7·7
08	9 02·0	9 03·5	8 37·3	0·8	0·5	6·8	4·1	12·8	7·8
09	9 02·3	9 03·7	8 37·5	0·9	0·5	6·9	4·2	12·9	7·8
10	9 02·5	9 04·0	8 37·8	1·0	0·6	7·0	4·3	13·0	7·9
11	9 02·8	9 04·2	8 38·0	1·1	0·7	7·1	4·3	13·1	8·0
12	9 03·0	9 04·5	8 38·3	1·2	0·7	7·2	4·4	13·2	8·0
13	9 03·3	9 04·7	8 38·5	1·3	0·8	7·3	4·4	13·3	8·1
14	9 03·5	9 05·0	8 38·7	1·4	0·9	7·4	4·5	13·4	8·2
15	9 03·8	9 05·2	8 39·0	1·5	0·9	7·5	4·6	13·5	8·2
16	9 04·0	9 05·5	8 39·2	1·6	1·0	7·6	4·6	13·6	8·3
17	9 04·3	9 05·7	8 39·5	1·7	1·0	7·7	4·7	13·7	8·3
18	9 04·5	9 06·0	8 39·7	1·8	1·1	7·8	4·7	13·8	8·4
19	9 04·8	9 06·2	8 39·9	1·9	1·2	7·9	4·8	13·9	8·5
20	9 05·0	9 06·5	8 40·2	2·0	1·2	8·0	4·9	14·0	8·5
21	9 05·3	9 06·7	8 40·4	2·1	1·3	8·1	4·9	14·1	8·6
22	9 05·5	9 07·0	8 40·6	2·2	1·3	8·2	5·0	14·2	8·6
23	9 05·8	9 07·2	8 40·9	2·3	1·4	8·3	5·0	14·3	8·7
24	9 06·0	9 07·5	8 41·1	2·4	1·5	8·4	5·1	14·4	8·8
25	9 06·3	9 07·7	8 41·4	2·5	1·5	8·5	5·2	14·5	8·8
26	9 06·5	9 08·0	8 41·6	2·6	1·6	8·6	5·2	14·6	8·9
27	9 06·8	9 08·2	8 41·8	2·7	1·6	8·7	5·3	14·7	9·2
28	9 07·0	9 08·5	8 42·1	2·8	1·7	8·8	5·4	14·8	9·0
29	9 07·3	9 08·7	8 42·3	2·9	1·8	8·9	5·4	14·9	9·1
30	9 07·5	9 09·0	8 42·6	3·0	1·8	9·0	5·5	15·0	9·1
31	9 07·8	9 09·2	8 42·8	3·1	1·9	9·1	5·5	15·1	9·2
32	9 08·0	9 09·5	8 43·0	3·2	1·9	9·2	5·6	15·2	9·2
33	9 08·3	9 09·8	8 43·3	3·3	2·0	9·3	5·7	15·3	9·3
34	9 08·5	9 10·0	8 43·5	3·4	2·1	9·4	5·7	15·4	9·4
35	9 08·8	9 10·3	8 43·8	3·5	2·1	9·5	5·8	15·5	9·4
36	9 09·0	9 10·5	8 44·0	3·6	2·2	9·6	5·8	15·6	9·5
37	9 09·3	9 10·8	8 44·2	3·7	2·3	9·7	5·9	15·7	9·6
38	9 09·5	9 11·0	8 44·5	3·8	2·3	9·8	6·0	15·8	9·6
39	9 09·8	9 11·3	8 44·7	3·9	2·4	9·9	6·0	15·9	9·7
40	9 10·0	9 11·5	8 44·9	4·0	2·4	10·0	6·1	16·0	9·7
41	9 10·3	9 11·8	8 45·2	4·1	2·5	10·1	6·1	16·1	9·8
42	9 10·5	9 12·0	8 45·4	4·2	2·6	10·2	6·2	16·2	9·9
43	9 10·8	9 12·3	8 45·7	4·3	2·6	10·3	6·3	16·3	9·9
44	9 11·0	9 12·5	8 45·9	4·4	2·7	10·4	6·3	16·4	10·0
45	9 11·3	9 12·8	8 46·1	4·5	2·7	10·5	6·4	16·5	10·0
46	9 11·5	9 13·0	8 46·4	4·6	2·8	10·6	6·4	16·6	10·1
47	9 11·8	9 13·3	8 46·6	4·7	2·9	10·7	6·5	16·7	10·2
48	9 12·0	9 13·5	8 46·9	4·8	2·9	10·8	6·5	16·8	10·2
49	9 12·3	9 13·8	8 47·1	4·9	3·0	10·9	6·6	16·9	10·3
50	9 12·5	9 14·0	8 47·3	5·0	3·0	11·0	6·7	17·0	10·3
51	9 12·8	9 14·3	8 47·6	5·1	3·1	11·1	6·8	17·1	10·4
52	9 13·0	9 14·5	8 47·8	5·2	3·2	11·2	6·8	17·2	10·5
53	9 13·3	9 14·8	8 48·0	5·3	3·3	11·3	6·9	17·3	10·5
54	9 13·5	9 15·0	8 48·3	5·4	3·3	11·4	6·9	17·4	10·6
55	9 13·8	9 15·3	8 48·5	5·5	3·3	11·5	7·0	17·5	10·6
56	9 14·0	9 15·5	8 48·8	5·6	3·4	11·6	7·1	17·6	11·0
57	9 14·3	9 15·8	8 49·0	5·7	3·5	11·7	7·1	17·7	10·8
58	9 14·5	9 16·0	8 49·2	5·8	3·5	11·8	7·2	17·8	10·8
59	9 14·8	9 16·3	8 49·5	5·9	3·6	11·9	7·2	17·9	10·9
60	9 15·0	9 16·5	8 49·7	6·0	3·7	12·0	7·3	18·0	11·0

37ᵐ

37	SUN PLANETS	ARIES	MOON	v or d	Corrⁿ	v or d	Corrⁿ	v or d	Corrⁿ
s	° ′	° ′	° ′	′	′	′	′	′	′
00	9 15·0	9 16·5	8 49·7	0·0	0·0	6·0	3·8	12·0	7·5
01	9 15·3	9 16·8	8 50·0	0·1	0·1	6·1	3·8	12·1	7·6
02	9 15·5	9 17·0	8 50·2	0·2	0·1	6·2	3·9	12·2	7·6
03	9 15·8	9 17·3	8 50·4	0·3	0·2	6·3	3·9	12·3	7·7
04	9 16·0	9 17·5	8 50·7	0·4	0·3	6·4	4·0	12·4	7·8
05	9 16·3	9 17·8	8 50·9	0·5	0·3	6·5	4·1	12·5	7·8
06	9 16·5	9 18·0	8 51·1	0·6	0·4	6·6	4·1	12·6	7·9
07	9 16·8	9 18·3	8 51·4	0·7	0·4	6·7	4·2	12·7	7·9
08	9 17·0	9 18·5	8 51·6	0·8	0·5	6·8	4·3	12·8	8·0
09	9 17·3	9 18·8	8 51·9	0·9	0·6	6·9	4·3	12·9	8·1
10	9 17·5	9 19·0	8 52·1	1·0	0·6	7·0	4·4	13·0	8·1
11	9 17·8	9 19·3	8 52·3	1·1	0·7	7·1	4·4	13·1	8·2
12	9 18·0	9 19·5	8 52·6	1·2	0·8	7·2	4·5	13·2	8·3
13	9 18·3	9 19·8	8 52·8	1·3	0·8	7·3	4·6	13·3	8·3
14	9 18·5	9 20·0	8 53·1	1·4	0·9	7·4	4·6	13·4	8·4
15	9 18·8	9 20·3	8 53·3	1·5	0·9	7·5	4·7	13·5	8·4
16	9 19·0	9 20·5	8 53·5	1·6	1·0	7·6	4·8	13·6	8·5
17	9 19·3	9 20·8	8 53·8	1·7	1·1	7·7	4·8	13·7	8·6
18	9 19·5	9 21·0	8 54·0	1·8	1·1	7·8	4·9	13·8	8·6
19	9 19·8	9 21·3	8 54·3	1·9	1·2	7·9	4·9	13·9	8·7
20	9 20·0	9 21·5	8 54·5	2·0	1·3	8·0	5·0	14·0	8·8
21	9 20·3	9 21·8	8 54·7	2·1	1·3	8·1	5·1	14·1	8·8
22	9 20·5	9 22·0	8 55·0	2·2	1·4	8·2	5·1	14·2	8·9
23	9 20·8	9 22·3	8 55·2	2·3	1·4	8·3	5·2	14·3	8·9
24	9 21·0	9 22·5	8 55·4	2·4	1·5	8·4	5·3	14·4	9·0
25	9 21·3	9 22·8	8 55·7	2·5	1·6	8·5	5·3	14·5	9·1
26	9 21·5	9 23·0	8 55·9	2·6	1·6	8·6	5·4	14·6	9·1
27	9 21·8	9 23·3	8 56·2	2·7	1·7	8·7	5·4	14·7	9·2
28	9 22·0	9 23·5	8 56·4	2·8	1·8	8·8	5·5	14·8	9·3
29	9 22·3	9 23·8	8 56·6	2·9	1·8	8·9	5·6	14·9	9·3
30	9 22·5	9 24·0	8 56·9	3·0	1·9	9·0	5·6	15·0	9·4
31	9 22·8	9 24·3	8 57·1	3·1	1·9	9·1	5·7	15·1	9·4
32	9 23·0	9 24·5	8 57·4	3·2	2·0	9·2	5·8	15·2	9·5
33	9 23·3	9 24·8	8 57·6	3·3	2·1	9·3	5·8	15·3	9·6
34	9 23·5	9 25·0	8 57·8	3·4	2·1	9·4	5·9	15·4	9·6
35	9 23·8	9 25·3	8 58·1	3·5	2·2	9·5	5·9	15·5	9·7
36	9 24·0	9 25·5	8 58·3	3·6	2·3	9·6	6·0	15·6	9·8
37	9 24·3	9 25·8	8 58·5	3·7	2·3	9·7	6·1	15·7	9·8
38	9 24·5	9 26·0	8 58·8	3·8	2·4	9·8	6·1	15·8	9·9
39	9 24·8	9 26·3	8 59·0	3·9	2·4	9·9	6·2	15·9	9·9
40	9 25·0	9 26·5	8 59·3	4·0	2·5	10·0	6·3	16·0	10·0
41	9 25·3	9 26·8	8 59·5	4·1	2·6	10·1	6·3	16·1	10·1
42	9 25·5	9 27·0	8 59·7	4·2	2·6	10·2	6·4	16·2	10·1
43	9 25·8	9 27·3	9 00·0	4·3	2·7	10·3	6·4	16·3	10·2
44	9 26·0	9 27·5	9 00·2	4·4	2·8	10·4	6·5	16·4	10·3
45	9 26·3	9 27·8	9 00·5	4·5	2·8	10·5	6·6	16·5	10·3
46	9 26·5	9 28·1	9 00·7	4·6	2·9	10·6	6·6	16·6	10·4
47	9 26·8	9 28·3	9 00·9	4·7	2·9	10·7	6·7	16·7	10·4
48	9 27·0	9 28·6	9 01·2	4·8	3·0	10·8	6·8	16·8	10·5
49	9 27·3	9 28·8	9 01·4	4·9	3·1	10·9	6·8	16·9	10·6
50	9 27·5	9 29·1	9 01·6	5·0	3·1	11·0	6·9	17·0	10·6
51	9 27·8	9 29·3	9 01·9	5·1	3·2	11·1	6·9	17·1	10·7
52	9 28·0	9 29·6	9 02·1	5·2	3·3	11·2	7·0	17·2	10·8
53	9 28·3	9 29·8	9 02·4	5·3	3·3	11·3	7·1	17·3	10·8
54	9 28·5	9 30·1	9 02·6	5·4	3·4	11·4	7·1	17·4	10·9
55	9 28·8	9 30·3	9 02·8	5·5	3·4	11·5	7·2	17·5	10·9
56	9 29·0	9 30·6	9 03·1	5·6	3·5	11·6	7·3	17·6	11·0
57	9 29·3	9 30·8	9 03·3	5·7	3·6	11·7	7·3	17·7	11·1
58	9 29·5	9 31·1	9 03·6	5·8	3·6	11·8	7·4	17·8	11·1
59	9 29·8	9 31·3	9 03·8	5·9	3·7	11·9	7·4	17·9	11·2
60	9 30·0	9 31·6	9 04·0	6·0	3·8	12·0	7·5	18·0	11·3

Extract Number A14

46ᵐ   INCREMENTS AND CORRECTIONS   **47ᵐ**

46ᵐ	SUN PLANETS	ARIES	MOON	v or d / Corrⁿ	v or d / Corrⁿ	v or d / Corrⁿ
s	° ′	° ′	° ′	′ ′	′ ′	′ ′
00	11 30·0	11 31·9	10 58·6	0·0 0·0	6·0 4·7	12·0 9·3
01	11 30·3	11 32·1	10 58·8	0·1 0·1	6·1 4·7	12·1 9·4
02	11 30·5	11 32·4	10 59·0	0·2 0·2	6·2 4·8	12·2 9·5
03	11 30·8	11 32·6	10 59·3	0·3 0·2	6·3 4·9	12·3 9·5
04	11 31·0	11 32·9	10 59·5	0·4 0·3	6·4 5·0	12·4 9·6
05	11 31·3	11 33·1	10 59·8	0·5 0·4	6·5 5·0	12·5 9·7
06	11 31·5	11 33·4	11 00·0	0·6 0·5	6·6 5·1	12·6 9·8
07	11 31·8	11 33·6	11 00·2	0·7 0·5	6·7 5·2	12·7 9·8
08	11 32·0	11 33·9	11 00·5	0·8 0·6	6·8 5·3	12·8 9·9
09	11 32·3	11 34·1	11 00·7	0·9 0·7	6·9 5·3	12·9 10·0
10	11 32·5	11 34·4	11 01·0	1·0 0·8	7·0 5·4	13·0 10·1
11	11 32·8	11 34·6	11 01·2	1·1 0·9	7·1 5·5	13·1 10·2
12	11 33·0	11 34·9	11 01·4	1·2 0·9	7·2 5·6	13·2 10·2
13	11 33·3	11 35·1	11 01·7	1·3 1·0	7·3 5·7	13·3 10·3
14	11 33·5	11 35·4	11 01·9	1·4 1·1	7·4 5·7	13·4 10·4
15	11 33·8	11 35·6	11 02·1	1·5 1·2	7·5 5·8	13·5 10·5
16	11 34·0	11 35·9	11 02·4	1·6 1·2	7·6 5·9	13·6 10·5
17	11 34·3	11 36·2	11 02·6	1·7 1·3	7·7 6·0	13·7 10·6
18	11 34·5	11 36·4	11 02·9	1·8 1·4	7·8 6·0	13·8 10·7
19	11 34·8	11 36·7	11 03·1	1·9 1·5	7·9 6·1	13·9 10·8
20	11 35·0	11 36·9	11 03·3	2·0 1·6	8·0 6·2	14·0 10·9
21	11 35·3	11 37·2	11 03·6	2·1 1·6	8·1 6·3	14·1 10·9
22	11 35·5	11 37·4	11 03·8	2·2 1·7	8·2 6·4	14·2 11·0
23	11 35·8	11 37·7	11 04·1	2·3 1·8	8·3 6·4	14·3 11·1
24	11 36·0	11 37·9	11 04·3	2·4 1·9	8·4 6·5	14·4 11·2
25	11 36·3	11 38·2	11 04·5	2·5 1·9	8·5 6·6	14·5 11·2
26	11 36·5	11 38·4	11 04·8	2·6 2·0	8·6 6·7	14·6 11·3
27	11 36·8	11 38·7	11 05·0	2·7 2·1	8·7 6·7	14·7 11·4
28	11 37·0	11 38·9	11 05·2	2·8 2·2	8·8 6·8	14·8 11·5
29	11 37·3	11 39·2	11 05·5	2·9 2·2	8·9 6·9	14·9 11·5
30	11 37·5	11 39·4	11 05·7	3·0 2·3	9·0 7·0	15·0 11·6
31	11 37·8	11 39·7	11 06·0	3·1 2·4	9·1 7·1	15·1 11·7
32	11 38·0	11 39·9	11 06·2	3·2 2·5	9·2 7·1	15·2 11·8
33	11 38·3	11 40·2	11 06·4	3·3 2·6	9·3 7·2	15·3 11·9
34	11 38·5	11 40·4	11 06·7	3·4 2·6	9·4 7·3	15·4 11·9
35	11 38·8	11 40·7	11 06·9	3·5 2·7	9·5 7·4	15·5 12·0
36	11 39·0	11 40·9	11 07·2	3·6 2·8	9·6 7·4	15·6 12·1
37	11 39·3	11 41·2	11 07·4	3·7 2·9	9·7 7·5	15·7 12·2
38	11 39·5	11 41·4	11 07·6	3·8 2·9	9·8 7·6	15·8 12·2
39	11 39·8	11 41·7	11 07·9	3·9 3·0	9·9 7·7	15·9 12·3
40	11 40·0	11 41·9	11 08·1	4·0 3·1	10·0 7·8	16·0 12·4
41	11 40·3	11 42·2	11 08·3	4·1 3·2	10·1 7·8	16·1 12·5
42	11 40·5	11 42·4	11 08·6	4·2 3·3	10·2 7·9	16·2 12·6
43	11 40·8	11 42·7	11 08·8	4·3 3·3	10·3 8·0	16·3 12·6
44	11 41·0	11 42·9	11 09·1	4·4 3·4	10·4 8·1	16·4 12·7
45	11 41·3	11 43·2	11 09·3	4·5 3·5	10·5 8·1	16·5 12·8
46	11 41·5	11 43·4	11 09·5	4·6 3·6	10·6 8·2	16·6 12·9
47	11 41·8	11 43·7	11 09·8	4·7 3·6	10·7 8·3	16·7 12·9
48	11 42·0	11 43·9	11 10·0	4·8 3·7	10·8 8·4	16·8 13·0
49	11 42·3	11 44·2	11 10·3	4·9 3·8	10·9 8·4	16·9 13·1
50	11 42·5	11 44·4	11 10·5	5·0 3·9	11·0 8·5	17·0 13·2
51	11 42·8	11 44·7	11 10·7	5·1 4·0	11·1 8·6	17·1 13·3
52	11 43·0	11 44·9	11 11·0	5·2 4·0	11·2 8·7	17·2 13·3
53	11 43·3	11 45·2	11 11·2	5·3 4·1	11·3 8·8	17·3 13·4
54	11 43·5	11 45·4	11 11·5	5·4 4·2	11·4 8·8	17·4 13·5
55	11 43·8	11 45·7	11 11·7	5·5 4·3	11·5 8·9	17·5 13·6
56	11 44·0	11 45·9	11 11·9	5·6 4·3	11·6 9·0	17·6 13·6
57	11 44·3	11 46·2	11 12·2	5·7 4·4	11·7 9·1	17·7 13·7
58	11 44·5	11 46·4	11 12·4	5·8 4·5	11·8 9·1	17·8 13·8
59	11 44·8	11 46·7	11 12·6	5·9 4·6	11·9 9·2	17·9 13·9
60	11 45·0	11 46·9	11 12·9	6·0 4·7	12·0 9·3	18·0 14·0

47ᵐ	SUN PLANETS	ARIES	MOON	v or d / Corrⁿ	v or d / Corrⁿ	v or d / Corrⁿ
s	° ′	° ′	° ′	′ ′	′ ′	′ ′
00	11 45·0	11 46·9	11 12·9	0·0 0·0	6·0 4·8	12·0 9·5
01	11 45·3	11 47·2	11 13·1	0·1 0·1	6·1 4·8	12·1 9·6
02	11 45·5	11 47·4	11 13·4	0·2 0·2	6·2 4·9	12·2 9·7
03	11 45·8	11 47·7	11 13·6	0·3 0·2	6·3 5·0	12·3 9·7
04	11 46·0	11 47·9	11 13·8	0·4 0·3	6·4 5·1	12·4 9·8
05	11 46·3	11 48·2	11 14·1	0·5 0·4	6·5 5·1	12·5 9·9
06	11 46·5	11 48·4	11 14·3	0·6 0·5	6·6 5·2	12·6 10·0
07	11 46·8	11 48·7	11 14·6	0·7 0·6	6·7 5·3	12·7 10·1
08	11 47·0	11 48·9	11 14·8	0·8 0·6	6·8 5·4	12·8 10·1
09	11 47·3	11 49·2	11 15·0	0·9 0·7	6·9 5·5	12·9 10·2
10	11 47·5	11 49·4	11 15·3	1·0 0·8	7·0 5·5	13·0 10·3
11	11 47·8	11 49·7	11 15·5	1·1 0·9	7·1 5·6	13·1 10·4
12	11 48·0	11 49·9	11 15·7	1·2 1·0	7·2 5·7	13·2 10·5
13	11 48·3	11 50·2	11 16·0	1·3 1·0	7·3 5·8	13·3 10·5
14	11 48·5	11 50·4	11 16·2	1·4 1·1	7·4 5·9	13·4 10·6
15	11 48·8	11 50·7	11 16·5	1·5 1·2	7·5 5·9	13·5 10·7
16	11 49·0	11 50·9	11 16·7	1·6 1·3	7·6 6·0	13·6 10·8
17	11 49·3	11 51·2	11 16·9	1·7 1·3	7·7 6·1	13·7 10·8
18	11 49·5	11 51·4	11 17·2	1·8 1·4	7·8 6·2	13·8 10·9
19	11 49·8	11 51·7	11 17·4	1·9 1·5	7·9 6·3	13·9 11·0
20	11 50·0	11 51·9	11 17·7	2·0 1·6	8·0 6·3	14·0 11·1
21	11 50·3	11 52·2	11 17·9	2·1 1·7	8·1 6·4	14·1 11·2
22	11 50·5	11 52·4	11 18·1	2·2 1·7	8·2 6·5	14·2 11·2
23	11 50·8	11 52·7	11 18·4	2·3 1·8	8·3 6·6	14·3 11·3
24	11 51·0	11 52·9	11 18·6	2·4 1·9	8·4 6·7	14·4 11·4
25	11 51·3	11 53·2	11 18·8	2·5 2·0	8·5 6·7	14·5 11·5
26	11 51·5	11 53·4	11 19·1	2·6 2·1	8·6 6·8	14·6 11·6
27	11 51·8	11 53·7	11 19·3	2·7 2·1	8·7 6·9	14·7 11·6
28	11 52·0	11 53·9	11 19·6	2·8 2·2	8·8 7·0	14·8 11·7
29	11 52·3	11 54·2	11 19·8	2·9 2·3	8·9 7·0	14·9 11·8
30	11 52·5	11 54·5	11 20·0	3·0 2·4	9·0 7·1	15·0 11·9
31	11 52·8	11 54·7	11 20·3	3·1 2·5	9·1 7·2	15·1 12·0
32	11 53·0	11 55·0	11 20·5	3·2 2·5	9·2 7·3	15·2 12·0
33	11 53·3	11 55·2	11 20·8	3·3 2·6	9·3 7·4	15·3 12·1
34	11 53·5	11 55·5	11 21·0	3·4 2·7	9·4 7·4	15·4 12·2
35	11 53·8	11 55·7	11 21·2	3·5 2·8	9·5 7·5	15·5 12·3
36	11 54·0	11 56·0	11 21·5	3·6 2·9	9·6 7·6	15·6 12·4
37	11 54·3	11 56·2	11 21·7	3·7 2·9	9·7 7·7	15·7 12·4
38	11 54·5	11 56·5	11 22·0	3·8 3·0	9·8 7·8	15·8 12·5
39	11 54·8	11 56·7	11 22·2	3·9 3·1	9·9 7·8	15·9 12·6
40	11 55·0	11 57·0	11 22·4	4·0 3·2	10·0 7·9	16·0 12·7
41	11 55·3	11 57·2	11 22·7	4·1 3·2	10·1 8·0	16·1 12·7
42	11 55·5	11 57·5	11 22·9	4·2 3·3	10·2 8·1	16·2 12·8
43	11 55·8	11 57·7	11 23·1	4·3 3·4	10·3 8·2	16·3 12·9
44	11 56·0	11 58·0	11 23·4	4·4 3·5	10·4 8·2	16·4 13·0
45	11 56·3	11 58·2	11 23·6	4·5 3·6	10·5 8·3	16·5 13·1
46	11 56·5	11 58·5	11 23·9	4·6 3·6	10·6 8·4	16·6 13·1
47	11 56·8	11 58·7	11 24·1	4·7 3·7	10·7 8·5	16·7 13·2
48	11 57·0	11 59·0	11 24·3	4·8 3·8	10·8 8·5	16·8 13·3
49	11 57·3	11 59·2	11 24·6	4·9 3·9	10·9 8·6	16·9 13·4
50	11 57·5	11 59·5	11 24·8	5·0 4·0	11·0 8·7	17·0 13·5
51	11 57·8	11 59·7	11 25·1	5·1 4·0	11·1 8·8	17·1 13·5
52	11 58·0	12 00·0	11 25·3	5·2 4·1	11·2 8·9	17·2 13·6
53	11 58·3	12 00·2	11 25·5	5·3 4·2	11·3 8·9	17·3 13·7
54	11 58·5	12 00·5	11 25·8	5·4 4·3	11·4 9·0	17·4 13·8
55	11 58·8	12 00·7	11 26·0	5·5 4·4	11·5 9·1	17·5 13·9
56	11 59·0	12 01·0	11 26·2	5·6 4·4	11·6 9·2	17·6 13·9
57	11 59·3	12 01·2	11 26·5	5·7 4·5	11·7 9·3	17·7 14·0
58	11 59·5	12 01·5	11 26·7	5·8 4·6	11·8 9·3	17·8 14·1
59	11 59·8	12 01·7	11 27·0	5·9 4·7	11·9 9·4	17·9 14·2
60	12 00·0	12 02·0	11 27·2	6·0 4·8	12·0 9·5	18·0 14·3

Extract Number A15

Appendix B

Extracts from *AP 3270 Sight Reduction Tables for Air Navigation Vols 1* and *3*

LAT 50°N

LHA γ	◆Dubhe Hc Zn	REGULUS Hc Zn	PROCYON Hc Zn	◆SIRIUS Hc Zn	RIGEL Hc Zn	ALDEBARAN Hc Zn	◆Mirfak Hc Zn
90	48 39 044	27 11 104	40 44 147	22 36 169	30 54 193	52 19 215	64 59 285
91	49 06 044	27 49 105	41 05 148	22 43 170	30 45 195	51 57 216	64 22 285
92	49 33 044	28 26 106	41 25 149	22 50 171	30 35 196	51 34 218	63 45 286
93	50 00 044	29 03 107	41 44 151	22 56 172	30 24 197	51 10 219	63 08 286
94	50 27 045	29 40 108	42 03 152	23 01 173	30 13 198	50 45 220	62 31 286
95	50 54 045	30 16 109	42 21 153	23 06 174	30 00 199	50 20 222	61 54 287
96	51 21 045	30 53 109	42 38 154	23 10 175	29 47 200	49 54 223	61 17 287
97	51 49 045	31 29 110	42 54 156	23 13 176	29 34 201	49 27 224	60 40 288
98	52 16 045	32 05 111	43 09 157	23 15 177	29 19 202	49 00 226	60 04 288
99	52 44 046	32 41 112	43 24 158	23 17 178	29 04 203	48 32 227	59 27 289
100	53 11 046	33 16 113	43 38 160	23 18 179	28 49 205	48 04 228	58 51 289
101	53 39 046	33 52 114	43 50 161	23 19 180	28 32 206	47 35 229	58 14 289
102	54 07 046	34 27 115	44 03 162	23 18 181	28 15 207	47 05 231	57 38 290
103	54 35 046	35 02 116	44 14 164	23 17 182	27 58 208	46 35 232	57 02 290
104	55 02 046	35 36 117	44 24 165	23 16 183	27 39 209	46 04 233	56 25 291

	◆Mirfak Hc Zn	Alpheratz Hc Zn	◆ALTAIR Hc Zn	Rasalhague Hc Zn	◆ARCTURUS Hc Zn	Alkaid Hc Zn	Kochab Hc Zn
285	20 03 034	29 57 079	47 32 162	48 38 213	26 35 269	41 48 301	54 55 335
286	20 24 034	30 35 080	47 44 163	48 17 214	25 56 270	41 15 302	54 39 335
287	20 46 035	31 13 081	47 54 164	47 55 215	25 17 270	40 42 302	54 23 335
288	21 09 036	31 51 082	48 04 166	47 32 217	24 39 271	40 10 303	54 07 335
289	21 31 036	32 29 082	48 13 167	47 08 218	24 00 272	39 37 303	53 50 335
290	21 54 037	33 07 083	48 21 169	46 44 219	23 22 273	39 05 304	53 34 335
291	22 17 037	33 46 084	48 28 170	46 19 221	22 43 273	38 33 304	53 18 335
292	22 41 038	34 24 084	48 34 172	45 54 222	22 05 274	38 01 305	53 02 335
293	23 05 038	35 02 085	48 39 173	45 28 223	21 26 275	37 30 305	52 45 335
294	23 29 039	35 41 086	48 43 175	45 01 224	20 48 276	36 58 306	52 29 335
295	23 53 040	36 19 087	48 46 176	44 34 226	20 10 276	36 27 306	52 13 335
296	24 18 040	36 58 087	48 48 178	44 06 227	19 31 277	35 56 307	51 56 335
297	24 43 041	37 36 088	48 49 179	43 37 228	18 53 278	35 25 307	51 40 335
298	25 08 041	38 15 089	48 49 181	43 08 229	18 15 279	34 54 308	51 24 335
299	25 34 042	38 54 090	48 48 182	42 39 230	17 37 279	34 24 308	51 08 335

	CAPELLA Hc Zn	◆Hamal Hc Zn	Alpheratz Hc Zn	Enif Hc Zn	◆ALTAIR Hc Zn	VEGA Hc Zn	◆Kochab Hc Zn
315	17 36 037	26 12 084	49 06 103	48 48 164	46 18 206	62 18 260	46 54 337
316	17 59 038	26 50 085	49 43 104	48 58 165	46 01 207	61 40 261	46 39 337
317	18 23 038	27 29 086	50 21 105	49 08 167	45 43 208	61 02 262	46 24 337
318	18 47 039	28 07 086	50 58 106	49 16 168	45 25 210	60 24 263	46 09 337
319	19 12 040	28 46 087	51 35 107	49 23 170	45 05 211	59 46 264	45 54 337
320	19 37 040	29 24 088	52 12 108	49 30 171	44 45 212	59 07 265	45 39 337
321	20 02 041	30 03 089	52 48 109	49 35 173	44 24 214	58 29 265	45 24 337
322	20 27 041	30 41 089	53 25 110	49 40 174	44 02 215	57 50 266	45 09 338
323	20 53 042	31 20 090	54 01 111	49 43 176	43 40 216	57 12 267	44 55 338
324	21 19 043	31 59 091	54 37 112	49 45 177	43 17 217	56 33 268	44 40 338
325	21 45 043	32 37 092	55 12 113	49 47 179	42 53 219	55 55 269	44 26 338
326	22 12 044	33 16 093	55 48 114	49 47 180	42 29 220	55 16 269	44 11 338
327	22 38 044	33 54 093	56 22 116	49 46 182	42 04 221	54 38 270	43 57 339
328	23 06 045	34 33 094	56 57 117	49 44 183	41 38 222	53 59 271	43 43 339
329	23 33 045	35 11 095	57 31 118	49 42 185	41 12 223	53 21 272	43 29 339

Extract Number A16

LAT 50°

A dense sight-reduction table with column headings 0°, 1°, 2°, 3°, 4°, 5°, 6°, 7°, 8°, 9°, 10°, 11°, 12°, 13°, 14° and latitude row labels from 0 to 69.

DECLINATION (0°–14°) CONTRARY NAME TO LATITUDE

S. Lat. { LHA greater than 180°........Zn=180−Z ; LHA less than 180°........Zn=180+Z }

LAT 50°

Extract Number A17

LAT 50°

N. Lat. {LHA greater than 180°....... Zn=Z
LHA less than 180°........... Zn=360−Z}

DECLINATION (0°-14°) SAME NAME AS LATITUDE

	0°			1°			2°			3°		
LHA	Hc	d	Z	Hc	d	Z	Hc	d	Z	Hc	d	Z
	° ′	′	°	° ′	′	°	° ′	′	°	° ′	′	°
0	40 00	+60	180	41 00	+60	180	42 00	+60	180	43 00	+60	180
1	40 00	60	179	41 00	60	179	42 00	60	179	43 00	60	179
2	39 58	60	177	40 58	60	177	41 58	60	177	42 58	60	177
3	39 56	60	176	40 56	60	176	41 56	60	176	42 56	60	176
4	39 53	60	175	40 53	60	175	41 53	60	175	42 53	60	175
5	39 49	+60	174	40 49	+60	173	41 49	+60	173	42 49	+59	173
6	39 44	60	172	40 44	60	172	41 44	60	172	42 44	59	172
7	39 39	59	171	40 38	60	171	41 38	60	171	42 38	59	171
8	39 32	60	170	40 32	59	170	41 31	60	169	42 31	59	169
9	39 25	59	168	40 24	60	168	41 24	59	168	42 23	60	168
10	39 16	+60	167	40 16	+59	167	41 15	+59	167	42 14	+60	167
11	39 07	60	166	40 07	59	166	41 06	59	165	42 05	59	165
12	38 57	60	165	39 57	59	164	40 56	59	164	41 55	59	164
13	38 47	59	163	39 46	59	163	40 45	59	163	41 44	58	163
14	38 35	59	162	39 34	59	162	40 33	58	161	41 31	59	161
15	38 23	+59	161	39 22	+58	160	40 20	+59	160	41 19	+58	160
16	38 10	58	160	39 08	59	159	40 07	58	159	41 05	58	159
17	37 56	58	158	38 54	58	158	39 52	58	158	40 50	59	157
18	37 41	58	157	38 39	58	157	39 37	58	156	40 35	58	156
19	37 26	58	156	38 24	57	156	39 21	58	155	40 19	58	155
20	37 10	+57	155	38 07	+58	154	39 05	+57	154	40 02	+58	154
21	36 53	57	153	37 50	57	153	38 47	58	153	39 45	57	152
22	36 35	57	152	37 32	57	152	38 29	57	151	39 26	57	151
23	36 17	57	151	37 14	57	151	38 11	56	150	39 07	57	150
24	35 58	56	150	36 54	57	149	37 51	57	149	38 48	56	149
25	35 38	+56	149	36 34	+57	148	37 31	+56	148	38 27	+56	147
26	35 18	56	148	36 14	56	147	37 10	56	147	38 06	56	146
27	34 56	57	146	35 53	55	146	36 48	56	146	37 44	56	145
28	34 35	56	145	35 31	55	145	36 26	56	144	37 22	55	144
29	34 13	55	144	35 08	55	144	36 03	56	143	36 59	55	143
30	33 50	+55	143	34 45	+55	143	35 40	+55	142	36 35	+55	142
31	33 26	55	142	34 21	55	141	35 16	55	141	36 11	54	140
32	33 02	55	141	33 57	54	140	34 51	55	140	35 46	54	139
33	32 37	55	140	33 32	54	139	34 26	55	139	35 21	54	138
34	32 12	54	139	33 06	55	138	34 01	54	138	34 55	53	137
35	31 46	+54	138	32 40	+54	137	33 34	+54	137	34 28	+54	136
36	31 20	54	137	32 14	53	136	33 07	54	136	34 01	53	135
37	30 53	54	136	31 47	53	135	32 40	53	134	33 33	53	134
38	30 26	53	134	31 19	53	134	32 12	53	133	33 05	53	133
39	29 58	53	133	30 51	53	133	31 44	53	132	32 37	52	132
40	29 30	+53	132	30 23	+52	132	31 15	+53	131	32 08	+52	131
41	29 01	53	131	29 54	52	131	30 46	52	130	31 38	52	130
42	28 32	52	130	29 24	52	130	30 16	52	129	31 08	52	129
43	28 03	52	129	28 55	51	129	29 46	52	128	30 38	52	128
44	27 33	51	128	28 24	52	128	29 16	51	127	30 07	52	127
45	27 02	+52	128	27 54	+51	127	28 45	+51	126	29 36	+51	126
46	26 31	52	127	27 23	51	126	28 14	51	125	29 05	51	125
47	26 00	51	126	26 51	51	125	27 42	51	124	28 33	50	124
48	25 29	50	125	26 19	51	124	27 10	51	123	28 01	50	123
49	24 57	50	124	25 47	51	123	26 38	50	123	27 28	50	122
50	24 24	+51	123	25 15	+50	122	26 05	+50	122	26 55	+50	121
51	23 52	50	122	24 42	50	121	25 32	50	121	26 22	50	120
52	23 19	50	121	24 09	50	120	24 59	49	120	25 48	50	119
53	22 46	49	120	23 35	50	119	24 25	49	119	25 14	50	118
54	22 12	50	119	23 02	49	119	23 51	49	118	24 40	49	117
55	21 38	+50	118	22 28	+49	118	23 17	+49	117	24 06	+49	116
56	21 04	49	117	21 53	49	117	22 42	49	116	23 31	49	116
57	20 30	49	116	21 19	48	116	22 07	49	115	22 56	49	115
58	19 55	49	116	20 44	48	115	21 32	49	114	22 21	48	114
59	19 20	49	115	20 09	48	114	20 57	49	114	21 46	48	113
60	18 45	+48	114	19 33	+49	113	20 22	+48	113	21 10	+48	112
61	18 09	49	113	18 58	48	112	19 46	48	112	20 34	48	111
62	17 34	48	112	18 22	48	112	19 10	48	111	19 58	48	110
63	16 58	48	111	17 46	48	111	18 34	48	110	19 22	47	109
64	16 22	48	111	17 10	48	110	17 58	47	109	18 45	48	109
65	15 46	+48	110	16 34	+47	109	17 21	+48	108	18 09	+47	108
66	15 09	48	109	15 57	47	108	16 44	48	108	17 32	47	107
67	14 33	47	108	15 20	48	107	16 08	47	107	16 55	47	106
68	13 56	47	107	14 43	48	107	15 31	47	106	16 18	47	105
69	13 19	47	106	14 06	47	106	14 53	47	105	15 40	47	105

	4°			5°			6°			7°		
LHA	Hc	d	Z	Hc	d	Z	Hc	d	Z	Hc	d	Z
	° ′	′	°	° ′	′	°	° ′	′	°	° ′	′	°
0	44 00	+60	180	45 00	+60	180	46 00	+60	180	47 00	+60	180
1	44 00	60	179	45 00	60	179	46 00	60	179	47 00	60	179
2	43 58	60	177	44 58	60	177	45 58	60	177	46 58	60	177
3	43 56	60	176	44 56	60	176	45 56	60	176	46 56	60	176
4	43 53	59	175	44 52	60	174	45 52	60	174	46 52	60	174
5	43 48	+60	173	44 48	+60	173	45 48	+60	173	46 48	+60	173
6	43 43	60	172	44 43	60	172	45 43	59	171	46 42	60	171
7	43 37	60	170	44 37	60	170	45 37	59	170	46 36	60	170
8	43 30	60	169	44 30	59	169	45 29	60	169	46 29	59	168
9	43 23	59	168	44 22	59	167	45 21	60	167	46 21	59	167
10	43 14	+59	166	44 13	+59	166	45 12	+60	166	46 12	+59	166
11	43 04	59	165	44 03	59	165	45 02	59	164	46 01	60	164
12	42 54	59	164	43 53	59	163	44 52	59	163	45 51	58	163
13	42 42	59	162	43 41	59	162	44 40	59	162	45 39	58	161
14	42 30	59	161	43 29	58	161	44 27	59	160	45 26	58	160
15	42 17	+59	160	43 16	+58	159	44 14	+58	159	45 12	+59	159
16	42 03	58	158	43 01	59	158	44 00	58	158	44 58	58	157
17	41 49	58	157	42 47	58	157	43 45	57	156	44 42	58	156
18	41 33	58	156	42 31	58	155	43 29	57	155	44 26	58	155
19	41 17	57	154	42 14	58	154	43 12	57	154	44 09	58	153
20	41 00	+57	153	41 57	+57	153	42 54	+58	152	43 52	+57	152
21	40 42	57	152	41 39	57	152	42 36	57	151	43 33	57	151
22	40 23	57	151	41 20	57	150	42 17	57	150	43 14	56	149
23	40 04	57	149	41 01	56	149	41 57	57	149	42 54	56	148
24	39 44	56	148	40 40	57	148	41 37	56	147	42 33	56	147
25	39 23	+57	147	40 20	+56	147	41 16	+55	146	42 11	+56	146
26	39 02	56	146	39 58	56	145	40 54	55	145	41 49	56	144
27	38 40	56	145	39 36	55	144	40 31	55	144	41 26	56	143
28	38 17	56	143	39 13	55	143	40 08	55	142	41 03	55	142
29	37 54	55	142	38 49	55	142	39 44	55	141	40 39	54	141
30	37 30	+55	141	38 25	+54	141	39 19	+55	140	40 14	+54	140
31	37 05	55	140	38 00	54	139	38 54	55	139	39 49	54	138
32	36 40	55	139	37 35	54	138	38 29	54	138	39 23	53	137
33	36 15	54	138	37 09	53	137	38 02	54	137	38 56	54	136
34	35 48	54	137	36 42	54	136	37 36	53	135	38 29	53	135
35	35 22	+53	135	36 15	+53	135	37 08	+53	134	38 01	+53	134
36	34 54	53	134	35 47	53	134	36 40	53	133	37 33	53	133
37	34 26	53	133	35 19	53	133	36 12	53	132	37 05	52	132
38	33 58	53	132	34 51	52	132	35 43	53	131	36 36	52	130
39	33 29	53	131	34 22	52	131	35 14	52	130	36 06	52	129
40	33 00	+52	130	33 52	+52	130	34 44	+52	129	35 36	+51	128
41	32 30	52	129	33 22	52	129	34 14	51	128	35 05	52	127
42	32 00	52	128	32 52	51	128	33 43	52	127	34 35	51	126
43	31 30	51	127	32 21	51	127	33 12	51	126	34 03	51	125
44	30 59	51	126	31 50	51	126	32 41	51	125	33 32	50	124
45	30 27	+51	125	31 18	+51	125	32 09	+50	124	32 59	+51	123
46	29 56	50	124	30 46	51	124	31 37	50	123	32 27	50	122
47	29 23	51	123	30 14	50	123	31 04	50	122	31 54	50	121
48	28 51	50	122	29 41	50	122	30 31	50	121	31 21	50	120
49	28 18	50	121	29 08	50	121	29 58	50	120	30 48	49	119
50	27 45	+50	120	28 35	+49	120	29 24	+50	119	30 14	+49	118
51	27 12	49	119	28 01	49	119	28 50	50	118	29 40	49	117
52	26 38	49	118	27 27	49	118	28 16	49	117	29 05	49	117
53	26 04	49	118	26 53	49	117	27 42	49	116	28 31	48	116
54	25 29	49	117	26 18	49	116	27 07	49	115	27 56	48	115
55	24 55	+49	116	25 44	+48	115	26 32	+49	114	27 21	+48	114
56	24 20	48	115	25 08	49	114	25 57	48	114	26 45	48	113
57	23 45	48	114	24 33	48	113	25 21	48	113	26 09	48	112
58	23 09	49	113	23 58	48	112	24 46	48	112	25 34	47	111
59	22 34	48	112	23 22	48	112	24 10	48	111	24 58	47	110
60	21 58	+48	111	22 46	+48	111	23 34	+47	110	24 21	+48	109
61	21 22	48	111	22 10	47	110	22 57	48	109	23 45	47	109
62	20 46	47	110	21 33	48	109	22 21	47	108	23 08	47	108
63	20 09	48	109	20 57	47	108	21 44	47	108	22 31	47	107
64	19 33	47	108	20 20	47	107	21 07	47	107	21 54	47	106
65	18 56	+47	107	19 43	+47	106	20 30	+47	106	21 17	+47	105
66	18 19	47	106	19 06	47	106	19 53	47	105	20 40	46	104
67	17 42	47	105	18 29	47	105	19 16	46	104	20 02	47	104
68	17 05	46	105	17 51	47	104	18 38	47	103	19 25	46	103
69	16 27	47	104	17 14	47	103	18 01	46	103	18 47	46	102

	8°			9°			10°			11°		
LHA	Hc	d	Z	Hc	d	Z	Hc	d	Z	Hc	d	Z
	° ′	′	°	° ′	′	°	° ′	′	°	° ′	′	°
0	48 00	+60	180	49 00	+60	180	50 00	+60	180	51 00	+60	180
1	48 00	60	179	49 00	60	179	50 00	60	179	51 00	60	178
2	47 58	60	177	48 58	60	177	49 58	60	177	50 58	60	177
3	47 56	59	176	48 55	60	176	49 55	60	175	50 55	60	175
4	47 52	60	174	48 52	60	174	49 52	60	174	50 52	60	174
5	47 48	+59	173	48 47	+60	173	49 47	+60	172	50 47	+60	172
6	47 42	60	171	48 42	60	171	49 42	59	171	50 41	60	171
7	47 36	59	170	48 35	60	170	49 35	59	169	50 34	60	169
8	47 28	60	168	48 28	59	168	49 27	60	168	50 27	59	168
9	47 20	59	167	48 19	60	167	49 19	59	166	50 18	59	166
10	47 11	+59	165	48 10	+59	165	49 09	+59	165	50 08	+59	165
11	47 01	59	164	48 00	59	164	48 59	58	163	49 57	59	163
12	46 49	59	163	47 48	59	162	48 47	59	162	49 46	58	162
13	46 37	59	161	47 36	59	161	48 35	58	160	49 33	59	160
14	46 24	59	160	47 23	58	159	48 21	58	159	49 19	59	159
15	46 11	+58	158	47 09	+58	158	48 07	+58	158	49 05	+58	157
16	45 56	58	157	46 54	58	157	47 52	58	156	48 50	57	156
17	45 40	58	156	46 38	58	155	47 36	57	155	48 33	58	154
18	45 24	57	154	46 21	58	154	47 19	57	153	48 16	57	153
19	45 07	57	153	46 04	57	152	47 01	57	152	47 58	57	152
20	44 49	+57	152	45 46	+57	151	46 43	+56	151	47 39	+57	150
21	44 30	57	150	45 27	56	150	46 23	57	149	47 20	56	149
22	44 10	57	149	45 07	56	148	46 03	56	148	46 59	56	147
23	43 50	56	148	44 46	56	147	45 42	56	147	46 38	56	146
24	43 29	56	146	44 25	56	146	45 21	55	145	46 16	56	145
25	43 07	+56	145	44 03	+55	145	44 58	+56	144	45 54	+55	143
26	42 45	55	144	43 40	55	143	44 35	55	143	45 30	55	142
27	42 22	55	143	43 17	54	142	44 11	55	141	45 06	55	141
28	41 58	55	141	42 53	54	141	43 47	55	140	44 42	54	140
29	41 33	55	140	42 28	54	140	43 22	54	139	44 16	54	138
30	41 08	+54	139	42 02	+54	138	42 56	+54	138	43 50	+54	137
31	40 43	54	138	41 37	53	137	42 30	54	137	43 24	53	136
32	40 16	54	137	41 10	53	136	42 03	54	135	42 57	53	135
33	39 50	53	135	40 43	53	135	41 36	53	134	42 29	53	134
34	39 22	53	134	40 15	53	134	41 08	53	133	42 01	52	132
35	38 54	+53	133	39 47	+53	133	40 40	+52	132	41 32	+52	131
36	38 26	52	132	39 18	53	131	40 11	52	131	41 03	52	130
37	37 57	52	131	38 49	52	130	39 41	52	130	40 33	51	129
38	37 28	52	130	38 20	51	129	39 11	52	129	40 03	51	128
39	36 58	51	129	37 49	52	128	38 41	51	127	39 32	51	127
40	36 27	+52	128	37 19	+51	127	38 10	+51	126	39 01	+51	126
41	35 57	51	127	36 48	51	126	37 39	50	125	38 29	51	125
42	35 26	50	126	36 16	51	125	37 07	50	124	37 57	51	124
43	34 54	51	125	35 45	50	124	36 35	50	123	37 25	50	123
44	34 22	50	124	35 12	51	123	36 03	49	122	36 52	50	122
45	33 50	+50	123	34 40	+50	122	35 30	+49	121	36 19	+50	121
46	33 17	50	122	34 07	50	121	34 57	49	120	35 46	49	120
47	32 44	50	121	33 34	49	120	34 23	49	119	35 12	49	119
48	32 11	49	120	33 00	49	119	33 49	49	118	34 38	49	118
49	31 37	49	119	32 26	49	118	33 15	49	117	34 04	48	117
50	31 03	+49	118	31 52	+49	117	32 41	+48	116	33 29	+49	116
51	30 29	48	117	31 17	49	116	32 06	48	115	32 54	48	115
52	29 54	49	116	30 43	48	115	31 31	48	115	32 19	48	114
53	29 19	49	115	30 08	48	114	30 56	48	114	31 44	48	113
54	28 44	48	114	29 32	48	113	30 20	48	113	31 08	48	112
55	28 09	+48	113	28 57	+48	112	29 45	+47	112	30 32	+48	111
56	27 33	48	112	28 21	48	112	29 09	47	111	29 56	47	110
57	26 57	48	111	27 45	48	111	28 33	47	110	29 20	47	109
58	26 21	48	110	27 09	47	110	27 56	47	109	28 43	47	108
59	25 45	47	110	26 32	48	109	27 20	47	108	28 07	46	108
60	25 09	+47	109	25 56	+47	108	26 43	+47	107	27 30	+46	107
61	24 32	47	108	25 19	47	107	26 06	47	106	26 53	46	106
62	23 55	47	107	24 42	47	106	25 29	46	106	26 15	47	105
63	23 18	47	106	24 05	47	105	24 52	46	105	25 38	46	104
64	22 41	47	105	23 28	46	105	24 14	47	104	25 01	46	103
65	22 04	+46	104	22 50	+47	104	23 37	+46	103	24 23	+46	102
66	21 26	47	104	22 13	46	103	22 59	46	102	23 45	46	102
67	20 49	46	103	21 35	46	102	22 21	46	101	23 07	46	101
68	20 11	46	102	20 57	47	101	21 44	46	101	22 30	45	100
69	19 33	47	101	20 20	46	101	21 06	45	100	21 51	46	99

	12°			13°			14°			
LHA	Hc	d	Z	Hc	d	Z	Hc	d	Z	LHA
	° ′	′	°	° ′	′	°	° ′	′	°	
0	52 00	+60	180	53 00	+60	180	54 00	+60	180	360
1	52 00	60	178	53 00	59	178	53 59	60	178	359
2	51 58	60	177	52 58	60	177	53 58	60	177	358
3	51 55	60	175	52 55	60	175	53 55	60	175	357
4	51 52	59	174	52 51	60	174	53 51	60	173	356
5	51 47	+59	172	52 46	+60	172	53 46	+60	172	355
6	51 41	60	171	52 41	59	170	53 40	60	170	354
7	51 34	60	169	52 34	59	169	53 33	59	169	353
8	51 26	59	167	52 25	60	167	53 25	59	167	352
9	51 17	59	166	52 16	60	166	53 16	59	165	351
10	51 07	+59	164	52 06	+59	164	53 05	+59	164	350
11	50 56	59	163	51 55	59	163	52 54	59	162	349
12	50 44	59	161	51 43	59	161	52 42	58	161	348
13	50 32	58	160	51 30	58	159	52 28	58	159	347
14	50 18	58	158	51 16	58	158	52 14	58	158	346
15	50 03	+58	157	51 01	+58	156	51 59	+57	156	345
16	49 47	58	155	50 45	57	155	51 42	58	154	344
17	49 31	57	154	50 28	57	153	51 25	58	153	343
18	49 13	57	152	50 10	57	152	51 07	57	152	342
19	48 55	57	151	49 52	57	151	50 49	56	150	341
20	48 36	+56	150	49 32	+57	149	50 29	+56	149	340
21	48 16	56	148	49 12	56	148	50 08	56	147	339
22	47 55	56	147	48 51	56	146	49 47	56	146	338
23	47 34	55	146	48 29	56	145	49 25	55	144	337
24	47 12	55	144	48 07	55	144	49 02	55	143	336
25	46 49	+55	143	47 44	+54	142	48 38	+55	142	335
26	46 25	55	142	47 20	54	141	48 14	54	140	334
27	46 01	54	140	46 55	54	140	47 49	54	139	333
28	45 36	54	139	46 30	54	138	47 24	53	138	332
29	45 10	54	138	46 04	53	137	46 57	54	136	331
30	44 44	+53	137	45 37	+53	136	46 30	+53	135	330
31	44 17	53	135	45 10	53	135	46 03	53	134	329
32	43 50	52	134	44 42	53	133	45 35	52	133	328
33	43 22	52	133	44 14	52	132	45 06	52	132	327
34	42 53	52	132	43 45	52	131	44 37	52	130	326
35	42 24	+52	131	43 16	+52	130	44 08	+51	129	325
36	41 55	51	129	42 46	51	129	43 37	51	128	324
37	41 24	52	128	42 16	51	128	43 07	51	127	323
38	40 54	51	127	41 45	51	127	42 36	50	126	322
39	40 23	51	126	41 14	50	125	42 04	50	125	321
40	39 52	+50	125	40 42	+50	124	41 32	+50	124	320
41	39 20	50	124	40 10	50	123	41 00	50	123	319
42	38 48	50	123	39 38	49	122	40 27	50	121	318
43	38 15	50	122	39 05	49	121	39 54	49	120	317
44	37 42	50	121	38 32	49	120	39 21	49	119	316
45	37 09	+49	120	37 58	+49	119	38 47	+48	118	315
46	36 35	49	119	37 24	49	118	38 13	48	117	314
47	36 01	49	118	36 50	48	117	37 38	49	116	313
48	35 27	48	117	36 15	49	116	37 04	48	115	312
49	34 52	49	116	35 41	48	115	36 29	47	114	311
50	34 18	+48	115	35 06	+47	114	35 53	+48	113	310
51	33 42	48	114	34 30	48	113	35 18	47	113	309
52	33 07	48	113	33 55	47	112	34 42	47	112	308
53	32 32	47	112	33 19	47	111	34 06	47	111	307
54	31 56	47	111	32 43	47	111	33 30	47	110	306
55	31 20	+47	110	32 07	+47	110	32 54	+46	109	305
56	30 43	47	109	31 30	47	109	32 17	46	108	304
57	30 07	47	109	30 54	46	108	31 40	46	107	303
58	29 30	47	108	30 17	46	107	31 03	46	106	302
59	28 53	47	107	29 40	46	106	30 26	46	105	301
60	28 16	+47	106	29 03	+46	105	29 49	+46	104	300
61	27 39	46	105	28 25	46	104	29 11	46	104	299
62	27 02	46	104	27 48	46	104	28 34	46	103	298
63	26 24	46	103	27 10	46	103	27 56	46	102	297
64	25 47	46	103	26 33	45	102	27 18	46	101	296
65	25 09	+46	102	25 55	+45	101	26 40	+46	100	295
66	24 31	46	101	25 17	45	100	26 02	46	99	294
67	23 53	46	100	24 39	45	99	25 24	46	99	293
68	23 15	46	99	24 01	45	99	24 46	45	98	292
69	22 37	46	98	23 23	45	98	24 08	45	97	291

LAT 50°

Extract Number A18

TABLE 5.—Correction to Tabulated Altitude for Minutes of Declination

Extract Number A19

Appendix C

Extracts from *NP 401 Vol 4, Sight Reduction Tables for Marine Navigation*

54°, 306° L.H.A. **LATITUDE SAME NAME AS DECLINATION**

N. Lat. { L.H.A. greater than 180°......Zn=Z
L.H.A. less than 180°..........Zn=360°−Z

Dec.	45°			46°			47°			48°			49°			50°			51°			52°			Dec.
	Hc	d	Z	Hc	d	Z	Hc	d	Z	Hc	d	Z	Hc	d	Z	Hc	d	Z	Hc	d	Z	Hc	d	Z	
°	° ′	′	°	° ′	′	°	° ′	′	°	° ′	′	°	° ′	′	°	° ′	′	°	° ′	′	°	° ′	′	°	°
0	24 33.5	+46.6	117.2	24 05.9	+47.2	117.6	23 37.9	+47.9	118.0	23 09.6	+48.4	118.4	22 40.9	+49.0	118.7	22 11.9	+49.6	119.1	21 42.6	+50.1	119.5	21 12.9	+50.7	119.8	0
1	25 20.1	46.3	116.5	24 53.1	47.0	116.9	24 25.8	47.6	117.3	23 58.0	48.3	117.7	23 29.9	48.9	118.1	23 01.5	49.4	118.5	22 32.7	50.0	118.9	22 03.6	50.5	119.2	1
2	26 06.4	46.2	115.8	25 40.1	46.8	116.2	25 13.4	47.5	116.7	24 46.3	48.1	117.1	24 18.8	48.7	117.5	23 50.9	49.3	117.9	23 22.7	49.9	118.3	22 54.1	50.4	118.6	2
3	26 52.6	45.9	115.1	26 26.9	46.6	115.5	26 00.9	47.2	116.0	25 34.4	47.9	116.4	25 07.5	48.5	116.8	24 40.2	49.1	117.2	24 12.6	49.7	117.6	23 44.5	50.3	118.0	3
4	27 38.5	45.7	114.4	27 13.5	46.4	114.8	26 48.1	47.1	115.3	26 22.3	47.7	115.7	25 56.0	48.4	116.2	25 29.3	49.0	116.6	25 02.3	49.5	117.0	24 34.8	50.1	117.4	4
5	28 24.2	+45.5	113.6	27 59.9	+46.2	114.1	27 35.2	+46.8	114.6	27 10.0	+47.5	115.1	26 44.4	+48.1	115.5	26 18.3	+48.8	116.0	25 51.8	+49.4	116.4	25 24.9	+50.0	116.8	5
6	29 09.7	45.2	112.9	28 46.1	45.9	113.4	28 22.0	46.7	113.9	27 57.5	47.3	114.4	27 32.5	48.0	114.8	27 07.1	48.6	115.3	26 41.2	49.2	115.8	26 14.9	49.8	116.2	6
7	29 54.9	44.9	112.1	29 32.0	45.7	112.6	29 08.7	46.3	113.2	28 44.8	47.1	113.7	28 20.5	47.7	114.2	27 55.7	48.4	114.7	27 30.4	49.1	115.1	27 04.7	49.7	115.6	7
8	30 39.8	44.7	111.4	30 17.7	45.4	111.9	29 55.0	46.2	112.4	29 31.9	46.9	113.0	29 08.2	47.6	113.5	28 44.1	48.2	114.0	28 19.5	48.8	114.5	27 54.4	49.4	115.0	8
9	31 24.5	44.3	110.6	31 03.1	45.2	111.1	30 41.2	45.9	111.7	30 18.8	46.6	112.2	29 55.8	47.3	112.8	29 32.3	48.0	113.3	29 08.3	48.7	113.8	28 43.8	49.3	114.3	9
10	32 08.8	+44.1	109.8	31 48.3	+44.8	110.4	31 27.1	+45.6	110.9	31 05.4	+46.3	111.5	30 43.1	+47.1	112.1	30 20.3	+47.8	112.6	29 57.0	+48.4	113.1	29 33.1	+49.1	113.7	10
11	32 52.9	43.8	109.0	32 33.1	44.6	109.6	32 12.7	45.4	110.2	31 51.7	46.1	110.8	31 30.2	46.8	111.3	31 08.1	47.5	111.9	30 45.4	48.2	112.5	30 22.2	48.9	113.0	11
12	33 36.7	43.4	108.2	33 17.7	44.2	108.8	32 58.1	45.0	109.4	32 37.8	45.9	110.0	32 17.0	46.6	110.6	31 55.6	47.3	111.2	31 33.6	48.0	111.8	31 11.1	48.7	112.3	12
13	34 20.1	43.1	107.3	34 01.9	44.0	108.0	33 43.1	44.8	108.6	33 23.7	45.5	109.2	33 03.6	46.3	109.9	32 42.9	47.0	110.5	32 21.6	47.8	111.1	31 59.8	48.4	111.6	13
14	35 03.2	42.8	106.5	34 45.9	43.6	107.1	34 27.9	44.4	107.8	34 09.2	45.2	108.5	33 49.9	46.0	109.1	33 29.9	46.8	109.7	33 09.4	47.5	110.3	32 48.2	48.2	110.9	14
15	35 46.0	+42.3	105.6	35 29.5	+43.2	106.3	35 12.3	+44.1	107.0	34 54.4	+44.9	107.7	34 35.9	+45.7	108.3	34 16.7	+46.5	109.0	33 56.9	+47.2	109.6	33 36.4	+48.0	110.2	15
16	36 28.3	42.0	104.7	36 12.7	42.9	105.5	35 56.4	43.7	106.2	35 39.3	44.6	106.8	35 21.6	45.4	107.5	35 03.2	46.2	108.2	34 44.1	47.0	108.9	34 24.4	47.7	109.5	16
17	37 10.3	41.6	103.8	36 55.6	42.4	104.6	36 40.1	43.4	105.3	36 23.9	44.2	106.0	36 07.0	45.0	106.7	35 49.4	45.9	107.4	35 31.1	46.6	108.1	35 12.1	47.4	108.8	17
18	37 51.9	41.1	102.9	37 38.0	42.1	103.7	37 23.5	42.9	104.4	37 08.1	43.9	105.2	36 52.0	44.8	105.9	36 35.3	45.5	106.6	36 17.7	46.4	107.3	35 59.5	47.2	108.0	18
19	38 33.0	40.7	102.0	38 20.1	41.6	102.8	38 06.4	42.6	103.6	37 52.0	43.5	104.3	37 36.8	44.3	105.1	37 20.8	45.2	105.8	37 04.1	46.0	106.5	36 46.7	46.8	107.2	19
20	39 13.7	+40.2	101.1	39 01.7	+41.2	101.9	38 49.0	+42.2	102.7	38 35.5	+43.0	103.4	38 21.1	+44.0	104.2	38 06.0	+44.9	105.0	37 50.1	+45.7	105.7	37 33.5	+46.5	106.5	20
21	39 53.9	39.7	100.1	39 42.9	40.8	100.9	39 31.2	41.7	101.7	39 18.5	42.7	102.5	39 05.1	43.6	103.3	38 50.9	44.4	104.1	38 35.8	45.4	104.9	38 20.0	46.2	105.7	21
22	40 33.6	39.2	99.1	40 23.7	40.2	100.0	40 12.9	41.2	100.8	40 01.2	42.2	101.6	39 48.7	43.1	102.4	39 35.3	44.1	103.3	39 21.2	44.9	104.1	39 06.2	45.8	104.8	22
23	41 12.8	38.7	98.1	41 03.9	39.8	99.0	40 54.1	40.8	99.8	40 43.4	41.8	100.7	40 31.8	42.8	101.5	40 19.4	43.7	102.4	40 06.1	44.6	103.2	39 52.0	45.5	104.0	23
24	41 51.5	38.2	97.1	41 43.7	39.2	98.0	41 34.9	40.2	98.9	41 25.2	41.2	99.7	41 14.6	42.2	100.6	41 03.1	43.2	101.5	40 50.7	44.2	102.3	40 37.5	45.1	103.2	24
25	42 29.7	+37.5	96.1	42 22.9	+38.6	97.0	42 15.1	+39.8	97.9	42 06.4	+40.8	98.8	41 56.8	+41.8	99.7	41 46.3	+42.8	100.5	41 34.9	+43.7	101.4	41 22.6	+44.6	102.3	25
26	43 07.2	37.0	95.0	43 01.5	38.1	95.9	42 54.9	39.1	96.9	42 47.2	40.3	97.8	42 38.6	41.3	98.7	42 29.1	42.3	99.6	42 18.6	43.3	100.5	42 07.2	44.3	101.4	26
27	43 44.2	36.3	93.9	43 39.6	37.5	94.9	43 34.0	38.6	95.8	43 27.5	39.7	96.8	43 19.9	40.8	97.7	43 11.4	41.8	98.6	43 01.9	42.8	99.6	42 51.5	43.8	100.5	27
28	44 20.5	35.7	92.8	44 17.1	36.8	93.8	44 12.6	38.0	94.8	44 07.2	39.1	95.7	44 00.7	40.2	96.7	43 53.2	41.3	97.6	43 44.7	42.3	98.6	43 35.3	43.3	99.5	28
29	44 56.2	35.0	91.7	44 53.9	36.2	92.7	44 50.6	37.4	93.7	44 46.3	38.5	94.7	44 40.9	39.6	95.6	44 34.5	40.7	96.6	44 27.0	41.8	97.6	44 18.6	42.8	98.6	29
30	45 31.2	+34.3	90.5	45 30.1	+35.5	91.5	45 28.0	+36.7	92.6	45 24.8	+37.9	93.6	45 20.5	+39.0	94.6	45 15.2	+40.1	95.6	45 08.8	+41.3	96.6	45 01.4	+42.3	97.6	30
31	46 05.5	33.5	89.3	46 05.6	34.8	90.4	46 04.7	36.0	91.4	46 02.7	37.2	92.5	45 59.5	38.4	93.5	45 55.3	39.6	94.5	45 50.1	40.6	95.6	45 43.7	41.8	96.6	31
32	46 39.0	32.8	88.1	46 40.4	34.1	89.2	46 40.7	35.3	90.3	46 39.9	36.5	91.3	46 37.9	37.8	92.4	46 34.9	38.9	93.4	46 30.7	40.1	94.5	46 25.5	41.2	95.5	32
33	47 11.8	32.0	86.9	47 14.5	33.2	88.0	47 16.0	34.6	89.1	47 16.4	35.8	90.2	47 15.7	37.0	91.2	47 13.8	38.2	92.3	47 10.8	39.4	93.4	47 06.7	40.6	94.5	33
34	47 43.8	31.1	85.7	47 47.7	32.5	86.8	47 50.6	33.7	87.9	47 52.2	35.1	89.0	47 52.7	36.3	90.1	47 52.0	37.6	91.2	47 50.2	38.8	92.3	47 47.3	39.9	93.4	34
35	48 14.9	+30.3	84.4	48 20.2	+31.6	85.5	48 24.3	+33.0	86.6	48 27.3	+34.2	87.8	48 29.0	+35.6	88.9	48 29.6	+36.8	90.0	48 29.0	+38.1	91.1	48 27.2	+39.3	92.3	35
36	48 45.2	29.4	83.1	48 51.8	30.8	84.2	48 57.3	32.1	85.4	49 01.5	33.5	86.5	49 04.6	34.7	87.7	49 06.4	36.1	88.8	49 07.1	37.3	90.0	49 06.5	38.6	91.1	36
37	49 14.6	28.4	81.8	49 22.6	29.8	82.9	49 29.4	31.2	84.1	49 35.0	32.6	85.2	49 39.3	34.0	86.4	49 42.5	35.2	87.6	49 44.4	36.6	88.8	49 45.1	37.8	89.9	37
38	49 43.0	27.5	80.4	49 52.4	28.9	81.6	50 00.6	30.3	82.7	50 07.6	31.6	83.9	50 13.3	33.0	85.1	50 17.7	34.5	86.3	50 21.0	35.7	87.5	50 22.9	37.1	88.7	38
39	50 10.5	26.4	79.0	50 21.3	27.9	80.2	50 30.9	29.3	81.4	50 39.2	30.8	82.6	50 46.3	32.2	83.8	50 52.2	33.5	85.0	50 56.7	34.9	86.3	51 00.0	36.2	87.5	39
40	50 36.9	+25.5	77.6	50 49.2	+26.9	78.8	51 00.2	+28.4	80.0	51 10.0	+29.8	81.2	51 18.5	+31.2	82.5	51 25.7	+32.7	83.7	51 31.6	+34.1	85.0	51 36.2	+35.5	86.2	40
41	51 02.4	24.3	76.2	51 16.1	25.8	77.4	51 28.6	27.3	78.6	51 39.8	28.8	79.8	51 49.7	30.3	81.1	51 58.4	31.6	82.4	52 05.7	33.1	83.6	52 11.7	34.5	84.9	41
42	51 26.7	23.3	74.7	51 41.9	24.8	75.9	51 55.9	26.2	77.2	52 08.6	27.7	78.4	52 20.0	29.2	79.7	52 30.0	30.7	81.0	52 38.8	32.1	82.3	52 46.2	33.6	83.6	42
43	51 50.0	22.1	73.2	52 06.7	23.6	74.5	52 22.1	25.2	75.7	52 36.3	26.7	77.0	52 49.2	28.1	78.3	53 00.7	29.7	79.6	53 10.9	31.2	80.9	53 19.8	32.6	82.2	43
44	52 12.1	20.9	71.7	52 30.3	22.5	73.0	52 47.3	24.0	74.2	53 03.0	25.5	75.5	53 17.3	27.1	76.8	53 30.4	28.5	78.1	53 42.1	30.0	79.4	53 52.4	31.6	80.8	44
45	52 33.0	+19.8	70.2	52 52.8	+21.2	71.4	53 11.3	+22.8	72.7	53 28.5	+24.3	74.0	53 44.4	+25.9	75.3	53 58.9	+27.5	76.6	54 12.1	+29.0	78.0	54 24.0	+30.5	79.3	45
46	52 52.8	18.5	68.6	53 14.0	20.1	69.9	53 34.1	21.5	71.1	53 52.8	23.1	72.4	54 10.3	24.7	73.8	54 26.4	26.2	75.1	54 41.1	27.9	76.5	54 54.5	29.4	77.8	46
47	53 11.3	17.2	67.0	53 34.1	18.7	68.3	53 55.6	20.3	69.6	54 15.9	21.9	70.9	54 35.0	23.4	72.2	54 52.6	25.0	73.5	55 09.0	26.6	74.9	55 23.9	28.2	76.3	47
48	53 28.5	15.9	65.4	53 52.8	17.5	66.7	54 15.9	19.1	68.0	54 37.8	20.6	69.3	54 58.4	22.2	70.6	55 17.7	23.8	72.0	55 35.6	25.4	73.3	55 52.1	27.0	74.7	48
49	53 44.4	14.5	63.8	54 10.3	16.1	65.1	54 35.0	17.6	66.3	54 58.4	19.3	67.6	55 20.6	20.9	69.0	55 41.5	22.5	70.3	56 01.0	24.1	71.7	56 19.1	25.7	73.1	49
50	53 58.9	+13.2	62.2	54 26.4	+14.7	63.4	54 52.6	+16.4	64.7	55 17.7	+17.9	66.0	55 41.5	+19.5	67.3	56 04.0	+21.1	68.7	56 25.1	+22.8	70.1	56 44.8	+24.5	71.5	50
51	54 12.1	11.9	60.5	54 41.1	13.4	61.7	55 09.0	14.9	63.0	55 35.6	16.5	64.3	56 01.0	18.1	65.6	56 25.1	19.7	67.0	56 47.9	21.4	68.4	57 09.3	23.0	69.8	51
52	54 24.0	10.4	58.8	54 54.5	11.9	60.0	55 23.9	13.4	61.3	55 52.1	15.0	62.6	56 19.1	16.7	63.9	56 44.8	18.3	65.3	57 09.3	19.9	66.7	57 32.3	21.7	68.1	52
53	54 34.4	8.9	57.1	55 06.4	10.5	58.3	55 37.3	12.1	59.6	56 07.1	13.6	60.9	56 35.8	15.2	62.2	57 03.1	16.9	63.5	57 29.2	18.5	64.9	57 54.0	20.1	66.4	53
54	54 43.3	7.5	55.4	55 16.9	9.0	56.6	55 49.4	10.5	57.8	56 20.7	12.1	59.1	56 51.0	13.6	60.4	57 20.0	15.3	61.8	57 47.7	17.0	63.2	58 14.1	18.7	64.6	54
55	54 50.8	+6.1	53.7	55 25.9	+7.5	54.9	55 59.9	+9.0	56.1	56 32.8	+10.6	57.3	57 04.6	+12.2	58.6	57 35.3	+13.7	60.0	58 04.7	+15.4	61.4	58 32.8	+17.1	62.8	55
56	54 56.9	4.6	52.0	55 33.4	6.0	53.1	56 08.9	7.5	54.3	56 43.4	9.0	55.5	57 16.8	10.6	56.8	57 49.0	12.2	58.1	58 20.1	13.8	59.5	58 49.9	15.5	60.9	56
57	55 01.5	3.0	50.2	55 39.4	4.5	51.4	56 16.4	5.9	52.5	56 52.4	7.4	53.7	57 27.4	8.9	55.0	58 01.2	10.6	56.3	58 33.9	12.2	57.7	59 05.4	13.8	59.1	57
58	55 04.5	1.6	48.5	55 43.9	2.9	49.6	56 22.3	4.4	50.7	56 59.8	5.9	51.9	57 36.3	7.4	53.2	58 11.8	9.0	54.4	58 46.1	10.5	55.8	59 19.2	12.2	57.2	58
59	55 06.1	+0.1	46.7	55 46.8	+1.5	47.8	56 26.7	2.8	48.9	57 05.7	4.2	50.1	57 43.7	5.7	51.3	58 20.7	7.2	52.6	58 56.6	8.8	53.9	59 31.4	10.5	55.2	59
60	55 06.2	−1.4	45.0	55 48.3	−0.2	46.0	56 29.5	+1.2	47.1	57 09.9	+2.6	48.2	57 49.4	+4.1	49.4	58 27.9	+5.6	50.7	59 05.4	+7.1	51.9	59 41.9	+8.7	53.3	60
61	55 04.8	2.9	43.2	55 48.1	1.6	44.3	56 30.7	−0.3	45.3	57 12.5	+1.0	46.4	57 53.5	2.3	47.6	58 33.5	3.8	48.8	59 12.5	5.4	50.0	59 50.6	6.9	51.3	61
62	55 01.9	4.4	41.5	55 46.5	3.2	42.5	56 30.4	2.0	43.5	57 13.5	−0.6	44.6	57 55.8	+0.8	45.7	58 37.3	2.2	46.8	59 17.9	3.6	48.1	59 57.5	5.2	49.3	62
63	54 57.5	5.9	39.8	55 43.3	4.8	40.7	56 28.4	3.5	41.7	57 12.9	2.3	42.7	57 56.6	−1.0	43.8	58 39.5	+0.4	44.9	59 21.5	1.9	46.1	60 02.7	3.3	47.4	63
64	54 51.6	7.4	38.0	55 38.5	6.2	38.9	56 24.9	5.1	39.9	57 10.6	3.9	40.9	57 55.6	2.6	41.9	58 39.9	−1.3	43.0	59 23.4	+0.1	44.1	60 06.0	+1.5	45.4	64
65	54 44.2	−8.8	36.3	55 32.3	−7.8	37.2	56 19.8	−6.6	38.1	57 06.7	−5.5	39.0	57 53.0	−4.3	40.0	58 38.6	−3.0	41.1	59 23.5	−1.7	42.2	60 07.5	−0.3	43.3	65
66	54 35.4	10.3	34.6	55 24.5	9.2	35.4	56 13.2	8.2	36.3	57 01.2	7.0	37.2	57 48.7	5.9	38.1	58 35.6	4.7	39.2	59 21.8	3.5	40.2	60 07.2	2.1	41.3	66
67	54 25.1	11.6	32.9	55 15.3	10.7	33.7	56 05.0	9.7	34.5	56 54.2	8.7	35.4	57 42.8	7.5	36.3	58 30.9	6.4	37.2	59 18.3	5.2	38.3	60 05.1	4.0	39.3	67
68	54 13.5	13.1	31.2	55 04.6	12.2	32.0	55 55.3	11.2	32.7	56 45.5	10.2	33.6	57 35.3	9.2	34.4	58 24.5	8.1	35.3	59 13.1	6.9	36.3	60 01.1	5.7	37.3	68
69	54 00.4	14.4	29.6	54 52.4	13.5	30.3	55 44.1	12.7	31.0	56 35.3	11.8	31.8	57 26.1	10.8	32.6	58 16.4	9.8	33.5	59 06.2	8.7	34.4	59 55.4	7.5	35.3	69
70	53 46.0	−15.8	27.9	54 38.9	−15.0	28.6	55 31.4	−14.2	29.3	56 23.5	−13.2	30.0	57 15.3	−12.3	30.8	58 06.6	−11.3	31.6	58 57.5	−10.4	32.5	59 47.9	−9.3	33.4	70
71	53 30.2	17.0	26.3	54 23.9	16.3	26.9	55 17.2	15.5	27.6	56 10.3	14.8	28.2	57 03.0	13.9	29.0	57 55.3	13.0	29.7	58 47.1	12.0	30.5	59 38.6	11.0	31.4	71
72	53 13.2	18.4	24.7	54 07.6	17.7	25.3	55 01.7	16.9	25.9	55 55.5	16.1	26.5	56 49.1	15.4	27.2	57 42.3	14.6	27.9	58 35.1	13.6	28.7	59 27.6	12.8	29.5	72
73	52 54.8	19.6	23.1	53 49.9	19.0	23.6	54 44.8	18.3	24.2	55 39.4	17.6	24.8	56 33.7	16.9	25.4	57 27.7	16.1	26.1	58 21.5	15.3	26.8	59 14.8	14.4	27.6	73
74	52 35.2	20.8	21.5	53 30.9	20.2	22.0	54 26.5	19.7	22.5	55 21.8	19.0	23.1	56 16.8	18.3	23.7	57 11.6	17.5	24.3	58 06.2	16.8	25.0	59 00.4	16.0	25.7	74
75	52 14.4	−22.0	20.0	53 10.7	−21.4	20.4	54 06.8	−20.8	20.9	55 02.8	−20.3	21.4	55 58.5	−19.6	22.0	56 54.1	−19.1	22.5	57 49.4	−18.4	23.2	58 44.4	−17.6	23.8	75
76	51 52.4	23.1	18.5	52 49.3	22.7	18.9	53 46.0	22.2	19.3	54 42.5	21.6	19.8	55 38.9	21.1	20.3	56 35.0	20.4	20.8	57 31.0	19.8	21.4	58 26.8	19.2	22.0	76
77	51 29.3	24.3	17.0	52 26.6	23.8	17.4	53 23.8	23.3	17.8	54 20.9	22.9	18.2	55 17.8	22.3	18.6	56 14.6	21.8	19.1	57 11.2	21.3	19.6	58 07.6	20.7	20.2	77
78	51 05.0	25.3	15.5	52 02.8	24.9	15.9	53 00.5	24.5	16.2	53 58.0	24.1	16.6	54 55.5	23.7	17.0	55 52.8	23.2	17.4	56 49.9	22.6	17.9	57 46.9	22.1	18.4	78
79	50 39.7	26.3	14.1	51 37.9	26.0	14.4	52 36.0	25.7	14.7	53 33.9	25.2	15.1	54 31.8	24.8	15.4	55 29.6	24.4	15.8	56 27.3	24.0	16.2	57 24.8	23.5	16.7	79
80	50 13.4	−27.4	12.7	51 11.9	−27.1	13.0	52 10.3	−26.7	13.2	53 08.7	−26.4	13.5	54 07.0	−26.1	13.9	55 05.2	−25.7	14.2	56 03.3	−25.3	14.6	57 01.3	−24.9	15.0	80
81	49 46.0	28.3	11.3	50 44.8	28.1	11.5	51 43.6	27.8	11.8	52 42.3	27.5	12.1	53 40.9	27.2	12.3	54 39.5	26.9	12.6	55 38.0	26.5	13.0	56 36.4	26.1	13.3	81
82	49 17.7	29.3	9.9	50 16.7	29.0	10.1	51 15.8	28.8	10.4	52 14.8	28.6	10.6	53 13.7	28.3	10.8	54 12.6	28.0	11.1	55 11.5	27.7	11.4	56 10.3	27.4	11.7	82
83	48 48.4	30.2	8.6	49 47.7	30.0	8.8	50 47.0	29.8	9.0	51 46.2	29.5	9.2	52 45.4	29.3	9.4	53 44.6	29.1	9.6	54 43.8	28.9	9.8	55 42.9	28.7	10.1	83
84	48 18.2	31.0	7.3	49 17.7	30.9	7.5	50 17.2	30.7	7.6	51 16.7	30.6	7.8	52 16.1	30.4	7.9	53 15.5	30.2	8.1	54 14.9	30.0	8.3	55 14.2	29.7	8.5	84
85	47 47.2	−31.9	6.0	48 46.8	−31.7	6.1	49 46.5	−31.7	6.3	50 46.1	−31.5	6.4	51 45.7	−31.3	6.5	52 45.3	−31.2	6.7	53 44.9	−31.0	6.8	54 44.5	−30.9	7.0	85
86	47 15.3	32.7	4.8	48 15.1	32.6	4.9	49 14.8	32.5	5.0	50 14.6	32.4	5.1	51 14.4	32.3	5.2	52 14.1	32.1	5.3	53 13.9	32.1	5.4	54 13.6	31.9	5.5	86
87	46 42.6	33.5	3.5	47 42.5	33.4	3.6	48 42.3	33.3	3.7	49 42.2	33.2	3.8	50 42.1	33.2	3.8	51 42.0	33.1	3.9	52 41.8	33.0	4.0	53 41.7	33.0	4.1	87
88	46 09.1	34.2	2.3	47 09.1	34.2	2.4	48 09.0	34.1	2.4	49 09.0	34.1	2.5	50 08.9	34.0	2.5	51 08.9	34.0	2.6	52 08.8	34.0	2.6	53 08.7	33.9	2.7	88
89	45 34.9	34.9	1.2	46 34.9	34.9	1.2	47 34.9	34.9	1.2	48 34.9	34.9	1.2	49 34.9	34.9	1.2	50 34.9	34.9	1.3	51 34.8	34.8	1.3	52 34.8	34.8	1.3	89
90	45 00.0	−35.6	0.0	46 00.0	−35.6	0.0	47 00.0	−35.6	0.0	48 00.0	−35.6	0.0	49 00.0	−35.7	0.0	50 00.0	−35.7	0.0	51 00.0	−35.7	0.0	52 00.0	−35.7	0.0	90
	45°			46°			47°			48°			49°			50°			51°			52°			

54°, 306° L.H.A. **LATITUDE SAME NAME AS DECLINATION**

Extract Number A20

LATITUDE CONTRARY NAME TO DECLINATION L.H.A. 54°, 306°

Dec.	45° Hc	d	Z	46° Hc	d	Z	47° Hc	d	Z	48° Hc	d	Z
°	° ′	′	°	° ′	′	°	° ′	′	°	° ′	′	°
0	24 33.5	−46.7	117.2	24 05.9	−47.3	117.6	23 37.9	−47.9	118.0	23 09.6	−48.6	118.4
1	23 46.8	46.9	117.9	23 18.6	47.6	118.3	22 50.0	48.2	118.6	22 21.0	48.7	119.0
2	22 59.9	47.1	118.6	22 31.0	47.7	118.9	22 01.8	48.3	119.3	21 32.3	48.8	119.6
3	22 12.8	47.3	119.2	21 43.3	47.8	119.6	21 13.5	48.4	119.9	20 43.5	49.0	120.3
4	21 25.5	47.4	119.9	20 55.5	48.0	120.2	20 25.1	48.6	120.6	19 54.5	49.2	120.9
5	20 38.1	−47.5	120.5	20 07.5	−48.2	120.9	19 36.5	−48.6	121.2	19 05.3	−49.2	121.5
6	19 50.6	47.7	121.2	19 19.3	48.2	121.5	18 47.9	48.9	121.8	18 16.1	49.3	122.1
7	19 02.9	47.9	121.8	18 31.1	48.4	122.1	17 59.0	48.9	122.4	17 26.8	49.5	122.7
8	18 15.0	47.9	122.5	17 42.7	48.5	122.8	17 10.1	49.0	123.0	16 37.3	49.6	123.3
9	17 27.1	48.1	123.1	16 54.2	48.6	123.4	16 21.1	49.2	123.6	15 47.7	49.6	123.9
10	16 39.0	−48.2	123.7	16 05.6	−48.7	124.0	15 31.9	−49.2	124.2	14 58.1	−49.7	124.4
11	15 50.8	48.3	124.4	15 16.9	48.9	124.6	14 42.7	49.3	124.8	14 08.4	49.9	125.0
12	15 02.5	48.4	125.0	14 28.0	48.9	125.2	13 53.4	49.4	125.4	13 18.5	49.9	125.6
13	14 14.1	48.4	125.6	13 39.1	49.0	125.8	13 04.0	49.5	126.0	12 28.6	49.9	126.2
14	13 25.7	48.6	126.2	12 50.1	49.0	126.4	12 14.5	49.6	126.6	11 38.7	50.1	126.7
15	12 37.1	−48.7	126.8	12 01.1	−49.2	127.0	11 24.9	−49.6	127.1	10 48.6	−50.1	127.3
16	11 48.4	48.7	127.4	11 11.9	49.2	127.6	10 35.3	49.7	127.7	9 58.5	50.1	127.9
17	10 59.7	48.8	128.0	10 22.7	49.2	128.1	9 45.6	49.7	128.3	9 08.4	50.2	128.4
18	10 10.9	48.8	128.6	9 33.5	49.4	128.7	8 55.9	49.8	128.8	8 18.2	50.3	129.0
19	9 22.1	48.9	129.2	8 44.1	49.4	129.3	8 06.1	49.9	129.4	7 27.9	50.2	129.5
20	8 33.2	−49.0	129.8	7 54.7	−49.4	129.9	7 16.2	−49.8	130.0	6 37.7	−50.4	130.1
21	7 44.2	49.0	130.3	7 05.3	49.5	130.4	6 26.4	50.0	130.5	5 47.3	50.3	130.6
22	6 55.2	49.1	130.9	6 15.8	49.5	131.0	5 36.4	49.9	131.1	4 57.0	50.4	131.2
23	6 06.1	49.1	131.5	5 26.3	49.5	131.6	4 46.5	50.0	131.6	4 06.6	50.4	131.7
24	5 17.0	49.1	132.1	4 36.8	49.6	132.1	3 56.5	50.0	132.2	3 16.2	50.4	132.2
25	4 27.9	−49.2	132.7	3 47.2	−49.6	132.7	3 06.5	−50.0	132.8	2 25.8	−50.5	132.8
26	3 38.7	49.1	133.2	2 57.6	49.6	133.3	2 16.5	50.0	133.3	1 35.3	50.4	133.3
27	2 49.6	49.2	133.8	2 08.0	49.6	133.8	1 26.5	50.1	133.9	0 44.9	−50.5	133.9
28	2 00.4	49.2	134.4	1 18.4	49.6	134.4	0 36.4	−50.0	134.4	0 05.6	+50.4	45.6
29	1 11.2	49.2	134.9	0 28.8	−49.6	135.0	0 13.6	+50.1	45.0	0 56.0	50.5	45.0
30	0 22.0	−49.2	135.5	0 20.8	+49.7	44.5	1 03.7	+50.0	44.5	1 46.5	+50.4	44.5
31	0 27.2	+49.3	43.9	1 10.5	49.6	43.9	1 53.7	50.0	43.9	2 36.9	50.4	44.0
32	1 16.5	49.2	43.3	2 00.1	49.6	43.4	2 43.7	50.0	43.4	3 27.3	50.4	43.4
33	2 05.7	49.1	42.8	2 49.7	49.6	42.8	3 33.7	50.0	42.8	4 17.7	50.4	42.9
34	2 54.8	49.2	42.2	3 39.3	49.6	42.2	4 23.7	50.0	42.3	5 08.1	50.3	42.3
35	3 44.0	+49.2	41.6	4 28.9	+49.5	41.7	5 13.7	+49.9	41.7	5 58.4	+50.3	41.8
36	4 33.2	49.1	41.0	5 18.4	49.5	41.1	6 03.6	49.9	41.2	6 48.7	50.3	41.2
37	5 22.3	49.1	40.5	6 07.9	49.5	40.5	6 53.5	49.9	40.6	7 39.0	50.3	40.7
38	6 11.4	49.0	39.9	6 57.4	49.4	40.0	7 43.4	49.8	40.0	8 29.3	50.2	40.1
39	7 00.4	49.0	39.3	7 46.8	49.4	39.4	8 33.2	49.7	39.5	9 19.5	50.1	39.6
40	7 49.4	+49.0	38.7	8 36.2	+49.4	38.8	9 22.9	+49.8	38.9	10 09.6	+50.1	39.0
41	8 38.4	48.9	38.1	9 25.6	49.2	38.2	10 12.7	49.6	38.3	10 59.7	50.0	38.5
42	9 27.3	48.9	37.6	10 14.8	49.3	37.7	11 02.3	49.6	37.8	11 49.7	49.9	37.9
43	10 16.2	48.7	37.0	11 04.1	49.1	37.1	11 51.9	49.5	37.2	12 39.6	49.9	37.3
44	11 04.9	48.8	36.4	11 53.2	49.1	36.5	12 41.4	49.5	36.6	13 29.5	49.8	36.8
45	11 53.7	+48.6	35.8	12 42.3	+49.0	35.9	13 30.9	+49.3	36.0	14 19.3	+49.7	36.2
46	12 42.3	48.6	35.2	13 31.3	48.9	35.3	14 20.2	49.3	35.5	15 09.0	49.7	35.6
47	13 30.9	48.4	34.6	14 20.2	48.8	34.7	15 09.5	49.2	34.9	15 58.7	49.5	35.0
48	14 19.3	48.4	34.0	15 09.0	48.8	34.1	15 58.7	49.1	34.3	16 48.2	49.4	34.4
49	15 07.7	48.3	33.4	15 57.8	48.6	33.5	16 47.8	48.9	33.7	17 37.6	49.4	33.8
50	15 56.0	+48.2	32.7	16 46.4	+48.5	32.9	17 36.7	+48.9	33.1	18 27.0	+49.2	33.2
51	16 44.2	48.0	32.1	17 34.9	48.4	32.3	18 25.6	48.8	32.5	19 16.2	49.1	32.6
52	17 32.2	48.0	31.5	18 23.3	48.3	31.7	19 14.4	48.6	31.8	20 05.3	48.9	32.0
53	18 20.2	47.8	30.9	19 11.6	48.2	31.0	20 03.0	48.5	31.2	20 54.2	48.9	31.4
54	19 08.0	47.7	30.2	19 59.8	48.0	30.4	20 51.5	48.3	30.6	21 43.1	48.7	30.8
55	19 55.7	+47.5	29.6	20 47.8	+47.9	29.8	21 39.8	+48.2	30.0	22 31.8	+48.5	30.2
56	20 43.2	47.4	28.9	21 35.7	47.7	29.1	22 28.0	48.1	29.3	23 20.3	48.4	29.5
57	21 30.6	47.2	28.3	22 23.4	47.6	28.5	23 16.1	47.9	28.7	24 08.7	48.2	28.9
58	22 17.8	47.1	27.6	23 11.0	47.4	27.8	24 04.0	47.7	28.0	24 56.9	48.1	28.2
59	23 04.9	46.9	26.9	23 58.4	47.2	27.1	24 51.7	47.5	27.3	25 45.0	47.8	27.6
60	23 51.8	+46.7	26.3	24 45.6	+47.0	26.5	25 39.2	+47.4	26.7	26 32.8	+47.7	26.9
61	24 38.5	46.6	25.6	25 32.6	46.9	25.8	26 26.6	47.1	26.0	27 20.5	47.5	26.2
62	25 25.1	46.3	24.9	26 19.5	46.6	25.1	27 13.7	47.0	25.3	28 08.0	47.2	25.5
63	26 11.4	46.1	24.2	27 06.1	46.4	24.4	28 00.7	46.7	24.6	28 55.2	47.0	24.8
64	26 57.5	45.9	23.4	27 52.5	46.2	23.7	28 47.4	46.5	23.9	29 42.2	46.8	24.1
65	27 43.4	+45.7	22.7	28 38.7	+46.0	22.9	29 33.9	+46.3	23.1	30 29.0	+46.6	23.4
66	28 29.1	45.4	22.0	29 24.7	45.7	22.2	30 20.2	46.0	22.4	31 15.6	46.3	22.6
67	29 14.5	45.2	21.2	30 10.4	45.5	21.4	31 06.2	45.7	21.7	32 01.9	46.1	21.9
68	29 59.7	44.9	20.5	30 55.9	45.1	20.7	31 51.9	45.5	20.9	32 48.0	45.7	21.1
69	30 44.6	44.6	19.7	31 41.0	45.0	19.9	32 37.4	45.2	20.1	33 33.7	45.5	20.4
70	31 29.2	+44.4	18.9	32 26.0	+44.6	19.1	33 22.6	+44.9	19.4	34 19.2	+45.1	19.6
71	32 13.6	44.0	18.1	33 10.6	44.3	18.3	34 07.5	44.6	18.6	35 04.3	44.9	18.8
72	32 57.6	43.8	17.3	33 54.9	44.0	17.5	34 52.1	44.2	17.7	35 49.2	44.5	18.0
73	33 41.4	43.4	16.5	34 38.9	43.6	16.7	35 36.3	43.9	16.9	36 33.7	44.1	17.1
74	34 24.8	43.0	15.7	35 22.5	43.3	15.9	36 20.2	43.5	16.1	37 17.8	43.8	16.3
75	35 07.8	+42.7	14.8	36 05.8	+42.9	15.0	37 03.7	+43.2	15.2	38 01.6	+43.4	15.4
76	35 50.5	42.3	14.0	36 48.7	42.6	14.2	37 46.9	42.7	14.3	38 45.0	43.0	14.5
77	36 32.8	42.0	13.1	37 31.3	42.1	13.3	38 29.6	42.4	13.4	39 28.0	42.5	13.6
78	37 14.8	41.5	12.2	38 13.4	41.7	12.4	39 12.0	41.9	12.5	40 10.5	42.2	12.7
79	37 56.3	41.1	11.3	38 55.1	41.3	11.4	39 53.9	41.5	11.6	40 52.7	41.6	11.8
80	38 37.4	+40.6	10.4	39 36.4	+40.8	10.5	40 35.4	+40.9	10.7	41 34.3	+41.2	10.8
81	39 18.0	40.2	9.4	40 17.2	40.3	9.5	41 16.3	40.5	9.7	42 15.5	40.6	9.8
82	39 58.2	39.7	8.4	40 57.5	39.8	8.6	41 56.8	40.0	8.7	42 56.1	40.2	8.8
83	40 37.9	39.1	7.5	41 37.3	39.3	7.6	42 36.8	39.4	7.7	43 36.3	39.5	7.8
84	41 17.0	38.7	6.5	42 16.6	38.8	6.6	43 16.2	38.9	6.7	44 15.8	39.0	6.8
85	41 55.7	+38.0	5.4	42 55.4	+38.2	5.5	43 55.1	+38.3	5.6	44 54.8	+38.4	5.7
86	42 33.7	37.5	4.4	43 33.6	37.5	4.5	44 33.4	37.6	4.5	45 33.2	37.7	4.6
87	43 11.2	36.9	3.3	44 11.1	37.0	3.4	45 11.0	37.0	3.4	46 10.9	37.1	3.5
88	43 48.1	36.3	2.2	44 48.1	36.3	2.3	45 48.0	36.4	2.3	46 48.0	36.4	2.4
89	44 24.4	35.6	1.1	45 24.4	35.6	1.2	46 24.4	35.6	1.2	47 24.4	35.6	1.2
90	45 00.0	+34.9	0.0	46 00.0	+34.9	0.0	47 00.0	+34.9	0.0	48 00.0	+34.9	0.0
	45°			46°			47°			48°		

49° Hc	d	Z	50° Hc	d	Z	51° Hc	d	Z	52° Hc	d	Z	Dec.
° ′	′	°	° ′	′	°	° ′	′	°	° ′	′	°	°
22 40.9	−49.1	118.7	22 11.9	−49.7	119.1	21 42.6	−50.3	119.5	21 12.9	−50.7	119.8	0
21 51.8	49.3	119.4	21 22.2	49.8	119.7	20 52.3	50.3	120.0	20 22.2	50.9	120.4	1
21 02.5	49.4	120.0	20 32.4	50.0	120.3	20 02.0	50.5	120.6	19 31.3	51.0	120.9	2
20 13.1	49.6	120.6	19 42.4	50.0	120.9	19 11.5	50.6	121.2	18 40.3	51.1	121.5	3
19 23.5	49.6	121.2	18 52.4	50.2	121.5	18 20.9	50.7	121.8	17 49.2	51.2	122.0	4
18 33.9	−49.8	121.8	18 02.2	−50.3	122.0	17 30.2	−50.8	122.3	16 58.0	−51.2	122.6	5
17 44.1	49.9	122.4	17 11.9	50.4	122.6	16 39.4	50.8	122.9	16 06.8	51.4	123.1	6
16 54.2	49.9	122.9	16 21.5	50.5	123.2	15 48.6	51.0	123.4	15 15.4	51.4	123.7	7
16 04.3	50.1	123.5	15 31.0	50.5	123.8	14 57.6	51.0	124.0	14 24.0	51.5	124.2	8
15 14.2	50.1	124.1	14 40.5	50.6	124.3	14 06.6	51.1	124.5	13 32.5	51.6	124.7	9
14 24.1	−50.3	124.7	13 49.9	−50.7	124.9	13 15.5	−51.2	125.1	12 40.9	−51.6	125.2	10
13 33.8	50.3	125.2	12 59.2	50.8	125.4	12 24.3	51.2	125.6	11 49.3	51.7	125.8	11
12 43.5	50.3	125.8	12 08.4	50.9	126.0	11 33.1	51.3	126.1	10 57.6	51.7	126.3	12
11 53.2	50.5	126.3	11 17.5	50.9	126.5	10 41.8	51.4	126.7	10 05.9	51.8	126.8	13
11 02.7	50.5	126.9	10 26.6	50.9	127.0	9 50.4	51.4	127.2	9 14.1	51.8	127.3	14
10 12.2	−50.5	127.4	9 35.7	−51.0	127.6	8 59.0	−51.4	127.7	8 22.3	−51.9	127.8	15
9 21.7	50.6	128.0	8 44.7	51.1	128.1	8 07.6	51.5	128.2	7 30.4	51.9	128.3	16
8 31.1	50.7	128.5	7 53.6	51.0	128.6	7 16.1	51.5	128.7	6 38.5	51.9	128.8	17
7 40.4	50.7	129.1	7 02.6	51.2	129.2	6 24.6	51.5	129.3	5 46.6	51.9	129.3	18
6 49.7	50.7	129.6	6 11.4	51.1	129.7	5 33.1	51.6	129.8	4 54.7	52.0	129.8	19
5 59.0	−50.8	130.1	5 20.3	−51.2	130.2	4 41.5	−51.6	130.3	4 02.7	−52.0	130.3	20
5 08.2	50.7	130.7	4 29.1	51.2	130.7	3 49.9	51.6	130.8	3 10.7	52.0	130.8	21
4 17.5	50.8	131.2	3 37.9	51.2	131.3	2 58.3	51.6	131.3	2 18.7	52.0	131.3	22
3 26.7	50.9	131.8	2 46.7	51.2	131.8	2 06.7	51.6	131.8	1 26.7	52.1	131.8	23
2 35.8	50.8	132.3	1 55.5	51.3	132.3	1 15.1	51.7	132.3	0 34.6	−52.0	132.3	24
1 45.0	−50.8	132.8	1 04.2	−51.2	132.8	0 23.4	−51.6	132.8	0 17.4	+52.0	47.2	25
0 54.2	50.9	133.3	0 13.0	−51.3	133.4	0 28.2	+51.7	46.6	1 09.4	52.0	46.7	26
0 03.3	−50.8	133.9	0 38.3	+51.2	46.1	1 19.9	51.6	46.1	2 01.4	52.0	46.2	27
0 47.5	+50.9	45.6	1 29.5	51.3	45.6	2 11.5	51.6	45.6	2 53.4	52.0	45.7	28
1 38.4	50.8	45.1	2 20.8	51.2	45.1	3 03.1	51.6	45.1	3 45.4	52.0	45.2	29
2 29.2	+50.9	44.5	3 12.0	+51.2	44.6	3 54.7	+51.6	44.6	4 37.4	+52.0	44.7	30
3 20.1	50.8	44.0	4 03.2	51.2	44.0	4 46.3	51.6	44.1	5 29.4	51.9	44.2	31
4 10.9	50.8	43.5	4 54.4	51.2	43.5	5 37.9	51.5	43.6	6 21.3	51.9	43.7	32
5 01.7	50.7	42.9	5 45.6	51.1	43.0	6 29.4	51.5	43.1	7 13.2	51.9	43.2	33
5 52.4	50.7	42.4	6 36.7	51.1	42.5	7 20.9	51.5	42.6	8 05.1	51.8	42.6	34
6 43.1	+50.7	41.9	7 27.8	+51.1	41.9	8 12.4	+51.4	42.0	8 56.9	+51.8	42.1	35
7 33.8	50.7	41.3	8 18.9	51.0	41.4	9 03.8	51.4	41.5	9 48.7	51.8	41.6	36
8 24.5	50.6	40.8	9 09.9	51.0	40.9	9 55.2	51.4	41.0	10 40.5	51.7	41.1	37
9 15.1	50.6	40.2	10 00.9	50.9	40.3	10 46.6	51.2	40.5	11 32.2	51.6	40.6	38
10 05.7	50.5	39.7	10 51.8	50.9	39.8	11 37.8	51.3	39.9	12 23.8	51.6	40.1	39
10 56.2	+50.4	39.1	11 42.7	+50.8	39.3	12 29.1	+51.1	39.4	13 15.4	+51.5	39.5	40
11 46.6	50.4	38.6	12 33.5	50.7	38.7	13 20.2	51.1	38.9	14 06.9	51.4	39.0	41
12 37.0	50.3	38.0	13 24.2	50.7	38.2	14 11.3	51.1	38.3	14 58.3	51.4	38.5	42
13 27.3	50.3	37.5	14 14.9	50.6	37.6	15 02.4	50.9	37.8	15 49.7	51.3	38.0	43
14 17.6	50.1	36.9	15 05.5	50.5	37.1	15 53.3	50.9	37.2	16 41.0	51.2	37.4	44
15 07.7	+50.1	36.3	15 56.0	+50.4	36.5	16 44.2	+50.7	36.7	17 32.2	+51.1	36.9	45
15 57.8	50.0	35.8	16 46.4	50.3	35.9	17 34.9	50.7	36.1	18 23.3	51.1	36.3	46
16 47.8	49.8	35.2	17 36.7	50.3	35.4	18 25.6	50.6	35.6	19 14.4	50.9	35.8	47
17 37.6	49.8	34.6	18 27.0	50.1	34.8	19 16.2	50.5	35.0	20 05.3	50.8	35.2	48
18 27.4	49.7	34.0	19 17.1	50.0	34.2	20 06.7	50.3	34.4	20 56.1	50.7	34.6	49
19 17.1	+49.6	33.4	20 07.1	+49.9	33.6	20 57.0	+50.3	33.8	21 46.8	+50.6	34.1	50
20 06.7	49.4	32.8	20 57.0	49.8	33.0	21 47.3	50.1	33.3	22 37.4	50.4	33.5	51
20 56.1	49.3	32.2	21 46.8	49.6	32.4	22 37.4	49.9	32.7	23 27.8	50.3	32.9	52
21 45.4	49.2	31.6	22 36.4	49.5	31.8	23 27.3	49.9	32.1	24 18.1	50.2	32.3	53
22 34.6	49.0	31.0	23 25.9	49.4	31.2	24 17.2	49.7	31.4	25 08.3	50.0	31.7	54
23 23.6	+48.9	30.4	24 15.3	+49.2	30.6	25 06.9	+49.5	30.8	25 58.3	+49.9	31.1	55
24 12.5	48.7	29.7	25 04.5	49.0	30.0	25 56.4	49.4	30.2	26 48.2	49.7	30.5	56
25 01.2	48.5	29.1	25 53.5	48.9	29.3	26 45.8	49.2	29.6	27 37.9	49.5	29.8	57
25 49.7	48.4	28.4	26 42.4	48.7	28.7	27 35.0	49.0	28.9	28 27.4	49.4	29.2	58
26 38.1	48.2	27.8	27 31.1	48.5	28.0	28 24.0	48.9	28.3	29 16.8	49.2	28.5	59
27 26.3	+48.0	27.1	28 19.6	+48.3	27.4	29 12.9	+48.6	27.6	30 06.0	+48.9	27.9	60
28 14.3	47.7	26.4	29 07.9	48.1	26.7	30 01.5	48.4	26.9	30 54.9	48.8	27.2	61
29 02.0	47.6	25.7	29 56.0	47.9	26.0	30 49.9	48.2	26.3	31 43.7	48.5	26.5	62
29 49.6	47.4	25.0	30 43.9	47.7	25.3	31 38.1	48.0	25.6	32 32.2	48.3	25.8	63
30 37.0	47.1	24.3	31 31.6	47.4	24.6	32 26.1	47.7	24.8	33 20.5	48.0	25.1	64
31 24.1	+46.8	23.6	32 19.0	+47.2	23.9	33 13.8	+47.5	24.1	34 08.5	+47.8	24.4	65
32 10.9	46.6	22.9	33 06.2	46.9	23.1	34 01.3	47.2	23.4	34 56.3	47.5	23.7	66
32 57.5	46.4	22.1	33 53.1	46.6	22.4	34 48.5	46.9	22.6	35 43.8	47.3	22.9	67
33 43.9	46.0	21.4	34 39.7	46.3	21.6	35 35.4	46.7	21.9	36 31.1	46.9	22.2	68
34 29.9	45.8	20.6	35 26.0	46.1	20.8	36 22.1	46.3	21.1	37 18.0	46.6	21.4	69
35 15.7	+45.4	19.8	36 12.1	+45.7	20.1	37 08.4	+46.0	20.3	38 04.6	+46.3	20.6	70
36 01.1	45.1	19.0	36 57.8	45.4	19.2	37 54.4	45.7	19.5	38 50.9	46.0	19.8	71
36 46.2	44.8	18.2	37 43.2	45.0	18.4	38 40.1	45.3	18.7	39 36.9	45.5	18.9	72
37 31.0	44.4	17.4	38 28.2	44.7	17.6	39 25.4	44.9	17.8	40 22.4	45.3	18.1	73
38 15.4	44.0	16.5	39 12.9	44.3	16.7	40 10.3	44.5	17.0	41 07.7	44.8	17.2	74
38 59.4	+43.6	15.6	39 57.2	+43.8	15.9	40 54.8	+44.2	16.1	41 52.5	+44.3	16.3	75
39 43.0	43.3	14.7	40 41.0	43.5	15.0	41 39.0	43.7	15.2	42 36.8	44.0	15.4	76
40 26.3	42.7	13.8	41 24.5	43.0	14.0	42 22.7	43.2	14.3	43 20.8	43.5	14.5	77
41 09.0	42.4	12.9	42 07.5	42.5	13.1	43 05.9	42.8	13.3	44 04.3	43.0	13.5	78
41 51.4	41.8	12.0	42 50.0	42.1	12.2	43 48.7	42.2	12.4	44 47.3	42.5	12.6	79
42 33.2	+41.4	11.0	43 32.1	+41.5	11.2	44 30.9	+41.8	11.4	45 29.8	+41.9	11.6	80
43 14.6	40.8	10.0	44 13.6	41.1	10.2	45 12.7	41.2	10.3	46 11.7	41.4	10.5	81
43 55.4	40.3	9.0	44 54.7	40.4	9.1	45 53.9	40.6	9.3	46 53.1	40.8	9.5	82
44 35.7	39.7	8.0	45 35.1	39.9	8.1	46 34.5	40.0	8.2	47 33.9	40.1	8.4	83
45 15.4	39.1	6.9	46 15.0	39.2	7.0	47 14.5	39.4	7.2	48 14.0	39.5	7.3	84
45 54.5	+38.5	5.8	46 54.2	+38.6	5.9	47 53.9	+38.7	6.0	48 53.5	+38.8	6.2	85
46 33.0	37.8	4.7	47 32.8	37.9	4.8	48 32.6	38.0	4.9	49 32.3	38.1	5.0	86
47 10.8	37.1	3.6	48 10.7	37.2	3.6	49 10.6	37.2	3.7	50 10.4	37.4	3.8	87
47 47.9	36.4	2.4	48 47.9	36.4	2.5	49 47.8	36.5	2.5	50 47.8	36.5	2.6	88
48 24.3	35.7	1.2	49 24.3	35.7	1.2	50 24.3	35.7	1.3	51 24.3	35.7	1.3	89
49 00.0	+34.9	0.0	50 00.0	+34.9	0.0	51 00.0	+34.8	0.0	52 00.0	+34.8	0.0	90
49°			50°			51°			52°			

S. Lat. { L.H.A. greater than 180° ...... Zn = 180° − Z; L.H.A. less than 180° .... Zn = 180° + Z

LATITUDE SAME NAME AS DECLINATION L.H.A. 126°, 234°

Extract Number A21

INTERPOLATION TABLE

Dec. Inc.	Tens 10'	20'	30'	40'	50'	Decimals	Units 0'	1'	2'	3'	4'	5'	6'	7'	8'	9'	Double Second Diff and Corr.
26.0	4.3	8.6	13.0	17.3	21.6	.0	0.0	0.4	0.9	1.3	1.8	2.2	2.6	3.1	3.5	4.0	0.8 — 0.1
26.1	4.3	8.7	13.0	17.4	21.7	.1	0.0	0.5	0.9	1.4	1.8	2.3	2.7	3.1	3.6	4.0	2.4 — 0.2
26.2	4.3	8.7	13.1	17.4	21.8	.2	0.1	0.5	1.0	1.4	1.9	2.3	2.7	3.2	3.6	4.1	4.0 — 0.3
26.3	4.4	8.8	13.1	17.5	21.9	.3	0.1	0.6	1.0	1.5	1.9	2.3	2.8	3.2	3.7	4.1	5.7 — 0.4
26.4	4.4	8.8	13.2	17.6	22.0	.4	0.2	0.6	1.1	1.5	1.9	2.4	2.8	3.3	3.7	4.2	7.3 — 0.5
26.5	4.4	8.8	13.3	17.7	22.1	.5	0.2	0.7	1.1	1.5	2.0	2.4	2.9	3.3	3.8	4.2	8.9 — 0.6
26.6	4.4	8.9	13.3	17.7	22.2	.6	0.3	0.7	1.1	1.6	2.0	2.5	2.9	3.4	3.8	4.2	10.5 — 0.7
26.7	4.5	8.9	13.4	17.8	22.3	.7	0.3	0.8	1.2	1.6	2.1	2.5	3.0	3.4	3.8	4.3	12.1 — 0.8
26.8	4.5	9.0	13.4	17.9	22.4	.8	0.4	0.8	1.2	1.7	2.1	2.6	3.0	3.4	3.9	4.3	13.7 — 0.9
26.9	4.5	9.0	13.5	18.0	22.5	.9	0.4	0.8	1.3	1.7	2.2	2.6	3.0	3.5	3.9	4.4	15.4 — 1.0
27.0	4.5	9.0	13.5	18.0	22.5	.0	0.0	0.5	0.9	1.4	1.8	2.3	2.7	3.2	3.7	4.1	17.0 — 1.1
27.1	4.5	9.0	13.5	18.0	22.6	.1	0.0	0.5	1.0	1.4	1.9	2.3	2.8	3.3	3.7	4.2	18.6 — 1.2
27.2	4.5	9.0	13.6	18.1	22.6	.2	0.1	0.5	1.0	1.5	1.9	2.4	2.8	3.3	3.8	4.2	20.2 — 1.3
27.3	4.5	9.1	13.6	18.2	22.7	.3	0.1	0.6	1.1	1.5	2.0	2.4	2.9	3.3	3.8	4.3	21.8 — 1.4
27.4	4.6	9.1	13.7	18.3	22.8	.4	0.2	0.6	1.1	1.6	2.0	2.5	2.9	3.4	3.8	4.3	23.4 — 1.5
27.5	4.6	9.2	13.8	18.3	22.9	.5	0.2	0.7	1.1	1.6	2.1	2.5	3.0	3.4	3.9	4.4	25.1 — 1.6
27.6	4.6	9.2	13.8	18.4	23.0	.6	0.3	0.7	1.2	1.6	2.1	2.6	3.0	3.5	3.9	4.4	26.7 — 1.7
27.7	4.6	9.3	13.9	18.5	23.1	.7	0.3	0.8	1.2	1.7	2.2	2.6	3.1	3.5	4.0	4.4	28.3 — 1.8
27.8	4.7	9.3	13.9	18.6	23.2	.8	0.4	0.8	1.3	1.7	2.2	2.7	3.1	3.6	4.0	4.5	29.9 — 1.9
27.9	4.7	9.3	14.0	18.6	23.3	.9	0.4	0.9	1.3	1.8	2.2	2.7	3.2	3.6	4.1	4.5	31.5 — 2.0
																	33.1 — 2.1
																	34.7

Extract Number A22

Appendix D

Extracts from *Reed's Nautical Almanac* and *Norie's Nautical Tables*

Reed's
Extract Number A23 Sun's True Bearing
Norie's
Extract Number A24 True Amplitudes
Extract Number A25 Traverse Table

SUN'S TRUE BEARING AT SUNRISE AND SUNSET
LATITUDES 0° to 66°   DECLINATIONS 0° to 11°

LAT.	DECLINATION											
	0°	1°	2°	3°	4°	5°	6°	7°	8°	9°	10°	11°
0° to 5°	90	89	88	87	86	85	84	83	82	81	80	79
6°	90	89	88	87	86	85	84	83	82	81	79.9	78.9
7°	90	89	88	87	86	85	84	83	81.9	80.9	79.9	78.9
8°	90	89	88	87	86	85	84	82.9	81.9	80.9	79.9	78.9
9°	90	89	88	87	86	85	83.9	82.9	81.9	80.9	79.9	78.9
10°	90	89	88	87	86	84.9	83.9	82.9	81.9	80.9	79.8	78.8
11°	90	89	88	87	86	84.9	83.9	82.9	81.9	80.8	79.8	78.8
12°	90	89	88	87	85.9	84.9	83.9	82.9	81.8	80.8	79.8	78.8
13°	90	89	88	86.9	85.9	84.9	83.8	82.8	81.8	80.8	79.7	78.7
14°	90	98	88	86.9	85.9	84.9	83.8	82.8	81.8	80.7	79.7	78.7
15°	90	89	88	86.9	85.9	84.8	83.8	82.8	81.7	80.7	79.7	78.6
16°	90	89	87.9	86.9	85.8	84.8	83.8	82.7	81.7	80.6	79.6	78.6
17°	90	89	87.9	86.9	85.8	84.8	83.7	82.7	81.6	80.6	79.5	78.5
18°	90	89	87.9	86.9	85.8	84.8	83.7	82.6	81.6	80.5	79.5	78.5
19°	90	89	87.9	86.8	85.8	84.7	83.7	82.6	81.5	80.5	79.4	78.4
20°	90	88.9	87.9	86.8	85.8	84.7	83.6	82.6	81.5	80.4	79.4	78.3
21°	90	88.9	87.9	86.8	85.7	84.7	83.6	82.5	81.4	80.4	79.3	78.2

Extract Number A23

TRUE AMPLITUDES

Lat.	Declination														
	16°	17°	18°	19°	20°	20½°	21°	21½°	22°	22½°	23°	23½°	24°	24½°	25°
2	16.0	17.0	18.0	19.0	20.0	20.5	21.0	21.5	22.0	22.5	23.0	23.5	24.0	24.5	25.0
4	16.0	17.1	18.1	19.1	20.1	20.6	21.1	21.6	22.1	22.6	23.1	23.6	24.1	24.6	25.1
6	16.1	17.1	18.1	19.1	20.1	20.6	21.1	21.6	22.1	22.6	23.1	23.6	24.1	24.6	25.1
8	16.2	17.2	18.2	19.2	20.2	20.7	21.2	21.7	22.2	22.7	23.2	23.7	24.1	24.6	25.1
10	16.3	17.3	18.3	19.3	20.3	20.8	21.4	21.8	22.4	22.9	23.4	23.9	24.4	24.9	25.4
12	16.4	17.4	18.4	19.4	20.5	21.0	21.5	22.0	22.5	23.0	23.6	24.1	24.6	25.1	25.6
14	16.5	17.5	18.6	19.6	20.6	21.2	21.7	22.2	22.7	23.2	23.8	24.3	24.8	25.3	25.8
16	16.7	17.7	18.8	19.8	20.9	21.4	21.9	22.4	22.9	23.5	24.0	24.5	25.0	25.6	26.1
18	16.9	17.9	19.0	20.0	21.1	21.6	22.1	22.7	23.2	23.7	24.3	24.8	25.3	25.9	26.4
20	17.1	18.1	19.2	20.3	21.4	21.9	22.4	23.0	23.5	24.0	24.6	25.1	25.7	26.2	26.7
22	17.3	18.4	19.5	20.6	21.7	22.2	22.7	23.3	23.8	24.4	24.9	25.5	26.0	26.6	27.1
24	17.6	18.7	19.8	20.9	22.0	22.5	23.1	23.7	24.2	24.8	25.3	25.9	26.4	27.0	27.6
26	17.9	19.0	20.1	21.2	22.4	22.9	23.5	24.1	24.6	25.2	25.8	26.3	26.9	27.5	28.0
28	18.2	19.3	20.5	21.6	22.8	23.4	24.0	24.5	25.1	25.7	26.3	26.8	27.4	28.0	28.6
30	18.6	19.7	20.9	22.1	23.3	23.9	24.5	25.0	25.6	26.2	26.8	27.4	28.0	28.6	29.2
31	18.8	20.0	21.1	22.3	23.5	24.1	24.7	25.3	25.9	26.5	27.1	27.7	28.3	28.9	29.5
32	19.0	20.2	21.4	22.6	23.8	24.4	25.0	25.6	26.2	26.8	27.4	28.0	28.7	29.3	29.9
33	19.2	20.4	21.6	22.9	24.1	24.7	25.3	25.9	26.5	27.1	27.8	28.4	29.0	29.6	30.3
34	19.4	20.6	21.9	23.1	24.4	25.0	25.6	26.2	26.9	27.5	28.1	28.7	29.4	29.9	30.7

Extract Number A24

	319° / 221°			TRAVERSE TABLE			41 Degrees						041° / 139°	2h 44m

D. Lon	Dep.		D. Lon	Dep.		D. Lon	Dep.		D. Lon	Dep.		D. Lon	Dep.	
Dist.	D. Lat.	Dep.	Dist.	D. Lat.	Dep.	Dist.	D. Lat.	Dep.	Dist.	D. Lat.	Dep.	Dist.	D. Lat.	Dep.
1	00.8	00.7	61	46.0	40.0	121	91.3	79.4	181	136.6	118.7	241	181.9	158.1
2	01.5	01.3	62	46.8	40.7	122	92.1	80.0	182	137.4	119.4	242	182.6	158.8
3	02.3	02.0	63	47.5	41.3	123	92.8	80.7	183	138.1	120.1	243	183.4	159.4
4	03.0	02.6	64	48.3	42.0	124	93.6	81.4	184	138.9	120.7	244	184.1	160.1
5	03.8	03.3	65	49.1	42.6	125	94.3	82.0	185	139.6	121.4	245	184.9	160.7
6	04.5	03.9	66	49.8	43.3	126	95.1	82.7	186	140.4	122.0	246	185.7	161.4
7	05.3	04.6	67	50.6	44.0	127	95.8	83.3	187	141.1	122.7	247	186.4	162.0
8	06.0	05.2	68	51.3	44.6	128	96.6	84.0	188	141.9	123.3	248	187.2	162.7
9	06.8	05.9	69	52.1	45.3	129	97.4	84.6	189	142.6	124.0	249	187.9	163.4
10	07.5	06.6	70	52.8	45.9	130	98.1	85.3	190	143.4	124.7	250	188.7	164.0
11	08.3	07.2	71	53.6	46.6	131	98.9	85.9	191	144.1	125.3	251	189.4	164.7
12	09.1	07.9	72	54.3	47.2	132	99.6	86.6	192	144.9	126.0	252	190.2	165.3
13	09.8	08.5	73	55.1	47.9	133	100.4	87.3	193	145.7	126.6	253	190.9	166.0
14	10.6	09.2	74	55.8	48.5	134	101.1	87.9	194	146.4	127.3	254	191.7	166.6
15	11.3	09.8	75	56.6	49.2	135	101.9	88.6	195	147.2	127.9	255	192.5	167.3
16	12.1	10.5	76	57.4	49.9	136	102.6	89.2	196	147.9	128.6	256	193.2	168.0
17	12.8	11.2	77	58.1	50.5	137	103.4	89.9	197	148.7	129.2	257	194.0	168.6
18	13.6	11.8	78	58.9	51.2	138	104.1	90.5	198	149.4	129.9	258	194.7	169.3
19	14.3	12.5	79	59.6	51.8	139	104.9	91.2	199	150.2	130.6	259	195.5	169.9
20	15.1	13.1	80	60.4	52.5	140	105.7	91.8	200	150.9	131.2	260	196.2	170.6
21	15.8	13.8	81	61.1	53.1	141	106.4	92.5	201	151.7	131.9	261	197.0	171.2
22	16.6	14.4	82	61.9	53.8	142	107.2	93.2	202	152.5	132.5	262	197.7	171.9
23	17.4	15.1	83	62.6	54.5	143	107.9	93.8	203	153.2	133.2	263	198.5	172.5
24	18.1	15.7	84	63.4	55.1	144	108.7	94.5	204	154.0	133.8	264	199.2	173.2
25	18.9	16.4	85	64.2	55.8	145	109.4	95.1	205	154.7	134.5	265	200.0	173.9
26	19.6	17.1	86	64.9	56.4	146	110.2	95.8	206	155.5	135.1	266	200.8	174.5
27	20.4	17.7	87	65.7	57.1	147	110.9	96.4	207	156.2	135.8	267	201.5	175.2
28	21.1	18.4	88	66.4	57.7	148	111.7	97.1	208	157.0	136.5	268	202.3	175.8
29	21.9	19.0	89	67.2	58.4	149	112.5	97.8	209	157.7	137.1	269	203.0	176.5
30	22.6	19.7	90	67.9	59.0	150	113.2	98.4	210	158.5	137.8	270	203.8	177.1
31	23.4	20.3	91	68.7	59.7	151	114.0	99.1	211	159.2	138.4	271	204.5	177.8
32	24.2	21.0	92	69.4	60.4	152	114.7	99.7	212	160.0	139.1	272	205.3	178.4
33	24.9	21.6	93	70.2	61.0	153	115.5	100.4	213	160.8	139.7	273	206.0	179.1
34	25.7	22.3	94	70.9	61.7	154	116.2	101.0	214	161.5	140.4	274	206.8	179.8
35	26.4	23.0	95	71.7	62.3	155	117.0	101.7	215	162.3	141.1	275	207.5	180.4
36	27.2	23.6	96	72.5	63.0	156	117.7	102.3	216	163.0	141.7	276	208.3	181.1
37	27.9	24.3	97	73.2	63.6	157	118.5	103.0	217	163.8	142.4	277	209.1	181.7
38	28.7	24.9	98	74.0	64.3	158	119.2	103.7	218	164.5	143.0	278	209.8	182.4
39	29.4	25.6	99	74.7	64.9	159	120.0	104.3	219	165.3	143.7	279	210.6	183.0
40	30.2	26.2	100	75.5	65.6	160	120.8	105.0	220	166.0	144.3	280	211.3	183.7
41	30.9	26.9	101	76.2	66.3	161	121.5	105.6	221	166.8	145.0	281	212.1	184.4
42	31.7	27.6	102	77.0	66.9	162	122.3	106.3	222	167.5	145.6	282	212.8	185.0
43	32.5	28.2	103	77.7	67.6	163	123.0	106.9	223	168.3	146.3	283	213.6	185.7
44	33.2	28.9	104	78.5	68.2	164	123.8	107.6	224	169.1	147.0	284	214.3	186.3
45	34.0	29.5	105	79.2	68.9	165	124.5	108.2	225	169.8	147.6	285	215.1	187.0
46	34.7	30.2	106	80.0	69.5	166	125.3	108.9	226	170.6	148.3	286	215.8	187.6
47	35.5	30.8	107	80.8	70.2	167	126.0	109.6	227	171.3	148.9	287	216.6	188.3
48	36.2	31.5	108	81.5	70.9	168	126.8	110.2	228	172.1	149.6	288	217.4	188.9
49	37.0	32.1	109	82.3	71.5	169	127.5	110.9	229	172.8	150.2	289	218.1	189.6
50	37.7	32.8	110	83.0	72.2	170	128.3	111.5	230	173.6	150.9	290	218.9	190.3
51	38.5	33.5	111	83.8	72.8	171	129.1	112.2	231	174.3	151.5	291	219.6	190.9
52	39.2	34.1	112	84.5	73.5	172	129.8	112.8	232	175.1	152.2	292	220.4	191.6
53	40.0	34.8	113	85.3	74.1	173	130.6	113.5	233	175.8	152.9	293	221.1	192.2
54	40.8	35.4	114	86.0	74.8	174	131.3	114.2	234	176.6	153.5	294	221.9	192.9
55	41.5	36.1	115	86.8	75.4	175	132.1	114.8	235	177.4	154.2	295	222.6	193.5
56	42.3	36.7	116	87.5	76.1	176	132.8	115.5	236	178.1	154.8	296	223.4	194.2
57	43.0	37.4	117	88.3	76.8	177	133.6	116.1	237	178.9	155.5	297	224.1	194.8
58	43.8	38.1	118	89.1	77.4	178	134.3	116.8	238	179.6	156.1	298	224.9	195.5
59	44.5	38.7	119	89.8	78.1	179	135.1	117.4	239	180.4	156.8	299	225.7	196.2
60	45.3	39.4	120	90.6	78.7	180	135.8	118.1	240	181.1	157.5	300	226.4	196.8
Dist.	Dep.	D. Lat.	Dist.	Dep.	D. Lat.	Dist.	Dep.	D. Lat.	Dist.	Dep.	D. Lat.	Dist.	Dep.	D. Lat.
D. Lon		Dep.	D. Lon		Dep.	D. Lon		Dep.	D. Lon		Dep.	D. Lon	Dep.	

49°	311° / 229°			49 Degrees								049° / 131°	3h 16m

Extract Number A25

Appendix E

Sight Reduction Forms

AP 3270 Vol. 1 STARS

DR _____   DATE _____

Initial Plan:	Twilight		LMT	d
	DR long	_____		
	_____		GMT	d

	Stars	Hc	Zn
GHA Aries h			
increment m s	_____		
DR long	_____		
LHA Aries	_____		

- -

Sights taken:			
Stars	_____	_____	_____
GMT	_____	_____	_____
GHA Aries h			
increment m s	_____ m s_____ m s_____		
chosen long.	_____	_____	_____
LHA Aries	_____	_____	_____
chosen lat.	_____		
Hc	_____	_____	_____
Zn	_____	_____	_____
SA	_____	_____	_____
IE	_____	_____	_____
dip	_____	_____	_____
AA			
corrn.	_____	_____	_____
TA			
CA	_____	_____	_____
INTERCEPT	_____	_____	_____

AP 3270 Vol. 3 STARS

DR _____   DATE _____

Twilight   LMT   d
DR long   _____
          _____ GMT   d

Star _____   GMT _____

SHA star
GHA Aries   h
increment   m s _____
GHA star
Chosen long.   _____
LHA star   _____   dec. _____

Chosen lat.   _____

        Hc   d   Z   Zn

        _____
        _____

SA
IE   _____

dip
AA
corrn.   _____
TA
CA   _____
INTERCEPT   _____

NP 401 SIGHT REDUCTION TABLES
FOR MARINE NAVIGATION

SUN

DR _____   DATE _____

GMT _____

GHA   h

increment   m s _____

chosen long.   _____

LHA   _____

chosen lat.   _____

	Hc	d	Z	Zn

dec. increment

_____

_____

SA

IE   _____

dip   _____

AA

corrn. UL/LL   _____

TA

CA   _____

INTERCEPT   _____

LATITUDE BY MERIDIAN ALTITUDE

SUN

DR _____   DATE _____

	MP	LMT	d
	DR long. _____		
	_____	GMT	d

dec.   SA
d   _____   IE   _____

             _____

                                 dip   _____
                                 AA
                                 corrn. UL/LL _____
                                 TA
                                 from 90°   _____
                                 TZD
                                 dec.   _____
                                 LATITUDE   _____

LATITUDE BY POLARIS

DR _____ DATE _____

Twilight   LMT   d
DR long. _____
                _____ GMT   d

GHA Aries   h
increment   m s   _____

DR   long   _____
LHA Aries   _____

                              SA
                              IE   _____

                              dip   _____
                              AA
                              corrn.   _____
                              TA
                              a_0
                              a_1
                              a_2 _____

                              $-1°$ _____
                              LATITUDE   _____

Appendix F

Shorebased Syllabus of RYA/DoT
Yachtmaster Ocean Certificate

SHOREBASED COURSE FOR THE RYA/DTp YACHTMASTER OCEAN CERTIFICATE

Item	*Subject*	*Broad detail to be covered*
1.	The earth and the celestial sphere	1. Definition of observer's zenith and position of a heavenly body in terms of latitude, longitude, GHA and declination 2. Right angle relationships, latitude and co-lat, declination and polar distance. Tabulation of declination in nautical almanac 3. Relationships between GHA, longitude and LHA. The tabulation of GHA in the almanac. Rate of increase of hour angle with time
2.	The PZX Triangle	1. The tabulated components of the triangle, LHA, Co-lat and polar distance 2. The calculable components, zenith distance and azimuth 3. Relationship between zenith distance and altitude 4. Introduction to the tabular method of solution in the air navigation tables and the basic sight form 5. The use of calculators for the solution of the PZX triangle
3.	The sextant	1. Practical guide to the use and care of a sextant at sea 2. Conversion of sextant altitude to true altitude, application of dip, index error and refraction 3. Correction of side error, perpendicularity, index error and collimation error
4.	Measurement of time	1. Definition of and relationship between UT, LMT, standard time and zone time 2. Rating of chronometers and watches
5.	Meridian Altitudes	1. Forecasting of time of meridian altitude 2. Reduction of meridian altitude sights
6.	Sun sights	1. The reduction and plotting of sun sights using air navigation tables 2. The plotting of a sun – run – meridian altitude
7.	Planet sights	1. Identification of planets from LHA and declination 2. Reduction of planet sights using air navigation tables – (twilight sights only)
8.	Starsight planning	1. Calculations of times of sunrise, sunset, civil and nautical twilights 2. Star identification using Air Navigation Tables and/or calculator
9.	Star sights	1. Reduction of star sights using Air Navigation Tables and/or calculator. (Seven selected stars only) 2. Plotting of star sights. Corrections to position for precession and nutation
10.	The pole star	1. Determination of latitude from sights of Polaris
11.	Moon sights	1. Special corrections applicable only to the moon
12.	Compass checking	1. Use of amplitude and azimuth tables and/or calculator
13.	Satellite navigation systems	1. Principles and limitations
14.	Great circle sailing	1. The comparison of rhumb lines and great circles 2. Vertices and composite tracks 3. The computation of a series of rhumb lines approximating to a great circle by use of the gnomonic and Mercator projections
15.	Meteorology	1. General Pressure distribution and prevailing winds over the oceans of the world 2. Tropical revolving storms, seasonal occurrence and forecasting by observation
16.	Passage planning	1. Publications available to assist with planning of long passages (routeing charts, *Ocean Passages for the World* and other publications)

Index